CULTURE SMART!

WESTERN
EUROPE

CULTURE SMART!

WESTERN EUROPE

Roger Jones

With contributions on clubbing and nightlife
by Maytal Kuperard

·K·U·P·E·R·A·R·D·

ISBN 978 1 85733 490 6
Also available as an e-book: eISBN 978 1 85733 628 3

British Library Cataloguing in Publication Data
A CIP catalogue entry for this book is available from the British Library

First published in Great Britain 2011
by Kuperard, an imprint of Bravo Ltd
59 Hutton Grove, London N12 8DS
Tel: +44 (0) 20 8446 2440   Fax: +44 (0) 20 8446 2441
www.culturesmart.co.uk
Inquiries: sales@kuperard.co.uk

Distributed in the United States and Canada
by Random House Distribution Services
1745 Broadway, New York, NY 10019
Tel: +1 (212) 572-2844   Fax: +1 (212) 572-4961
Inquiries: csorders@randomhouse.com

Series Editor Geoffrey Chesler
Design Bobby Birchall

Printed in Malaysia

Cover images: © Fotolia.com
Image on page 3: *Vasco Da Gama Bridge, Lisbon.* © Fotolia.com

About the Author

ROGER JONES is an English writer and translator who is a specialist in careers, education, music, and preparing others for the practical and psychological adjustments of living abroad. A graduate in modern languages from King's College, University of London, he also holds qualifications in management and education. He has traveled widely in Europe and worked in education for extended periods in a number of foreign countries. He has also worked in refugee welfare, as a bookseller, and as an examiner.

His published work includes two novels and many non-fiction guides. These include handbooks offering practical advice and insights into local traditions, behaviors, and attitudes for people planning to live or travel abroad. He is also the author of *Culture Smart! Thailand* and *Culture Smart! Libya*, published by Kuperard.

Roger Jones lives in Gloucestershire, England. He is an active member of the Society of Authors, and in his spare time he is closely involved in community organizations promoting heritage, the arts, and improvements to the built environment.

The Culture Smart! series is continuing to expand.
For further information and latest titles visit
www.culturesmart.co.uk

The publishers would like to thank **CultureSmart!**Consulting for its help in researching and developing the concept for this series.

CultureSmart!Consulting creates tailor-made seminars and consultancy programs to meet a wide range of corporate, public-sector, and individual needs. Whether delivering courses on multicultural team building in the USA, preparing Chinese engineers for a posting in Europe, training call-center staff in India, or raising the awareness of police forces to the needs of diverse ethnic communities, it provides essential, practical, and powerful skills worldwide to an increasingly international workforce.

For details, visit www.culturesmartconsulting.com

CultureSmart!Consulting and **CultureSmart!** guides have both contributed to and featured regularly in the weekly travel program "Fast Track" on BBC World TV.

CHAPTER 2: BELGIUM AND LUXEMBOURG

CHAPTER 3: BRITAIN

CHAPTER 4: FRANCE

CHAPTER 5: GERMANY

CHAPTER 6: IRELAND

CHAPTER 7: ITALY

CHAPTER 8: THE NETHERLANDS

culture smart! **western europe**

CHAPTER 9: PORTUGAL

CHAPTER 10: SPAIN

CHAPTER 11: SWITZERLAND

Western Europe: An Introduction

The countries of Western Europe described in this book cover an area that is 25 percent of the size of the United States and have a population that is 25 percent greater. While all these countries have some elements in common—all are democracies, for example, and all but one are members of the European Union—their similarities are vastly outweighed by their national differences.

Cross a border in Europe, and although the landscape may not change you will immediately notice some striking differences: the road signs, the architecture, the food, the life style, and in most cases the language, to name but a few. Bring an Irishman, a German, and an Italian together, and they may look similar, but they are very different indeed. This can be disconcerting to the innocent visitor from afar.

In unfamiliar surroundings it is not unusual to experience some stress and anxiety—"culture shock." This often affects Western Europeans who visit their neighboring countries just as much as people from other continents. The most obvious cause of culture shock is the language—at least fifteen languages and a multitude of dialects are spoken in Western Europe. Aside from this, when you visit another country you may find that people's attitudes toward others, their values, their standards, and their way of life are quite different from your own. Some countries set great store by punctuality, for instance, while in others people may express surprise if you arrive on time for an appointment. Even their body language may be different—they may gesticulate wildly when they speak, and become very animated in company, while you hardly move your hands and maintain a cool detachment.

This book attempts to describe how the people of Western Europe differ, both from you and from each other. It also attempts to explain *why* they are different. Whereas people who emigrate from Europe often shake off their past and assume a new identity, those who remain behind are still conditioned by it, and history is therefore an important clue to understanding the present.

Only seventy years ago most of these countries, not for the first time, were engaged in mortal combat. Although they have now discarded past rivalries, it would be too much to claim that they have forged a common identity. Their national characters remain essentially unchanged. Their political and educational systems diverge, their assumptions and reactions differ, and so do their eating and leisure habits.

So visitors to Western Europe, unless they are on a conducted tour, need to pick their way carefully as they move from one country to another. This book is in essence a survival guide, designed to point you in the right direction, alerting you to issues that you need to be aware of, and offering you an insight into how Europeans live and see themselves. While most of them welcome visitors from abroad, you will receive a warmer welcome if they feel you are making some effort to fit in with their way of life.

In each section of the book you will find a brief description of the country and the key historical events that shaped the way its people think today—essential reading. Then follows an attempt to define national values and attitudes. Such pronouncements are generalizations, of course. Nobody is a stereotype. To some extent the values and behavior described here may not be typical of the younger generation, many of whom are open to different influences from their parents, and may be more open-minded, cosmopolitan, and dynamic. But there are also young people who are more conservative, more extreme, and less tolerant than their parents.

Everyone, young and old, shares some of the traits of their fellow-countrymen and women but, at the same time, possesses a unique identity. Life would be very dull if all Spaniards were identical and all Belgians had the same tastes. *Culture Smart! Western Europe* fills in the cultural background; but it cannot predict with any accuracy how an individual will behave in every situation. We are all of us, first and foremost, individuals.

Every country in Western Europe is a treasure trove of art and culture, represented by galleries and museums, theaters and concert halls, and great architecture both historical and modern. Festivals and traditions are included here, since they are not only fascinating in themselves but go to the heart of a country's culture. Some are religious in origin but secular in spirit, and may differ from country to country and region to region. Today many of Europe's large urban areas are constantly being enriched by the traditional celebrations of their changing ethnic and religious minorities.

The book also looks at how Europeans behave in their daily lives, at their attitudes to work, at how they interact with their families, and at how they enjoy their leisure. It suggests ways that a stranger can approach them and begin to get to know them. Don't be put off if developing a relationship is a slow process; Europeans often take time to engage with new people.

Readers visiting Europe for business or professional reasons will find a number of tips that we hope will prove useful. In much of Europe business or professional life is not completely separate from a person's daily life, but rather an extension of it, so getting to grips with national values and attitudes could be time well spent.

So here we have eleven countries, each with its own different values, traditions, and life styles. The prospect of becoming familiar with all of these may be daunting; yet, armed with some basic human information you will be able to start a journey of exploration into the richness and complexity of these important and influential national cultures. *Culture Smart! Western Europe* is here to help you along the way.

A note on place names. *We have used English versions of European place names (such as Florence for Firenze or Munich for München) throughout the book, but pair them with the national names or spellings in the first instance.*

MAP OF EUROPE

Aberdeen •

Glasgow • • Edinburgh

Belfast •

IRELAND

Dublin •

• Manchest
Liverpool •

Birmingham •

Cardiff • **BRITAIN**

London •

ENGLISH CHANNEL

*ATLANTIC
OCEAN*

Paris •

• Nantes

FRANCE

BAY OF BISCAY

• Bordeaux

Oviedo • Bilbao •

Tolouse •

Oporto •

Saragossa •

Barcelona •

PORTUGAL   **SPAIN**

• Madrid

Lisbon •

Valencia •

BALEARIC ISLAN

• Seville

Malaga •

NORWAY

ESTONIA

RUSSIA

SWEDEN

LATVIA

LITHUANIA

NORTH
SEA

DENMARK

RUSSIA

BELARUS

• Hamburg

NETHERLANDS

• Bremen

Berlin •

POLAND

• Amsterdam
Rotterdam

GERMANY

Leipzig •

UKRAINE

• Brussels

• Cologne

CZECH REPUBLIC

BELGIUM

SLOVAKIA

• Stuttgart

Munich •

Vienna •

HUNGARY

ROMANIA

Zurich •
• Bern

AUSTRIA

SWITZERLAND

Geneva •

SLOVENIA

CROATIA

Lyon •

• Milan Venice •

• Turin

BOSNIA AND
HERZEGOVINA

SERBIA

• Genoa

• Monaco

• Florence

BULGARIA

CORSICA

ITALY

ADRIATIC
SEA

MACEDONIA

MEDITERRANEAN
SEA

• Rome

ALBANIA

SARDINIA

• Naples

GREECE

• Cagliari

Palermo •

SICILY

Chapter 1

AUSTRIA

Key Facts

Official Name	Republik Österreich	**Radio and TV**	The national state radio and TV network is Österreichischer Rundfunk (ÖRF). There are several local radio stations and commercial satellite stations. The PAL B system is used.
Capital City	Wien (Vienna)		
Major Cities	Graz, Linz, Salzburg, Innsbruck, Klagenfurt, Bregenz, Eisenstadt, St. Pölten		
Area	32,430 sq. miles (84,000 sq. km)		
Terrain	Mountainous in west; lowlands and hills in the north and east	**Press**	Vienna: *Die Presse, Neue Kronenzeitung, Der Standard, Kurier, Wiener Zeitung.* Provinces: *Kleine Zeitung, Salzburger Nachrichten, Tiroler Tageszeitung*
Climate	Temperate and Alpine		
Currency	Euro		
Population	8.2 million		
Language	German; Slovene- and Croatian-speaking minorities	**English-language Media**	*Die Presse* and *Austria Today* have Web sites with local and international news.
Ethnic Makeup	Austrian 90.2%; others 9.8 %. Other nationalities include Turks, former Yugoslav nationals, and Germans	**Electricity**	230 volts, 50 Hz. Two-prong plugs used. Adaptors are needed for US appliances.
Religion	Roman Catholic 74%; Protestant 4.7%; Muslim 4.7%; Jewish 4.2%; others 12.4%	**Internet Domain**	.at
		Telephone	Country code: 43 For international calls dial 00. Private companies may have their own codes.
Government	Democratic federal republic (*Bundesrepublik*) with eight provinces (*Bundesländer*) and Vienna, where the two houses of parliament (*Nationalrat, Bundesrat*) are based	**Time Zone**	Central European Time (CET), which is one hour ahead of GMT and UTC. There is daylight saving in summer.

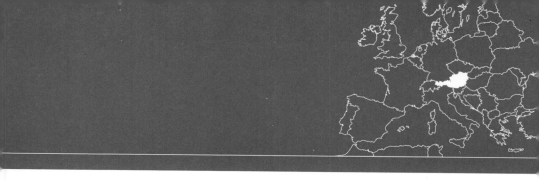

Map of Austria

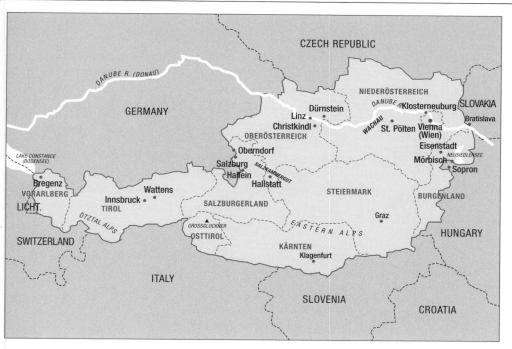

CZECH REPUBLIC

DANUBE R. (DONAU)

GERMANY

NIEDERÖSTERREICH

DANUBE R. Klosterneuburg SLOVAKIA

Dürnstein

Linz

Christkindl

WACHAU

St. Pölten Vienna (Wien)

Bratislava

OBERÖSTERREICH

Eisenstadt

Oberndorf

NEUSIEDLERSEE

LAKE CONSTANCE (BODENSEE)

Salzburg

Mörbisch

SALZKAMMERGUT

Hallein

Sopron

Bregenz

Wattens

Hallstatt

VORARLBERG

STEIERMARK

BURGENLAND

Innsbruck

LICHT.

TIROL

SALZBURGERLAND

ÖTZTAL ALPS

Graz

SWITZERLAND

GROSSGLOCKNER

EASTERN ALPS

HUNGARY

OSTTIROL

KÄRNTEN

ITALY

Klagenfurt

SLOVENIA

CROATIA

The Country
and Its People

Austria is a small, landlocked country of just over eight million people, with a musical, intellectual, and literary importance that seems out of all proportion to its size. Its capital, Vienna (Wien), has been a leading musical center and intellectual powerhouse for many generations.

In the heyday of the Austro–Hungarian Empire in the nineteenth century, people flocked to Vienna from all the Habsburg territories, making it one of the most cosmopolitan cities in Europe. In this respect Vienna stands apart from provincial Austria, where people tend to be conservative by nature and to cling to their local roots.

The vicissitudes of the twentieth century caused many Austrians to become introverted and defensive: there was a reluctance until recently to face up to the country's actions in the Second World War and the years leading up to it. But today's Austrians seem to have regained their self-confidence and are ready to grasp the opportunities on offer. In business they are efficient, flexible, and canny. Austria is an economic success story.

The Austrians excel in winter sports, and the country's impressive Alpine scenery makes it popular with skiing enthusiasts, mountaineers, and less active tourists. Austria's other excellence is music, and its musical life is remarkably vibrant, as befits the country that has been home to so many leading composers—notably Haydn, Mozart, Schubert, and the Strauss family.

Austria has borders with Germany, the Czech Republic, Hungary, Slovenia, Italy, Liechtenstein, and Switzerland. Although the Alps account for a large area of the terrain, the northern and eastern parts are flat or gently sloping. The highest peak is the

Mount Grossglockner, Hohe Tauern Natonal Park

Grossglockner (12,460 feet, or 3,798 meters) and the main river is
the Danube (Donau), but there are many other smaller rivers,
such as the Mur, the Salzach, and the Inn. The climate is
temperate, but the Alpine region is colder and subject to extensive
snowfalls in winter. The southeastern part of the country has a
warmer, more Mediterranean climate.

A HISTORICAL PERSPECTIVE

Austria first emerged as a distinct entity in the eleventh and
twelfth centuries, when it was ruled by the Babenberg family.
Later Rudolf of Habsburg became its ruler, establishing a dynasty
that lasted for more than five hundred years and at its greatest
extent controlled large swathes of Europe, including the
Netherlands, Poland, Romania, Ukraine, and Spain.

Danger threatened in 1683 with the advance of Ottoman
Turkish forces into the Habsburg territories, leading to the siege
of Vienna; but the threat was repulsed and in the following
century the Empress Maria Theresa transformed Austria into a
modern state and established Vienna as an important center for
culture, especially music.

In the early nineteenth century Austria was overrun by
Napoleon's troops, but these met with resistance in a number
of quarters, notably in the Tyrol (Tirol), where an innkeeper,
Andreas Hofer, led a successful rebellion.

ANDREAS HOFER

Andreas Hofer, who led the rebellion against the Napoleonic forces occupying his native Tyrol, is one of Austria's most celebrated heroes. He defeated Napoleon's Bavarian allies at Berg Isel near Innsbruck in 1809, forcing them out of the province and appointing himself commander-in-chief in the Tyrol with the agreement of the Austrian emperor. However, two months later the Tyrol was ceded to Napoleon, and Hofer was captured and executed on Napoleon's orders. He is commemorated in the Tyrolese anthem "Sandwirth Hofer."

In 1815 the post-Napoleonic settlement of the Congress of Vienna restored Austrian power, but Prussian ambition and nationalist aspirations among the subject nations of the Habsburg Empire led to Prussia's defeat of Austria in 1866. Subsequently a dual Austro–Hungarian monarchy was created, and the Empire enjoyed a period of prosperity and artistic creativity.

This proved to be the calm before the storm. In 1914 the Archduke Franz Ferdinand, the heir to the Habsburg throne, was assassinated by a Serbian nationalist, which led to Austro–Hungary's declaration of war on Serbia and precipitated the First World War. The effects of the war were devastating: Austria witnessed the end of the Habsburg Empire and the loss of substantial amounts of territory.

The 1920s and 1930s were characterized by economic hardship and political instability, with intense rivalry between the left- and right-wing political factions. Anti-Semitism was rife, especially in Vienna. In 1933 the Christian Socialist Chancellor Engelbert Dollfuss dissolved parliament and ruled by decree, only to be assassinated the following year in an attempted Nazi putsch. His successor, Kurt von Schuschnigg, attempted to preserve Austria's independence by signing the German–Austrian Agreement, but in 1938 Hitler annexed Austria—a move that was greeted with approval by many Austrians. Austria entered the Second World War as part of the German Reich.

At the end of the war the victorious Allies divided Austria (and its capital) into four zones of occupation. The atmosphere of postwar Vienna is captured graphically in Carol Reed's film *The Third Man*. In 1955 the Allies signed a treaty granting Austria its independence on the understanding that the country should be politically and militarily neutral.

KEY HISTORICAL DATES

1192	Duke Leopold V imprisons King Richard the Lionheart of England in Durnstein Castle.
1278	Rudolf of Habsburg defeats Otakar of Bohemia and founds an imperial dynasty that will last over five hundred years.
1571	Maximilian II grants his subjects religious freedom.
1576	Rudolf II reimposes Catholicism, which leads to the Thirty Years War in Protestant areas.
1683	The Turks besiege Vienna but are eventually repulsed.
1740	Maria Theresa becomes Empress; during her reign Austria becomes a modern state and important cultural center.
1805	Austria is overrun by Napoleon's forces.
1809	Andreas Hofer inflicts defeat on Napoleon's forces.
1815	Congress of Vienna.
1866	Prussia defeats Austria.
1867	Formation of the dual monarchy of Austria and Hungary.
1914	Assassination of Archduke Franz Ferdinand, heir to the imperial throne, leads to the First World War.
1918	Austria and Germany defeated. End of Habsburg rule. Austria becomes a republic.
1934	Chancellor Dollfuss dissolves parliament and rules by decree.
1935	Dollfuss is assassinated by Nazis.
1936	Chancellor Schuschnigg attempts to appease Hitler by signing the German–Austrian Agreement.
1938	The Anschluss. Germany annexes Austria.
1939–45	The Second World War, leading to the defeat of Germany and its allies.
1945	Austria is placed under Allied occupation, including Russian occupation.
1955	Treaty establishes Austria's independence and neutrality.
1960	Austria joins the European Free Trade Association.
1995	Austria becomes a full member of the European Union.

Austria Today

Many Austrians felt relieved to have escaped the fate of neighboring countries that had become part of the Communist bloc, and in the postwar period Austria increased in stability and prosperity. For much of this period the country was governed by a coalition of the two major parties, the People's Party (ÖVP) and the Socialists (SPÖ). Other parties include the right-wing Freedom Party (FPÖ), the Greens, and the Communists.

The collapse of Communism in Eastern Europe has proved a boon for Austria. No longer isolated on the edge of the free world, it now finds itself at the center of a dynamic economic region where its can act as a bridge between Western and Eastern Europe.

GOVERNMENT

Austria is a federal state of nine provinces, each with its own government and legislature. They are as follows:

Wien (Vienna) (population 1.55 million) is the capital of the country, and its mayor also has the title of governor of the province. The magnificence of its palaces, cultural institutions, and other architecture is an indication of its former importance as the hub of the Habsburg Empire.

Burgenland is the easternmost province. Its administrative center is the small town of Eisenstadt (approx. 12,750), once home to the Esterhazy Court, where Haydn was active.

Kärnten (Carinthia) is the southernmost province. Its capital, Klagenfurt (90,000), is situated on the shore of the Wörthersee.

Niederösterreich (Lower Austria) is the northeastern province, which surrounds Vienna. Its capital is St. Pölten (49,000).

Oberösterreich (Upper Austria) is situated between Niederösterreich and Salzburg. Its capital, Linz (185,000), is Austria's third-largest city and an important industrial center.

Salzburg is a picturesque province (immortalized in the film *The Sound of Music*) with many lakes and mountains. The capital is the city of Salzburg (143,000), the birthplace of Mozart.

Steiermark (Styria) is a substantial province that is often separated into the mountainous area of Upper Styria and the eastern part of Lower Styria. The capital, Graz (226,000), is the second-largest city in Austria.

Tirol (Tyrol), with its numerous mountain ranges, is an important area for winter sports. Its capital is Innsbruck (113,000).

Vorarlberg is the small, westernmost province of Austria, bordering Switzerland and Liechtenstein. Its capital is Bregenz (125,000), situated on Lake Constance.

Seefeld, Tyrol

Values and Attitudes

The twentieth century was a turbulent time for Austria, during which it lost its large empire and became a shadow of its former self. The initial shock led to some unpleasant outcomes between the wars—notably rabid anti-Semitism, as Austrians sought scapegoats for the tragedy that had befallen them.

Defeat in the Second World War led to a great deal of reassessment. There was some relief at the final outcome of the war for Austria, and many Austrians accepted their neutral status without demur. Gradually they became reconciled to their diminished role on the European stage and attempted to build on their strengths, with considerable success. Today the country boasts the second-highest per capita income in the euro-zone, and there is a greater confidence and optimism among Austrians.

PROVINCIALISM

Austrians have a tendency to identify themselves more with their region than with their country. A Viennese considers himself first and foremost to be Viennese rather than Austrian. In fact, many Viennese seem still to identify with the glory days of empire, and look on the provinces with disdain.

For their part, provincial Austrians nurse an antipathy for the Viennese, whom they regard as being too big for their boots. Their great love is for the regions they come from, so much so that a Tyrolean is unlikely to feel entirely comfortable in Styria, and vice versa. Many residents of Vorarlberg feel they have more in common with the Swiss, who speak a similar dialect to theirs.

RELIGION

Austria does not have an official state religion, and all religious groups are allowed to practice freely. Vienna, in particular, has a wide range of churches as well as mosques, synagogues, and Buddhist temples.

Around three-quarters of Austrians, however, are Roman Catholic. The country was at the forefront of the Counter-Reformation in the sixteenth century, the Emperor regarded himself as the secular protector of the Church, and Protestantism was discouraged. Churchgoing has declined in recent years.

Vierbergelauf *pilgrimage at Soerg, Carinthia*

COMING TO TERMS WITH THE PAST

In the postwar Potsdam Agreement of 1945 the Allies declared Austria to have been the victim of Nazi aggression, although a large number of Austrians had welcomed the Nazis and actively collaborated with them.

For decades the Austrians took refuge behind this declaration and denied any culpability for what had taken place. As a consequence no significant denazification program was instituted, as it had been in Germany, and politicians and civil servants implicated in atrocities were able to continue working as before.

It is only in recent years that Austria has started to atone for its conduct. The Austrian government has apologized to the victims of the Nazis, notably the Jews, and Austria's involvement in the Holocaust is now being taught in schools.

CONFORMITY AND CONSERVATISM

However much they like to criticize authority—and especially their politicians—Austrians are reasonably content with their lot and see no reason to rock the boat. They are conservative by temperament, and distrust change. *"Alles bleibt beim Alten"* ("Things stay as they are") is their favorite motto.

They are proud of their traditions, no more so than in Vienna, where the glories of their imperial past are all around them. Even young Austrians, while professing to espouse radical or unconventional views, tend to be more conformist than other Europeans of their age.

This conformity is also combined with prudence, particularly in financial matters. Austrians are thrifty with their money and hesitant to take risks with it. Memories of the financial hardships the country suffered between the two world wars clearly still linger, and they have no desire to repeat those times.

INTELLECTUALISM

A tendency to conform does not necessarily signify a reluctance to think critically, and Austria has a long tradition of questioning received values and opinions. In the declining years of the Austro–Hungarian Empire, writers such as Arthur Schnitzler and Karl Kraus questioned and satirized the society they lived in, and figures such as Freud and Adler were among the pioneers of modern psychology. This tradition continues, particularly in the country's universities. Austrians admire scholarship and respect those with good educational attainments.

ATTITUDES TO OTHER NATIONALITIES

In the years after the First World War there was resentment about the loss of certain territories, notably South Tyrol to Italy and German-speaking cities such as Maribor/Marburg and Ljubljana/Laibach to what was then Yugoslavia. At the time the province of Salzburg wanted to become part of Germany, and Vorarlberg to join Switzerland.

After the Second World War there was a large influx of refugees from Communist Eastern Europe, and many Turks and Yugoslavs migrated to the industrial centers to work. Apart from the occasional outburst in Carinthia against the Slovene minority there, most foreign nationals feel at home in Austria.

Attitudes are far more relaxed now. Vienna is a cosmopolitan European city and the Alpine resorts welcome tourists from around the world. The German media may dominate, but the Austrians, far from feeling inferior, still reckon they have the cultural edge.

STATUS

In the social hierarchy of the Habsburg Empire people were obsessed with titles and forms of address, and this tradition is still alive. Pupils address their teachers as "*Herr Professor*" or "*Frau Professor*" rather than by their surnames, and this is found throughout society, where the forms "*Herr Direktor*," "*Herr Doktor*," and "*Herr Meister*" are commonly used. Although the aristocracy has been abolished, aristocratic titles are still used— for example, "*Herr Graf*" ("Mr. Count"). Wives often take the title of their husbands in conversation, such as "*Frau Doktor*."

SUCCESS

While Austrians are proud of their achievements they seem reluctant to trumpet them, for fear of inspiring envy. That does not mean, however, that they deny themselves material comforts, and most aspire to a nice home and car. Although respect is generally accorded to people who reach high positions, they are suspicious of successful people, feeling that their success may have come about because of whom, rather than what, they know. Often membership of a political party acts as a stepping-stone to promotion.

WORK

Austrians are good, reliable workers who like to start early and finish early. They erect clear boundaries between work and leisure time, and rarely take work home with them. It is unusual for people to discuss work matters at home or in any social context, and bosses and employees rarely mix away from the workplace.

GEMÜTLICHKEIT

You will often hear the term "*gemütlich*" used by Austrians and Germans to describe both people and places. After the tensions of the working day they like to relax in cosy, sympathetic surroundings with friendly, cheerful company. *Gemütlichkeit* is, in essence, an attitude of mind that embraces a feeling of comfort and contentment, and a sense of belonging.

Festivals and Traditions

National festivals are standard throughout the country, and include all the major religious celebrations. Many are Catholic in origin, and are popularly attended. The tradition of going on pilgrimages to places such as Maria Zell in northern Styria is well entrenched, and people might join an organized religious group or just go for a day by themselves or with their families. You will also notice religious shrines along the roadsides.

Choir in traditional dress in Carinthia

THE FESTIVE YEAR
New Year

The New Year is a time for celebration, particularly Sylvesterabend (New Year's Eve). In some places people take to the streets with bottles of champagne and greet each other with the words *"Prosit Neujahr"* when the midnight hour strikes.

One of the most popular events of New Year's Day is a concert of light classical music by the Vienna Philharmonic Orchestra from the famous Musikvereinsaal, which reaches international audiences via radio and television.

HOLIDAYS AND FESTIVALS

January 1	Neujahrstag	New Year's Day
January 6	Dreikönigstag	Epiphany
*March/April:	Palmsonntag	Palm Sunday
*March April:	Ostersonntag	Easter Sunday
*March/April:	Ostermontag	Easter Monday
May 1	Tag der Arbeit	May Day/Labor Day
*May/June	Christihimmelfahrtstag	Ascension Day
*May/June	Pfingstsonntag	Whit Sunday
*May/June	Pfingstmontag	Whit Monday
*May/June	Fronleichnam	Corpus Christi
August 15	Mariä Himmelfahrt	Assumption
October 26	Nationalfeiertag	National holiday
November 1	Allerheiligen	All Saints' Day
December 8	Mariä Empfängnis	Immaculate Conception
December 25	Weihnachtsfeiertag	Christmas Day
December 26	Weihnachtsfeiertag (2)	Boxing Day

*The dates of these days are movable, and vary from year to year.

Epiphany

At Epiphany, or the Feast of the Three Kings, children go from door to door and collect sweets.

Fasching

Fasching is the equivalent of Mardi Gras, and is a season for partying in February before the beginning of Lent. Many formal balls are held, three hundred in Vienna alone, including the Physician's Ball (*Ärzteball*), the Flower Ball (*Blumenball*), and, most prestigious of all, the Opera Ball (*Opernball*) at the Vienna State Opera. Austrians take their dancing seriously, and many take courses in ballroom dancing.

Easter

Easter starts with a service on Palm Sunday when *Palmkätzchen* (branches of pussy willow) are blessed, and many people decorate their houses with these. Prayers are held at the Seven Stations of the Cross in Holy Week, and a vigil is held on the Saturday leading to the first Mass of Easter Day. Children hunt decorated hard-boiled eggs rather than chocolate eggs, but they are also given a chocolate Easter hare (*Osterhase*).

Easter eggs on sale in Vienna

In some areas bonfires are lit on Easter Eve, the relic of a pagan ritual to celebrate the arrival of spring. Bands of musicians process through the towns playing Easter music.

Corpus Christi and the Feast of the Assumption

These feast days, celebrating the Last Supper and the Assumption of the Virgin Mary, are marked by special Church masses, colorful processions through the streets, flowers, and brass bands.

Austrian National Day

Austrian National Day, in October, commemorates the day in 1955 when Austria regained its full independence. Schools often hold special ceremonies for their pupils.

St. Nicholas' Day

St. Nicholas is now widely known, of course, as a benevolent old man with a white beard who rewards good children with presents. His day on December 6 is celebrated in many countries of continental Europe, but in Austria the celebration has a twist. The evening before, a figure with horns, resembling the Devil and known as Krampus, goes around dragging a chain and carrying a birch rod, with which to administer punishment to children who have been naughty.

Advent market in front of the Town Hall, Vienna

Advent

During the Advent period, Christmas markets spring up in town and city centers, selling seasonal goods and gifts, tree decorations, mulled wine, and food specialties, while bands and choirs entertain the crowds with Christmas music and carols.

Christmas

Christmas itself is a family affair. Shops and businesses close early on Christmas Eve. Presents, which have been brought by the Christkindl (Christ Child), are exchanged, and the family sits down to a light meal, which usually includes carp. Many people then go out to attend midnight mass.

Christmas Day is a quiet day, when people go visiting or take part in leisure pursuits.

"SILENT NIGHT"

This popular Christmas carol originated in Austria. On Christmas Eve, 1818, Josef Mohr, the curate of St. Nicholas' Church in Oberndorf, near Salzburg, gave the church organist, Franz Gruber, a poem he had written and asked him to compose a melody for it for two voices, a choir, and guitar accompaniment. This carol continues to be sung at Christmas at the church in Oberndorf and all around the world.

Tradition is important to Austrians; it gives them a sense of identity. Many women wear the traditional *Dirndl* (a dress with a full skirt, tightly laced bodice, and an apron, as seen in the picture on page 45) on special occasions; in the countryside you may notice it worn as a working uniform by, for example, waitresses and shop assistants. In parts of Austria men wear the traditional Styrian jacket and hat, but *Lederhosen* (leather shorts) are less common than they were.

Many villages and small towns have brass bands, which play at festivals, weddings, and funerals.

FAMILY OCCASIONS

Birthdays

Austrians celebrate both birthdays and name days—the feast day of the saint after whom they are named. While children often receive presents, congratulations are usually enough in the case of adults, unless it is an important birthday. Some people bring refreshments in for a small celebration with their workmates, or invite people to their homes.

Weddings

Austrians often have two weddings—a civil ceremony and a church ceremony. Customs differ, but the most colorful events tend to be village weddings, where the lucky couple and their guests may be entertained by the local brass band.

Funerals

Funerals tend to be solemn occasions with a procession, often accompanied by local dignitaries and a brass band. Black is the usual dress code, and burial, rather than cremation, tends to be the norm.

Getting to Know the Austrians

Austrians make a clear distinction between friends and acquaintances. They tend to have a small circle of friends, often dating from their school or college days, and it takes time for an outsider to penetrate this tight circle. Once you become accepted as a friend you are a friend for life, but until that happens you should observe the formalities in your relationships.

FORMALITY

At work relationships tend to be formal, and people prefer not to discuss their private affairs with their colleagues. Often people work together for years without knowing anything about each other's private lives.

Like Germans, the Austrians value their personal space, and have a liking for order and decorum. They are not especially demonstrative, and would not normally appreciate excessive shows of affection.

FORMS OF ADDRESS

People tend to address one another formally, using *Sie* rather than the familiar *du* for "you," though now younger people tend to greater informality. You should only use the word *du* (or its plural, *ihr*) when addressing small children or close friends.

As people get to know you better they may start to use the *du* form, but it is up to the older person to give the lead. The change of relationship may be celebrated in a little ritual by linking arms and drinking glasses of wine or beer.

When referring to people within an organization it is usual to refer to them by their title—"*Frau Doktor* Schmidt," or "*Herr*

Generaldirektor Hoffmann," for example—rather than their first name. When addressing people you should also use their title— "*Herr Professor*," "*Frau Diplom-Ingenieur*," and so on—or, if they are of equal rank with you, "*Herr Kollege*" or "*Frau Kollegin*."

GREETINGS

Most people greet each other with a handshake, and the greeting "*Grüss Gott*" ("May God greet you") is very common. "*Guten Morgen*," "*Guten Tag*," and "*Guten Abend*" are also used, according to the time of day. It is quite usual to greet everyone in this way when entering a shop or restaurant, and to bid them farewell with "*Auf Wiedersehen*" or "*Auf Wiederschauen*." The more informal greeting "*Servus*" is also used in both contexts.

It is customary to wish people a good meal, and you may hear "*Mahlzeit*," "*Gesegnete Mahlzeit*" ("A blessing on your meal"), or "*Guten Appetit*."

MEETING PEOPLE

One way to meet people is to use public transport. Train journeys are often a good way to make acquaintances, particularly if you are conversant in German.

Going on a trip is another way of getting to know people. If

you are on a short visit, why not join an excursion to an interesting place that is not exclusively for foreigners?

Those in the country for an extended stay could look around for a club to join. Most towns have a good selection of clubs and groups catering to every sort of activity, including sports, mountaineering, and cultural pursuits.

For those attached to an organization such as a university or company, the staff will often organize excursions to places of interest. These days usually end with drinks or a meal in a *Gasthaus* (pub/restaurant).

Another way to meet people is to enroll in a course at the local further education institute (*Volkshochschule*). Ballroom dancing courses are ubiquitous and popular.

INVITATIONS HOME

Austrians like to meet their friends in a restaurant or coffee house, and it is quite usual on these occasions for everyone to pay their own way. If, as host, you are intending to pay for the party this needs to be made clear from the outset.

For a special occasion you may receive an invitation to someone's home. Austrians are hospitable people, and will do their very best to please. It is a good idea to dress smartly and arrive fairly punctually. In some houses you may be expected to remove your shoes on entry.

Small gifts are appreciated on these occasions, such as chocolates or flowers for the hostess. Different kinds of flowers often have a particular significance in Austrian tradition, so it would be a good idea to tell the florist the reason for the gift, to avoid a possible gaffe.

GOOD MANNERS

The Austrians set great store by good manners, and old-fashioned courtesy is still much appreciated. Men will stand up as a sign of respect when a guest arrives, precede a woman into a restaurant, and hold the door open for her. They help her on and off with her coat and offer her a seat before they sit down themselves.

It is *de rigueur* to dress smartly for all but the most informal occasions. When going out to the opera or the theater or even to the office, no Austrian would dream of wearing a T-shirt and jeans, for example. Although in some offices the younger members of staff are starting to dress down a little, they certainly don't look scruffy.

The tradition of good manners is also found among younger people. Generally speaking, young women like to be treated with respect by their escorts, and sexual advances are not usually acceptable early in a relationship. Drunkenness is also frowned on.

THE LANGUAGE

In order to get to know the Austrians really well, it is important to get to grips with German. Although in the more cosmopolitan areas of the country people are fluent in English, elsewhere people may have little occasion to speak it, and may regard visitors who do not speak German with suspicion. If you make the effort to communicate, however slight your German, they will be pleased.

German is the mother tongue of most Austrians, but there are certain differences between Austrian German and the language as spoken in Northern Germany.

Although standard German is taught in schools, Austrians tend to speak in their local dialect with one another, which a German speaker from north Germany might find hard to follow. Generally, Austrian German has softer consonants, and the vocabulary can be different.

REMEMBER WHERE YOU ARE!	Germany	Austria
Bread roll	Brötchen	Semmel
Tomato	Tomate	Paradeiser
Potato	Kartoffel	Erdapfel
This year	dieses Jahr	heuer
January	Januar	Jänner
Boy	Junge	Knabe
Girl	Mädchen	Mädel*
(*Austrians often affix the diminutive -l to words.)		

There are also a few grammatical differences, but these need not worry the visitor. If you speak German you will be understood.

The German language has been subject to a spelling reform in recent years, with mixed results. Older people tend to stick with the spelling they are used to.

CONVERSATION

The Austrians can be excellent company once you get to know them, and their conversation outside the workplace is usually lighthearted, witty, and well informed. Many have a strong sense of the absurd and enjoy poking fun at politicians and other people in the public eye—a tradition that goes back to writers such as Nestroy and the satirist Karl Kraus, who wrote the biting satire *Die letzten Tage der Menschheit* ("The Last Days of Mankind").

Most subjects are allowed, though as a foreigner it would be bad form to make fun of Austrian foibles in the way that the Austrians do themselves. Avoid discussing the Second World War with older people, for whom it will bring back unfortunate memories and perhaps expose skeletons in cupboards.

Daily Life

HOUSING

Until recently many people lived in rented accommodation, and in the postwar years, particularly in Vienna, housing was scarce. With increasing prosperity home ownership is rising, though at 56 percent the proportion is low compared with other European countries. Today most people in towns and cities live in apartments, while houses are more usual in more rural districts.

Older apartments are spacious, with high ceilings, and can be expensive to keep warm in winter. The traditional ceramic stove powered by coal and wood is being replaced by central heating. Many apartment buildings have cellars for storage.

THE HOUSEHOLD

Austria, like many Roman Catholic countries, was once very family-oriented, but over recent decades the birth rate has declined and families are now smaller. This has been caused by people choosing to remain single, couples deciding not to have children, and divorce. Traditional values are more persistent in rural areas, especially in the Alps, where households with larger families are still very much the norm.

DAILY ROUTINE

Austrians get up early, because much of the country lies east of the Central European Time zone. Breakfast consists of coffee or tea, with bread or rolls and slices of cheese, cold meats, sausage, and preserves (which are called *Marmelade*). Children usually take a lunch box to school with them.

Lunch is the main cooked meal of the day for many Austrians, and in the afternoon they often have a snack, called a *Jause*. Supper is usually a light meal served at 6:00 p.m. or soon after, and on weekdays people retire to bed early.

SHOPPING

Although supermarkets are becoming ubiquitous, many Austrians still prefer to shop at small specialty stores and market stalls. There is a preference for food produced in Austria, which

Market day in Wiener Neustadt

is of a very high standard. Most towns and villages have markets for fresh produce, attracting plenty of customers.

The supermarkets don't give you free bags with your purchases, so you need to remember to bring your own bags or otherwise buy them from the stores. Shops are normally open from 8:00 or 9:00 a.m. to 6:00 p.m.—bakeries may open earlier—but they are normally closed on Sundays.

EDUCATION

State involvement in education goes back to the time of the Empress Maria Theresa, who in 1774 introduced six years of compulsory schooling for all. Most schools are run by the provincial governments and equip their pupils with a good all-round education. Private schools are relatively rare.

Formal education starts at six years old, when a child enters the *Volkschule*. At the age of ten children move either to a *Hauptschule* (comprehensive secondary school), which offers a four-year course and may be followed by up to four years at a vocational college; or to a *Gymnasium*, which offers a four-year junior course followed by a four-year senior course. At the age of eighteen or nineteen pupils can take the *Matura*, a school-leaving exam which will entitle them to enter higher education.

THE ARMED FORCES

National service is compulsory for all Austrian men, and is very unpopular. It consists of six months' service followed by sixty days' refresher training in the reserves. Those with leadership potential may opt to serve longer to attain noncommissioned officer status, and there is always the option to make a career in the armed services. There are nine officer ranks, corresponding to civil service grades.

It is possible for conscientious objectors to be assigned work in other occupations in lieu of national service.

NEWSPAPERS

The Austrians are voracious newspaper readers and enjoy discussing the latest events. The country has sixteen daily newspapers, of which the most influential (and serious) is *Die Presse*, and the most popular *Neue Kronungzeitung* and *Kurier*. *Wiener Zeitung* was established in 1703 and is reckoned to be the

world's oldest newspaper. *Wirtschaftsblatt* is a financial newspaper. *Die Presse* has a Web site with news in English. *Austria Today* is an English-language paper.

In the provinces readers often prefer to read their local papers, such as *Salzburger Nachrichten, Tiroler Tageszeitung, Oberösterreichische Nachrichten,* and *Kleine Zeitung.*

TV AND RADIO

The state broadcaster, Österreichischer Rundfunk (ÖRF), which is financed through license fees, broadcasts two TV channels. Many Austrians also watch German and Swiss TV programs, thanks to satellite and cable transmissions. There are also a few private TV stations that have localized transmissions. There is a network of both ÖRF and private radio stations.

Austrian TV uses the PAL-B/G system which differs from the British PAL system and America's NTSC. A license fee is payable for each radio and TV you use.

MAIL AND TELECOMMUNICATIONS

Post offices have long opening hours (8:00 a.m. to 6:00 p.m. on weekdays, and 8:00 a.m. to 12:00 noon on Saturdays) and offer a wide range of services. You can post your letters in the pale yellow mailboxes seen outside post offices and in other prominent positions. The postal system is very efficient.

The telephone system, run by Telekom AT, is also efficient. To use public telephones you need a phone card, which can be bought from Tabak Trafik shops (state tobacconists)and vending machines, and you can make international calls from post offices.

There is a high rate of computer ownership, and there are a number of Internet service providers. Most hotels provide free Internet connection.

Leisure Time

Time off is important to the Austrians, who are very fond of the outdoor life and enjoy walking, mountaineering, and cycling in the summer, and skiing in the winter. During the year there are many public holidays, and people like to get away for long weekends as often as possible. Since it is quite common to take retirement at the age of fifty-five, you will observe plenty of energetic pensioners making the most of their free time.

Austrians like to make trips not only within the country itself but also to Italy, Germany, and Croatia, which are on Austria's doorstep, and further afield.

EATING OUT

Eating out is a pleasure in Austria, as the standard of cuisine is normally very good. You find well-appointed inns and restaurants in the smallest places, and even at the tops of mountains. Look for the word *Gasthaus.*

Not all eating establishments offer meals in the evenings. Many of them close on either Mondays or Tuesdays to give their staff a day off (*Ruhetag,* or rest day).

Lunch is usually the main meal of the day, and the Austrians tend to eat early—12:00 noon or 12:30 p.m. is quite normal.

Before ordering you should look at the *Speisekarte* (bill of fare). The word *Menu* is used for fixed-price set meals, which are usually good value even if not always as substantial as the *à la carte* dishes.

Normally the waiter or waitress will greet you as you enter, escort you to a table, bring you the *Speisekarte* and wine list, and take orders for drinks. If this does not happen, you can sit at a table and attract attention by calling out *"Herr Ober"* to a waiter or *"Fräulein"* to a waitress. To ask for the bill call out, *"Zahlen, bitte."*

FOOD

Austrian food is good and plentiful, and Viennese cuisine has a reputation for appealing to the most discerning palate. Although Austria is particularly famous for its meat dishes, most restaurants offer a variety of fish dishes, usually serving fish caught in the many local lakes and rivers, and also cater to vegetarians. Some of the Austrian specialties are as follows.

Wiener Schnitzel	veal escalope
Goulasch	spicy Hungarian-style beef stew
Tiroler Gröstl	pan-fried potatoes, onions, meat
Rindsuppe	beef bouillon
Grammelknödel	pork dumplings
Tafelspitz	boiled beef, potatoes, horseradish sauce
Frittatensuppe	clear soup, chives, pancake strips
Schinkenfleckerl	baked ham and noodle casserole
Bauernschmaus	cold meat platter

Many larger towns now have a range of international fast food outlets, but it pays to be adventurous. Everywhere you will find the *Wurstlstand*, the Austrian equivalent of a hot-dog stall, which sells spicy sausage served with mustard in a roll.

DRINK

Austria produces a number of very palatable wines from vineyards in the Danube Basin and the southern and eastern regions of the country. Most are white wines produced from the Riesling or Gewürztraminer grape. The most celebrated are Grüner Veltliner, Welschriesling, and Schilcher. Burgenland, with its milder climate, produces good red wines, including Zweigeld and Blaufränkisch.

Some decades ago certain Austrian vineyards and wine merchants were found guilty of adulterating their wine. The scandal prompted the government to introduce some of the strictest wine laws in the world, with the result that Austrian wines are as safe as you can get. The country is also a major producer of organic wines.

Heuriger is the name given to the newly harvested wine, and it is available for drinking from Martinmas (November 11) onwards. Bars where the wine is served are also called *Heurige;* the district of Grinzing in Vienna is particularly famous for these, and music often accompanies the drinking. In winter mulled wine (*Glühwein*) is very popular. *Eiswein*, made from the frozen grapes picked after a frost, is a sweet dessert wine.

Austria boasts a large number of breweries, large and small, which produce excellent lager and specialty beers that are available in bottles or on draught (*vom Fass*). One just outside Graz claims to brew the strongest beer in the world. Cider (known as *Most*) is made in the Danube Valley, Styria, and Carinthia, and another drink made of slightly fermented grape juice (known as *Sturm*) is equally popular.

Schnapps (brandy) is often drunk to round off the meal. Austria boasts a number of distilleries, some very small, which produce an interesting range of fruit brandies.

Be warned, however. Penalties are severe for drunken driving, and the Austrians, as a whole, do not deliberately set out to get drunk during the course of an evening.

Apart from the internationally known soft drinks, Austria makes a good range of fruit juices (*Saft*), and mineral water is also available. Austrians are great coffee drinkers—read on. As for tea, it tends to be served weak, and if you add milk it will have no color at all.

COFFEE HOUSES

Coffee houses are part of Austrian culture. They are places where people can relax, read newspapers, meet their friends, play a game of cards—and drink coffee, of course. When ordering your coffee you need to specify which type you would like. Some examples are as follows.

Ein kleiner Brauner	a small cup of espresso coffee with a dash of milk
Ein grosser Brauner	the same, doubled
Ein Verlängerter	espresso, but much weaker
Ein Cappuccino	espresso with frothy hot milk
Ein Mokka	strong black coffee
Ein Fiaker	hot coffee with rum or brandy, and perhaps whipped cream
Ein Eiskaffee	iced coffee with whipped cream, and perhaps vanilla ice cream

It is quite common to have a cake or dessert with your coffee, often topped with whipped cream (*Schlag*), and there are many Austrian specialties, including the following.

Apfelstrudel	apple strudel
Kaiserschmarren	chopped sweet pancake with fruit
Kompott	stewed fruit
Krapfen	doughnut
Palatschinke	pancake filled with preserves
Sachertorte	rich chocolate cake
Salzburger Nockerl	soufflé
Topfenstrudel	curd strudel
Weichselstrudel	sour cherry strudel

One can also indulge a taste for cakes and pastries in a *Café-Konditorei*—a bakery that also serves tea and coffee.

Sachertorte

CULTURE AND ENTERTAINMENT

The Austrians are proud of their cultural heritage, and a larger proportion of the population, from every social class, attends operas and concerts and visits museums and art galleries than elsewhere in Europe. They are also avid readers, as befits a country with a strong literary tradition.

Mozart

Vienna Opera House

Many important composers were born in Austria or Austro–Hungary, notably Josef Haydn, Wolfgang Amadeus Mozart, Franz Schubert, Anton Bruckner, Hugo Wolf, Johann Strauss II (composer of "The Blue Danube"), and Gustav Mahler. The founders of the Second Viennese School—Schoenberg, Berg, and Webern—were all Austrian, and Vienna also attracted talents from further afield, including Beethoven and Richard Strauss.

Austria has given birth to some major literary figures. One of the greatest German poets of the Middle Ages, Walter von der Vogelweide, served at the Viennese Court, and the famous *Nibelungenlied*, which inspired Richard Wagner to compose the *Ring* cycle, emanates from Austria. Hugo von Hofmannsthal and Georg Trakl were early twentieth-century exponents of this tradition. Leading dramatists include Franz Grillparzer, Johann Nestroy, Ferdinand Raimund, and Arthur Schnitzler, famous for the play *Reigen* (*La Ronde*). Schnitzler was also a fiction writer, along with Franz Werfel, Stefan Zweig, and Robert Musil.

Austrian artists made a significant contribution to modern art at the beginning of the twentieth century, notably Gustav Klimt, whose example encouraged, among others, Oskar Kokoschka, Alfred Kubin, and Egon Schiele.

Many are the Austrian scientists and thinkers who have had a powerful impact on our present age. They include Sigmund Freud, Wolfgang Pauli, Konrad Lorenz, Gregor Mendel, Karl Popper, Ferdinand Porsche, Erwin Schrödinger, and Ludwig Wittgenstein, to name but a few.

The list of Hollywood film stars and directors born in Austria who became Hollywood names is equally impressive. It includes Billy Wilder, Erich von Stroheim, and the thirty-eighth governor of California, Arnold Schwarzenegger.

STUDENTS, CLUBBING, AND CLOSE ENCOUNTERS

Vienna has a vibrant nightlife, as do Graz, Salzburg, and Linz. In the capital comfortable bars, nightclubs, and international DJs are easy to find, but what sets the Vienna scene apart from other European cities is its little, quirky *tanz* bars, where you are sure to find wonderful music and good wine. Vienna specializes in intimate bars with piano players, authentic Gypsy violin music, or live jazz. The best ones are found in the so-called Bermuda Dreieck (Bermuda Triangle), which is the old Jewish quarter. There are other good nightspots in the Fourth (Naschmarkt), Seventh (Spittelberg), and Eighth (Amerlinghaus) districts. The general rule in Vienna is that the most interesting and alternative venues are located outside the tourist centers.

Graz, Austria's second city, is bustling with students and therefore has a young, interesting, and eclectic nightlife scene. You can dance into the morning hours, hear a concert, attend an opera or a festival, go to the theater, or simply sit and talk over a drink in a local tavern or cocktail bar. Bars are concentrated around the old town as well as the Karl-Franzens University to the west of it. Clubs don't usually fill up till around midnight and they tend to be found close to Griesplatz.

At ski resorts, also, there is usually plenty going on after dark, though the music may tend to be traditional Austrian folk music rather than the newest international sounds.

Young Austrians prefer to go out in a group rather than in pairs. Until you get to know a person particularly well, it is advisable to stay with the crowd. As we have seen, young Austrians are quite restrained in their sexual behavior, and in any case don't demonstrate affection as publicly as is sometimes seen today in other countries, such as Britain.

SPORTS

Austrians are sports enthusiasts. Skiing, of course, is the national obsession, and most young people are on skis almost as soon as they can walk. The country has been at the top of the international competition table for many years, and events are keenly followed.

Other popular outdoor activities include walking, hiking, cycling, jogging, and swimming, and there is plenty of scope for all these in Austria's extensive, beautiful, and easily accessible countryside. Team sports, such as soccer, have an eager following.

Getting Around

The country has an excellent public transport system, so there is really no need to rent a car in order to get around. If you do, however, you will find the roads are well maintained, though in the early spring after a hard winter you may find some of them cracking up due to frosts.

The Österreichische Bundesbahnen (ÖBB; Austrian Federal

Railways), which are mostly electrified, link most parts of Austria with frequent IC (Intercity) and ICE (Intercity Express) train services. Express trains have first and second-class carriages, and it is usually possible to break your journey if you are traveling more than 100 km. Some routes tend to be slower than others, particularly in the mountainous areas.

There are also, of course, trains on shorter routes that make more stops, and local trains that stop at every station.

You can buy tickets at stations or travel agents, or through the ÖBB Web site. Discounts are often available in the form of travel passes of varying duration from four days to two weeks, and there are sometimes special offers available if booked at Austrian tourist offices in other countries.

Bus services are available to places not served by trains. In rural areas they are called Post Buses, but are in fact operated by the state railways. If there is no ticket machine, payment can be made when you board the bus. However, it is wise to check beforehand.

URBAN TRANSPORTATION

All Austrian towns have efficient public transport systems. Larger ones, such as Vienna, Graz, Linz, and Innsbruck, have trams/street cars (*Strassenbahn*), supplemented by buses. Vienna also boasts a new and efficient subway (*U Bahn*) and an urban rail system (*Schnellbahn*).

Smaller urban centers, like Salzburg and Klagenfurt, rely on buses and electrically operated trolley buses. Usually you need to buy your ticket in advance, from a ticket machine or Tabak Trafik kiosk, and punch it before getting on a bus or subway train or as you enter a tram.

This is a system that operates on trust. However, if an inspector boards the vehicle anyone caught without a valid ticket will have to pay a not inconsiderable fine.

In towns the public transport system operates from early in the morning until quite late in the evening. Only Vienna has an all-night bus service.

TAXIS

Taxis must be booked by telephone, and journeys are normally metered. As we have seen, it is usual to give a tip by rounding up the amount you pay.

DRIVING

Austrian roads are good and well maintained, and the country has a number of fast freeways. Some of these are toll roads, and you need to purchase a toll card (*vignette*) at a gas station or Tabak Trafik kiosk in advance in order to use them. Tolls are levied on tunnels and some mountain roads.

You need to proceed carefully in Alpine regions, as some of the roads through and over the mountains have treacherous hairpin bends. Many Austrians have a devil-may-care attitude to driving and like to drive fast even along twisting roads. Bear in mind that they are used to these roads and know how to negotiate them, and it is unwise to follow their example. The speed limit on expressways is 130 kmph (80 mph), on open roads 100 kmph (62 mph), and in towns 50 kmph (31 mph). The drink-driving limit is 0.5 mg per ml.

Traffic laws are strictly enforced, and on-the-spot fines may be imposed for illegal parking and other traffic contraventions. You must carry your car documents (driver's license, certificate of insurance, vehicle registration document) and a red-and-white warning triangle in the car. It is compulsory to wear seat belts, and spectacle wearers are obliged by law to keep a spare pair in the car.

You should drive with dipped headlights at all times. In cities, streetcars have priority over other vehicles, and if one stops in front of you, you must not pass until passengers have alighted. When approaching a traffic circle give priority to vehicles already on it; otherwise, those coming from the right at a junction have priority.

Drivers' Licenses

European Union residents can drive on their existing license (*Führerschein*). Other nationals can drive for up to one year on their own license or international driving license, after which they have to apply to the *Verkehrsamt* (traffic office) of the province they are living in for an Austrian license.

For this it is necessary to complete an application form (*Führerscheinantrag*) and provide supporting documentation: birth certificate, residence form, passport, medical report, original driver's license, and two passport-size photographs.

CYCLING AND WALKING

Cycling is common in some urban areas, but cyclists and pedestrians need to comply with the rules of the road. Jay walking is illegal, and can result in a fine.

WHERE TO STAY

High-quality, inexpensive, comfortable accommodation is available everywhere in hotels and guesthouses (*Pension*) displaying a *Zimmer frei* ("rooms available") sign. A star rating is in place.

If you want to book accommodation in advance, the local tourist offices (*Verkehrsbüro*) can usually help you. You find them at main railway stations and often at town halls (*Rathaus*). A number of hotel chains have Web sites, and the Austrian National Tourist Office can advise (www.austria.info).

The tourist offices can also provide information on campsites (or see www.campsite.at for information and bookings). Members of the Youth Hostel Association or Hostelling International can find details of Austrian hostels run by the Österreichischer Jugendherbergsverband (www.oejhv.or.at). The Österreichischer Alpenverein (Austrian Alpine Club) can provide you with details of accommodation in the mountains—and even at the top of some of them.

LAW AND ORDER

Generally speaking, Austrians are law-abiding and Austria is a fairly safe place to live and visit. There are pockets of crime in the cities, often in areas populated by immigrants from Eastern Europe, but provided you take sensible precautions, such as locking your car and keeping your valuables safe, your experience should be crime free.

MEDICAL MATTERS

There is a state health service in Austria that is good, but not entirely free, so medical insurance is advisable. EU citizens can get emergency care with their European Health Insurance Card, but this will not cover every eventuality.

If you intend to stay in Austria for a lengthy period you will be expected to pay social security contributions to the *Krankenkasse* (social insurance organization) of the area.

For those studying or working in Austria, hospital treatment may be free, or inexpensive, but you should check with your insurance company for details.

PLACES TO VISIT

Vienna

Vienna is a must. You could spend a week here and scarcely scratch the surface. It is home to the world-famous Staatsoper (Vienna State Opera) and the Volksoper; to two important theaters, the Burgtheater (the most famous theater in the

German-speaking world, founded in 1776), and the Theater in der Josefstadt (founded 1788); and to the Musikvereinsaal, the concert hall that hosts the Vienna Philharmonic's New Year's Day Concert.

Another important attraction is the Spanish Riding School at the Hofburg, and if you like funfairs, the Prater is perhaps the most famous one in Europe. There are plenty of marvellous buildings to see, such as St. Stephen's Cathedral (Stefansdom), Schloss Belvedere, and Schloss Schönbrunn (Vienna's answer to Versailles), which is a World Heritage Site.

The capital has a number of world-class museums and art galleries, such as the Museum of Modern Art and the Museum of Fine Arts, as well as more specialist institutions, such as the Railway Museum and the Medical Museum. The city is a great place to stroll around—its center is a World Heritage Site—and if you feel like a walk in the country, the attractive scenery of the Vienna Woods is close by.

Provincial Pleasures

Visitors to Austria shouldn't spend all their time in Vienna. The provinces (*Bundesländer*) have their attractions, not least their magnificent scenery. Salzburg is a most attractive town, the center of which is also a World Heritage Site. Mozart's birthplace is here, and it is host to one of the most famous of all European music festivals, the Salzburger Festspiele, founded in 1920 by Richard Strauss and Hugo von Hofmannsthal. Not far away are pleasant lakeside towns, such as Sankt Wolfgang.

Graz, despite its size, is relatively unspoiled, and has many fine buildings. Some of these date from Renaissance times, and include the largest armory of medieval weaponry in Europe. The center of Graz is another World Heritage Site. Like many of the large Austrian cities, it has a fine opera house and theater and some attractive parks. Outside Graz, at Stübing, is an open-air museum devoted to traditional houses, and to the east are historic fortresses designed to keep out the Ottoman invaders.

Innsbruck is surrounded by spectacular Alpine scenery, and many of the most famous ski resorts of the Tyrol are within striking distance. Carinthia is popular because of its mild climate and the opportunities for sailing and other aquatic sports on the Wörthersee.

If you need a rest cure, do as the Austrians do and spend some time at a spa. One of the best-known ones is Baden bei Wien, south of Vienna, and Bad Gastein, and there are others, often amid spectacular scenery, including Bad Ischl and Bad Aussee.

Innsbruck, Mariahilf quarter

Business and Professional Life

Austria has a buoyant economy and a well-educated and hard-working workforce. It is regarded as one of the best business locations in Europe and is at the forefront of efforts to reduce greenhouse emissions and promote renewable energy sources.

BUSINESS PRACTICE

This is not unlike doing business in Germany. Business is done in a formal, matter-of-fact, structured manner, with little in the way of small talk. Businesspeople adopt a direct approach and like to get down to details quickly. The younger generation may come across as pushy and impatient in their keenness to get a deal done. Older people may operate in a slightly more relaxed manner and have more time for pleasantries. Generally, senior business and professional people are remarkably adaptable, and skillful in their dealings with people of other nationalities.

Austria has a few large corporations, but the majority of businesses tend to be family-owned, and in such cases you may need to establish who makes the decisions in the firm—father or son. Some of these are nationalized industries, which can be as bureaucratic as the civil service, but in recent decades a number have been privatized.

THE WORKING DAY

Working hours in businesses, government departments, schools, and colleges are from 8:00 a.m. to 5:00 p.m., but some may start before that. Austrians are early risers, and many like to get to the office before time. They also like to leave early, and on Fridays many take the afternoon off. If you are arranging a business meeting, avoid scheduling it for late in the afternoon or on a Friday after 12:00 noon.

The Austrians tend to separate work and pleasure into two distinct compartments, so don't expect to talk business over dinner or on the ski slopes. The idea of taking work home is alien to them. A person who does this may be thought not to be able to manage his time in the workplace effectively.

MAKING CONTACT

If you are making contact for the first time you should send a formal letter introducing yourself—not an e-mail, which may be ignored. This can be followed up with a telephone call, but the telephone should not be used for the first approach.

PREPARING FOR MEETINGS

It is important to prepare carefully for a formal meeting, whatever its nature, and to make sure you take any relevant documentation along with you—preferably translated into German.

It is customary to exchange business cards at a first meeting, so it is sensible to have some made in preparation for this. They should state your title—sales manager, consultant engineer, chief accountant, for example— and include your degree(s) or other qualifications—the more the merrier. Austria is a meritocracy.

Although most Austrians speak English, it is a good idea, if you don't speak German, to take someone with you who does, to act as an interpreter if there are difficulties with the language.

Finally, make sure you dress appropriately for the meeting. This will usually mean formal clothes and a tidy appearance.

MEETINGS

Austrians are sticklers for punctuality, and are unimpressed by people who arrive late for a meeting, however legitimate the excuse. Indeed, it is best to arrive early, since this could indicate greater commitment on your part.

On arrival, be prepared to shake hands with everyone in the room. Make it a firm handshake and establish eye contact from the first.

As mentioned earlier, you should use honorific titles in formal situations rather than a person's first name or surname, hence "Herr Doktor" rather than "Herr Schmidt," and "Frau Direktor" rather than "Frau Hofer," unless the person in question does not have a title, in which case "Herr Schmidt" and "Frau Hofer" would be correct. If a person has two doctorates this would be reflected in their title, such as "Herr Doktor Doktor Moser." Some younger Austrians may have studied abroad, in which case they will be less formal in the way they address you in private. However, in the presence of other Austrians they will keep to a more formal style.

PRESENTATIONS

Austrians expect clear, factual presentations. They put great emphasis on the need for supporting data to illustrate the points being made. They are not impressed by flashy presentations with little substance.

They will be meticulous about detail and will subject any negotiator to close questioning. You therefore need to ensure that your facts and arguments are correct and are not open to challenge. If your presentation is not followed by questions, it is possible that it has failed to make an impact.

NEGOTIATIONS

In negotiations it is essential to make a good impression on the most senior person in the room. Austrian institutions are, for the most part, hierarchical, and superiors and subordinates tend to keep their distance.

However, this is not always the case, and there are workplaces, often where managers have received some of their training abroad, where decisions are arrived at more democratically.

It is important to work out who the real decision makers are in the meeting. You will find a clue in the titles by which they are addressed. Even if you are being questioned by subordinates it is important to address your remarks partly to the senior person or people.

Avoid small talk. A business meeting is not a social occasion for Austrians but something to be conducted as efficiently and expeditiously as possible.

THE LEGAL SYSTEM

Austria's General Civil Code (*Das Allgemeine Bürgerliche Gesetzbuch*) dates from 1811, making it one of the oldest codes of civil law in the world. It is based on Roman law.

Since 2007 a new commercial law code (*Unternehmens-gesetzbuch*) has been in force that conforms to European Union requirements. All contracts have equal standing, whether they re in writing, sent by e-mail, or agreed verbally. Austria is also a member of the UN convention on contracts.

WOMEN IN BUSINESS

Women are making their mark in business and particularly in public service. If you have to obtain permissions from a local authority, for instance, you may well find you are dealing with a woman. If there is a woman with a notepad in a meeting, it would be a mistake to assume that she is a secretary.

Austrian men are especially polite and courteous to their female colleagues, treating them with a courtesy that in some countries might be regarded as old-fashioned.

Chapter 2

BELGIUM AND LUXEMBOURG

Key Facts

BELGIUM

Official Name	Royaume de Belgique (French)/Koninkrijk Belgie (Dutch). Short form Belgique/Belgie
Capital City	Bruxelles/Brussel (Brussels)
Major Cities	Anvers/Antwerpen (Antwerp), Liège/Luik, Gand/Gent (Ghent), Louvain/Leuven, Bruges/ Brugge, Namur
Area	30,528 sq. km; 11,781 sq. miles
Terrain	Coastal plain, more hilly toward the south
Climate	Temperate
Currency	Euro
Population	10.4 million
Language	Dutch 60%; French 39%; German 1%
Religion	Roman Catholic 75%; Protestant/others 25%
Government	Constitutional Monarchy, bicameral legislature
Radio and TV	Two public TV and radio networks, one Dutch, one French
Press	*De Standard, De Morgen, Le Soir, La Libre Belgique, The Bulletin* (English), *La Dernière Heure des Sports* (sports news)
Electricity	230 volts, 50 Hz. Two-prong plugs used
Internet Domain	.be
Telephone	Country code: 32. For international calls dial 100.
Time Zone	CET (GMT/UTC + 1)

LUXEMBOURG

Official Name	Grand-Duché de Luxembourg
Capital City	Luxembourg
Area	2,586 sq. km.
Terrain	Gently rolling uplands, slightly mountainous
Climate	Temperate
Currency	Euro
Population	497,000
Language	Lëtzebuergesch, French, German
Religion	Roman Catholic 87%; others 13%
Government	Constitutional Dukedom, Chamber of Deputies
Radio and TV	RTL broadcasts throughout Europe.
Internet Domain	.lu
Telephone	Country code: 352 International calls: 00
Time Zone	As Belgium
Electricity	As Belgium

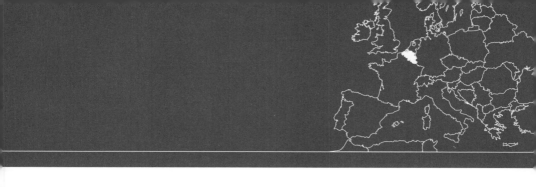

Map of Belgium and Luxembourg

NORTH SEA

THE NETHERLANDS

Knokke-Heist
Zeebrugge
Ostend
Bruges
Veurne
WEST
FLANDERS
Roeselare
Ieper
(Ypres)
Kortrijk
Mouscron
Tournai

Turnhout
Antwerp
ANTWERP
Ghent SCHELDT RIVER
Mechelen
EAST
FLANDERS
Aalst
FLEMISH
BRABANT
Brussels
Waterloo
WALLOON
BRABANT
Wavre
Louvain-la-Neuve

LIMBURG
GERMANY
Leuven
Hasselt

Liège
Verviers
Eupen

HAINAUT
La Louvière
Mons
Binche
Charleroi

Namur
NAMUR
Dinant

MEUSE RIVER
LIÈGE
Spa
Malmédy
M T S
Saint-Vith

A R D E N N E S

FRANCE

Bastogne
Troisvierges

LUXEMBOURG
Bouillon
Diekirch

LUXEMBOURG
Arlon
Grevenmacher
Virton
Luxembourg
City

The Countries and Their People

Old houses on the Grand' Place, Brussels

Belgium is on the northwestern seaboard of northwest Europe, and shares frontiers with the Netherlands, Germany, France, and Luxembourg. Its landscape ranges from the flat lands of the coastal plain to hills in the south. The climate is temperate, but becomes more extreme in the Ardennes region in the southeast.

There are two distinct communities in the country—the Dutch- (or Flemish-) speaking Flemings in the north, and the French-speaking Walloons in the south—and an intense rivalry exists between them. There is also a tiny German-speaking minority in the province of Liège; the Brussels region, although geographically part of Flanders, is bilingual.

Belgium stands at a crossroads of Western Europe, which has not always been the most comfortable position. For much of its history it has been ruled by foreign powers, and in the last century it turned into a major battlefield on two occasions. Since the Second World War life has been more peaceful, the country has prospered, and its cosmopolitan capital, Brussels, has become the heart of the European Community.

As for the Belgians, forget Hercule Poirot, the fictional creation of Agatha Christie. The real people of Belgium are much more interesting. They are hospitable, fun-loving, witty, tolerant, and slightly subversive—and they make excellent beer and chocolate. They tend to be less nationalistic than their neighbors, and identify more closely with their linguistic community than with the nation state.

Belgian (or Flemish) art is world famous through the names of Jan Van Eyck, Rogier Van der Weyden, Hans Memling, the Brueghel family, Pieter Paul Rubens, Anthony Van Dyck, and the Surrealist René Magritte. Belgians who have distinguished themselves in other disciplines include the architect Victor Horta, creator of the Art Nouveau style; the composer César Franck; the poet and dramatist Maurice Maeterlinck; the cartoonist Hergé, of Tintin fame; the detective novelist Georges Simenon; the satirical cabaret singer Jacques Brel; and Adolphe Sax, inventor of the saxophone.

Luxembourg is mentioned briefly in this chapter because its history and fortunes have been closely identified with those of Belgium. This small country, roughly the size of the American state of Rhode Island, has frontiers with Belgium, Germany, and France, and, like Belgium, plays a pivotal role in the affairs of the European Union.

A HISTORICAL PERSPECTIVE
The Path to Prosperity

Belgium derives its name from the Belgae, a Celtic tribe that put up stiff resistance to Julius Caesar in his conquest of Gaul. As the Roman Empire collapsed the Germanic Franks moved in, and in 843 the area was divided between two of the Frankish King Charlemagne's grandsons—Charles the Bald and Lothar.

Local rulers wielded considerable power, notably the counts of Flanders based in Ghent (Gent/Gand), whose territory extended into France. In the thirteenth century trade flourished, with Bruges and Antwerp developing into major trading ports. When

Flanders became virtually a French province in the fourteenth century, the English king Edward III halted wool exports, placing the Flemish weaving industry in jeopardy.

At the end of the 1300s most of the present-day territory of Belgium, the Netherlands, and Luxembourg was brought under the rule of the Duchy of Burgundy, heralding an age of prosperity in which the arts flourished. The centralizing policies of a later ruler, Philip the Good, were resisted, and under Mary Duchess of Burgundy the cities regained their freedoms and privileges.

Spanish, Austrian, and French rule

On Mary's death the Low Countries—the expanse of low-lying lands around the Rhine, Scheldt, and Meuse River deltas—came into the possession of the Habsburgs and eventually became subject to the most powerful ruler in Europe, the Holy Roman Emperor Charles V, who had actually been born in Ghent.

Charles imposed heavy taxes to finance his military campaigns and also sought to stem the tide of Protestantism that had engulfed the Low Countries.

His son Philip II of Spain took even more drastic action against the Protestants, provoking a rebellion led by William of Orange. (See chapter on the Netherlands.) Eventually an agreement that guaranteed religious freedom was signed (the Pacification of Ghent, 1576), and when the northern provinces formed a union the southern ones—present-day Belgium and Luxembourg—allied themselves with Spain, and Brussels became the capital. Protestant traders and craftsman fled north.

The Thirty Years War (1618–48), fought throughout Europe between Catholics and Protestants, concluded with the Peace of Westphalia, in which more territory was ceded to the northern United Provinces and Antwerp's importance as a port declined.

More territory was lost to the northern Netherlands and France when Louis XIV of France invaded, and the country eventually came under Austrian rule in 1713. The Belgians rebelled and established the United States of Belgium in 1790, but four years later Revolutionary French troops occupied the country and, despite a rebellion by the peasants, remained in control until Napoleon's defeat—on Belgian soil—at Waterloo in 1815.

Independence and War

The Congress of Vienna amalgamated Belgium with the northern Netherlands into the United Kingdom of the Netherlands, but despite the efforts of the king, William I, the political, cultural, and religious differences between the two proved insurmountable. Revolts broke out that led to Belgium's gaining independence in 1831, with Prince Leopold of Saxe-Coburg as its first king.

In 1815 Luxembourg was created a Grand Duchy, becoming the personal possession of William I, who negotiated its inclusion within the German Confederation. In 1839 it lost its French-speaking areas to Belgium, but gained a number of concessions. In 1867 it became fully independent.

Belgium became for a time the second leading industrial power in the world. The Flemings, however, felt they were the poor relations of the French-speaking Walloons and became restive. A compromise was reached with the adoption of Dutch as an official language and equal rights for both communities, which went some way towards alleviating these grievances.

In the twentieth century Belgium became a battleground when it was invaded twice by Germany. Some of the bloodiest battles of the First World War were fought on Belgian soil, with considerable loss of life. During the Second World War the country was run by a German military administration after its government fled to England to form a government-in-exile there.

Belgium and Luxembourg Today

Belgium recovered quickly after the war, yet Wallonia's economy with its reliance on heavy industry declined just as that of Flanders improved. A linguistic frontier was drawn up between the French and Dutch-speaking parts, and a large amount of political power was devolved to the regions.

Currently, the Flemish districts are West Flanders, East Flanders, Flemish Brabant, Antwerp, and Limberg. The Walloon districts are Hanaut, Namur, Liège, Walloon Brabant, and Luxembourg (not the Grand Duchy of Luxembourg). The Brussels region, as mentioned above, has bilingual status.

The postwar years witnessed an upsurge in cooperation with neighboring countries. Belgium and Luxembourg established a customs union with the Netherlands in 1948. A few years later all

three states became founder members of the
European Coal and Steel Community, and
then of the European Economic Community
(now the European Union).

Brussels (Bruxelles/Brussel) became the
headquarters of NATO and the European Economic
Community, and a quarter of its residents are non-Belgians.
Luxembourg is also an important center for EU institutions.

European Parliament building, Brussels

GOVERNMENT

Belgium is a constitutional monarchy with a bicameral legislature
consisting of the Senate (seventy-one members) and a fully
elected Chamber of Representatives (150 members). The King as
head of state appoints the prime minister and the cabinet, which
must contain an equal proportion of French- and Dutch-
speakers. There are numerous political parties, and governments
tend to be coalitions.

Much of the political power has been devolved to the lower
levels of government, notably the regional administrations and
assemblies and also the communes, and each linguistic group
has its own institutions.

Luxembourg has a single-chamber legislature (sixty members,
elected for five years). The country is divided into three districts:
Diekirch, Grievenmacher, and Luxembourg.

KEY HISTORICAL DATES

843	Belgium is divided between two grandsons of Charlemagne.
867	Baldwin Iron Arm establishes Ghent as his capital.
963	Count Siegfried establishes an independent state of Luxembourg.
12th cent.	Trade and industry start to flourish in Belgium.
1398	Belgium comes under Burgundian rule.
1464	Regional assemblies meet in Bruges to protest against centralization of power.
1477	The Great Privilege restores rights and freedoms to cities.
1550	Emperor Charles V decrees death sentence for Protestants.
1576	Pacification of Ghent guarantees freedom of religious belief.
1579	Union of Arras, in which the southern provinces ally themselves with Spain.
1618–48	The Thirty Years War.
1648	The Peace of Westphalia transfers parts of Belgium to the Netherlands.
1713	Belgium comes under Austrian rule.
1789	The Brabant Revolution, leading to the formation of the United States of Belgium in 1790.
1794	France occupies the Low Countries (including Belgium).
1798	The Peasants' Revolt fails to stop French reforms.
1815	Battle of Waterloo followed by the Congress of Vienna. Belgium and the Netherlands amalgamated. The Grand Duchy of Luxembourg created.
1830	Revolution breaks out, leading to Belgium's secession from the Netherlands in 1831.
1867	Luxembourg gains full independence.
1898	Law gives equal rights to Flemish and Walloon communities.
1914–18	First World War. Belgium becomes a battleground.
1922	Belgium and Luxembourg form tariff union.
1939–40	Second World War.
1948	Formation of the Benelux customs union.
1958	Belgium and Luxembourg become members of the European Economic Community (later EU).

Values and Attitudes

Despite its small size, Belgium often feels as if it is two or more countries, partly because of the linguistic divide and partly because of its devolved administration, which gives each area a substantial amount of autonomy. Because of its strategic position, it has been exposed to a variety of different traditions and influences. It has therefore become adaptable and cosmopolitan, and at the same time wary and distrustful.

Luxembourg is a more homogeneous and tightly knit society, naturally proud to be the only Grand Duchy in the world, and enjoying a prosperity that other nations can only envy.

ATTITUDES TO ONE ANOTHER

The fact that Belgium is one country divided by two languages has already been mentioned. But how does this affect relationships between the two linguistic communities?

For much of Belgian history the Flemings could be described as the underdogs. Flanders was much poorer and less developed than the French-speaking region of Wallonia. Moreover, French was the language of choice of the Flemish nobility, who looked down on the Flemish dialects as the language of the peasantry.

So, apart from the period from 1815 to 1830, when Belgium was under Dutch rule, French was the dominant language and French-speakers took the most prestigious jobs—in government, the professions, and industry. It was not until 1886 that Dutch gained official recognition.

Today the Flemings outnumber the Walloons, and their economy is the more buoyant of the two. Yet each community continues to have an antipathy to the other's mother tongue, although all public officials are expected to be conversant in both.

Considering this intense rivalry, how does Belgium survive as a single nation? Three main unifying elements are suggested.

First, having been under foreign rule for most of their history, the Belgians value their independence. They have no desire to be absorbed by one of their neighbors, as could happen if they split up.

Second, the institution of the royal family is a stabilizing force, and King Albert is a much respected head of state, as well as a symbol of the nation.

The third unifying force is Catholicism. Both communities have been strongly Catholic historically, and were not persuaded to change their allegiance to Protestantism in the sixteenth century, as the Dutch did so readily.

There are no social tensions to speak of in Luxembourg. The locals speak Luxembourgish, which gives them a strong sense of local identity, as well as French and German.

DISTRUST OF AUTHORITY

For much of its history Belgium has been ruled or occupied by other nations: the Franks, the Burgundians, the Spanish, the Austrians, the French, the Dutch, and the Germans. Having their destiny determined by others inevitably caused resentment, and the Belgians mounted several rebellions over the centuries against their different overlords.

Although the country is now an independent sovereign state, this lack of regard for authority persists. The Belgians dislike being told what to do, have a hearty contempt for bureaucracy, and are cynical about politicians and the political process. They are one of the most heavily taxed nations in the world, and have few qualms about evading taxes and disregarding, or circumventing, petty regulations.

COMPROMISE AND TOLERANCE

One reason that Belgium has not split into two is its people's ability to compromise, both in politics and in industrial relations. The Belgians prefer to resolve issues amicably rather than resort to conflict, even if the result is complicated and far from ideal. In politics, for instance, this has resulted in a cumbersome, multi-tiered bureaucracy. In Belgian companies regular meetings are held between employers and employees and monitored by the government in order to avoid confrontation and to ensure that industry runs smoothly.

Because they have been involved in international trade for centuries, the Belgians are remarkably adaptable to working with people from different cultures and are open to new ideas and challenges. They tolerate diversity, their laws are remarkably liberal, and there are few subjects or practices that are taboo. Here, for example, euthanasia is legal, and so is limited possession of drugs.

MODESTY

The Belgians are self-deprecating and unassuming to a fault. They seem almost ashamed of the small size of their country, comparing it unfavorably with its larger neighbors. Is it because they suffer from a lack of self-esteem or because they simply do not wish to draw attention to themselves?

One would not realize from talking to them that their country is a major exporter or that their industry is highly efficient. Before the First World War it was an industrial colossus, and although larger countries have now overtaken it, Belgium is still a force to be reckoned with.

One suspects that beneath the veneer of modesty lies a quiet self-confidence. Having learned from two world wars that a state of this size is powerless to resist incursions, the Belgians are happy to get on with their lives away from the limelight.

CAUTION AND PRAGMATISM

You might say that the Belgians like a quiet life and are extremely risk-averse. They are often reluctant to change jobs, even if offered a position with better prospects, and are not likely to put themselves out to get promotion. They like a good working environment, and once they have found one they prefer to stay with it.

The Belgians are careful with their money, particularly the Flemings, who have higher levels of savings than any other Europeans. That does not mean they are stingy, but they like to have enough cash by them in case of emergencies and are reluctant to indulge in extravagant spending sprees.

One could regard this as a manifestation of a pragmatic, down-to-earth mentality. The Belgians are first and foremost practical people, rather than dreamers, and this has long been so: if you look at the paintings of some of the great Flemish masters you will find a good deal of matter-of-fact earthiness and humor in them.

RELIGION

Throughout its history Belgium has been staunchly Catholic, for which reason it did not wish to amalgamate with the Netherlands. The country is, however, a secular state, allowing people to worship freely—yet the Catholic Church continues to exert an influence on politics, business, and intellectual life. Most people subscribe to its teachings, and the tradition of baptizing children into the Church remains strong. However, it is reckoned that only around 12 percent of the populace attend mass regularly, and only half of all weddings take place in church—many fewer in the Brussels region. The divorce rate is the second-highest in Europe, though divorce is less common among practicing Catholics.

MORALITY

A visit to the red-light districts of Brussels, Antwerp (Anvers/Antwerpen), and other cities, with their brothels and lesbian/gay clubs and bars, might suggest to the casual foreign observer that Belgians have turned their backs on morality.

Certainly the Belgian laws are liberal, tolerating homosexuality and prostitution and sanctioning same-sex unions and euthanasia. But it would be erroneous to conclude that all Belgians necessarily approve of such behavior. Indeed, many of them feel uneasy about it, since it conflicts with deeply held religious beliefs.

MULTICULTURALISM

Nearly 10 percent of Belgium's population is of foreign origin while in Brussels itself this rises to 30 percent, the number being made up by foreign diplomats and officials in the international organizations based in the capital, as well as substantial numbers of Spaniards and Portuguese.

Thanks to the booming jobs market, there has also been a considerable influx of immigrants from outside the European Union, notably Turkey, North Africa, and Zaire (formerly the Belgian Congo). While the Congolese, who share a common heritage with the Belgians, are accepted—more or less—the others are not made to feel so welcome, and live separate lives. In this respect they resemble the two major linguistic communities.

A disturbing trend in the current century has been the rise of a far-right party that advocates the repatriation of all immigrants and has stirred up prejudice against Muslims. Although racism runs contrary to Belgium's traditionally tolerant outlook, the party has attracted substantial support.

HUMOR

It is always a delight to watch a visitor encountering for the first time the surrealism that infuses so much of Belgian wit, art, and life—for instance while watching a TV program by Les Snuls, a group of actors whose humor is based on wild satire of all aspects of Belgian life. Surrealism was not a Belgian invention, but you could be forgiven for thinking that it was, so ubiquitous is it in Belgian culture.

Jokes, cartoons, and the highly popular comic strips all have a strong anarchic flavor, echoing the Belgians' deep-rooted skepticism of authority and rules and regulations. There are few superheroes—rather, ordinary folk will be caught up in weird adventures or situations, and be made to look foolish.

There is a great deal of humor based on wordplay—not surprising in a multilingual country—and also on poking fun at others. Several Flemish TV programs consist entirely of jokes in which people from Antwerp, Limburg, and West Flanders cheerfully make fun of each other.

Festivals and Traditions

Belgians like to have fun, and they have an abundance of festivals, some national, some local, and some that go back to the Middle Ages. A number are religious in character.

On public holidays, public offices and businesses are closed. If a holiday falls on a Sunday, people take the following Monday off; if it falls on a Tuesday or Thursday some organizations take two days off in order to lengthen the weekend.

HOLIDAYS AND FESTIVALS

January 1	Nouvel An/Nieuwjaar	New Year's Day
January 6	Driekoning/Épiphanie	Epiphany
March/April	Lundi de Pâques/Paasmaandag	Easter Monday
May 1	Fête du Travail/Dag van de Arbeid	Labor Day
May	Ascension/Hemelvaart	Ascension
May	Lundi de Pentecôte/Pinkstermaandag	Whit Monday
June 18	Waterloo	Waterloo Day
June 23 (Lux.)	Fête Nationale/Nationale Feestdag	National Day
July 21 (Bel.)	Fête Nationale/Nationale Feestdag	National Day
August 15	Assomption/OLV Hemelvaart	Assumption
November 1	La Toussaint/Allerheiligen	All Saints' Day
November 11	Armistice/Wapenstilstand	Armistice Day
November 15	Fête du Roi/Konigsdag	King's Day
December 6	Saint Nicholas /Sinterklaas	St. Nicholas' Day
December 25	Noël/Kerstmis	Christmas Day

THE FESTIVE YEAR

New Year

On New Year's Eve the Flemings like to have a large dinner with their friends, which sometimes lasts into the early hours of New

Year's Day. At midnight toasts are drunk, fireworks are set off, and the ships in Antwerp's harbor blow their horns. On New Year's Day children visit their grandparents to read out their New Year resolutions, and are usually rewarded with a gift.

Epiphany

This commemorates the visit of the Magi to the infant Christ, and it is customary in Flemish areas for children to dress up as the three kings and go around the houses singing traditional songs and being rewarded with sweets or fruit. Shops sell Epiphany cakes, which contain sweets or small porcelain figures.

Carnival/Carnaval

This is the last big celebration before the Lenten fast, and it is customary to have parties and fancy-dress parades through the streets. Local customs vary. Ostend has its Procession of a Thousand Lamps, while in Binche men ("Gilles") parade in traditional shirts, masks, ostrich-feather hats, and clogs to the beat of a drum, throwing oranges to—or at—the onlookers.

Masked procession, Binche

Easter

Both Good Friday and Easter Day are marked by church services, and children hunt for Easter eggs in the garden.

April Fools' Day

Belgians enjoy playing pranks on one another on this day, in common with other countries in northern Europe.

Labor Day (May Day)

Trees are planted in some towns as a symbol of renewal around this time.

On the second Sunday of the month the city of Ypres/Ieper remembers the old Festival of Cats, when cats were thrown from the belfry of the Cloth Hall. For six centuries live cats were used, as they were believed to personify evil spirits. Nowadays toy cats have taken their place.

Ascension Day

Bruges stages the famous Holy Blood Procession, when the relic of Christ's blood, which the Count of Flanders brought home from the Crusades in 1149, is paraded through the city.

Waterloo Day

On June 18 in 1815 the Duke of Wellington defeated Napoleon on the field of Waterloo just outside Brussels, and every five years sees a reenactment of this famous battle.

National Day of Luxembourg

This is an occasion for parades and speeches.

Belgian National Day

This public holiday is marked by a military parade in front of the Royal Palace in Brussels and firework displays around the country.

All Saints' Day

People honor the dead by bringing candles and chrysanthemums to their graves. The day after, the Day of the Dead, it is traditional to eat "soul cakes."

St. Nicholas' Day

This is the day when children receive presents, which may include a spiced cookie depicting St. Nicholas, the patron saint of children.

Christmas

Life becomes festive as Christmas approaches, with special markets in town squares and depictions of the Nativity in churches.

Christmas is very much a family affair, and on Christmas Eve families dine together. They will often attend mass at the local church at midnight, or else on Christmas morning. Presents are exchanged, and lunch usually consists of goose or turkey, sausages, and a chocolate cake in the shape of a yule log.

FAMILY OCCASIONS

The important stages of a person's life call for celebrations, and the first of these is a child's baptism in church. This is normally followed by a small party at which the guests give presents (often clothes) for the baby and traditionally receive sugared almonds from the godparents to mark the occasion. Confirmation, followed by first communion, is another important rite of passage in Catholic families.

Weddings consist of a civil ceremony, which takes place at the local town hall, followed by a reception in the afternoon and a big party at night. Around half of all weddings include a church ceremony after the civil ceremony has been conducted.

Usually wedding invitations specify which parts of the wedding you are invited to. Normally only close family members attend the civil ceremony. There is often a gift list from which guests can choose a present to give the couple.

Deaths are usually announced in the newspapers with details of the funeral arrangements. Cremation is becoming more popular than burial, but people still prefer to have a church funeral. Refreshments are usually served after the ceremony.

Church at Strud

Getting to Know the Belgians

The Belgians are a friendly people, but may give the impression at first of being somewhat reserved. The reason is that in their overcrowded country they value their privacy and personal space. They regard their home as a place where they can retreat from the outside world to be with their family and where they do not like to be disturbed. Luxembourgers tend to be of a similar disposition.

However, that does not mean they will never open up to you, but it will take time. In fact they often get on better with foreigners than with compatriots from across the linguistic divide. Young people, by contrast, tend to form friendships more speedily.

THE EXPATRIATE LIFE

It is not difficult to make friends, particularly if you are living in Brussels, but these will not necessarily be Belgians. More than a quarter of all the capital's residents come from other countries, and there are plenty of expatriate clubs offering opportunities to socialize. Many of the expatriates will be "birds of passage," with no roots in Belgium, who find fellow expats easier to get to know than the indigenous population.

Foreign residents who have lived in the country over a period of time are likely to have local friends, to whom they may well be willing to introduce you.

WHICH LANGUAGE SHOULD I USE?

About 60 percent of Belgians speak Dutch (in Belgium sometimes referred to Flemish), and the rest speak French. Few foreigners visiting Belgium will know any Dutch, but the

Flemings will accept this as a matter of course, and will be happy to speak to you in English, in which they are likely to be fairly fluent. If you know a few words of Dutch, so much the better, but in no circumstances should you address them in French!

If you speak French, by all means use it in Wallonia and Brussels, where 75 percent of the populace speak it. However, many people have a sound working knowledge of English, which they generally much prefer to Dutch.

If you find yourself in the company of both Walloons and Flemings, the lingua franca will be English, which is completely neutral.

Fortunately the residents of Luxembourg have no language hangups. Their national language is Luxembourgish, or Lëtzebuergesch, which has been described as a mixture of French and German spoken with a Dutch accent—but they won't expect visitors to speak it. They are fluent in German and French (also official languages) and are normally proficient in English, too.

FORMS OF ADDRESS

Both Dutch and French use different words for "you." In Dutch the formal "*u*" is both singular and plural, and is safest to use in a formal setting or with someone you don't know well; you will hear it frequently in phrases such as "*Dank u*" (thank you). The informal forms *je* (singular) and *jullie* (plural) are used for children, family, and close friends. If you've been invited to call someone by their first name, you can use *je*.

In French the usage is much the same—use the formal *vous* until invited to use the informal *tu*.

Although it is increasingly common for colleagues to use first names and informal pronouns at work, it is far less often done when there is a significant difference in age or seniority, or when talking to clients, suppliers, or visitors. It is best to wait until invited to move on to the informal level of address with any Belgian acquaintance. The French-speakers in Brussels are the least likely to initiate familiarities, perhaps because so many encounters in Brussels are professional and transitory.

JOINING IN

If you are in Belgium or Luxembourg for professional reasons—as an employee or a student, for example—you will have a ready-made circle of acquaintances. However, forming friendships calls for a little effort on your part. If you are invited to an informal occasion, such as a birthday party, do accept it if you can. Small social occasions are a means whereby Belgians encourage harmony in the workplace.

A great many people belong to clubs or attend evening classes in a range of subjects from languages to flower arranging. If you are spending some time in the country, to follow their example would not only help you to develop new interests but open up opportunities to socialize with your fellow-learners. If you are dedicated enough to join an evening class to learn Dutch, you may find there is an added bonus in meeting Walloons who are learning it for professional reasons.

HANGING OUT

The café culture tradition so common in most Latin countries is very much a part of the Belgian scene. At all times of day you will find people sitting in cafés, or outside on the terrace, chatting or just watching the world go by. Here you will find people from the whole spectrum of society at their most relaxed. Unless they are

Café in the Galeries Royales Saint-Hubert

obviously engrossed in a book or in a discussion with colleagues, they may be quite happy to converse with you, but it will be up to you to make the first move. A casual remark could lead to an interesting discussion.

A convivial time can also be had in bars and various live music venues in the evening, though loud music can severely inhibit conversation.

MAKING CONVERSATION

Most subjects are permissible, but people are often averse to talking about personal matters with strangers, and visitors should steer away from these unless they happen to crop up. It is best to avoid questions about their job, their family, or their salary, as they are unlikely to wish to discuss these.

Belgians, as we have seen, are modest people, and distrust people who boast about themselves or their achievements. Nor do they take kindly to people who criticize their institutions or find fault with the way their country is run (such as the dual language policy), particularly if they do so with little knowledge of why things are as they are. They enjoy humor, especially satire and slapstick, and their jokes often make fun of people from other parts of the country—though such jokes would not be well received coming from foreign visitors, so be aware of this and err on the side of caution. Sometimes their remarks can be anarchic or surreal, but they should all be taken with a pinch of salt.

The weather, food, drink, and current events are good openers. Bear in mind that Belgians in general have sophisticated tastes and can hold their own in discussions on art and other cultural matters. What else would you expect of a country with so many world-famous artists?

INVITATIONS HOME

If you are invited to dinner in someone's home, expect the evening to be fairly formal. If you receive a written invitation with the letters *RSVP* (or *VGA,* the Dutch equivalent) you should reply immediately.

To be on the safe side it is a good idea to dress smartly. "Smart casual," for instance, rules out jeans or T-shirts, and usually signifies jackets for men and a dress or suit for women. It is a good idea to bring your hosts a gift, such as flowers (but not lilies, chrysanthemums, or red roses), wine, chocolates, or a memento from your own country. If you know they have children, it is a nice gesture to bring a small present for them, too.

You should wait for your host to designate a place for you before sitting down, and refrain from eating or drinking until a toast is proposed. As in other countries in Europe, it is customary to use the knife and fork together and to place them neatly side-by-side on your plate when you have finished. Ideally, you should not leave any food on your plate. Do compliment your host and hostess on the food, even if you know they were not responsible for cooking it!

Sending a handwritten note of thanks after the event is always good manners.

Daily Life

Belgium is possibly the most urbanized country in Europe, and its population density is second only to that of the Netherlands.

HOUSING

Some 60 percent of Belgians outside the capital own their own homes, and houses are the dwelling of choice. Many people choose to remain for most of their lives in the town or village where they were born, and, given the country's small size and excellent transportation system, getting to the workplace is easy from wherever you live.

Young Belgians usually start by renting until they have accumulated enough capital to invest in a house of their own. Most houses are individually built, rather than put up by a

housing estate developer. Many young families are moving out of the cities into the country areas, which is putting tremendous pressure on green spaces.

In Brussels the accommodation pattern is different, and 60 percent of housing is rented, mainly because of the high proportion of foreign residents living there.

House in Laforêt

THE HOUSEHOLD

Although the divorce rate is high, most Belgians value traditional family life. In a small country with good transportation links nobody lives far from the rest of their family, and it is possible to visit parents and grandparents on a regular basis. Belgian parents are devoted to their children, and young fathers today are playing a much greater role in their upbringing.

At the other end of the life spectrum, Belgium has a large cohort of active elderly people who are enjoying better health and living longer than their predecessors.

Nowadays couples are getting married later, and some are deciding not to have children. As in many other European countries, the birth rate has declined, and women with children find they are able to continue their careers thanks to the extensive child-care provision available.

No mention of the family would be complete without reference to family pets. The Belgians adore animals, especially cats and dogs, and there is a higher proportion of pet ownership here than in any other country in Europe.

DAILY ROUTINE

Most families rise early in order to get to work or school by 8:00 or 8:30 a.m. The 350,000 or so commuters who work in Brussels have a particularly early start.

Breakfast varies, depending on which linguistic community a family belongs to, with the Flemish meal being more substantial than the Wallonian *petit déjeuner*. Many people lunch with their work colleagues, and, if they are not in a rush to get home, may go out with them for a drink after work.

People like to shop at markets, of which there are at least a hundred in Brussels alone. Here you can find everything —food, flowers, bric-à-brac, even pets—and the quality of the produce is uniformly good. The Sunday market near the Gare Du Midi/Zuidstation is especially popular.

Shopping hours are approximately 9:30 a.m. to 6:00 p.m. Monday to Saturday, with extended hours on Fridays.

While supermarkets stay open all day, smaller shops sometimes either close for lunch or close early on one day of the week, and there are convenience stores (*magasins de nuit/avondwinkels*) which stay open until 1:00 a.m.

School ends at 4:00 p.m., but children often participate in after-school activities. Parents are increasingly fearful of letting their children travel around on their own, and may find themselves operating a taxi service for their offspring.

When work ends for the day, Belgians like to switch off and resume their private lives. If they do not go out in the evening, for entertainment, evening classes, and so on, people stay in and mainly watch TV. Weekends are generally reserved for outings and visits to friends and family.

EDUCATION

In Belgium children start school when they are six years old, and stay until they are eighteen, but many enter the system after the age of two and a half by attending an *école maternelle/kleuterschool*. In Luxembourg preschool facilities are also available. Primary school lasts for six years and secondary school for seven.

Schools, which reflect the linguistic divide, are of three kinds: state schools, provincial or communal schools, and independent (mainly Church) schools. All receive state support to a greater or lesser degree. In Wallonia around half of primary and secondary pupils attend state schools, while in Flanders this proportion drops to around 30 percent.

At the age of eleven children start lessons in a second language, which used to be the national language that is not their mother tongue, but many now opt instead to learn English first and then go on to learn the other national language. Around 80 percent achieve a secondary education diploma, which allows them to go on to higher education, an option that around 60 percent take.

Students may enter most higher education institutions in Belgium provided they have a diploma. The country has a well-established university system which is organized by the two main language communities. The oldest university is the Catholic University of Leuven/Louvain, founded in 1425. Other notable institutions are Ghent University, Antwerp University, the Free University of Brussels, and Liège University. Students from the German-speaking enclave normally study in Germany.

*University Law Faculty,
Louvain-la-Neuve*

Luxembourg acquired its own university more recently, in 2003. The University of Luxembourg teaches through the media of German and French. As in Belgium, the first degree is the bachelor's degree, which normally takes three years; the second level is the master's, which takes a further one or two years. The choice of subjects is currently limited, so students of certain disciplines study abroad.

THE ARMED FORCES

Conscription has been abolished in Belgium, but volunteers aged eighteen are recruited for the armed services. Luxembourg is similar, but its minimum age for recruits, both male and female, is seventeen.

MAIL AND TELECOMMUNICATIONS

Post Offices open from 9:00 a.m. to 5:00 p.m. on weekdays, but close on Saturday afternoons, They offer banking and other services. The mail service to places outside Belgium is considered to be slower than it ought to be.

The telephone service, now privatized, is run by Belgiacom. Public telephones take credit cards or phone cards, obtainable from newsagents and post offices. Cell phones are in general use.

As elsewhere, Internet use is common.

NEWSPAPERS, TV, AND RADIO

Newspaper readership is on the decline, although sports papers and local newspapers remain popular. The main quality newspapers in Flanders are *De Standaard* and *De Morgen,* while the leading French-language newspapers are *Le Soir* and *La Libre Belgique.* The weekly English-language newspaper *Le Bulletin* provides foreign residents with news and information on forthcoming events in Belgium.

Two public broadcasting networks in Belgium serve the two main linguistic communities, RTBF providing programmes in French, and VRT in Dutch. There are also commercial and satellite channels. Digital TV is also available.

Leisure Time

Belgians are able to enjoy their time off amid comfortable surroundings with plenty of good food and drink. Hardworking they may be, but they appreciate their leisure time as it gives them a chance to unwind and enjoy the fruits of their labors. The people of Luxembourg also appreciate the good life.

SHOPPING FOR PLEASURE

Shopping in Belgium is a positive delight, and Brussels leads the way for the sophisticated shopper with the Avenue Louise, the Anspach Center at De Brouckère, and the Galeries Royales St. Hubert, the world's first shopping mall, which was built in 1847.

The Belgians, however, favor Antwerp which, in addition to smart stores and boutiques, offers antique and secondhand shops, and, of course, diamond dealers.

Most traders prefer cash to credit or debit cards, so it's advisable to carry plenty of banknotes. You will find ATMs at most banks if you run short. Banking hours are usually from 9:00 a.m. to 4:00 or 5:00 p.m.

EATING OUT

With more restaurants per capita than any other country in the world, Belgium is a gourmet's paradise. You have two national cuisines and a score of others to choose from.

Even breakfasts vary, depending on which part of Belgium you are in. In Flanders you will be served cold meats along with various breads, jams, fruit juices, and coffee, while in the French-speaking parts a more frugal "continental breakfast" is served.

Restaurants are open from around 11:00 a.m. until 3:00 p.m. for lunch, and from 6.30 to 10.30 p.m. for dinner. Brasseries, which are more casual eateries, open at 11:00 a.m. and usually stay open all day and evening.

There are also plenty of cafés around, but not all of them serve food. You can usually get a meal in an *estaminet/eetcafé*, a *grand café*, or (in Flanders) a *herberg*. If you are in the market for fast food, try one of the kiosks selling *frites/fritures* (chips/French fries) or *gaufres/wafels* (waffles).

Eating out is a social occasion for most Belgians, so it doesn't matter to them if the service is a bit slow. Even dogs are frequently included in the family parties.

TIPPING

In restaurants and cafés a service charge is normally added to the bill but, if it is not, a 5 or 10 percent tip is considered sufficient.

In theaters and cinemas the usherette who shows you to your seat will expect a one-euro tip, and the cloakroom attendant will expect a similar amount.

Café-restaurant on the Grand' Place

FOOD

Belgian food caters to every taste. Being a maritime country, Belgium has excellent seafood, and there is a wide range of fresh vegetables. There are several specialties for which Belgium is famous, including the following dishes:

bisque d'homard	poached lobster in seafood stock
sole Ostendaise	fresh fillet of sole served with lemon and butter
carbonnades flamandes	beef fillets braised in beer
faisan à la Brabançonne	pheasant roasted with braised chicory, herbs, and bacon
anguilles au vert	eels cooked in butter served with herbs
ragout d'agneau	braised lamb with chicory, onions, and herbs
Genste stoverij	beer and beef stew with mustard
waterzooi	chicken or fish stew with cream and white wine

Luxembourg cuisine has elements of German cuisine and Franco-Belgian cuisine. Among its specialties are:

carré de porc fumé	smoked pork and broad beans
cochon de lait en gelée	jellied suckling pig
jambon d'Ardennes	smoked Ardennes ham
tarte aux quetsches	plum tart

One of the most famous products of Belgium is its chocolate, and all over the country you will find chocolate specialists selling their delectable wares. Belgian chocolate manufacturing dates back to the 1880s when cocoa was first imported from the plantations of the Belgian Congo. Dark chocolate made here has a very high cocoa content. Known as pralines, the chocolates have fillings of cream, nuts, or rich, dark chocolate.

DRINK

The favored drink in Belgium is beer, which is not restricted to just a few brands, such as Stella Artois, Leffe, and Jupiter. The average Belgian downs ninety-three liters of beer annually, and the country boasts around 125 breweries that reputedly produce more than 8,700 different beers, including seasonal beers. Some of these are brewed to recipes devised by Trappist monks who fled to Belgium during the French Revolution.

Apart from table beer (with an alcoholic strength of around 1.5 percent) most specialty beers are strong. There are various types that normally come in bottles, such as amber ale, blonde ale, brown ale, Dubbel (a Trappist beer), Flemish Red, Oud Bruin (a Flemish sour brown ale), Tripel, and white beer (made from wheat). Lambic beers, from a region southwest of Brussels, are normally served straight from the barrel, and may contain fruit. Luxembourg also boasts some excellent local brews.

There are vineyards in both Wallonia and Flanders, but the wine (90 percent white) is mainly for local consumption. Luxembourg produces white Moselle wines, which tend to be drier than the German equivalent and are exported to Belgium.

CULTURE AND ENTERTAINMENT

Belgium's art galleries and museums number almost three hundred, and there are more than seventy in Brussels alone. The range of subject matter they cover is vast.

The Théâtre Royale de la Monnaie is not only Belgium's leading opera house but it also witnessed a turning-point in the country's

history. On August 25, 1830, the aria "Amour sacré de la patrie" ("Sacred Love of the Fatherland") from Auber's opera *La muette de Portici* provoked a riot against Dutch rule and paved the way to independence.

The Palais des Beaux-Arts boasts the capital's largest concert hall, and puts on concerts by the acclaimed Belgian National Orchestra; like most arts organizations it receives a generous subsidy from the government. The Art Deco Kaaitheater is a center for dance and the Théâtre Marionettes de Toone specializes in puppet shows presented by the same family since 1830.

Film aficionados are well catered to by the twenty-eight-screen Kinepolis to the north of the city, the Musée du Cinema in the Palais des Beaux-Arts complex, and other venues.

The Kaaitheater, Brussels

Note that usherettes and cloakroom attendants expect one-euro tips (see box on Tipping on page 103).

The Forêt National arena, southeast of Brussels city center, hosts rock, folk, and pop concerts, and the Ancienne Belgique near the center puts on smaller-scale events of this type. As you would expect of the country that gave birth to the inventor of the saxophone, there are several venues specializing in jazz and blues, such as Travers, Sounds, and L'Archiduc.

There is a vibrant cultural life outside Brussels, notably in Antwerp, Ghent, and Liège, each of which boasts an opera house whose seasons run from September to May. The country has a number of world-class dance companies, notably the contemporary Les Ballets C de la B, based in Ghent, and the Royal Flanders Ballet, based in Antwerp.

Music features prominently in several of the festivals held throughout the country, such as the Flanders Festival, the Brussels Jazz Marathon at the end of May, the Festival of Wallonia from June to October, and the Bosella Folk and Jazz Festival in July. Werchter, near Leuven, hosts the country's largest rock festival (June–July), and a similar festival, Pukkelpop, takes place at Hasselt in late August.

Luxembourg's modern Grand Theatre with its two auditoria provides opera, dance, and drama performances, while the Philharmonie Concert Hall provides a wide spectrum of music.

STUDENTS, CLUBBING, AND CLOSE ENCOUNTERS

Brussels is world unto itself, with a very mixed and vibrant nightlife. There is something for everyone here. Along the Avenue Louise or Chaussée de Waterloo you will find an array of champagne and cocktail bars and clubs, for which the dress code is designer. The central Sablon area is frequented by an older expatriate crowd. The Saint-Géry quarter is much more chilled out and casual, with bars clustered around the square, and in the summer the terraces overflow with revellers.

The students and the more dressed-down and hip crowd head for the district of Ixelles for live music, or to the Matonge district for live African music and dancing. Some of the side streets off the Avenue Louise and the sleazier Schaerbeek area near the Gare du Nord are the red light districts. Single women should avoid the latter.

In Brussels' gay district, located in the St. Jacques quarter, there are Latino nightclubs, techno music, and the great Chez Maman's drag club in which to glitter the night away. The trendy rue Antoine Dansaert is where locals meet to while away their evenings in cocoon-like bars, and where the famous 1930s jazz café, L'Archiduc, still stands. The international community, which is quite cut off from Belgian society, will find a familiar crowd in the Irish pubs and continental bars in the Place du Luxembourg.

Possibly overwhelmed by the number of foreigners in their midst, young Belgians tend to socialize separately, within their own language groups, and it can be hard to break into a circle of friends. Typically new friends are made at work, through clubs and societies, and especially at house parties. A distinctive social activity is the drinking game Cantus, which has strict rules involving traditional songs and drinking beer and is divided by gender. Although Ghent and Leuven/La Neuve are the liveliest student towns, good places to meet a student and bohemian crowd in Brussels are Parvis de Saint-Gilles and the Université Libre de Bruxelles (ULB) in Etterbeek. Brussels municipality also organizes lots of very popular free events and festivals.

Young Belgians are more conservative and family minded— polite and well-brought-up—than Anglo-Saxons. Dating etiquette may be a little more formal than Americans and British people are used to, though Dutch-speakers may be less strait-laced than their Francophone counterparts.

SPORTS

The Belgians are passionate about cycle racing, and one of the main events of the year is De Gordel (the Ring), a 100-meter (62-mile) ride around the outer suburbs of Brussels, along which participants can also jog or walk.

Tennis and football are also popular sports, and the leading football clubs, such as Anderlecht, Club Brugge, and Standard Liège, have an enthusiastic following. Belgians are also fond of hiking, for which specialist hiking maps are available.

Horse riding, rock climbing, kayaking, water skiing, and yachting are other popular pastimes, and in the winter when the Ardennes are covered with snow the more energetic like to undertake skiing and other winter sports.

Getting Around

Belgium is a compact country, and journeys between even the most distant places take only a matter of hours. Public transport in both Belgium and Luxembourg is efficient, frequent, and reliable. Belgian trains are clean and fast (except for the *stoptreinen*). Brussels is the hub of the network and is particularly well served by high-speed international expresses linking it to Paris, Amsterdam, Cologne, and London. There is seldom any need to pay the full price for a ticket, as there are various types of discounted tickets, which can be bought up to five days in advance and are well worth enquiring about.

There are bus services, which often connect with rail services, and the waterways also provide transportation possibilities, but these are mainly for tourists.

URBAN TRANSPORTATION

Brussels has an efficient transport system comprising a metro (subway), buses, and trams. The metro has signs in both French and Dutch. Tickets can be used over the entire transport network, and it is cheaper to buy a five- or ten-ticket card. Each ticket is valid for an hour, with no restriction on the number of changes you make, and must be inserted in a validation machine each time you enter a metro station or board a bus or tram.

There are tram networks in Antwerp and Ghent, and also along the coast. Other cities rely on buses.

Taxis are very expensive, and charge an initial fee plus an additional charge for the distance traveled. They charge double rates outside the city boundaries, and premium rates apply after 10:00 p.m. Tips and taxes are included in the price shown on the meter, but even so many drivers expect an additional tip.

DRIVING

Driving in Brussels itself may be hair-raising at times, but elsewhere in Belgium it can be a pleasure. However, the country was late to introduce driving tests, which didn't come in until 1967, and even people who have passed their test often drive in a cavalier fashion.

Be warned. Belgium has twice as many fatal accidents per head of population as its neighbors, and although there are speed limits—120 kmph (75 mph) on expressways, 90 kmph (56 mph) on other roads, 50 kmph (31 mph) in towns, and 30 kmph (18 mph) in some residential streets—they are not always scrupulously observed. The drink-drive limit is 0.5 mg per ml, but the police are more lenient than elsewhere, and a driver can ask for a thirty-minute delay before taking a breathalyser test.

Road signs can be confusing. Priority should be given to trams and traffic coming from the right at junctions, even out of side roads. If you see an orange-yellow diamond surrounded by white it means the main road has priority. Look out for cyclists when turning right over a cycle path.

As in other European countries, seat belts are compulsory, and children under twelve should sit in the back. Warning triangles should be carried for use in a breakdown, and so should car documents.

CYCLING AND WALKING

Although cycling is not as popular in Belgium as in the Netherlands, Flanders in particular has good facilities, such as cycle lanes, especially in the cities, and cycles can be rented at many railway stations. The towns of Wallonia are less cycle-friendly, and central Brussels can be dangerous. Always lock your bicycle, since cycle theft is common.

Pedestrians need to take care at designated crossings near junctions as cars are allowed to filter round corners even when the green man symbol is flashing. Also, many drivers are reluctant to stop at pedestrian crossings.

PLACES TO VISIT

Brussels (meaning "village on the marshes") has its particularly grand Grand' Place, dominated by the Gothic Hôtel de Ville (town hall) with its 320-foot belfry, and surrounded by seventeenth-century guild houses. Other sights are the Cathedral of Saint Michel and Sainte Gudule and the Art Deco Sacré-Coeur Basilica, the world's fifth-largest church. The Musées Royaux des Beaux Arts (Royal Fine Arts Museums—one specializing in art of the fifteenth to the eighteenth centuries, the other specializing in modern art of the nineteenth century onwards) are the best in the country. The Centre Belge de la Bande Dessinée celebrates the work of comic-strip cartoonists, many of them Belgian. To the south of Brussels is Waterloo, site of the famous battle that changed the face of Europe.

Antwerp is the principal city of Flanders, Belgium's largest port, an industrial center, and the hub of the world's diamond trade. It boasts a fine central square (Grote Markt) with an ornate sixteenth-century town hall (Stadhuis), a cathedral (Onze Lieve Vrouwe Kathedraal), and St. Paul's Church (Sint Pauluskerk). A mile away from the Grote Markt is the impressive Koninklijk Museum voor Schone Kunsten (Royal Fine Arts Museum), which traces Flemish painting from the Middle Ages to the present. In Wappen Square you will find the Rubenshuis, where the artist Rubens lived and worked.

The Stadhuis, Bruges

Bruges/Brugge is an unspoilt medieval town that is often described as "the Venice of the North" because of its canal network. Like other cities it has a fine town hall (Stadhuis) dating from around 1400, and its cathedral has the tallest spire in the country. The Groeninge Museum contains an extensive collection of early Flemish and Dutch masters.

Ghent was second in size only to Paris in the middle of the fourteenth century. It was the center of the cloth trade, and continues to have an important textile industry. Here you will find many Renaissance buildings and a great Gothic cathedral, Sint Baafskathedraal, which houses the famous Ghent altarpiece by Jan and Hubert Van Eyck.

Belgium has some beautiful beaches along its coastline, and the south of the country is full of attractive scenery.

PLACE NAMES

As we have seen, many places in Belgium have two names—a Dutch name and a French name, and the signs tend not to be bilingual. So, if you are heading for Liège (which is in the French-speaking region) you will not find that name on any signpost in Flanders. Instead you should look out for its Dutch name, Luik.

The following are some of the major towns that have dual names; in each case the French name is given first.

Anvers/Antwerpen; Bruxelles/Brussel; Bruges/Brugge; Contrai/Kortrijk; Gand/Gent; Liège/Luik; Louvain/Leuven; Malines/Mechelen; Mons/Bergen; Ostende/Oostende, Saint-Trond/Sint-Truiden; Tongres/Tongeren, Tournai/Doornik; Ypres/Ieper.

HEALTH AND SAFETY

Belgium boasts one of the best healthcare systems in Europe, and EU citizens are entitled to use the state service on the same terms as Belgians on production of the European Health Insurance Card. This involves paying for treatment, then applying for partial reimbursement from the local Mutualité/Ziekefonds office. However, travel insurance is recommended. A similar system operates in Luxembourg.

WHERE TO STAY

The standard of accommodation in Belgium and Luxembourg is generally good, and both countries use the Benelux Standard method of classifying hotels and guest houses, based on a star system.

Bed-and-breakfast establishments (*chambres d'hôtes/ gastenkamer*) are very popular, as are residential apartment hotels (*résidences*) offering weekly or monthly rates for those contemplating a longer stay.

In the countryside accommodation is available in *gîtes ruraux/landelijke verbliyven*, which are often attached to farms. Youth hostels (*auberges de jeunesse/jeugdherbergen*) are run by two organizations, one for Wallonia and the other for Flanders. Campsites are numerous, and are classified in the same way as hotels.

LAW AND ORDER

Belgium is a relatively safe country with a low crime rate, but beware of pickpockets in the main railway stations and public spaces of Brussels. If you are robbed or burgled you should report the crime to the nearest police station to obtain the necessary documentation for making an insurance claim.

Business and Professional Life

Belgium's strategic position has made it an important trading nation ever since the Middle Ages. Today its cosmopolitanism has been reinforced by the presence of a large number of multinational companies, many of which employ expatriates as well as Belgian nationals. These and the various international organizations based in Brussels, such as the European Commission and NATO, have a culture of their own and are therefore not considered here.

A third of Belgian industry is reputed to be owned by the Société Générale de Belgique. Seventy per cent of small to medium-sized businesses are family firms. Flemish companies usually have the letters NV or BVBA after their names, and Walloon firms have the initials SA or SPRL.

Luxembourg's economy was once dominated by the steel industry, but it has since diversified, especially into financial services. In terms of per capita income it ranks third in the world. Sixty per cent of the labor force are not Luxembourgers, and often live in neighboring countries.

THE ROLE OF GOVERNMENT

Although the Belgian government is keen to encourage inward investment, would-be investors are sometimes deterred by the levels of bureaucracy through which they have to wade. Another problem lies in the fact that in the past public appointments were made on the basis of political affiliation rather than competence.

Belgian businesspeople often have a Belgian solution to overcoming problems with their bureaucracy: they simply circumvent the rules and regulations. Foreigners are strongly advised not to try the same thing.

The government is keen to foster good labor relations and corporate social responsibility. Disagreement can break out over how to achieve these goals, but after much discussion a compromise of sorts is eventually reached.

BUSINESS PRACTICE

By now the reader of this book will be aware of Belgium's linguistic divide. English tends to be the lingua franca in the Dutch- and German-speaking areas, and although the Walloons are usually proficient in English they will prefer to speak French, unless they see you are struggling.

The Flemings are fairly direct, but couch their language in politer tones than their Dutch neighbors. In this respect their style comes closer to that found in the French-speaking community. When addressing German- and Dutch-speakers it would be quite in order to use the English terms Mr., Mrs., and Miss; but in the French-speaking area *Monsieur*, *Madame*, and *Mademoiselle* are more appropriate.

First names are usually used only between friends, though at work if you are speaking to someone at a similar level to yours it may be permissible. However, a strict hierarchy exists in most firms and it is best to address older and more senior staff members formally. When speaking formally to one another the Flemings use the formal *u* (you) and French-speakers *vous*.

REGIONAL DIFFERENCES

There are a few subtle differences between businesses in Wallonia and those in Flanders. Those in the French-speaking part tend to be more formal and hierarchical, with top-down leadership. People are aware of their place in the organization and don't generally venture outside the boundaries of their position.

Flemish companies usually have less hierarchical structures, and responsibility is delegated to a greater degree. Senior managers tend to be more consultative and to work more closely with the rest of the workforce.

The business atmosphere in Luxembourg is not markedly different from that found in Belgium, with a particular emphasis on consensus and collaboration. Business is conducted in a low-key fashion and the Luxembourgers are unimpressed by extravagant claims or high-pressure tactics.

PREPARING FOR MEETINGS

Written communications are couched in formal and elegant prose, and, whatever language you are using, you should express yourself as politely as possible. Even e-mails can be quite formal.

When addressing a letter you should note that in Belgium the "Van" prefix in Dutch names is spelled with a capital letter, whereas in the Netherlands it begins with a lower-case "v." Professional titles should be included, if known.

It is sensible to propose an initial meeting well in advance, as people have busy schedules; and you should ask them to suggest a suitable date and time. The appointment should be confirmed by e-mail or telephone a day or so before it is due to take place.

Business cards are usually exchanged at meetings, and it will make a favourable impression if you have yours translated into the target language of your counterpart, and don't omit to include your qualifications.

It should go without saying that you need to brief yourself thoroughly beforehand, and ensure you have detailed documentation to hand out, preferably in French or Dutch, whichever is appropriate. Bear in mind that you will be expected to be formally dressed.

MEETINGS

Punctuality is essential in Belgium, and you should double-check the time you have agreed upon, both in your language and in that of your hosts, since mistakes are possible. For instance, the Dutch *half negen* (half-nine) means half past eight, not half past nine. The Walloons are as much sticklers for time as the Flemings are.

A firm handshake gets the meeting off to a good start, and if there are several people present they should all be greeted in a similar fashion, and names and titles exchanged.

As in Latin countries, the first meeting is often reserved for getting to know one another and establishing mutual trust. It is unusual to get down to business straight away, as in the Netherlands, though it occasionally happens.

People like meetings to be well structured and focused. Having an agenda is a good idea and can keep a meeting on track, though you should be flexible enough to allow for deviations if they could prove fruitful.

PRESENTATIONS

Marshal your facts and figures, and be prepared to present them clearly. Your audience will appreciate concrete ideas, practical solutions, and good empirical evidence to back up your case. Choose common sense and a low-key approach over spin every time. A hard sell is likely to be resisted.

NEGOTIATIONS

Your interlocutors are likely to seek compromise and consensus rather than be confrontational. Some Belgians say that this is a key difference between them and the Dutch. A calm negotiating style, patience, and readiness to concede points will always move your case ahead more safely than aggression or a rigid bottom line. This can mean, however, that decision making is slow, as every point of view is considered and consensus is built.

DECISIONS

Establishing trust is one key to a successful outcome, and achieving consensus is another, especially in Flanders, and can be time-consuming. In Wallonia, by contrast, the ultimate decision tends to lie in the hands of a single individual.

Once an agreement has been reached it is essential to have adequate follow-up. Letters should be sent confirming the agreements made and thanking individuals for their help and participation, and you should issue progress reports, as well as keeping in touch by sending Christmas cards, for example.

BUSINESS ENTERTAINMENT

Dinners are purely social occasions. Lunches are a different matter, and if you are invited out to lunch in the middle of serious negotiations, you should not feel put out. Working lunches are quite common, and offer an opportunity to discuss business in a more informal manner than in the boardroom. If you have a late morning appointment, you could be whisked away for lunch immediately.

By all means enjoy the food, but at a business lunch it is best to stick to mineral water. If you relax or behave carelessly you could miss out on an important deal. A successful lunch meeting might clinch it.

Belgians like to forget about business once they are at home. If you are invited to a business contact's home for dinner, this will be a purely social occasion.

WOMEN IN BUSINESS

Women and men are equal in the sight of the law, and good maternity-leave provision and child-care facilities mean that those women who wish to pursue their careers after marriage are well catered to; but while women account for a substantial proportion of the workforce their average remuneration falls well below what men earn.

Despite gaining full voting rights in 1948, there are very few women who hold high political office. However, in both business and professional life well-educated women are starting to make their mark and are particularly well represented in the professions.

Chapter 3

BRITAIN

Key Facts

Official Name	United Kingdom of Great Britain and Northern Ireland. Short forms United Kingdom, Britain	**Government (cont.)**	Scotland has its own Scottish Parliament and Wales a National Assembly.
Capital City	London	**Radio and TV**	The British Broadcasting Corporation (BBC) is non-commercial, funded through a license fee. Commercial broadcasters include ITV, Channel 4, Channel 5, BSkyB. There are numerous radio stations, both national and local, many of which are operated by the BBC. Wales has a TV channel and radio stations broadcasting in Welsh. TV uses the PAL system.
National Capitals	*Scotland:* Edinburgh; *Wales:* Cardiff; *Northern Ireland:* Belfast		
Major Cities	*England:* Manchester, Birmingham, Liverpool. *Scotland:* Glasgow, Aberdeen. *Wales:* Wrexham, Newport. *N. Ireland:* Londonderry		
Area	93,822 sq. miles (9243,000 sq. km)		
Terrain	Lowlands and hills; mountainous in Scotland, Wales, and the north of England	**Press**	National: *The Times, Guardian, Daily Telegraph, Independent, Daily Mail, Sun,* and many others. Regional: *The Scotsman, Glasgow Herald, Western Mail, Yorkshire Post, Liverpool Daily Post,* etc.
Climate	Temperate		
Currency	Pound sterling		
Population	61 million		
Language	English. Also Welsh in Wales, some Scots Gaelic in Scotland	**Electricity**	230–240 volts, 50 Hz. 3-prong plugs used
Religion	Christian 72%; Muslim 2.7%; Hindu 1%; Sikh 0.6%; Jewish 0.5%; Buddhist 0.3%	**Internet Domain**	.uk
		Telephone	Country code: 44 For international calls dial 00.
Government	Constitutional monarchy. Bicameral parliament: House of Commons (elected) and House of Lords (unelected)	**Time Zone**	Greenwich Mean Time (GMT/UTC), with summer daylight saving

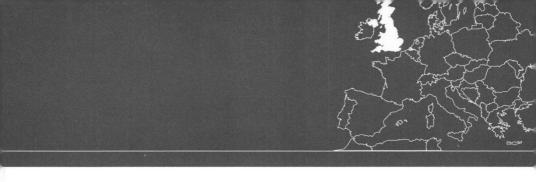

Map of Britain

SCOTLAND

Aberdeen

Glasgow
Edinburgh

Londonderry

Belfast
NORTHERN IRELAND
Armagh
Newry

Newcastle-
upon-Tyne

NORTH SEA

ISLE OF MAN

ENGLAND

Blackpool   Leeds

Liverpool

Manchester Sheffield

Wrexham

Nottingham

Norwich

WALES

Birmingham   Leicester

Carmarthen

Coventry   Cambridge

Swansea Newport

Oxford   Ipswich

Cardiff

London

Bristol Reading

Southampton Portsmouth
Bournemouth

Plymouth

Brighton

ISLE OF WIGHT

The Country and Its People

Great Britain (the epithet "great" is used to differentiate it from Brittany in France) consists of England, Scotland, and Wales, and stretches from the Shetland Islands in the north to the Scilly Isles in the southwest. Together with Northern Ireland these countries form the United Kingdom. (Northern Ireland is covered in the section on Ireland on page 244.)

It is situated in the northwest corner of Europe and is entirely surrounded by sea. The terrain is generally fairly flat or gently

The white cliffs of Dover

undulating in the south, but becomes increasingly hilly and mountainous the further north you go. Thanks to the Gulf Stream, Britain enjoys a temperate climate, generally with little snow in winter except in the uplands, and its maritime location causes the weather to be changeable.

England accounts for well over four-fifths of the population of Great Britain (61 million), and most of the people can claim mixed blood—Anglo-Saxon, Norman French, Scandinavian, and Celtic. Over the past half-century there has been an influx of people from the Commonwealth. Afro-Caribbeans have favored the London area, while Asians from the Indian subcontinent have settled predominantly in London, Birmingham, Manchester, Leicester, and Bradford.

Both the Scots and the Welsh take pride in their Celtic ancestry and like to emphasize their distinctiveness. Although they remain part of the United Kingdom, they have also achieved some measure of political autonomy in recent years. A substantial minority would like complete independence from England.

Britain has changed considerably since the Second World War. It is no longer an imperial power, although it still has many overseas interests. The influx of people from all over the world has made it more cosmopolitan and multicultural—and more open to new ideas. This is no longer the country of Bertie Wooster and Mary Poppins. It is changing—and changing fast.

A HISTORICAL PERSPECTIVE

Many of Britain's foundations were laid in the first millennium CE with waves of invasions. First the Romans came and civilized the country—England, at least—with straight roads and underfloor heating, and built a wall (still in existence) to keep out the Scots. Then came the Anglo-Saxon invasions and England became a predominantly Anglo-Saxon society, with the indigenous Celtic population pushed to the extremities.

The next invaders were the Vikings, who established their rule over considerable areas of the country. Finally, in 1066, the Normans, led by William the Conqueror, imposed their rule on the English. For the next three centuries French was the language of the ruling classes and the Conqueror's successors ruled large swathes of France as well as England.

During this era the English legal system was established and the first steps to curb the powers of the monarch were implemented when King John was forced to sign Magna Carta by the rebellious barons in 1215. Edward I sought to bring both Scotland and Wales under his control, but later the country was torn apart as the rival royal houses of York and Lancaster battled it out for the English throne. (Shakespeare's history plays give many of the details.)

Expansion, Prosperity, and Civil War

The Wars of the Roses ended with Henry Tudor's victory at the Battle of Bosworth. Henry VII's second son, Henry VIII, was to change England for ever by breaking off relations with the Pope and establishing a separate English Church, thus paving the way for the Reformation in England. He appropriated all the lands belonging to the monasteries and married six times, each time in an attempt to leave a male heir to the throne.

With the accession of his Catholic daughter, Mary, the Protestant Reformation threatened to go into reverse. But her half-sister, Elizabeth I, ushered in a period of peace and prosperity during which the arts flourished and the foundations of Britain's overseas empire were laid. England emerged as a preeminent naval power after it defeated an armada of ships from Spain.

The kingdoms of Scotland and England were united when Mary, Queen of Scots' son, James Stuart (VI of Scotland, I of England) succeeded Elizabeth. During his reign the first successful English colony was established in America and a monumental translation of the Scriptures was commissioned: the King James Bible.

James' successor, Charles I, was less successful; civil war broke out in 1642 between Parliament and the king, culminating in his execution in 1649 and the creation of a Commonwealth (republic), with Oliver Cromwell as Lord Protector (equivalent to President).

Monarchy and Democracy

The republican experiment lasted until 1660, when the exiled heir to the throne, Charles II, was invited to return to England (the Restoration), resulting in the reinstatement of the House of Lords and the Anglican Church. In 1688 his brother, James II, was dethroned on account of his Catholic beliefs and the Protestant

KEY HISTORICAL DATES

43 CE	Roman conquest of England begins.
9th century	Picts and Scots unite to form Kingdom of Scotland.
1066	Battle of Hastings; the victorious William of Normandy gains the English throne.
1085	A survey of England is announced, recorded in the Domesday Book.
1215	English Barons force King John to sign Magna Carta, limiting royal power and binding the king to the law of the land.
1455–85	The Wars of the Roses between rival royal houses, ending with Henry VII's accession to the throne.
1534	Henry VIII breaks off relations with the Pope and founds the Church of England.
1553	Henry's daughter, Mary, becomes queen and tries to reinstate Catholicism.
1558–1603	Reign of Elizabeth I stabilizes the country.
1603	King James VI of Scotland becomes King of England, uniting the two countries.
1642	Start of English Civil War, which leads to the beheading of King Charles I.
1660	Restoration of the Monarchy.
1688	The Glorious Revolution; William of Orange replaces the Catholic James II.
1707	Act of Union unites English and Scottish Parliaments.
1783	Britain loses its thirteen American colonies.
1801	Act of Union unites Great Britain and Ireland.
1815	Wellington defeats Napoleon at the Battle of Waterloo.
1837–1901	Reign of Queen Victoria.
1914–1918	First World War, ending in victory for Britain and its allies.
1939–45	Second World War, ending in victory for Britain and its allies.
1947	Britain grants independence to India and Burma.
1948	National Health Service established.
1952	Elizabeth II becomes Queen.
1973	Britain becomes a member of the European Community.

William of Orange was invited to rule England with his wife Mary, who was James' sister.

The following century witnessed the union of the English and Scottish parliaments, the beginnings of the modern parliamentary system, the industrial revolution, and the loss of Britain's American colonies during the reign of George III. At the close of the eighteenth century Napoleon posed a military threat to most of Europe, but in 1815 he was eventually defeated by the coalition forces under the Duke of Wellington at the Battle of Waterloo.

Winged Victory, Victoria
Memorial, London

The nineteenth century was a time of progress and reform. Railways were built, the British Empire expanded, slavery was abolished, voting rights were extended, and universal education was introduced. But the optimistic belief in progress was shattered with the outbreak of the First World War in 1914.

The postwar period brought many changes: Irish independence, an economic crisis, and agitation for better working conditions. But, with Hitler's rise to power in Germany, the peace was short-lived. The Second World War resulted in victory again for Britain and its allies, but it was in many ways a hollow one. Subsequent years saw the dismantling of the Empire and economic decline, but on the positive side the development of the welfare state ensured that henceforth nobody would live in penury.

GOVERNMENT

Britain is a constitutional monarchy, in which the monarch's role is largely ceremonial. Although the Queen may choose her prime minister, in effect it is the leader of the party commanding the majority of seats in the House of Commons who gets the job. The House of Commons consists of 645 members elected by the "first past the post" system, although election through proportional representation is sometimes mooted. There are currently moves under consideration to reduce the number of MPs and introduce a fairer voting system known as AV (the Alternative Vote). No one party won a clear majority of seats in the 2010 General Election, so the party with the most MPs—the Conservatives—formed a coalition government with the Liberal Democrats. Members of the House of Lords are appointed, but there are moves afoot to make this an elected chamber.

The lower tier of government is provided by county and district councils, metropolitan borough councils, or unitary authorities. The main political parties are the Conservative Party (sometimes known as the Tories), the Labour Party, and the Liberal Democrats. Others include the Green Party, the British National Party (BNP)—an extreme right-wing group—and the United Kingdom Independence Party (UKIP), which campaigns for Britain's withdrawal from the European Union.

Scotland has its own parliament, which sits in Edinburgh and is responsible for domestic matters. Wales has an Assembly, which sits in Cardiff, but its powers are less extensive than those of the Scottish parliament. Both countries have large nationalist parties campaigning for complete independence from the rest of the United Kingdom.

There are a number of islands that have links with Britain for the purposes of foreign policy and defense, but are otherwise independent. The Isle of Man, in the Irish Sea between Britain and Ireland, boasts the world's oldest parliament, the Tynwald. The Channel Islands (Guernsey, Jersey, Sark, and Alderney), close to the coast of northern France, are also self-governing, and serve as a reminder of Britain's historical ties with Normandy.

Houses of Parliament, London

Values and Attitudes

One needs to start by accepting that no two British people think alike. They pride themselves on their individualism, which some might consider eccentricity. They are generally tolerant, self-deprecating, and creative. They distrust intellectuals, dislike pomposity, and may often appear aloof.

There are national and regional differences: the Scots are extremely proud of their Scottishness; the Welsh are sometimes distrustful of strangers; people from the north of England have a reputation for being bluff and friendly; the southerners are more introverted and cautious. However, all these are mere generalities.

HUMOR

British people have a sense of humor that other nations do not always readily understand. Much of what they say is laced with irony, and such comments as "Charming!" or "Lovely day!" may mean just the opposite of what they say.

The British enjoy satire, especially political satire, often found in publications such as *Private Eye*. Stand-up comedians are popular, and so are TV situation comedies, especially those that deal with class differences. Some of the most popular ones, such as *Yes Minister*, *Dad's Army*, and *Fawlty Towers*, were made decades ago.

The English, especially, are masters of the understatement. So be warned should you ever challenge a person to a game of poker, for example. When you ask him if he has ever played before and he replies, "I've played a game or two," that could mean that he is the poker champion of Great Britain.

FAIRNESS AND COMPROMISE

Most people think sports are just about winning a match. For English people, it is how the game is played that really matters, and they dislike players who use devious methods to achieve their ends. They have a strong sense of fair play.

Allied with this is a feeling of sympathy with the underdog. People express delight when someone achieves success despite the odds against them. They are just as pleased when a person who enjoys more success than they feel he deserves experiences a sudden downfall.

In the best of worlds everyone wants to have his own way, but on a crowded island this would only lead to anarchy. For this reason British people are very keen to arrive at some form of consensus, even if this involves compromising their beliefs. They still have the habit of waiting patiently in queues (lines) to take their turn.

CLASS AND STATUS

British society used to consist of the upper class (aristocracy and landed gentry), the middle class (professional and managerial), and the working class. After the Second World War greater social mobility started to blur the boundaries between the classes, but in recent years that process seems to have stalled.

At one time members of the upper class tended to look down on people involved in business, or "trade," as it was called, but this kind of snobbery has almost disappeared, especially since many businessmen have made a great deal of money and enjoy the same lifestyle as those who were once considered their superiors. Class divisions have not disappeared altogether, because class is not just to do with money. Education at a good public (that is, private) school can enhance your prospects in life. If you have a title—a peerage or a knighthood—you are treated with respect, while people who lack good manners, or speak in a style or with an accent that marks them as having working-class origins or lacking a good education, still tend to be looked down on by those who speak "the Queen's English."

In some quarters status is defined by what you have rather than by what you are. Some people like to drive expensive cars and have stylish houses and possessions in order to "keep up with the Joneses." Other people dislike this materialism.

One disturbing phenomenon of recent years is the emergence of an underclass—households dependent entirely on state benefits with no member of working age actually in work.

ORDER AND TOLERANCE

The British are on the whole an orderly lot; they stand in lines at bus stops, outside football grounds, and in shops. The idea of pushing forward ahead of others who were there before them (jumping the queue) is anathema to them; this would be bad manners. Most like to have order and routine in their lives.

They are also tolerant to a fault. Their toleration extends to crowded and unreliable trains, rubbish in the streets, and poor service. Many prefer not to complain, being resigned to the fact that complaining will not make one bit of difference.

ALTRUISM AND DUTY

British people may seem aloof, but they are not self-centered. There are no fewer than 167,000 organizations registered with the Charities Commission, and perhaps a further 200,000 voluntary bodies that are not. Half the population make regular donations to charity, either by dipping into their own purses or by devoting their time and energy to raising funds—taking part in sponsored walks or runs, doing street collections, organizing events, and selling goods in charity shops. This altruism is fostered in schools, where children are encouraged to raise money in various ways for good causes.

Many people are also involved with their local community on a voluntary basis, helping the elderly and handicapped, organizing events, performing music, drama, and dance, and providing extracurricular activities for children.

This feeling of responsibility for others stems from an earlier age when social welfare depended on private initiatives, and the better-off felt they had a duty to assist the poor.

HIGHBROW AND LOWBROW

In many European countries the arts are regarded by all as the mark of civilized life. In Britain, by contrast, some of the population dismiss classical music, opera, the fine arts, and high-class drama as elitist, and prefer pop music, TV soap operas, comedy acts, and reality TV shows with no intellectual content.

Despite this apparent neglect, Britain has a number of world-class symphony orchestras and drama and opera companies, as well as hundreds of excellent museums and art galleries, funded partly out of the public purse. These tend to be visited by the better educated, the more prosperous, the elderly, and tourists. Many people are content with less demanding fare.

IDENTITY

Unlike most other nations, the English do not have a particular day to celebrate their nationhood, and they would be hard pressed to define what Britain stands for. Under Tony Blair's premiership an attempt was made to define "Britishness," and classes were set up to teach this to new immigrants. The Scots and the Welsh both have a clearer sense of identity than the English.

In many respects the symbol of British identity is the Queen. Many public displays of national identity have royal associations, such as the ceremony of Trooping the Colour on the Queen's Official Birthday and the pageantry associated with the State Opening of Parliament in November. It is expressed in the patriotism shown at Remembrance Day ceremonies held in November at the Cenotaph in London and at war memorials up and down the country; and on such occasions as the "Last Night of the Proms"—the performance concluding the annual series of Promenade Concerts at the Royal Albert Hall in London, in which patriotic songs, such as "Land of Hope and Glory" and "Jerusalem," are sung with fervor by all present.

The Albert Hall, London

THE ROYAL FAMILY

The British Royal Family is an essential ingredient in the British sense of nationhood. While undercurrents of republicanism exist among those who resent the privileged status of the Queen and her family, most people profess loyalty to the Crown and are content to accept the status quo. There is a general consensus that the Queen and her Consort, Prince Philip, do a good job. Feelings have been more mixed about the heir to the throne, Prince Charles, especially after his failed marriage to the much-loved Diana, but his reputation has partially recovered in recent years. His charity, the Prince's Trust, has achieved outstanding results among disadvantaged young people. His sons, both serving in the armed forces, also enjoy good approval ratings.

Although their role is mainly ceremonial, members of the Royal Family always draw a crowd, and charities are eager to enlist a royal personage among their patrons.

RELIGION

Although Britain has a wealth of religious buildings, British people, for the most part, tend to be lukewarm about religion. This was not always the case, and in the post-Reformation period religious differences were a source of intense conflict.

Some people are referred to as "four-wheel Christians" because they are carried to church in a vehicle, probably only three times in their life: in a pram to be christened, in a bridal car to be wed, and in a hearse for their funeral. These days there are some who never enter a church at all. It is no longer the norm for every child to be christened or confirmed; people often opt for civil wedding ceremonies; and humanist funerals with no religious content are becoming more common.

Despite this the leader of the Anglican Church, the Archbishop of Canterbury, commands considerable respect, as does his deputy, the Archbishop of York. The Roman Catholic Archbishop of Westminster is also highly regarded.

Regular attendance in most churches may be declining, but the majority of the population (around 70 percent) still consider themselves Christians and act according to Christian principles. Some charismatic congregations are bucking the trend, and

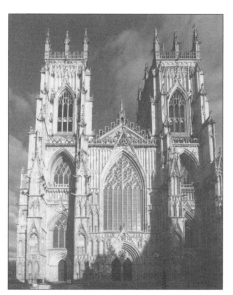

York Minster

other religions are flourishing, as can be seen from the growing number of mosques and temples in most of the major conurbations. There are active Jewish congregations, both liberal and orthodox, in many towns and cities.

The Church of England enjoys a unique position. Since Henry VIII's break with the Roman Church it has been the established (state) Church of England, and the monarch continues to be its official head. It embraces two traditions: the Catholic tradition (High Church), which lays greater stress on liturgy and ceremonial; and the evangelical tradition (Low Church), which puts greater emphasis on the Bible. There is a range of other Protestant denominations, described collectively as Nonconformist, including Methodists, Baptists, United Reformed Church, and Quakers.

The Church in Wales is Episcopalian, but is no longer tied to the state. The Church of Scotland is Presbyterian, and that country also has a number of strict Calvinist sects, which are opposed to any nonreligious activity on Sundays.

Although Catholicism was suppressed for around three centuries after the Reformation, the Roman Catholic Church now operates freely. Relations between the Churches—and with other religious groupings—are generally cordial.

LOVE OF ANIMALS

The British pride themselves on being animal lovers, and many households have at least one pet, usually a cat or a dog, other popular pets being rabbits, hamsters, and birds. It is said that the British think more of their pets than of their wives or children!

While most pet owners are responsible people, a minority are not, with the result that thousands of pets are abandoned each year and end up in animal shelters, which often depend on charity for their existence.

PREJUDICE

New arrivals get the impression that the British have a superiority complex and regard all foreigners with suspicion. However, apart from a minority of xenophobes, this is not the case. Admittedly, there has been some alarm, particularly among the working classes, about the numbers of immigrants entering the country, as it is felt they help to depress wages and put a strain on housing and health services.

Another cause for concern has been the development of immigrant ghettoes whose residents make little or no effort to integrate with the rest of society. The rise of the right-wing British National Party has served to increase tension in these areas.

However, in the boom years following the start of the millennium Britain benefited from the influx of migrant workers, especially those from Eastern Europe, who were able to bring skills into the country that were in short supply.

The British are a tolerant people and many people from abroad, including those from ethnic minorities, have become accepted as part of the fabric of British society. Proof of this lies in the growing number of intermarriages.

Festivals and Traditions

Apart from Easter and Christmas, statutory holidays are not connected with religious festivals, although up to 1834 they were—and there were thirty-three of them! Many public holidays are described as Bank Holidays—an innovation brought in by Sir John Lubbock in 1871 to give bank employees days off to play cricket matches.

HOLIDAYS AND FESTIVALS	
January 1	New Year's Day
January 2	New Year (Scotland only)
March/April	Good Friday
March/April	Easter Monday (not Scotland)
First Monday in May	May Day Bank Holiday
Last Monday in May	Spring Bank Holiday
First Monday in August	August Bank Holiday (Scotland only)
Last Monday in August	August Bank Holiday (not Scotland)
November 30	St. Andrew's Day (Scotland only)
December 25	Christmas Day
December 26	Boxing Day Bank Holiday.
(When Christmas Day and/or Boxing Day fall on a weekend, the following day or days are observed as public holidays.)	

THE FESTIVE YEAR

Burns Night

This is a Scottish celebration held on January 25, when Scots celebrate their national poet, Robert Burns, with suppers at which they propose a toast to his immortal memory and eat haggis (a tasty "pudding" of minced meat, offal, onions, oatmeal, and spice, sewn up into a sheep's stomach and boiled for three hours).

Valentine's Day

February 14 is when people send cards and flowers to their sweethearts, or anonymously to their secret loves. Couples may go out for a romantic candlelit dinner.

Shrove Tuesday

This is the day before Ash Wednesday, which marks the beginning of the Christian period of Lent, leading up to Easter. Whereas most European countries celebrate Carnival at this time, the British observe the occasion in a less extravagant manner by making pancakes.

St David's Day

March 1 is when the Welsh celebrate their patron saint, and wear leeks or daffodils.

Maundy Thursday

In an ancient ceremony the Queen dispenses "Maundy money" to the poor and deserving in a church service.

Easter Sunday

On this most important Christian festival, observers celebrate Christ's resurrection at Church services. Families may exchange small presents, and children receive chocolate Easter eggs.

St. George's Day

The English do not normally celebrate the festival of their patron saint, whose day is April 23, except in Stratford-upon-Avon, where it coincides with Shakespeare's birthday.

Battle of Britain Sunday

Services are held in most towns on the third Sunday in September to commemorate one of the turning points of the Second World War, when the Royal Air Force repulsed a sustained aerial attack by Germany.

Hallowe'en

Children have long celebrated All Hallows' Eve on October 31 with parties involving witches, ghosts, bats, magic, and carved pumpkins (jack o'lanterns); more recently the American custom of "Trick or Treat" has become popular.

Guy Fawkes Night

In 1604 a group of Catholics plotted to blow up the Houses of Parliament at the time when the King was due to open the new parliamentary session. The plot—to be executed by Guy Fawkes—was foiled. Since then, traditionally, on November 5, people would light bonfires on which a "guy"—an effigy of Guy Fawkes— was burned and fireworks set off. Nowadays, this happens less, and the day is mainly an excuse for a fireworks display.

Remembrance Sunday

Armistice Day, when the agreement was signed ending the First World War, falls on November 11. Nowadays, on the Sunday closest to that date, special services are held in churches, and ceremonies are held at the Cenotaph in London and at war memorials throughout the land to commemorate those who lost their lives in war.

St. Andrew's Day

St. Andrew is the patron saint of Scotland and this day, November 30, is a public holiday there.

Christmas Eve

Before they go to bed on December 24, children hang up stockings in the hope that Santa Claus (Father Christmas) will come and fill them with gifts during the night. Many people attend midnight church services, or watch these on television.

Christmas Day

Many people attend Christmas Day services in church. The rest of the day is a family affair, given over to exchanging presents, eating, and merrymaking. The food consumed is rich in calories and usually includes roast turkey, roast potatoes, Christmas pudding (made from flour, dried fruit, and nuts), mince pies (a cooked dried-fruit mixture encased in pastry), and a special iced fruit cake or a chocolate yule log.

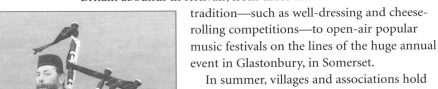

New Year's Eve

This is celebrated with particular gusto in Scotland, where the New Year is known as Hogmanay. Firework displays are common, especially in Edinburgh, where the celebrations are particularly impressive. People join hands at the stroke of midnight and sing the song, "Auld Lang Syne."

LOCAL FESTIVALS

Britain abounds in festivals, from those that have their roots in

tradition—such as well-dressing and cheese-rolling competitions—to open-air popular music festivals on the lines of the huge annual event in Glastonbury, in Somerset.

In summer, villages and associations hold garden fêtes, despite the uncertainties of the British weather. In many rural counties agricultural shows are organized at which farmers exhibit their finest animals in the hope of winning awards. Flower shows, which also have a competitive element, are also popular—none more so than the annual Chelsea Flower Show in London, which is a highlight of the social calendar.

Wales has its musical and literary festivals (*eisteddfods*), and Scotland its Highland Games, in which people compete in a variety of rustic sports. The three-week-long Edinburgh Festival, a celebration of all the arts, is Britain's biggest festival.

Every August, on the Bank Holiday weekend, the two-day Notting Hill Carnival in London is led by members of the British Afro-Caribbean community. A riot of music, dance and costume, it is the second-largest street festival in the world.

FAMILY OCCASIONS

Birthdays and Anniversaries

Children look forward to their birthdays, and often have parties. These are sometimes elaborate and expensive occasions, with well-off parents hiring entertainers or arranging parties in restaurants. Adults tend to confine their celebrations to parties for notable birthdays such as coming of age at eighteen or twenty-one, or wedding anniversaries.

Weddings

At one time wedding ceremonies were held either at register offices or in churches, but now various venues, including hotels and country houses, are licensed for weddings. Nonetheless, church weddings remain popular with Christians, and if the couple marries in an Anglican church there is no need for a civil ceremony.

At the wedding ceremony the bride's father generally gives his daughter away, while the bridegroom's brother or friend supports him and looks after the wedding rings. A reception normally follows, after which the newlyweds leave for their honeymoon. It is a tradition for the bridegroom to go out with his male friends before the wedding to celebrate his last night as a bachelor, and for the bride to do likewise with her own friends, though in practice this would now rarely happen on the night before the wedding day.

People are marrying much later these days: the average age of first marriage is twenty-nine for women and thirty-two for men.

Funerals

Funeral services are held in churches or in cemetery chapels, after which the deceased is either buried or cremated. The ceremony often includes tributes to the deceased by members of the family or close friends. It is normal to have a reception (sometimes known as a wake) afterward to enable friends and relations of the deceased to meet and share their reminiscences.

Getting to Know the British

British people have a reputation for being cold, reserved, and difficult to get to know. They certainly do not exhibit the warmth and friendliness one might experience in Spain, for example. This is because most of them value their privacy—demonstrated by their preference for living in houses with gardens surrounded by hedges or fences.

However, that should not deter you from approaching someone in the street to ask for directions, or from starting a conversation in a pub or on a train if you think they look friendly.

JOIN A CLUB

If you are in the country for some time, and are having problems in getting to know the British, why not join a club or enroll on a course? There are clubs, associations, or classes for all pastimes—sports, amateur dramatics, country dancing, bridge, chess, and choral singing, to name but a few. Churches and other religious organizations offer opportunities for people to meet one another on a social basis. Local further education colleges and adult education centers offer evening courses in all manner of subjects from arts and crafts to car maintenance.

FORMS OF ADDRESS

If you are introduced to someone, it is normal to shake hands and for both people to say "How do you do?" (which needs no answer) or, less formally, "Hello," or "Hi." People do not stand on ceremony these days, and while you might start off addressing people politely by using their title, for example "Mr. Smith," "Mrs. Jones," or "Miss Brown," it may not be long before you are on first-name terms with them. However, older people may still prefer to be addressed formally.

It is becoming less common to use or hear the term "Sir" or "Madam" except in schools and the armed forces, and in a situation of service such as in a shop or a restaurant. In formal settings a subordinate might address a person by his job title, for example, "Professor," or "Prime Minister."

Newcomers to Britain are sometimes uncertain how to address a peer (Lord, Lady) or a knight (with the title Sir). You generally use the surname in the case of a peer ("Lord Smith" or "Lady Smith"), but address a knight using his first name ("Sir George," whose wife would be addressed as Lady Smith); Dame Monica Smith would be addressed as "Dame Monica."

If you should happen to meet the Queen of England, the proper form of address is "Your Majesty" (or "Ma'am"). For the other royals it is "Your Royal Highness" (or "Sir" or "Ma'am").

Don't be alarmed if people—particularly tradespeople—address you using words such as dear, duck, love, darling, pet, or chuck. These are general terms of endearment.

GOOD MANNERS

Most British people are polite. They unfailingly say "please" and "thank you." They don't say "You're welcome," as the Americans do in response to thanks; a smile will suffice.

They use the expression "sorry" a great deal to apologize for the slightest inconvenience. "I'm sorry" or "I'm very sorry" is an appropriate response to hearing bad news. The expression "I beg your pardon?" or "What did you say?" may be used if a person has misheard what you have said and wants the sentence repeated.

The expression "Excuse me" is appropriate if you have to interrupt a conversation or need to pass someone who is standing in your way.

INVITATIONS HOME

The British, on the whole, are happy to show off their homes, so don't be surprised to be invited to a drinks party, cocktails, a buffet meal, or a barbecue. Normally these are informal affairs, since both partners are likely to lead busy lives and will not be able to arrange an elaborate spread, except at weekends and during holidays, unless they hire private caterers. But you could receive an invitation to a very formal dinner, which may specify the mode of dress for the evening. It may also give the time in the form of, for example, "7:30 for 8:00 p.m.," which you can take to mean that drinks will be served from the earlier time, and dinner at or soon after the later time—you need not arrive exactly at 7:30, but should arrive by 8:00. Whatever the occasion, you should reply, whether you are accepting or declining, as soon as possible.

It is a nice idea to take along a small gift, such as flowers or good chocolates, for your hosts. You could also enquire beforehand whether this is a special occasion, such as a birthday or wedding anniversary, and if so bring or send a card.

At the end of the party make sure to thank your hosts sincerely and tell them how much you enjoyed the event.

MAKING CONVERSATION

British people are sometimes slow to initiate a conversation, and it may be up to the visitor to make the first move. Although they feign modesty, they are not averse to flattery, and you cannot go wrong if you praise a person's home, children, garden, or pets.

Most topics are permissible, notably the weather (which is an endless source of interest), sport, and travel. You should avoid talking about money and yourself, unless invited to do so, and then you should take care not to boast about your achievements.

Political discussions can be tricky unless you are acquainted with the political leanings of the people you are with. It is not sensible to probe into people's personal lives, or they might suspect your motives.

Daily Life

People's lives vary a great deal. Naturally, a Scottish crofter is likely to live a less hectic and complicated life than a banker in the City of London, for instance, but there is a discernible pattern common to most people living in Britain.

HOUSING

The overwhelming majority of British people aspire to own their own homes, and many are prepared to scrimp and scrape in order to be able to afford a mortgage on a house. Around 70 percent own their homes, and the preference is for a house—detached, semi-detached, or terraced—with a garden. The British like to have plenty of space around themselves.

Terraced houses in Moss Side, Manchester

Mansion flats in Page Street, London

The cost of owning a home soared in the early years of the twenty-first century, which meant that more people had to settle for rented accommodation. In large cities this often means apartments (flats). However, there is also an extensive range of houses for rent owned by private landlords, councils, and independent housing associations.

THE HOUSEHOLD

The average British family has two children; many have more, but this is balanced against the fact that one in four couples has no children at all. One in four children lives in a one-parent family, usually headed by a mother.

Although marriage is popular, there are 2.3 million unmarried couples in Britain, and 44 percent of children live with parents who are unmarried, though some may eventually tie the knot. A large proportion of marriages end in divorce, and it is interesting to note that 40 percent of marriages are second marriages. As a consequence, a large number of children live in families with only one natural parent and with stepbrothers and stepsisters.

Most households consist of parent(s) and children, but you may find three generations living under the same roof, particularly among ethnic minorities. A modern tendency is for children to live at home for longer; for instance, 60 percent of young men aged twenty-four are still living with their parents. Seven million people in Britain live alone.

DAILY ROUTINE

People tend to rise between 7:00 and 8:00 a.m., though long-distance commuters into London may have to get up earlier.

The extensive "English breakfast" that one encounters in hotels is rarely the norm, except perhaps on weekends. Most families have a light breakfast of cereals, toast and marmalade, and coffee or tea, and then rush off. Some do not have time even for this.

Children normally have to be at school by 9:00 a.m., and this is also when most shops and offices open. Factory workers usually start work earlier.

Many British people make a major food shopping expedition once a week to a large supermarket; local markets are also popular for fresh fruit and vegetables. Most stores are open between 9:00 a.m. and 5:30 p.m., Monday to Saturday, and often for six hours on Sundays. Some large supermarkets are open twenty-four hours a day, and in busy areas local neighborhood shops may be open earlier and until quite late.

It is rare for people to go home for lunch. For this reason, many larger establishments (including schools) have canteens, or people take a lunchbox to work.

School is usually over at 3:30 p.m. or soon after, but some schools put on extracurricular activities for their pupils. Factories and offices finish at around 5:00 p.m. Since members of the household may well arrive home at different times, the custom of sitting down to dinner as a family has become rarer—though most families eat at least one meal together on weekends.

AFTER WORK

Watching television is a popular means of passing the evening, but families no longer watch it together. Many children now have TV sets in their bedrooms where they can watch their favorite programs undisturbed—or else they play games or access chat lines on their computers.

There is a range of channels available, including five non-commercial channels operated by the British Broadcasting Corporation and financed by the (compulsory) TV license. The BBC also has five national radio stations (Radio 1, mainly pop music; Radio 2, general; Radio 3, classical music and culture; Radio 4, speech and news; Radio 5, news and sport); and a network of local stations. There are also a number of commercial TV and radio broadcasters, such as ITV, BSkyB, and Channels 4 and 5. The general feeling is that as TV channels have proliferated the overall standard has gone down. That is perhaps why a substantial minority of people go out in the evenings—to clubs and societies, to the theater or cinema, to evening classes, to the gym, or to the pub.

CHILDREN AND TEENAGERS

At one time there was a general feeling that "children should be seen and not heard." Some parents still feel awkward about taking children into restaurants, and there are establishments that exclude children. But most parents want their children to lead happy and successful lives, and that includes giving them experience of the world around them.

Among middle-class parents there is a tendency to want their children to "get on" at school, so school classes are sometimes supplemented with private lessons. Many parents encourage their children to learn to play musical instruments, though working-class parents often take a less proactive approach to their children's progress.

On the whole children are not subject to strict discipline, except perhaps among certain ethnic minorities. When they become teenagers some become rebellious and susceptible to "peer pressure," rejecting parental advice and spending their leisure time fraternizing with friends, often staying out and drinking until late. Lack of parental supervision at this stage has led to the worrying problem of teenage pregnancy. In the past teenage mothers often gave their babies up for adoption, willingly or not, but nowadays many girls bring up their babies themselves or with the help of their own mothers.

EDUCATION

Education is compulsory between the ages of five and eighteen, and children may go to nursery or preschool classes from the age of three or even younger. Many primary schools in England have links with the Church of England, since state provision of education arrived much later than in the rest of Europe and the Church was the main providers of education. That legacy continues, although most of the funds for running the schools are now provided by the local councils with a grant from central government.

The majority of pupils go to state schools and usually move on to secondary education around the age of eleven. Most secondary schools are comprehensive these days, which means they cater to the whole range of abilities; but in some areas there are also a number of selective schools, known as grammar schools, which take the most academically able pupils.

Private education is popular with parents who can afford it, and some enroll their offspring in preparatory (prep) schools from the age of eight. Most of these are day schools, but some are boarding schools. They are intended to prepare their pupils for entry to "public" schools (which are actually private) at the age of thirteen. Most public schools (which include such prestigious establishments as Eton, Harrow, and Winchester) offer boarding facilities. Unlike state schools, they are not obliged to follow the National Curriculum laid down by the government. At the age of sixteen most pupils take the General Certificate of Secondary Education (GCSE) in a number of subjects.

After GCSE, students may continue their schooling in the sixth form, or at a separate sixth-form college, to prepare for A (Advanced) Level examinations, often in two stages: AS (Advanced Subsidiary) and A2, for university entrance. The International Baccalaureate is favored by some public schools because it is considered to offer a more rigorous and broadly based education. Others leave school to enter colleges of further education for vocational courses, take up apprenticeships, or drop out of education.

Higher Education

More students than ever now go on to higher education—currently around 40 percent, though the former Labour Government once mooted plans to raise this to 50 percent. There is keen competition for places at the more prestigious universities, such as Oxford, Cambridge, London, Durham, Bristol, and Birmingham, which enjoy a worldwide reputation. Scottish students tend to study at Scottish universities.

British students are eligible for student loans at preferential rates, and those from low-income families receive grants to see

Pembroke College, Cambridge

them through university. Concern has been expressed that a disproportionate number of students from public schools obtain places in the better universities compared with pupils from state schools.

THE ARMED FORCES

The UK abolished conscription half a century ago, and now has a fully professional army. There is also a volunteer force, known as the Territorial Army, which is called upon to assist the professionals from time to time.

MAIL AND TELECOMMUNICATIONS

Britain was the first country to have a universal letter delivery service, for which the cost of sending a letter to anywhere in the United Kingdom was one penny. The postal service, with its distinctive red vans bearing the Royal Mail logo, is far pricier now, but is efficient.

Post offices, open on weekdays from 9:00 a.m. to 5:00 p.m. and on Saturdays until 12:00 noon, offer services including banking and bill payments, and act as a cash point for some banks.

The telecommunications network now has a number of providers both for fixed line phones and for cell phones. The dominant presence in fixed line telephones is British Telecom, once a state-owned corporation.

The Internet is very popular and can be accessed in Internet cafés and libraries, and there are many internet service providers.

Leisure Time

The British appreciate their leisure time, and enjoy eating out, going to the cinema, the theater, concerts, and sporting events, and going away for a long weekend. They subscribe to the axiom that "All work and no play makes Jack a dull boy."

SHOPPING FOR PLEASURE

Many people enjoy shopping—"retail therapy," as it is sometimes called. Over the past thirty years large shopping malls and out-of-town shopping centers have sprung up everywhere, seducing customers away from the traditional downtown shopping areas.

One strange phenomenon in Britain's high streets, as the main shopping streets are called, is the charity shop. These small stores are the trading arms of some of the country's major charities, and do brisk business in donated secondhand goods such as clothing, books, and bric-à-brac, and in some cases stock handicrafts and food items from countries that receive their aid. They are staffed mainly by volunteers and often yield good bargains.

EATING OUT

Britain used to have a reputation for uninteresting food, but over the past fifty years there has been a revolution spurred on by the arrival of Italians, Hong Kong Chinese, and Asians from the Indian subcontinent who opened restaurants that stay busy until midnight. Nowadays, there is an astonishing range of cuisines from all over the world on offer, as well as restaurants and hotels serving much improved British food, and there are plenty of American-style fast food outlets as well, which find favor with the young.

Fish and chips

Not everyone wants to eat out, but nor do they necessarily want to cook. Help is at hand in takeaways (or carry-outs, as they are known in Scotland), from which you can buy cooked food or have it delivered to your door. Takeaways specialize in pizza, kebabs, hamburgers, pies, Chinese, and Indian food, as well as the ubiquitous KFC (Kentucky Fried Chicken).

The most quintessentially British of the takeaways is the fish and chip shop, which has been around for a century and a half, and of which there are around eight thousand in Britain. Favorite fishes are cod, haddock, and plaice. Once the fish and chips were wrapped in newspaper to keep them warm; nowadays more hygienic containers are used. Your order may be doused with salt and vinegar unless you specify otherwise!

Lancashire hotpot, Welsh rarebit, Cornish pasty, Scotch broth, and Cumberland sausage are some of the simple, homely dishes associated with certain regions, and often available in modest eateries and pubs anywhere in the country.

TIPPING

Restaurants often add a service charge to the bill; you can leave a little extra if you had especially good service. If a service charge is not added, it is usual to leave 10 or 12.5 percent.

A similar amount is usual for taxi drivers. A small tip, say £1, is usual to thank someone who has given you a personal service, such as in a hairdresser's salon.

It is not necessary to tip in a pub where you have only bought drinks at the bar.

PUBS

Once public houses (pubs) were mainly drinking establishments, where you would drink your pint of beer and perhaps have a game of darts, skittles, or billiards, but there was often little on offer to eat. Nowadays, many pubs serve food, which may be cheaper than in a restaurant but is probably just as good, though the quality may vary. Some establishments have adopted the title "gastropub;" these specialize in good-quality ingredients and interesting cuisine, and not surprisingly their prices are likely to be higher. Country pubs are particularly congenial, but the strict drink-driving laws have meant fewer customers and some have been forced to close. In many pubs you order your food at the bar and then find a table to sit at. The food will be brought to you.

Pubs are often "tied" to a particular brewery whose name will be prominently displayed on the inn sign. Others are designated "free houses," which means they are independent—not that the drinks are free!

Pub in Hainford, Norfolk

At one time Britain had strict licensing laws, which obliged pubs to close by a certain time. In recent years pubs' opening hours have been liberalized in the hope of encouraging a "continental café culture", though the effect of the legislation has been to increase incidences of drunkenness late at night.

One deeply engrained habit, especially with the young, is to go on a "pub crawl", which involves visiting a number of different pubs in an area and having a drink in each.

FOOD

Good-quality food is widely available from markets and supermarkets; Britain's temperate climate and fertile land means that local produce is plentiful and deliciious. The "great British breakfast" of eggs and bacon is generally available, though the health-conscious may not indulge. Fine smoked fish and meats are a specialty, and a meal of roast meat or poultry "with all the trimmings" is often enjoyed by the family together on weekends—typically on Sundays.

DRINK

The national drink of England is ale—or beer. While younger people tend to drink lager from cans, and bottles are popular, those with more discriminating tastes choose what are known as real ales, straight from the barrel, which often have a local provenance. Some of the more traditional breweries offer tours.

Cider is a popular drink, made from apples, which is produced mainly in the counties of Herefordshire, Somerset, and Devon. Hereford has a cider museum devoted to the stuff. Bottled varieties, still or sparkling, sweet or dry, and with a fairly low alcoholic content, can be bought anywhere in the country, but those in the know will order draught cider in the areas where it is made. Beware—it can be strong!

The most famous spirit, and Scotland's major export, is Scotch

whisky (spelled without an "e" in the UK). Many of the well-known Scotches are blended, but the more expensive ones, known as single malts, are not. Visitors to the northeast of Scotland can travel by steam train to the distilleries in the area. Gin is a spirit distilled from grain and flavored with juniper berries.

Wine production is not traditionally associated with England, but there are a number of vineyards in the south that

Whisky barrels

make predominantly white wine. There are also excellent country wines using such ingredients as plums, blackberries, rhubarb, and elderberries, which are worth trying.

A wide range of non-alcoholic beverages is available in Britain, ranging from international brands to delicious elderflower cordial.

CULTURE AND ENTERTAINMENT

Britain has a dominant position in the world of culture and entertainment, with a wide range of art galleries and museums, theaters, concert halls, opera houses, and cinemas. In London, the theaters are mostly in the West End, and there are three within the National Theatre complex on the South Bank of the Thames. Concert halls include the Royal Festival Hall, also on the South Bank, and the Royal Albert Hall, in Kensington. The Royal Opera House in Covent Garden is world famous for opera and ballet, and the Coliseum, a few streets away, is the home of the English National Opera.

Some British cities, such as Birmingham, Manchester, Edinburgh, and Cardiff, have concert halls or other venues that surpass those of London; most of the larger towns have their own theaters, which tend to put on touring productions. Cinemas in nearly every town show the latest blockbusters, and there is a network of art cinemas and cinema clubs for the more specialized movies.

The summer is a time for open-air pop concerts and theater productions. Many localities put on festivals devoted to literature, music, and other branches of the arts. Over the Christmas holiday period many theaters put on pantomimes. These productions are generally aimed at children and based on fairy tales, such as *Cinderella*, *Puss in Boots*, and *Mother Goose*, and often star well-known comedians, singers, or actors from TV soap operas. Don't expect great drama; this is entertainment in the vaudeville tradition, with lots of slapstick humor interspersed with songs and dancing.

STUDENTS, CLUBBING, AND CLOSE ENCOUNTERS

Most of the larger towns have nightclubs and other drinking establishments, particularly favored by the young. Some of these stay busy into the early hours of the morning. Some offer live entertainment—from a solitary guitarist or singer to a line-up of bands—and others function as discos with a DJ.

London is world famous for its parties and nonstop nightlife. After-hours drinking dens and dancing realms of all shapes and sizes cater to all music and social tastes. You can while away a pleasant evening in any of the numerous pubs around the city, many of which serve food too. There are lots of cultural activities and performances on offer seven days a week, such as live music, theatrical shows, gallery events, and comedy nights. There are DJ bars, elegant nightclubs, cabarets, and burlesque events.

The London club scene is bursting at the seams, and the list of places and areas is long. Old Street and Shoreditch in East London is the current trendy night spot, with big clubs, quirky bars, and excellent restaurants; this provides great people-watching and a glimpse at London's subculture. The famous Soho still hasn't lost its charm. Although rather commercial, it is always bustling with people, has all sorts of venues open till late, and plays host to London's gay scene. In the West End and Mayfair you will need to dress in your finest, and to enter some of the more exclusive clubs in the city you will have to get yourself on to a guest list. In West London, Notting Hill plays host to some great music venues and in North London, Islington is the spot where young people hang out at trendy restaurants, with lots of pubs and bars to choose from. In South London, Brixton holds down its own cultural scene with its large Afro-Caribbean community, some good music bars, and a few clubs; it makes for a great alternative to central or East London.

One of the less savory aspects of nightlife is the tendency for certain elements to go out not so much to have a good time as to get drunk, and sometimes fights break out. Beware of the drug pushers who hang around some of the clubs and pubs.

The British don't strike up a conversation easily, so be prepared to make the first move if you want to get to know someone. Don't be put off by this—it's just the nature of social communication here. Once contact is made, a person of the opposite sex is more likely to start up a witty text-message conversation to flirt, test the waters, and even ask you out, than do it face-to-face.

On the other hand, you may find it easy to "hook up" with someone when you are out on the town, and one-night stands have become relatively common for the British, who can be rather promiscuous and sexually spontaneous on a night out. However, a pub is not like a bar, in that people are there for socializing with their friends, as opposed to looking for possible new partners.

The gender roles are still relatively traditional in the UK, and the man takes on his role as gentleman gallantly. He is expected to instigate a date, and on a first date a girl usually expects the man to pay as well as to fix the location and possibly the travel arrangements, though if the meeting is more casual the girl will usually offer to split the bill. A typical first date in London might be to meet for a drink in a bar, or to have a meal in a restaurant followed by a few drinks out later if the date has gone well.

SPORTS

The British have always been a sporting nation, and this is reflected in the sheer variety of sports they indulge in—whether as spectators or participants. Many sports, such as tennis, football, and cricket, originated in Britain, though this does not mean that the British always excel in these today.

Football

There are basically two varieties of football: association football (soccer), with teams of eleven players, and rugby, which fields teams of thirteen or fifteen players and in which the (oval) ball is thrown, caught, and carried, as well as kicked.

Soccer as a spectator sport has a huge following, and football teams such as Manchester United, Chelsea, and Liverpool are famous throughout the world. England and Wales have four principal leagues: the Premier, the Championship, and Leagues One and Two. Scotland has its own league, which is dominated by two Glasgow teams: Rangers and Celtic. In international football and rugby matches each country—England, Wales, and Scotland—fields its own national team.

Cricket

While both types of football are regarded as winter games, cricket is played in the summer. The basic principle of the game is that a bowler hurls the ball at the wicket (three wooden stumps with two wooden bails balanced on top), and the player standing and wielding a bat in front of the wicket seeks to deflect the ball so that the bails don't fall off. Some matches take up to five days to play, but a more modern version can be played in less than a day. Cricket is also popular in former countries of the British Empire, such as Australia, New Zealand, South Africa, the West Indies, India, and Pakistan.

Rowing and Sailing

Britain has excelled in some water sports, particularly these. Rowing clubs are found in many riverside locations, and this team sport is particularly associated with the universities of Oxford and Cambridge, which have an annual boat race on the Thames in London. Another famous event is the Henley Royal Regatta, in Oxfordshire.

Intrepid yachtsmen and women think nothing of competing in round-the-world races or the famous Fastnet Race from the Isle of Wight in the south of England, around the Fastnet Rock off southwestern Ireland, finishing at Plymouth. Cowes Week on the Isle of Wight is among the leading events for the sailing fraternity.

Equestrian Sports

Horse racing is regarded as "the sport of kings," and every day

races are held at race tracks around the country. Among the most famous races are the Cheltenham Gold Cup, the Derby (at Epsom) and the Grand National (at Liverpool). For Royal Ascot week, near London, the spectators dress up in all their finery, just as in the musical *My Fair Lady*.

"Eventing" is another equestrian

The Derby, Epsom

occasion, in which riders compete to see who can maneuver around an obstacle course in the fastest time. The Horse Trials at Badminton near Bristol are particularly well known.

Tennis

Tennis has a large following among the British, even if they are not active players themselves. The great event of the year is the tournament at Wimbledon, in south London, from which the whole country hopes that a British champion will emerge— something that has not happened for some time.

Other Sports

There are opportunities to participate in virtually every sport imaginable, from archery and badminton to volleyball and weightlifting. Facilities for these sports are found in private clubs and public leisure centers.

If team sports do not appeal, other activities, such as swimming, mountaineering, potholing (exploring underground caves), hang-gliding, hiking, and marathon running are widely practiced. Coastal areas offer a range of activities, such as windsurfing.

You don't need to be at the peak of fitness in order to play certain sports, and one finds people playing croquet, golf, bowls, and even cricket and tennis into old age.

Getting Around

Britain has a comprehensive public transport system, and you can travel by air, rail, or road to most corners of the country.

For the longest distances, air would be the transport of choice, and if you book well in advance you may be able to snap up a bargain airfare from a low-cost, no-frills airline.

Although the rail network was severely pruned back in the 1960s, the railways are experiencing a revival, especially commuter lines into London. Since the 1990s the rail services have been run by private rail companies. Standard rail fares in Britain are the highest in Europe, but if you are smart you will avoid paying the full amount by booking in advance and not traveling during the peak hours. To find timetables and fares, access the Web site www.nationalrail.co.uk.

A cheaper alternative, if you are not in a hurry, is to travel by bus or coach, where there are often excellent bargains to be had if you book in advance. The company with the most comprehensive network is National Express, which serves all the airports and has a particularly busy terminus at Heathrow Airport. Its website is www.nationalexpress.com. There are a number of competitors in the field, which means that fares between popular destinations are likely to remain low. Bear in mind, however, that roads into and out of cities, especially London, can get very congested at peak travel times, causing some services to arrive later than scheduled.

URBAN TRANSPORTATION

Most towns and cities have efficient bus services, and trams are making a comeback in some places, such as Manchester. The

Newcastle-upon-Tyne area has a light railway system, and Liverpool has an urban railway that runs partly underground. Glasgow has its own subway.

London has a good public transport system, with many bus services operating through the night. For speedy travel the

underground train (Tube) is the transport of choice. London's subway is the oldest in the world, and parts of it are showing their age. The fares are quite expensive, unless you take advantage of concessions, like the one-day travel card available after the morning rush hour is over. Most Tube stations have ticket offices and ticket machines. An electronic card, the Oyster Card, can be used for storing credit, obviates the need for payment each time you travel, and gives a considerable discount, so is well worth having. It can be used on buses, Tube trains, trams, the Docklands Light Railway (DLR), London Overground, and National Rail services in London.

DRIVING

Australians, Indians, Japanese, New Zealanders, South Africans, and Thais have no problems when driving in Britain. Other nationals do, because the British drive on the left, not on the right as in continental Europe and the Americas.

Remember to pass other vehicles on their right (not left), and drive around traffic circles (roundabouts) in a clockwise direction, giving priority to vehicles coming from your right, already on the traffic circle, or at junctions such as crossroads where no other priority is marked. Otherwise the rules are broadly similar to those in other Western European countries.

Speed limits must be observed. The general rule is 70 mph (112.6 kmph) on motorways (expressways); 60 mph (96.5 kmph) on other open roads; and 30 mph (48 kmph) in built-up or residential areas. Be aware of signs indicating otherwise— sometimes, for example, the speed limit within a town has been reduced to 20 mph (32 kmph). Stay within the limits to avoid incurring a fine. Speed cameras are common.

The UK's legal drink-driving limit is 0.8 mg per ml. Driving while over this limit can incur very severe penalties. Note that it is illegal to use a cell phone while driving. Seat belts must be worn, and young children must be strapped into special seats in the back of the car. You should drive carefully if there are pedestrians about, since they tend to cross the road where they want to, rather than at special crossings. Another problem at night is cyclists riding around illegally without lights.

Britain's road system is adequate, but the motorways near the big cities can get very congested. There are virtually no tolls to pay, unless you are going through certain tunnels, over a suspension bridge, or along a short section of toll motorway around Birmingham. Some "A" roads are divided highways, and good; but be prepared for plenty of bends in the others.

Driving into central London is not recommended. If it is necessary to do so on a weekday, you will have to pay a congestion charge, and you are advised to do this in advance or before midnight on the same day (or incur a heavier charge); some other cities are considering introducing a similar scheme.

On the positive side, most British drivers are courteous and do not honk their car horns impatiently. If they flash their headlights at you, this could mean they are either beckoning you on or warning you of a hazard (or a speed camera!) ahead, but whatever is the case you should always proceed with caution.

WHERE TO STAY

Accommodation in Britain can be good, bad, or indifferent. Local tourist information offices can usually recommend accommodation and make bookings for you, or will send you brochures listing accommodation in their area.

Most cities have five-star hotels—some independent, others belonging to international chains such as Hilton and Holiday Inn. Lower down the range there are so-called budget chains, such as Travelodge and Premier Inn, which have centralized booking systems, and many small independent hotels. Country hotels range from the luxurious to the modest.

If you want something cheaper, you should investigate guest houses or bed and breakfast establishments. You can find these in advance on the Internet, but if you have left it until the last minute keep your eyes open along the main roads into towns and cities. If you see a "Vacancies" sign displayed in the window you could be in luck. Note that not all of the rooms will necessarily have private bathrooms.

For the more intrepid there are camping and caravan sites. The Youth Hostel Association has hostels all over the country, and the YMCA and YWCA offer accommodation at modest rates.

If you are going to live in an area for some time, consult a reputable letting agent, who will be able to find you longer-term accommodation.

MEDICAL MATTERS

Citizens of the EU (and EEA) are entitled to the same treatment under the same terms as UK citizens if they produce a European Health Insurance Card. If you come from a country that does not have a reciprocal health agreement with the UK, it would be best to take out private health insurance for the duration of your stay.

For minor ailments a pharmacist in any chemist's shop is qualified to offer advice. If you need to see a doctor, make an appointment to see a local GP (general practitioner), who will prescribe a remedy or make arrangements for you to see a specialist. If necessary, you can walk into the accident and emergency department ("A and E") of the nearest hospital. In the case of a serious accident or emergency, if you need to summon an ambulance, call 999 or 112.

LAW AND ORDER

Britain is a relatively safe place, and providing you take sensible precautions with yourself and your belongings, no harm should befall you. Keep your valuables safe, and your doors locked. Some areas are designated Neighbourhood Watch Areas, which means that local residents keep their eyes open for any suspicious activities and call the police if they are worried. The police are generally polite and helpful if people want advice or directions or experience trouble. They are less tolerant of people who break the law.

It is best not to visit city centers late at night, and certainly not alone, since people spilling out of clubs and pubs are sometimes drunk and can become violent. Fortunately, the police are usually out in force at such times.

PLACES TO VISIT

Many people come to Britain not for sunshine and beaches but for the country's considerable cultural and architectural heritage. There is a lot to see, from internationally famous museums and galleries to spectacular Gothic cathedrals and elegant stately homes.

London is a particular draw, with its museums and art galleries, such as the British Museum, the Victoria and Albert Museum, the National Gallery, Tate Britain, Tate Modern, the Wallace Collection, the National Portrait Gallery, St. Paul's Cathedral, Westminster Abbey, and the Houses of Parliament. On the fringe of London are the Royal Botanic Gardens at Kew, Hampton Court Palace, and Greenwich.

Visitors to England often take in some of the picturesque cities and towns such as Bath, Canterbury, and Stratford-upon-Avon, Shakespeare's home town. However, there are many other places of interest, including areas of outstanding natural beauty such as the Lake District, the Peak District, and the Cotswolds.

Remote inn at Glen Coe, in the Scottish Highlands   Caernarvon Castle, North Wales

Scotland has many attractions, from rugged mountain scenery, beautiful lochs, and islands, to the delights of its capital, Edinburgh, with Holyrood House (the palace of the Kings of Scotland) and the Royal Mile, leading to the imposing castle that dominates the city. The highest mountain in Britain is Ben Nevis (4,409 ft, or 1,344 m), in the west of Scotland.

Wales, too, is famous for its massive medieval castles, such as Chepstow, Harlech, and Caernarvon, and the more modern edifice in its busy capital, Cardiff. It boasts spectacular scenery as well, notably the Black Mountains in the south and the area around its highest mountain, Snowdon, in the north.

Beauty spots and places of interest in Northern Ireland are suggested in the chapter on Ireland.

Business and Professional Life

Britain was once known as the "workshop of the world," but nowadays only about 10 percent of the workforce is involved in manufacturing. Notwithstanding, manufacturing makes a considerable contribution to national wealth and is an important export earner. Indeed, the United Kingdom consistently ranks

among the top six trading nations. There was a stage when British manufacturing had a reputation for outdated practices and sloppy workmanship, but this is, happily, no longer the case. As a result of increasing competition from abroad, many manufacturers have become more efficient and require fewer employees.

City of London skyline

Another point of interest is that a significant swathe of British manufacturing is foreign-owned. The automobile industry, for example, is dominated by Japanese, American, German, and French companies. The country boasts some of the most productive automobile plants in Europe.

In recent years the financial service sector, based in the City of London, has grown in importance.

COMPANY CULTURE

In the bad old days of the 1960s and 1970s, a number of British companies failed because both managers and employees were resistant to change and were content just to "muddle through." In some dreadful instances management and trade unions were at loggerheads, and strikes were all too frequent.

Things have changed, partly because of more enlightened management styles and partly because of greater pragmatism on the part of trade unionists. Both management and unions realized that Britain was losing jobs to other countries where both sides of industry cooperated.

Another factor has been the impact of the foreign businesses that have opened branches in the UK. Japanese, German, and American companies, for instance, have different management styles from those found in many British companies, whose workforces have had to adapt to radically different practices.

When dealing with a business in Britain, you need to bear in mind who owns the company and be prepared to adjust your approach accordingly.

THE WORKING DAY

In London offices the working day may start as early as 8:30 a.m., or as late as 10:00 a.m., taking into account the fact that many members of staff have to make long journeys from home. In the provinces a 9:00 or 9:30 a.m. start is the norm, though factories may well start an hour earlier. Some companies, however, have flexible arrangements.

The working day normally ends between 5:00 and 6:00 p.m. Where possible, people like to leave their workplace early on Fridays in anticipation of the weekend, and some factories shut down at 1:00 p.m. on Fridays, unless it is necessary to stay on to complete an order.

The British tend to work longer hours than people elsewhere in Europe. The average vacation entitlement is twenty days, and at Christmas and the New Year many companies close down for a ten-day holiday—a point worth noting for business partners.

MAKING CONTACT

When writing letters the British do not use the elaborate formulae common in some other European countries. The tendency is to be brief, succinct, and polite.

It is important to use the person's title, unless you are on first-name terms. So you address the letter to "Mr. Jack Robinson," and begin "Dear Mr. Robinson," or "Dear Sir" (or "Dear Madam" in the case of a woman). A letters that starts with "Dear Jack Robinson" may suggest that a computer has written it rather than a real person—or that it is a circular. In the address you might follow the person's name with his or her position within the organization, for example Marketing Manager, Principal, or Head of Finance. The top person within a company would normally be referred to as Managing Director or Chief Executive (CEO)—not President.

MEETINGS

If you have a meeting it is important to arrive on time, but not too early. It is advisable to dress formally: pin-striped trousers and bowler hats went out decades ago, but dark suits are advisable, for both men and women.

On meeting for the first time it is usual to shake hands, but you should note that British people do not shake hands with the same frequency as many continental Europeans do. If you are meeting with a number of people a nod of acknowledgment will probably suffice.

You should take your cue from your hosts as to how to address them. If they address you by your first name, it will be quite in order to reciprocate. Older people and those with a military background may well be more formal.

It is usual to start off with a few pleasantries before getting down to business. You may be asked if you are enjoying your visit, and this will be an opportunity to establish a rapport. If you can say something complimentary about your experience of the country, this will invariably meet with approval.

If there are several people in the room, it may be difficult to work out who the real decision-maker is. The matter is to some extent irrelevant, since decisions are often arrived at through consensus.

PRESENTATIONS

On the whole British people appreciate presentations that are informative, and dislike a "hard sell". They are likely to listen intently, and it is a good idea to pause occasionally and invite questions. The best policy is to be relaxed and, if possible, deferential, and it helps if you can spice your sentences with humor. Avoid shows of arrogance or impatience.

Do not expect an instant response. The British like to chew ideas over, and might decide to set up a committee to investigate your proposals in greater detail. While there may be managers who can make quick decisions, most people are aware of the consequences of making a mistake and prefer to proceed more cautiously.

NEGOTIATIONS

The British negotiating style tends to be affable, relaxed, understated, and much less direct than the American style. The British like to feel that they are buying something, rather than being sold it, and they may take some time to make up their minds. It's best not to try to hurry things along.

THE WORK/LEISURE DIVIDE

The British generally separate the world of work from their personal life. While they may take their contacts out for a business lunch from time to time, or accompany their colleagues for a drink, this is often because they regard it as one of the requirements of the job.

On weekends and on vacation they generally like to cut themselves off completely from the workplace. This means they are out of reach outside business hours, and you would be well advised not to intrude on their privacy.

WOMEN IN BUSINESS

Although women are still outnumbered by men in chief executive posts, you will find them increasingly in senior management positions in most walks of life, including business, commerce, politics, the judiciary, the civil service, and academia.

Although it is rare to find women in major posts in manufacturing or engineering companies, they have managed to break through the "glass ceiling" in service industries such as retailing and publishing—more so than in most other countries in Europe. Women head several major companies, and women have also been prominent in the founding of new businesses. Many have risen through the ranks by dint of merit, and are highly competent. As such, they naturally expect to be treated as equals.

Chapter 4

FRANCE

Key Facts

Official Name	République Française	**Government (cont.)**	Two houses of parliament based in Paris: Assemblée Nationale (National Assembly) and Senat (Senate)
Capital City	Paris		
Major Cities	Bordeaux, Grenoble, Lille, Lyon, Marseille, Montpellier, Nice, Strasbourg, Toulouse		
Area	210,000 sq. miles (544,000 sq. km)	**Radio & TV**	The national state radio and TV network is supplemented by commercial stations. The SECAM transmission system is used.
Terrain	Varied: flat, hilly, mountainous, high central plateau		
Climate	Temperate, varying with terrain, to Mediterranean in south	**Press**	Paris: *Le Monde, Le Figaro, Le Parisien, L'Humanité, Liberation, France-Soir.* Provinces: *La Dépêche du Midi, Nice-Matin, La Voix du Nord, Presse-Ocean, Le Progrès*
Currency	Euro		
Population	64 million		
Language	French. Also regional languages, including Basque, Breton, Catalan, Provençal, and Flemish		
Ethnic Makeup	86% French (of Celtic and Latin descent); Basque minority in the southwest. 14% foreign (including other EU nationals and North African immigrants)	**English-language Media**	*Le Monde* carries a weekly English-language supplement from the *New York Times*.
		Electricity	230 volts, 50 Hz. Two-prong plugs used
		Internet Domain	.fr
Religion	Roman Catholic 88%; Protestant 2%; Muslim 5%; Jewish 1%; others 4%	**Telephone**	Country code: 33. For international calls dial 00.
Government	Unitary republic with an elected president who appoints the prime minister	**Time Zone**	CET (GMT/UTC + 1), with daylight saving in summer

Map of France

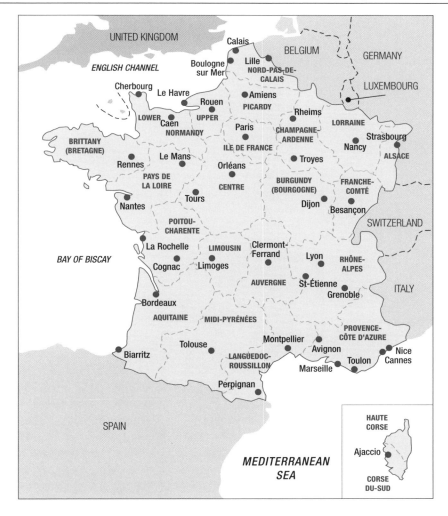

UNITED KINGDOM

ENGLISH CHANNEL

Calais

BELGIUM

GERMANY

Boulogne
sur Mer

Lille

NORD-PAS-DE-
CALAIS

LUXEMBOURG

Cherbourg

Le Havre

Amiens

PICARDY

Rouen

LOWER

UPPER

Caen

NORMANDY

Paris

Rheims

LORRAINE

Strasbourg

Nancy

BRITTANY
(BRETAGNE)

ILE DE FRANCE

CHAMPAGNE-
ARDENNE

ALSACE

Le Mans

Rennes

Troyes

PAYS DE
LA LOIRE

Orléans

CENTRE

BURGUNDY
(BOURGOGNE)

FRANCHE-
COMTÉ

Tours

Dijon

Besançon

Nantes

POITOU-
CHARENTE

SWITZERLAND

La Rochelle

LIMOUSIN

Clermont-
Ferrand

Lyon

BAY OF BISCAY

Cognac

Limoges

RHÔNE-
ALPES

AUVERGNE

St-Étienne

ITALY

Grenoble

Bordeaux

AQUITAINE

MIDI-PYRÉNÉES

PROVENCE-
CÔTE D'AZURE

Tolouse

Montpellier

Avignon

Nice

Biarritz

LANGUEDOC-
ROUSSILLON

Toulon

Cannes

Marseille

Perpignan

SPAIN

HAUTE
CORSE

Ajaccio

MEDITERRANEAN
SEA

CORSE
DU-SUD

The Country
and Its People

France is the largest country by area in Western Europe, and throughout history it has played an important political role, thanks to outstanding leaders such as Charlemagne, Louis XIV, Napoleon, and Charles de Gaulle. Once an important colonial power, France continues to play a leading role in international affairs, and was one of the founding members of the European Union.

France has led the way in other areas also, and has a cultural legacy second to none—in literature, music, and, above all, art. It has produced some of the great European philosophers, such as Descartes, Diderot, Montesquieu, Pascal, and Sartre. The French Revolution, with its slogan of *Liberté, Egalité, Fraternité*, has

Conques, Aveyron

inspired revolutionary movements throughout the world. The French language became, after the demise of Latin, the language of diplomacy, and remains an important world language.

While France has land boundaries with Belgium, Luxembourg, Germany, Switzerland, Italy, Monaco, Spain, and Andorra, it also has a lengthy coastline, of approximately 2,130 miles (3,430 km). It is washed by the English Channel to the north, by the Atlantic Ocean, along the Bay of Biscay, to the west, and by the Mediterranean Sea to the south.

The climate is temperate, with a maritime climate in the north and west affected by the Gulf Stream, a continental climate in the center and east of the country, and a warm Mediterranean climate in the south. At certain times of the year many parts of the country are affected by the Mistral, a cold, dry wind that blows strongly from the north and northwest.

France has a wide range of geographical features, ranging from plains and rolling hills in the north to the plateau of the Massif Central in the center and the mountainous regions of the Pyrenees, the Jura, and the Alps to the south and east.

A HISTORICAL PERSPECTIVE
France before Napoleon

In Roman times France was known as Gaul and inhabited by Celtic tribes. Roman rule established the Latin language, which developed into modern French. In the fifth century the Franks, a German tribe from the Baltic, ruled the country. The Carolingian dynasty arose in the eighth century, and its greatest king, Charlemagne, established a Christian Roman Empire, comprising France, large parts of Germany, and what is now northern Italy.

Duke William of Normandy (in northern France) invaded and conquered England in 1066, and this led to a long-standing rivalry between the two countries. William and his successors, as kings in their own right, with substantial possessions on the French mainland, often came into conflict with the kings of France. In the course of the Hundred Years War (1337–1453), the English King Henry V won a famous victory at Agincourt, and an English-controlled clerical tribunal burned the French resistance leader Jeanne d'Arc (Joan of Arc) at the stake for witchcraft and heresy. It was only in 1558 that the English Crown relinquished its last possession in France—Calais.

THE SUN KING
Louis XIV was known as "Le Roi Soleil" (the Sun King) and his absolutism is epitomized in his words "*L'État—c'est moi*" (I am the state.) Apart from being a powerful political figure, he was a great patron of the arts, building himself a sumptuous palace at Versailles, and employing a glittering array of dramatists and musicians, including Corneille, Racine, Molière, and Lully.

The Reformation led to considerable religious ferment in France, but the Edict of Nantes (1598) granted French Protestants freedom to worship until its revocation in 1685 by Louis XIV. He reigned for nearly seventy-three years (1643–1715), attaining absolute control over the country and becoming the most powerful monarch in Europe.

The Sun King's successors were far less capable—Louis XV made his mistress Madame de Pompadour prime minister—and within seventy-five years of his death the Bourbon monarchy came to an abrupt end with the French Revolution.

The French Revolution
When Louis XVI called a meeting of the long-dormant parliament (the States-General) to discuss reform of the country's finances, the representatives of the third of the three "estates" (nobles, clergy, and commons) set themselves up as L'Assemblée Nationale (the National Assembly). Riots broke out in Paris as rumors spread of royal plans to suppress the Assembly, and the army joined the revolutionaries. A republic was declared in 1792, and the king was executed.

The Assembly abolished the feudal system and published a "Declaration of the Rights of Man and of the Citizen." In order to bring in revenue it confiscated Church property, placing the clergy on the state payroll. Local government was reformed, and the separation of legislative, executive, and judicial powers was enshrined in Europe's first written constitution, based on the rational ideas and beliefs developed by the eighteenth-century French philosophers.

Power was seized by the radical republican Jacobin party, and in 1793 the Jacobin extremist Robespierre instituted a reign of terror, executing both aristocrats and revolutionaries. Robespierre himself ended up under the guillotine when a more moderate executive took over, but this was replaced in a coup d'état by the brilliantly successful Corsican general Napoleon Bonaparte.

The chronology of French history from 1789 to 1870 can be summarized as follows: Revolution, Republic, Empire, Monarchy, Revolution, Monarchy, Republic, Empire, Republic.

The Nineteenth Century

Napoleon was an extraordinary leader who crowned himself Emperor of France and dominated most of Europe until defeated at the Battle of Waterloo (1815). But his most enduring legacy is his implementation of the principles of the Revolution in all the territories conquered by France, and the introduction of the Code Napoléon, which is still in force today.

The Bourbon monarchy was restored in 1815, but the seeds of reform had been planted and in 1848 a second revolution led to the establishment of the Second French Republic. Napoleon's nephew was elected president and four years later founded the Second Empire, taking the title Napoleon III. He restored France's preeminence, but was eventually defeated by Prussia in 1870 at the Battle of Sedan.

A Third French Republic was proclaimed and Prussian troops besieged Paris. The government signed a peace treaty that ceded Alsace Lorraine to Germany, while revolutionary socialists set up a provisional assembly in Paris, known as the Paris Commune, which was brutally put down.

The Twentieth Century

Twice in the following century France found itself fighting against Germany, with appalling losses. In the First World War 1.4 million Frenchmen were killed and another four million wounded. The subsequent peace treaty returned Alsace Lorraine to France.

In 1940 Nazi Germany invaded France, eventually occupying the whole of the country. In the southern half of the country the French government under Marshal Pétain collaborated with the Germans. In London General de Gaulle set up a government in exile known as the Free French and organized the French Resistance to wage guerrilla warfare against the German occupation.

KEY HISTORICAL DATES

51 BCE	Julius Caesar conquers Gaul.
732 CE	Charles Martel repels Moorish invasion at Poitiers and paves way to the establishment of the Carolingian dynasty.
800	Charlemagne is crowned Holy Roman Emperor.
1337–1453	Hundred Years War between England and France.
1431	Joan of Arc is burned at the stake.
1643	Louis XIV accedes to the throne.
1789	The French Revolution.
1792	Declaration of the First French Republic.
1793	Committee of Public Safety set up under Robespierre.
1794	Robespierre executed and replaced by a five-man executive known as the Directory.
1799	Coup d'état overthrows the Directory. Napoleon is appointed First Consul.
1804	Napoleon crowns himself Emperor of France in Notre Dame.
1806	Napoleon dissolves the Holy Roman Empire.
1812	Napoleon's abortive invasion of Russia.
1815	Napoleon defeated at Waterloo. Bourbon monarchy is restored.
1821	Napoleon dies in exile on St. Helena.
1848	Second French Republic is established. Prince Louis-Napoléon Bonaparte is elected president.
1852	Louis-Napoléon proclaims the Second Empire and takes the title Napoleon III. France prospers.
1870	France is defeated by Prussia at Sedan. Napoleon III is captured. Proclamation of the Third French Republic.
1871	The Paris Commune.
1914–18	First World War costs many lives.
1919	Treaty of Versailles.
1940	Nazi Germany invades and occupies France.
1944	France is liberated following the Allied invasion of Normandy.
1954–62	Algerian War of Independence.
1956	France becomes a founder member of the European Economic Community (EEC).
1958	Charles de Gaulle becomes Prime Minister, proclaims the Fifth French Republic, and becomes its president.

After the Allied victory in 1945 France's Fourth Republic experienced considerable political and social turbulence, not least because of liberation struggles in the former colonies in Indo-China and the Algerian War of Independence. On the positive side, reconciliation with Germany led to the formation of the European Economic Community.

When the French government collapsed in 1958, the French called on De Gaulle to take over as prime minister. He proclaimed the Fifth Republic, becoming its first president, with considerable executive powers. He granted independence to Algeria, and to most of France's other colonies. Since this time and under De Gaulle's successors, Presidents Pompidou, Giscard d'Estaing, Mitterand, and Sarkozy, France has thrived.

GOVERNMENT

The Fifth French Republic has a president as head of state who is elected for five years. It is the president who appoints the prime minister, who is responsible for national policy.

The French Parliament comprises the Senate (Sénat) of 321 members elected for a nine-year term and the National Assembly (Assemblée Nationale) with 577 members elected for five years. Within both houses are members representing France's overseas departments: French Guiana, Guadeloupe, Martinique, and La Réunion.

The country is divided into ninety-six departments grouped into twenty-two administrative regions, of which the most populous is the Île de France, with Paris at its hub.

At the international level France belongs to NATO (North Atlantic Treaty Organization), is a permanent member of the UN Security Council, and is a leading player in the European Union.

Values and Attitudes

"How can one be expected to govern a country that has 246 different kinds of cheese?" President de Gaulle's words may offer a clue to the personality of the French people. They are essentially individualists—as different as Camembert from Roquefort, and as Port-Salut from Saint Agur.

We must beware of making sweeping generalizations about the French. For one thing, French national identity is a relatively new phenomenon. In the past most of the population identified with their local area or region; and as recently as 1880 only 20 percent of them spoke French, as opposed to local languages and dialects.

Nowadays, thanks to better communications, the media, and a national educational system, things have changed, and even the fiercely individualistic Bretons have developed characteristics that one could define as typically French.

A QUESTIONING MIND

The French philosopher and mathematician René Descartes (1596–1650) is known as "the father of modern philosophy." He codified the French system of logical thinking—Cartesian logic. His most famous dictum is "I think, therefore I am."

At school, French children are taught to think matters through to a logical conclusion. Reason is paramount, and whereas other nationalities look for practical solutions, the French look for consistency in an argument. If they discover flaws in a proposition they are likely to raise objections.

The desire for abstraction and order is reflected in the many formal gardens to be found in France. Intellectuals are highly respected in France, whereas other countries tend to view them with a modicum of suspicion.

STYLE, ELEGANCE, AND WIT

The French attach considerable importance to style. It is no coincidence that many of the world's major fashion houses are in Paris. French women dress well, and so do their menfolk. There is no room for slovenliness in French society.

Elegance is also reflected in the way the French interact with people. They express themselves with style and wit, striving always for *le mot juste* (the correct word), and expect an equally clever and quick rejoinder.

NATIONAL PRIDE

French people often give the impression of having a superiority complex. They prefer French food and wine and feel their methods of government and business, as well as their cultural life, are superior to those of other nations.

This is no doubt because pride in being French is instilled in the young from an early age. They learn of the country's glorious history—of Napoleon and Charlemagne, and of the importance of the French Revolution.

They are steeped in French literature, including writers such as Molière, Voltaire, Hugo, De Balzac, Baudelaire, Zola, Daudet, Flaubert, Verlaine, and Jules Verne. They are taken to art galleries to admire French painters including Gauguin, Toulouse-Lautrec, Matisse, Renoir, Monet, and Pissarro. Roads and squares are named after famous French people, and a station in Paris commemorates a famous French victory (Gare d'Austerlitz).

As a consequence, the French are well acquainted with their country's cultural and historical heritage. This pride is also boosted by prestigious modern projects, such as their high-speed trains (TGVs) and the new National Library (Bibliothèque Nationale).

THE LANGUAGE

The French are especially proud of their language. Until the early part of the twentieth century it was the international lingua franca, and although its role has been supplanted to a large extent by English, they expect foreign visitors not only to be able to speak French, but to speak it well.

Great emphasis is put on speaking and writing French correctly in French schools, with particular importance accorded to spelling, grammar, and punctuation. According to the Loi Toubon (Toubon's Law) of 1994, all signs, advertisements, and product descriptions have to be in French. Forty per cent of the music played on the radio must be French, as must 40 percent of the films transmitted by TV stations.

The French have considered themselves to have a civilizing mission (*mission civilisatrice*) to promote their language and culture to the world, and to that end the government invests heavily in cultural centers in other countries, such as the Alliance Française.

SOCIAL CLASS

Napoleon wanted government service to be open to all, no matter how lowly their origins. This was his interpretation of equality, the second of the ideals of the French Revolution. Yet, while the Revolution removed one elite (the monarchy and the aristocracy), to all intents and purposes it replaced it with another. Nowadays France is run by the graduates of the *Grandes Écoles*, the elite higher educational establishments outside the main university framework (see page 187), who form a tight, upper-middle-class group (*haute bourgeoisie*) that dominates the civil service, business, and politics. It is a self-perpetuating association that is prepared to exercise nepotism as and when called for.

Below this class is the professional middle class, and below that *la petite bourgeoisie* (traders and shopkeepers). On the bottom rung of the social ladder comes the working class. It is unusual for a person to marry above or below his or her station.

FAMILY VALUES

The family is a strong social unit, and it is not unusual for two or three generations of the same family to live in the same household or close to each other, or for children to live with their parents until they marry.

Families like to keep themselves to themselves, and usually only very intimate friends are invited to family gatherings. Members are very supportive of one another, and nepotism is not frowned on.

MORALITY

Parisian nightlife, with its nightclubs and theaters featuring scantily clad ladies, may suggest that sexual relations are very free and easy.

In fact, the French have a more conservative attitude toward sex than other nationalities, though the younger generation is more relaxed about such matters.

On the other hand, illegitimacy and marital infidelity are tolerated. At President Mitterand's funeral, for instance, both his wife and his mistress were in attendance. French people cannot understand why the Americans and the British make such a fuss when prominent figures are found to be having extramarital affairs.

RELIGION

Although Church and state are separate in France, the Church continues to have a strong influence on the lives and traditions of many French people. Most of them consider themselves Roman Catholic, even though many attend church infrequently. Church attendance is falling, especially in the cities and among the younger generation, and the priesthood is declining in numbers.

GOOD MANNERS

The French appreciate good behavior, and bring their children up quite strictly. They frown on inappropriate dress, excessive informality, and riotous behavior. They do not smile much, and may give the impression of being aloof. In the south of the country people have the reputation of being warmer and friendlier.

Festivals and Traditions

Each day of the ecclesiastical year is associated with a saint, and very many French parents give their children saints' names. Most children are baptized in church, and a child's first communion is a big event in his or her life.

Most villages and towns have a patron saint—St. Denis in the case of Paris—and the day of that saint is a time of celebration. Several national holidays are religious in origin.

HOLIDAYS AND FESTIVALS

January 1	Jour de l'An	New Year's Day
March/April	Pâques	Easter
May 1	Fête du Travail	Labor Day
May 8	Fête de la Victoire 1945	Victory in Europe Day
May	Ascension	Ascension Day
May	Pentecôte	Pentecost/Whitsun
July 14	Fête Nationale	Bastille Day
August 15	L'Assomption de Marie	Assumption
November 1	Toussaint	All Saints' Day
November 11	Armistice	Remembrance Day
December 25	Noël	Christmas Day

THE FESTIVE YEAR

New Year

The New Year is a time for celebration with a party (*reveillon*) on New Year's Eve and a big meal on the day itself. People greet each other with the words "*Bonne Année.*"

Epiphany
This day, January 6, commemorates the visit of the three Magi (wise men, or kings) to the infant Jesus. People often bake a special cake—*la galette des Rois*—and may put a small charm in it to be discovered by one lucky person.

Holy Week and Easter
Good Friday commemorates Christ's crucifixion, and there are processions and church services. The churches are full on Easter Sunday, and mass is usually followed by a big family meal. Easter Monday is a public holiday.

Ascension
A religious feast commemorating Christ's ascension into heaven, this is marked by masses in church and religious processions.

Pentecost
This two-day festival commemorates the coming of the Holy Spirit to Christ's disciples, inspiring them in their mision to spread his teachings. Masses are said and processions take place.

Fête Nationale
July 14, or *le quatorze juillet,* as it is often called, is a secular festival that commemorates the storming of the Bastille during the French Revolution. There are normally parades, speeches—including one by the President—fireworks, and other celebrations, and performances of the French national anthem.

Feast of the Assumption
This feast day celebrates the Virgin Mary's ascent into heaven, and is a time for family celebrations and religious ceremonies.

All Saints' Day
On this day, November 1, the French remember their dead. They visit the graves of dead relatives, and often place chrysanthemums on them.

Remembrance Day

Remembrance Day takes place on November 11, the eleventh day of the eleventh month, the day in 1918 when the Armistice was signed, bringing the First World War to an end. People hold ceremonies of remembrance and lay wreaths at war memorials throughout France. In Paris the President lays a wreath at the grave of the Unknown Soldier at the Arc de Triomphe.

Christmas

Stores mark the approach of Christmas by putting up lavish decorations designed to entice shoppers in to buy Christmas presents. Christmas cribs depicting Christ's nativity are erected in churches and public squares.

It is very much a family festival, and on Christmas Eve the family decorates a Christmas tree and attends midnight mass in the local church. This is followed by a festive supper (*reveillon*), which varies according to the region, but would typically consist of oysters, cold meats (charcuterie), goose, capon, or turkey, salad, cheese, and a yule log cake. Presents are exchanged around the tree on either Christmas Eve or Christmas Day, and people wish each other "*Joyeux Noël.*"

Santa Claus, or "Père Noël," traditionally fills children's shoes with sweets and small gifts on Christmas Eve.

Christmas decorations

LOCAL FESTIVALS

A hundred and fifty years ago many people in provincial France lived in isolated communities and had little sense of national identity. Even today local and regional allegiances are very strong, and as a result France has a rich variety of local festivals. Nice is famous for its Mardi Gras festival in February, and in May Rouen puts on the Festival de Jeanne d'Arc. The Avignon Festival is one of a number of summer festivals for which France is renowned. November sees the wine festival in Burgundy and in December Lyon celebrates with its Festival of Lights.

ETHNIC FESTIVALS

France has a number of significant ethnic minorities, notably Jews (historically European, but now also of North African origin), Muslims (mainly from North Africa), and Indo-Chinese. The largest communities are found in Paris. Muslims celebrate Milad un-Nabi, the Birthday of the Prophet Mohammed, Eid ul-Fitr at the end of Ramadan, and Eid ul-Adha (the Feast of the Sacrifice). The Chinese New Year, which occurs between the end of January and the end of February, is celebrated with great gusto, especially in the thirteenth district of Paris, which has a large concentration of Indo-Chinese.

FAMILY OCCASIONS

France is a secular state, but the Church, particularly the Roman Catholic Church, continues to play a pivotal role in the lives of many French families. Soon after a child is born he or she is taken to the church to be baptized, a rite that formally marks their entry into the Christian community. Many parents then hold a celebration party at which family and friends are introduced to the infant.

At around the age of twelve, children are confirmed and take their First Communion after a period of preparation. This confms their full membership of the Church, and in the family's eyes this confers on them a sense of adulthood and offers an excuse for further celebration.

Church weddings remain popular, but have no legal status in France, so couples are required to attend the local *mairie* or *préfecture* for the official marriage ceremony, usually following it with the church wedding. As in many other countries, wedding celebrations are becoming elaborate and expensive affairs.

The French take death very solemnly, and church funerals offer an opportunity for the family and friends to pay their respects to the deceased.

Getting to Know the French

Newcomers to France often feel ill at ease. The local people may seem coldly polite and not particularly welcoming. They seldom return a smile, not out of rudeness but because it is not the done thing in France if you want to be taken seriously. Formality needs to govern relationships, certainly in the early stages.

THE LANGUAGE

Although many French people speak English and other languages quite well, that does not mean that they are always willing to do so—perhaps out of shyness, which is why it should be your priority to learn some French.

There are many institutions offering French courses both in France and abroad—notably the Alliance Française—and a number of French universities have courses that will introduce you to French language and culture. You will quickly develop greater fluency if you also make regular efforts to watch French TV, read French newspapers and magazines, and communicate with French people in their own language—shopkeepers, hairdressers, and everyone you come across.

French is a Romance language, which means that it is an offshoot of Latin that has become modified over the centuries. In 1635 the Académie Française was founded to regulate the French language and remove all colloquialisms and foreign words. It has achieved some success in that the language is a good vehicle for expressing ideas clearly, but it has not been able to keep it as pure as it would like. English has made deep inroads into French, which has adopted such Anglicisms as "le look," "le camping," "le weekend," and "le self" (self-service cafeteria). The arrival of the Internet has intensified the invasion of foreign vocabulary, and most French IT users prefer to use English terms rather than coin new French words for them.

DIALECTS AND OTHER LANGUAGES

Everyone is taught standard French at school, but at home they tend to lapse into their local dialect with friends and family. Since France is a large country it has a rich variety of regional dialects that use words and expressions that are native only to that region.

In addition a few local languages still thrive, mainly on the outer fringes of the country. The most important of these is Breton, a Celtic language that is still spoken widely in Brittany. Italian is spoken close to the Italian border, and German in Alsace-Lorraine, especially among the older folk, since this was once occupied by Germany. Basque and Catalan are spoken in the areas of France adjoining Spain, and Provençal is still spoken in parts of the south.

However, this should not present a problem for the visitor, since people will use standard French—and perhaps even English—if they know if you are not from their area.

MEETING PEOPLE

Sometimes it is possible to strike up a relationship in a café-bar, especially if you frequent a particular one on a regular basis.

Another idea is to check if there is a welcome center (*accueil*) for new residents in your area, such as Nice-Acceuil, or Lyon-Acceuil. The local town hall (*mairie*) can give you details of this, and also information about activities such as organized rambles in the area—another good way of meeting people.

As in most countries, there are many clubs specializing in all kinds of activities, from sports to bridge, and friendships develop more easily among people with interests in common.

GREETINGS

When meeting a person or a group, it is quite normal to shake hands and even to kiss. If you do not know them by name, start by saying "*Bonjour, Monsieur*," or "*Bonjour, Madame*." You never use "*Bonjour*" on its own. When greeting a group of people you say "*Bonjour, Messieurs Dames*." "Good evening" is "*Bonsoir*."

When taking your leave, you should say "*Au revoir, Monsieur/Madame*," and wish the person "*Bonne journée*" ("Have a nice day") or "*Bonne soirée*" ("Have a nice evening"), to which the reply is "*Merci*" or "*Je vous remercie*" ("Thank you").

Note that you should address a person as *vous* (the formal word for "you") until you get to know them more intimately, when *tu* becomes permissible.

When you are on first-name terms with someone, note that many people have hyphenated names, and it is normal to address people by their full name, such as Jean-Christophe or Marie-Claire, rather than Jean or Marie.

COMMON COURTESIES

Habits that some might regard as old-fashioned still prevail in France. A man will open a door to let a woman through first, and people will rise from their seats to greet a visitor, unless bidden not to. Also, it is important to dress in a manner appropriate to the occasion, which will generally mean smartly and elegantly.

If you want to see someone, don't assume that you can drop in on them at home. Instead, call them in advance to see if it would be convenient, or arrange to meet at a café in the neighborhood. Dropping by unannounced is perfectly acceptable in southern areas of the country, however.

INVITATIONS HOME

If you receive an invitation from a French person to a meal in their home, this is a great honor, so do accept it with alacrity.

You will be expected to arrive not exactly on time, but ten or fifteen minutes late. Any gift you take along will be much appreciated. Chocolates are generally welcome, but be careful in your choice if you decide to give flowers, since chrysanthemums are associated with death, and carnations are regarded as unlucky. Ask the florist for advice.

Before the meal, people will wish one another "*Bon appétit.*" Your host will raise his glass of wine and wish his guests "*À votre santé*," and the meal will commence.

Avoid adding a lot of condiments (salt, pepper, or sauces) to the food, as this may suggest that you think it has not been well prepared. Make polite conversation (but not so polite that you sound boring), and steer away from money matters.

Sending a note of thanks afterwards is preferable to thanking the host or hostess by phone.

MAKING CONVERSATION

The French enjoy stimulating conversation, especially about current events, food, wine, sports, and culture. They prefer not to talk about personal matters, such as health, religion, money, and their own family. They dislike people who dominate the conversation, and like to switch topics to avoid boredom.

They often sound opinionated, but that is because they like offering new insights into matters of the moment and they will not take offense if people disagree. They will be interested in your impressions of France, but may be less interested in hearing about your own country. Conversations have to be sparkling and witty, but irony does not go down well.

Daily Life

Apartment buildings, Le Havre

HOUSING

Most city dwellers live in rented apartments, typically five stories high, but social housing projects, especially those on the fringes of Paris, are much, much higher. Some of the older ones have a concierge, or caretaker, who has a ground-floor apartment next to the entrance to enable her (rarely a man) to keep an eye on people coming in and out of the block. The concierge keeps the public areas clean and may handle the mail.

More modern apartment blocks have bells and intercoms enabling visitors to communicate with the apartment they want. When you hear a buzz, push open the entrance door. If it is dark inside you will need to press a succession of light switches or buttons that work on a timer. The interiors of apartments are often more lavish than the exteriors, but for the impecunious there are always garrets, especially in Paris.

Increasingly French people are opting to live in suburbia, where houses, either to buy or to rent, are more readily available. Second homes are becoming popular, particularly in rural areas where people have a family link. In villages and small towns living in houses is much more common.

Most bathrooms have modern toilets, but some have what is known as *un WC à la turque* consisting of a hole with a platform on each side on which you place your feet to squat. Before using the flush it is sensible to stand back as your feet may be drenched with water. A bidet is a feature of most French bathrooms. French plumbing, which was once notoriously bad, is much improved these days.

DAILY ROUTINE

Usually the weekday starts at 7:00 a.m. with a light breakfast of croissants and bread with butter and preserves and a bowl of white coffee (*café au lait*) or hot chocolate. If there is a bakery nearby, people pop out early to buy fresh bread or croissants. Some families have cereal, such as corn flakes, for breakfast.

Offices usually open around 9:00 a.m. and operate until 6:00 p.m. or later. The school day normally lasts from 8:30 a.m. to 4:30 p.m., with Wednesday afternoons off. Two-hour lunches between 12.30 and 2.30 p.m. are still the norm in many places. The evening meal starts at 7:00 or 8:00 p.m.

Weekends are less regimented and are a time for people to pursue their own interests. Lunch tends to be a leisurely affair, and people enjoy making trips. On Sunday mornings a dwindling minority go to church.

SHOPPING

Like most people, the French are enthusiastic shoppers. While they flock to supermarkets these days for life's essentials, they also patronize specialist shops and markets. Bakeries (*boulangeries*) tend to open earlier than other shops, at 7:00 or 7:30 a.m., so that people can purchase freshly baked goods for breakfast.

Cheeses in a Paris market

Most shoppers frequent street markets, particularly food markets, where they can buy fresh fruit and vegetables as well as meat, cheese, and seafood. There are also specialist markets selling antiques and bric à brac, such as the famous Flea Market (*Marché aux Puces*) in Paris.

FAMILY LIFE

French families tend to be paternalistic, with the husband wielding authority in the household. What he says goes, and this affects the way the children are brought up.

Children are expected to be well behaved and not interrupt or contradict their elders. Their upbringing—both at home and at school—is designed to ensure they become model citizens. This does not always work, and there are plenty of instances of young people rebelling against authority.

Parents can be quite critical of their children if they do not toe the line. Relationships remain close, and even when they leave the parental roost, sons and daughters pay frequent visits and dine with their parents on a regular basis. They also keep in touch with a network of relations living in the neighborhood.

EDUCATION

France is a meritocracy, and most parents want their children to have a good education. Education is compulsory between the ages of six and sixteen, though most children attend a nursery school first of all and study until they are eighteen.

The state educational system has a good reputation and provides education for the majority of children. Others go to private schools, which are often denominational, but not normally expensive since teachers' salaries and certain other costs are paid by the government. However, parents have to foot the bill for school textbooks and stationery.

All schools follow a national curriculum, which prescribes in detail what should be taught. It is alleged that a French Minister of Education once pointed to the clock in his office and boasted that he could tell exactly what was being taught at each level on each day to within the hour.

Children are expected to study hard, and those who fail to make the grade in the *concours* (a public exam held at the end of each year) have to repeat the year. Wednesday afternoons are normally free, but children may have to attend school on Saturday mornings. The summer vacation lasts two months. Mathematics is accorded particular importance, and older pupils have to study philosophy. The school leaving examination is the *Baccalauréat*, known as the *Bac*, and those who pass become *bacheliers*.

Having attained the *Bac* at the right level, the student is eligible to go to university to study for a bachelor's degree (*licence*)—three years—or a master's degree (*master*)—a further two years. However, the more ambitious will opt to take a competitive examination to enter one of the *Grandes Écoles*, such as L'École Nationale de l'Administration (ENA) or L'École Polytechnique. These represent the top tier of the educational system, and virtually all the members of the French cabinet and the country's captains of industry have been educated at one of these establishments.

THE ARMED FORCES

Formerly young men over eighteen were expected to do twelve months' military service or community service. This rule no longer applies, although registration is still compulsory. The age range for volunteering for military service is seventeen to forty.

NEWSPAPERS

French people like to keep up to date with events, and are well served by their newspapers. The most serious of the Paris newspapers is *Le Monde* (which does not normally publish photographs), followed by *Le Figaro*. Others include *Le Parisien*, *L'Humanité*, *Libération*, and *France-Soir*. The *International Herald Tribune* is also published in

Paris. *Les Échos* is a business paper, and *L'Équipe* concentrates on sports news.

In addition to these there are several weekly magazines that are news oriented, such as *Paris Match, Le Point, L'Express,* and the satirical *Le Canard Enchaîné.*

Although newspapers published in Paris circulate in the provinces, many of the locals prefer to buy their own regional newspapers. such as *La Dépêche du Midi, La Voix du Nord, Le Progrès, L'Est Républicain, Nice-Matin,* and *Paris-Normandie.*

TELEVISION AND RADIO

France has a plethora of TV channels, both terrestrial and satellite. The terrestrial ones are obliged to ensure that a certain proportion of their program content is French in origin, and this regulation applies to radio stations as well. The transmission system is SECAM, which means that sets operating on the PAL or NTSC systems do not work in France.

MAIL AND TELECOMMUNICATIONS

The postal system in France is efficient. Post offices (*Bureaux de poste*), which offer a range of services including banking and currency exchange, are open between 8:00 a.m. and 7:00 p.m. on weekdays, closing at noon on Saturdays. Postage stamps can also be purchased from a café-tabac.

When addressing an envelope, write the person's name and title in full. Remember to add the five-digit post code.

The French telephone system is also very efficient. Telephone numbers have ten digits. The first digits are the dialing code of the geographical area: Paris 01, western France 02, east 03, southeast 04, southwest 05. When dialing France from abroad, add 33 at the beginning and ignore the initial zero. Mobile numbers usually begin with 06, and Freephone numbers with 0800. Some telephone companies offer a facility to dial most numbers in France and abroad free of charge using an 09 number.

In 1983 the French telephone service (France Télécom) pioneered Minitel, an online minicomputer providing access to a range of services such as directory enquiries and train bookings. Minitel is still in existence, but has now been overtaken by the Internet.

Leisure Time

The French enjoy their leisure actively, and make full use of their free time, whether it is *le weekend*, a public holiday, or the *grandes vacances* (the main holiday of the year), when Paris would become a ghost town were it not for the tourists.

EATING OUT

The French are proud of their cuisine and consider it superior to any other in the world. They like to dine out and take time over a good meal. On weekends they often dine out *en famille*. They enjoy discussing food and trying out new dishes, and like to hand on their appreciation of good food to their children.

Each region of France has a typical range of dishes, and in large urban centers there are many restaurants specializing in Italian, Chinese, Vietnamese, Indian, Lebanese, and North African cuisine. Fast food outlets, such as McDonald's and Quick, find favor with the young, while self-service cafeterias are popular in cities with people in a hurry.

Café culture is strong in France and everywhere there are cafés or café-bars where people can sit and watch the world go by—or indulge in lengthy discussions about how to change it. Apart from serving drinks these establishments often offer light snacks, such as a *croque-monsieur* (grilled cheese and ham on toast), a *croque-madame* (the same topped with an egg), an *omelette*, a *crêpe* (pancake), or a *salade*.

It is worth noting that you either sit at the bar to have your drink or sit at a table and be waited upon. You cannot order your drink at the bar and then move over to a table, as is the custom in Britain.

Salons de thé are similar to cafés but are a little more elegant and have a wider range of food. *Brasseries* are open all day and offer a limited menu. *Bistrots* here do not have the same cachet as they do in English-speaking countries; generally they are small, local restaurants serving good, basic meals. If you want a good, reasonably priced meal, try a *relais routier*—originally a café for truck drivers.

Many restaurants offer a fixed-price menu with three or four courses and perhaps a carafe or *pichet* (jug) of wine, known as a *menu touristique* or *menu à prix fixe*.

TIPPING

Service compris means that a service charge is included in the bill, and this will be the case in most restaurants and cafés today. It is, however, usual to leave a coin or two in the saucer.

A FORMAL FRENCH MEAL

If you are invited out to dine, either in a restaurant or in a person's home, the meal is likely to follow a certain order. Here are the elements you can expect:

L'apéritif. This could be gin and tonic, Martini, Campari (a bitter herbal drink), or *pastis* (an aniseed drink like the Greek *ouzo*, mixed with water to produce a cloudy white liquid—Pernod and Ricard are the best-known brands).

Hors d'oeuvre. This is a starter, which might be raw vegetables (*crudités*) with a dressing, or a plate of cold meats. *Une assiette anglaise* combines the two. Some restaurants offer a free *amuse-bouche* of pâté or fish to whet the appetite.

L'entrée. Often fish.

Le plat principal. This is the main course. Note that vegetables are often served separately from the main course, unlike most other countries, where everything is served on the same plate.

La salade. This is usually eaten after the main course.

Les fromages. This is usually a small selection of cheeses.

Le dessert. Perhaps a specialty such as *poire Belle Hélène*, or fruit, or ice cream.

Le café. Coffee at this time is normally served black, but some people opt for herbal tea (tisane).

Le digestif. A glass of brandy or liqueur.

If you find an array of cutlery at your place, you normally start at the outside and work inward, but it is wise to check what others are doing. There may be three glasses—for water, red wine, and white wine. Bread is served with the meal and should be broken, not cut. Wine is normally drunk during the meal and may be served by the bottle or half-bottle, or by the carafe.

DRINK

French wine is famous throughout the world, and none is more famous than Champagne, the effervescent dry white wine grown in the area centered on Reims, east of Paris. Other notable winegrowing areas are Burgundy, Bordeaux, Alsace, the Loire Valley, and the Rhône Valley, which produces such famous wines as Muscadet, Chablis, Entre-deux-Mers, Châteauneuf du Pape, and Beaujolais.

The best-quality wines bear the designation *Appellation Contrôlée*, showing that their provenance, varietal make-up, and production methods are strictly regulated. Wines with the *Vin de pays* designation are usually from the southern wine regions of France, such as Languedoc-Roussillon and Provence, and are very drinkable.

French brandies also have a worldwide reputation. Grapes from the Charente region are distilled to make Cognac, and grapes from the Gers region Armagnac. There are numerous liqueurs such as *crème de menthe*, flavored with mint, and *cassis*, made from blackcurrants.

Beer-drinkers are well served by a wide range of breweries producing lager-type beers. Beer from Alsace is particularly prized. Much of the cider produced in France comes from Normandy, which also distils cider to make cider brandy known as Calvados.

A full range of soft drinks is available in France, including famous mineral waters, such as Evian, Perrier, and Vittel, which may be sparkling (*gazeuse*) or still (*non gazeuse*). Plain water is also available in restaurants if you specify *une carafe d'eau*. Fruit juices are readily available, and a popular drink in hot weather is *citron pressé* (squeezed fresh lemon and water, served with sugar).

CULTURE AND ENTERTAINMENT

France has a strong cultural tradition with art galleries, museums, concert halls, opera houses, and theaters in all the main urban centers and many festivals devoted to a wide range of music, including jazz, classical, and pop. Paris is the Mecca for all things cultural and boasts the Louvre, the Opéra-Garnier, which inspired the story *The Phantom of the Opera*, and the newer Opéra-Bastille. The Salle Pleyel hosts major orchestral concerts, and L'Olympia is an important center for

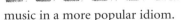

music in a more popular idiom.

Paris is also home to the Comédie Française, France's national theater founded in 1680, and a number of other theaters that put on operettas, drama, and ballet. There is also, of course, the famous Moulin Rouge.

Cinema-going is a popular pastime. The French have always been proud of their film industry, which can boast internationally renowned directors such as Jean Renoir, Jean-Luc Godard, Robert Bresson, Alain Resnais, Luc Besson, and François Truffaut. The industry continues to thrive, producing around twenty-five new films each year. Yet the most popular films tend to be from Hollywood and are either dubbed into French or given subtitles. La Cinémathèque in Paris is a film theater that shows mainly classic films.

STUDENTS, CLUBBING, AND CLOSE ENCOUNTERS

Paris, divided into twenty "arrondissements", promises something for everyone. Whether you are looking for an academic, arty or chic scene, you will find that each district, characterized by its residents and what it has on offer, will provide you with something different.

The best places for going out and getting a real taste for the nightlife and subculture are Belleville and Ménilmontant, in east Paris. They are two of the city's multicultural areas and have an authentic Parisian nightlife scene bursting with sophistication and eclecticism.

The Bastille, once the hub of the Revolution, is now the heart of Paris' creative community, full of music venues and quirky bars; it can get a little mainstream at weekends.

In the heart of the city, the Marais offers an array of chic cafés and an active gay and lesbian scene.

Pigalle, better known as the seedy sex center of Paris, is home to some good music venues, namely the Moulin Rouge cabaret, Clichy and 18th, where the cancan is still performed.

The Latin Quarter in the south of Paris caters for a more academic scene, located between the Sorbonne and the Panthéon, while the Montparnasse, reminiscent of its 1920s artistic heyday, offers a refreshing change from the mainstream nightlife spots .

Your chances of getting a date in France are probably based on your ability to speak French, particularly in Paris where the locals may feign an inability to speak English just for the fun of it. Love and the exploration of it is not taboo in France, so don't be afraid and play hard to get. It is straightforward. If he or she is asking you out, they like you.

Although the French can be very formal, the initial date should be unintimidating—perhaps a long walk in the city followed by going to a café and getting to know each other over coffee and cigarettes; simple yet intimate.

French people have tight social groups, and it is quite likely that a couple will "date" in the company of their friends until they know each other better.

SPORTS

The French enjoy sports both as spectators and as participants. The Tour de France, the famous cycle race, takes place every July, the Le Mans twenty-four-hour car race is in June, and there is also the Monte Carlo Rally. Both soccer and rugby football have an enthusiastic following.

The Tour de France

Winter sports are very popular, as are water sports along France's extensive coast. Cycling and traveling by barge are gaining favor in the plains of northern France, and there are many opportunities for walkers and mountaineers.

Boules is a popular activity, particularly with older men. It differs from the English game of bowls in that the iron *boule* is thrown toward a wooden ball, known as the *cochonnet*. The game is known as *pétanque* in the south of France.

Getting Around

Back in the nineteenth century communications were so bad that many French people scarcely ever ventured outside the confines of their own towns and villages. Today every place is linked to a vast, well-maintained road network, and there is an extensive rail network, of which over half is electrified. National and regional bus and coach services connect places that are inaccessible by rail.

The French have an efficient railway system run by the national rail company SNCF (Société Nationale des Chemins de Fer Français), which links into the rail systems of neighboring countries. Before boarding the train you have to validate (*composter*) your ticket by pushing it into a machine that stamps the date and time on it. Keep it on your person to show the ticket inspector on the train.

Normal express trains are good and comfortable, but there are also high-speed trains linking Paris to the provinces known as *trains à grande vitesse* (TGV), for which advance booking is necessary.

URBAN TRANSPORTATION

Paris has an integrated public transport system run by RATP (Régie Autonome des Transports Parisien), which comprises buses, subway trains (*le Métro*), and suburban lines (RER). You can obtain a map of the routes from any metro station.

If you are staying in Paris for a while, it is best to buy a book (*carnet*) of ten tickets, which is much cheaper than buying tickets singly for each journey. For bus and RER journeys beyond the central zone you may have to use more than one ticket.

There are also day passes (*Mobilis*), and visitors' travel passes (*Paris Visites*) lasting for one to five days that can be bought at the airport if you arrive by air. Otherwise you can obtain a weekly *Passe Navigo Découverte* (residents can get a *Passe Navigo*), which runs from Monday to Sunday, for which you need to supply a passport photograph.

Tickets must be validated as you enter the bus or to gain access to the metro platform before you start your journey.

Many French cities and large towns have light rail or tram systems as well as buses.

DRIVING

France has a comprehensive road system, and away from the main conurbations the roads are generally not crowded, except when the annual summer holidays begin and end. There are toll expressways, with tollbooths (*péages*) at various intervals, highways, and minor roads, which are free.

The speed limit is 130 kmph (80 mph) on the expressways, 90 kmph (56 mph) on open roads, and 50 kmph (31 mph) in built-up areas. Formerly, drivers had to yield to traffic coming from the right on traffic circles, but now vehicles on the traffic circles have priority. The wearing of seat belts is compulsory, and children below the age of ten are not allowed to sit in the front seat. The drink-drive limit is 0.5 mg per ml.

Drivers must carry (in case of accident or breakdown) red warning triangles, a first-aid box, and a spare set of headlamps in their cars, as well as a fluorescent jacket.

WHERE TO STAY

There is plenty of accommodation in France, from one-star hotels through hotel chains that provide good, inexpensive accommodation, such as Ibis and ETAP Hotels, to very luxurious establishments. It is advisable to book in advance at peak periods, but this is not always necessary.

Alternatives to hotels are guesthouses, known as *chambres d'hôtes*, offering bed and breakfast, and self-catering holiday cottages, known as *gîtes*. There are plenty of camping sites (*camping*), which are equipped to a high standard, and a network of youth hostels (*auberges de jeunesse*—see www.fuaj.com).

Local tourist offices (*offices du tourisme*) can provide information and make bookings for you, as can French tourist offices abroad.

MEDICAL MATTERS

France offers a high standard of health care, and citizens of the EU and EEA are entitled to use the health service on the same terms as French residents on production of a European Health Insurance Card (EHIC). Provided you use a health service doctor (*médecin conventionné*) you will be able to claim a partial refund on presentation of a signed statement describing the treatment given (*feuille de soins*). If you need a prescription you will have to attach the *vignettes* the pharmacist gives you to get a refund. Hospital charges also work on the reimbursement system. Applications for refunds should be sent to the local health insurance office (Caisse Primaire d'Assurance-Maladie).

Because of the bureaucracy involved many people prefer to take out private medical insurance. Citizens from outside the EEA and EU should certainly do so.

LAW AND ORDER

France is no worse than any other country in Europe with respect to crime, and provided you take reasonable precautions, such as keeping your money, credit cards, and passport safe, and do not leave valuables in a car, you should have a trouble-free stay. If you do have the misfortune to be robbed, report this to the police in the district (*arrondissement*) where it happened, who will fill out a statement (*constat de vol*).

The French police can be severe and unsmiling. They are able to issue on-the-spot fines for offenses such as speeding, and possession of illegal drugs could land you in jail.

PLACES TO VISIT

Paris

Paris is one of the great cities of the world, with plenty of wonderful architecture and the River Seine flowing through the middle. Many people are content just to stroll along the wide boulevards built by Baron Haussmann a hundred and fifty years ago, along the banks of the Seine, where there is always plenty of activity, or through parks such as the Jardin des Tuileries.

The Cathedral of Notre Dame on the Île de la Cité on the Seine, Paris

For a view over the city you can nip to the top of the Eiffel Tower or the Basilica of the Sacred Heart (Sacré-Coeur) in Montmartre. Paris is full of splendid churches, notably the cathedral of Notre Dame de Paris, the Madeleine, the Trinité, and St. Eustache.

The art galleries of Paris are, of course, renowned throughout the world. Among the leading ones are the Louvre (home to the *Mona Lisa*), the Musée d'Orsay (once a railway terminus), the Musée National d'Art Moderne, and the Centre Pompidou, named after a former president, which some say looks more like an oil refinery from the outside.

Just outside the city are the Palace of Versailles, with its magnificent gardens, and Disneyland Paris.

Provincial Pleasures

France is a large country, and contains considerable variety within its borders. It has spectacular Alpine scenery, which includes Mont Blanc and many fashionable skiing resorts, and the rugged terrain of the Massif Central.

The French Riviera on the Mediterranean has been a playground for holidaymakers for over a century and a half, and has stylish resorts such as Nice and Cannes, home to the famous film festival. But there are many attractive beaches and resorts all along the long coastlines, including the once fashionable Deauville, in the north.

Throughout the country there are architectural jewels that are well worth a visit. Cluny Abbey, the cathedrals of Rouen, Amiens, Strasbourg, Chartres, and Reims, and the medieval fortifications of Carcassonne are all well worth investigation.

The provinces come alive with jazz and classical music festivals during the summer. On a more somber note there are the battles and military cemeteries of the two World Wars, including the Normandy landing beaches.

View of the French Alps, from Savoie

Business & Professional Life

France is one of the world's leading economic powers, and plays a significant role in international affairs. It is also a country where the worlds of government and business are closely intertwined. Politicians and leaders in industry and commerce have nearly all been through the elite *Grandes Écoles* and know one another well. Individuals frequently move seamlessly between the two worlds, so today's President-Director General of Electricité de France could well become tomorrow's Minister of Commerce. On top of this the state holds a substantial stake in several firms, which means the person you have to deal with is likely to be a combination of bureaucrat and businessperson.

Headquarters of the Société Générale, Paris

MAKING CONTACT

As has already been mentioned, the French are quite formal in their dealings with other people, and this is certainly true in business and professional matters.

Timing is important. Meetings are held during office hours between 9:00 a.m. and 7:00 p.m. The period from late July to the end of August is not a good time to seek a meeting, since this is when most French people take their holidays.

Your initial approach needs to be by letter, couched in formal terms, and preferably in French. It is important to address the person you wish to see by the right title (for example, "Monsieur le Directeur"), and the hard-sell approach should be avoided at all costs. A follow-up telephone call to the person's office is quite in order, but do not expect a secretary to make an appointment for you without consulting the boss.

It is also sensible to aim high. French organizations are hierarchical, and there is no point in starting to deal with a person who does not possess any decision-making powers. Top managers are authoritarian, and rarely delegate; they issue instructions to their subordinates and tend to ignore any suggestions from them.

PREPARING FOR MEETINGS

Remember that you will be dealing with people who are intelligent, knowledgeable, and powerful, who will want to discuss the merits of any proposition you have to make in some detail. So it is essential to be well prepared and to know all about the company or institution with which you will be dealing. If your French is rudimentary, take along an interpreter.

Dress smartly and soberly, and look well-groomed. The French always judge people by their appearance, and the smarter you look the higher the status they will accord you. This applies to both men and women.

Aim to get to the meeting on time. However, the French are not great sticklers for punctuality, as the Germans are, and you may have to wait for a while for everyone to gather.

Don't be disappointed if there is no agenda for the meeting. Even if there is one, you can regard it as a guide to the points the meeting is likely to cover, rather than as a firm schedule that will be followed strictly.

ESTABLISHING TRUST

On the whole, French people in business or public service prefer to deal with people they know well and can trust—and who speak their language. A foreigner therefore starts at a disadvantage since the chances are that he or she does not belong to the close-knit network of *Grandes Écoles* graduates. This will mean trying that much harder and being prepared for the long haul.

An understanding of French business etiquette will help to open doors; excessive familiarity in your approach will not. If you have had experience of France or French people or—best of all—if you have studied in France, it might be helpful to mention this, as it will demonstrate that you are not a total stranger, but avoid name dropping.

Once trust is established, doing business becomes much easier, and it is worth developing a lasting relationship through regular contacts.

PRESENTATIONS

These need to be logical and detailed, setting out clearly the outline of any proposal. Avoid hyperbole; the French prefer low-key presentations that present the arguments clearly and precisely. Ideally they should be conducted in French, with supporting material also in French.

NEGOTIATIONS

Negotiations are usually formal affairs and, once again, you should avoid seeming over-friendly, as this could offend or annoy people. Your patience and powers of diplomacy might be tested, particularly if discussions get protracted and seem to be wandering away from the point.

Yet long discussions are not necessarily a bad thing; the French like to be thorough. They are also more interested in coming to a logical decision through argument rather than simply adopting a proposition purely on practical grounds.

Sometimes discussions can turn into heated arguments, but you should endeavor to remain polite and courteous at all times and not be put off by detailed probing. The French are not trying to catch you out.

Make sure you have good explanations and counter-arguments that will satisfy them. And if one line of argument does not seem to be working, or the French seem to be stalling over a particular point, be prepared to change tack. Present your proposals from another angle and point to flaws in their objections, without appearing to be critical. You will find they are susceptible to well-reasoned arguments.

WOMEN IN BUSINESS

Although Frenchwomen were late in achieving voting rights, they are prominent in all sectors of business and public life. One of the leading candidates in the last presidential election was a woman.

Their participation is encouraged through the provision of generous maternity benefits and leave, yet they tend to miss out on the best-paid jobs, and two out of three working women earn only the minimum wage.

If you are a female executive, you can expect to be treated with old-fashioned courtesy by your male counterparts. Sexual harassment is uncommon, and incurs heavy punishments.

Chapter 5

GERMANY

Key Facts

Official Name	Bundesrepublik Deutschland, German Federal Republic	**Radio and TV**	ARD is the national TV and radio network, comprsing North German, Bavarian, and South German State TV and radio. There are also numerous local and commercial satellite stations. The PAL B system is in use.
Capital City	Berlin		
Major Cities	Hamburg, Köln (Cologne), Dresden, Düsseldorf, Frankfurt am Main, Leipzig, München (Munich), Stuttgart		
Area	138,000 sq. miles (357,000 sq. km)	**Press**	Most of the newspapers are regional, including *Die Welt, Frankfurter Allgemeine Zeitung, and Süddeutsche Zeitung*. The tabloid *Bild Zeitung* has a national circulation.
Population	82 million		
Terrain	Flat plains in the north, hilly in the center, mountainous in the south		
Climate	Temperate		
Currency	Euro	**English-language Media**	*Frankfurter Allgemeine Zeitung* has a Web site with local and international news in English.
Language	German		
Religion	Christian (Lutheran and Roman Catholic) 72%; Muslim 1.7%; others 26.3%		
		Electricity	230 volts; 50 Hz. Two-prong plugs used
Government	A democratic federal republic of sixteen states (or *Länder*). There is an elected president and an elected prime minister who commands the majority of the seats in Parliament. There are two parliamentary chambers: the Bundestag (lower house) and the Bundesrat (upper house).	**Internet Domain**	.de
		Telephone	Country code: 49. For international calls dial 00.
		Time Zone	CET (GMT/UTC + 1), with daylight saving in summer

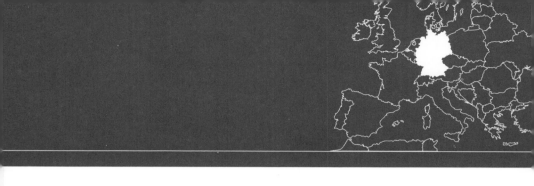

Map of Germany

The Country and Its People

Germany lies at the heart of Europe. It has borders with Poland, the Czech Republic, Austria, Switzerland, France, Luxembourg, Belgium, the Netherlands, and Denmark, and its shores are washed by the North Sea and the Baltic Sea.

Its landscape varies from the lowlands of the north to the Alpine regions of the south, where its highest mountain, the Zugspitze (9,152 feet; 2,962 meters,) is to be found. The country is crisscrossed by many great rivers, such as the Main, Elbe, Neckar, Danube (Donau), and, most important of all, the Rhine (Rhein).

Berlin, with 3.4 million people, is the country's capital, followed by Hamburg with 1.7 million and Munich (München) with 1.2 million. The country has a temperate continental climate, except in

Hohenzollern Castle, Baden-Württemberg

the areas close to the sea, which means that summers can be hot and winters cold. The south sometimes experiences the Föhn, a warm, dry wind from the Alps, which can cause headaches.

Germany is an industrial powerhouse and one of the world's leading exporters of a very wide range of manufactured and processed goods. Its intellectual and cultural life is second to none. It boasts a number of leading universities and research institutes; several of the world's finest orchestras and musicians are based here; and it has an impressive array of concert halls and opera houses.

Some of the greatest composers of classical music—the Bach family, Handel, Beethoven, Schumann, Mendelssohn, Brahms, Richard Strauss, and Wagner—were German. Goethe, Schiller, Heine, Brecht, Thomas Mann, and Gunther Grass are just a few of the German writers who are known throughout the world. Thinkers such as Leibnitz, Schopenhauer, Kant, Hegel, and Nietzsche were born on German soil, as was that key figure of the Reformation, Martin Luther.

It is unfortunate that outsiders often overlook the huge positive contribution that Germany has made to Western civilization and dwell on the relatively brief period in the twentieth century when the Nazis held power. The image of the jackbooted, ruthless, and arrogant SS officer portrayed in so many war films is quite unrepresentative of Germans today. However, this dark period— when Hitler's armies dominated Europe, when Jews and other minorities faced total extermination—scarred Europe for a generation, and it will take time for memories of the evils perpetrated by the Nazis to fade completely.

Germans now live in one of the best-governed, most democratic countries in Europe. They play a leading role in the affairs of the European Union, and their strong sense of social responsibility is an example to other nations.

A HISTORICAL PERSPECTIVE

For much of its history the name "Germany" represented a geographical area rather than a political entity. There was political cohesion of a sort when Charlemagne, the King of the Franks, brought the German tribes together and imposed order on much of continental Europe after being crowned "Emperor of the Romans" by Pope Leo III in 800 CE. He did not rule the territories as a unified whole, however. According to the laws of inheritance he divided the empire among his sons. Strife among his grandsons ended in the Treaty of Verdun (843), which split the empire into eastern, western, and central parts. The eastern realm later became Germany and the western France, while the central region never attained a separate national identity.

The imperial title lapsed until 962, when Otto I, King of the Saxons, was crowned Emperor in Rome. The new line of "Roman emperors" lasted for more than a thousand years, although they seldom had any powers outside the boundaries of Germany. Nevertheless, a series of vigorous German kings tried to convert the Roman Empire of the West into reality, which brought them into conflict with the Popes and the revived city-republics of Italy. Frederick Barbarossa was a notable emperor, who gave Bavaria to the Count Palatine of Wittelsbach in 1180, a dynasty that was to rule that territory until 1918.

In the thirteenth century the northern German city states of Hamburg, Bremen, and Lübeck rose to prominence when they formed the Hanseatic League to protect their trading interests. This was to dominate the commercial activity of northern Europe for the next two centuries.

During the Middle Ages the German princes consolidated their land holdings, originally held as fiefs granted by the Holy Roman Emperor. Gradually these principalities became more independent, uniting only to elect one of their number as Holy Roman Emperor on the death of his predecessor. By the sixteenth century, the title had become hereditary, and had passed to the Austrian House of Habsburg. After the Thirty Years War (1618–48) between Protestants and Catholics in central Europe, the Holy Roman Emperor's authority in Germany was greatly reduced.

What we know today as Germany was thus a patchwork of three hundred and fifty small autonomous principalities, duchies, kingdoms, and a few free cities, owing loose allegiance to the Emperor. This situation lasted until the Holy Roman Empire was dissolved by Napoleon in 1806.

Reformation, War, and the Rise of Prussia

Martin Luther's protest in 1517 against the sale of papal indulgences heralded the start of the Protestant Reformation

that was to set principality against principality. Most of the north German states adopted Protestantism, while others stayed with the old faith.

Religious differences played themselves out in the devastating Thirty Years War that engulfed Germany, Austria, Sweden, and the Netherlands. Today a religious divide still exists between the Protestant north and the Catholic south.

One important development in the seventeenth century was the rise of Prussia, which had passed into the hands of the Hohenzollern family of Brandenburg. When Frederick II of Prussia—Frederick the Great—

Statue of Martin Luther, Dresden

came to the throne in 1740 he built up a powerful army, which was to prove crucial in Europe's struggle against Napoleon, notably in the Battle of Waterloo in 1815. The victorious Allies decided to set up, in place of the Holy Roman Empire, the German Confederation, a loose association of the German states.

Prussia soon became the leading state within the Confederation, accounting for 60 percent of its area, and after it defeated its rival Austria in 1866, and France in 1870, it became the dominant power in the German-speaking world.

A United Germany and Two World Wars

In 1871, Prince Otto von Bismarck, a brilliant military and political strategist, brought the northern Confederation and four

southern states of Germany together to form the German Empire under Kaiser Wilhelm I. Bavaria became part of the union, but retained considerable autonomy and its own king.

The new Germany became an industrial colossus, eclipsing both the United States and Great Britain and forming an alliance with the Habsburg monarchy. The next Kaiser, Wilhelm II,

Otto von Bismarck

dispensed with Bismarck's services and concentrated on turning Germany into a global military power.

When the Austrian Archduke Franz Ferdinand was assassinated in 1914, Germany allied itself with Austria against Russia, France, and Britain. The calamitous First World War that ensued led to the eventual defeat of Germany and Austria, the demise of the Kaiser, and the establishment of the Weimar Republic. The postwar Treaty of Versailles imposed heavy reparations payments on Germany and stripped the country of some of its territories.

The demands of the Treaty caused considerable resentment, and it was partly this reaction, coupled with the desperation caused by the Great Depression, that led Germans to fall for the nationalistic rhetoric and promises of Adolf Hitler's National Socialist German Workers' Party. Hitler came to power in 1933, proclaiming the Third Reich as successor to the Holy Roman Empire and the modern German Empire.

Under the Nazis Germany sought to regain its lost territory and more, remilitarizing the Rheinland, then annexing Austria, the Sudetenland in western Czechoslovakia, and the rest of Czechoslovakia. The invasion of Poland was a step too far for Britain and France, and they declared war on Germany. The Second World War proved truly global in nature, and led eventually to the defeat of Germany, at tremendous cost. The country was decimated, with many German cities, including Berlin, reduced to rubble.

The Postwar Period

Germany emerged from the war a shadow of its former self, with its cities in ruins and its people facing starvation. The country was divided into four occupation zones, each under the control of one of the Allied powers (USA, France, USSR, and Britain) with its capital, Berlin, divided into four zones.

Differences of opinion between the Soviet Union and the Western powers led to the Soviet blockade of Berlin in 1948 and 1949. In 1949 the country was partitioned: the zones controlled by the Western powers became the German Federal Republic (West Germany) with its capital in the Rhineland city of Bonn, and the Soviet-controlled zone became the Communist German Democratic Republic (East Germany).

West Germany received large amounts of aid from the USA's Marshall Plan and quickly reestablished its industrial base. Its

KEY HISTORICAL DATES

410 CE	Germanic tribes sack Rome.
800	Frankish king Charlemagne is crowned Holy Roman Emperor.
1241	Formation of the Hanseatic League.
1517	Martin Luther's protests start the Protestant Revolution.
1555	The Peace of Augsburg acknowledges the division of Germany into Protestant and Catholic states.
1618–48	The Thirty Years War—a religious conflict in which one-third of the population perishes.
1701	Prussia becomes a kingdom and grows in importance.
1712	Frederick the Great becomes King of Prussia.
1806	Napoleon dissolves the Holy Roman Empire.
1815	After Napoleon's defeat the German Confederation is created.
1834	The German states set up a customs union.
1866	Bismarck instigates war against Austria in which Prussia is victorious.
1871	Unification of Germany under Kaiser Wilhelm I.
1888	Wilhelm II becomes Kaiser and seeks to increase German political power.
1914	Outbreak of First World War.
1918	Defeat of Germany leads to territorial losses.
1919	Formation of the Weimar Republic.
1933	Adolf Hitler becomes Chancellor and Head of State.
1939	Hitler's invasion of Poland precipitates Second World War.
1945	Germany is defeated and occupied by four Allied powers.
1948	Soviet blockade of Berlin. The Berlin Airlift.
1949	Germany is partitioned into the German Federal Republic (West Germany) and the German Democratic Republic (East Germany).
1956	West Germany becomes a founder member of the European Community.
1961	East Germany builds a wall in Berlin to prevent people escaping the regime.
1989	The Berlin Wall comes down.
1990	East Germany joins the German Federal Republic.

production started to exceed that of any other European country in what was described as an economic miracle (*Wirtschaftswunder*). Some of this success can be attributed to immigrant workers from southeast Europe who became known as *Gastarbeiter* (guest workers).

The Soviet Union, which had suffered enormous casualties at the hands of the Germans during the Second World War, was determined to keep a firm grip on the German territory under its control and installed a puppet regime. East Germany was very much a police state, and its economy was stagnant. In the 1960s the East German authorities erected a wall in Berlin and a fence dividing the west from the east to prevent their citizens from escaping the regime.

Germany Today

In 1989 the Soviet President Mikhail Gorbachev withdrew support from the East German regime, and the Berlin Wall came down. The following year East and West Germany were reunited, and the prosperous western provinces were faced with the task of absorbing impoverished East Germany into the Federal Republic and raising social and economic standards to equal those of the West. Today, a reunited Germany is the most economically powerful member of the EU.

Breach in the Wall at the Reichstag

GOVERNMENT

Nowadays the country is a federal republic consisting of sixteen provinces (*Länder*), each of which has a considerable measure of self-government.

The seat of government is once again Berlin. There is an elected president. The president is responsible for appointing the prime minister, who is the leader of the majority in the Bundestag, the lower chamber, whose members are elected for four years. His or her appointment must be ratified by both houses of parliament.

The electoral system is based on the Party List system of proportional representation, and since it is rare for one party to gain an absolute majority, most postwar governments in the German Federal Republic have been coalitions. The main parties are the Christian Democrats (CDU), the Socialists (SPD), the Free Democrats (FDP), the Christian Social Union (a Bavarian party allied with CDU), the Greens, and the Communists (PDS). The rise of the Far Right, which has attacked immigrants, sometimes gives cause for concern.

The upper chamber (Bundesrat) consists of representatives from the provincial governments, which each have between three and six seats according to their population.

the country and its people

GERMANY'S PROVINCES (*LÄNDER*)

Eleven provinces have belonged to the German Federal Republic since its inception:

Province	Capital
Schleswig-Holstein	Kiel
Hamburg	Hamburg
Bremen	Bremen
Niedersachsen (Lower Saxony)	Hannover (Hanover)
Berlin	Berlin
Nordrhein-Westfalen	Düsseldorf
Saarland	Saarbrücken
Rheinland Pfalz (Rhineland Palatinate)	Mainz
Hessen (Hesse)	Wiesbaden
Baden-Württemberg	Stuttgart
Bayern (Bavaria)	München (Munich)

Five were until 1989 in the German Democratic Republic (East Germany):

Mecklenburg-Vorpommern	Schwerin
Brandenburg	Potsdam
Sachsen-Anhalt	Magdeburg
Sachsen (Saxony)	Dresden
Thüringen (Thuringia)	Erfurt

Values and Attitudes

One has to be careful when attempting to describe the German national character. For one thing, Germany has been a nation on and off for less than a century. Until 1871 it was a collection of autonomous states, and from 1945 to 1989 it was divided again into East and West; so any generalizations about the German character need to be taken with a pinch of salt.

As a result of living under Communism for nearly half a century, the attitudes of people from what used to be East Germany differ in some respects from those of their counterparts from the West. Older people are not familiar with the workings of the market economy, and some long for the days when state institutions offered a sense of security. Some "Ossis," as they are called, regard unification as tantamount to a takeover by the more prosperous Federal Republic, and feel they are the poor relations of their richer compatriots living in the West. They lack the confidence of the children of the *Wirtschaftswunder*.

There is also a significant difference between the north and the south Germans. The Prussians of the north are seen as thrifty, careful, orderly, and followers of the Protestant work ethic. The south Germans, as represented by the Bavarians, are more gregarious, extravert, Catholic, and conservative. The Rhinelanders in the west have a reputation for being cosmopolitan and jolly, and the Saxons in the east are thought of as earnest and stolid.

LOVE OF ORDER
On the whole, the Germans like order, and a sense of neatness and regulation is inculcated into children from an early age.

Order represents security, and is achieved by planning ahead and keeping to the rules. Germans do not improvise, and the idea of "muddling through" is quite alien to them. Part of the reason for this devotion to tidiness may stem from the huge disruption of the period after the First World War, when the country was subjected to rampant inflation and money became worthless.

On a social level, this love of order can be seen in ecological awareness, responsible behavior, and respect for authority.

PURPOSEFULNESS

Linked with this liking for order is a certain rigidity of attitude. Germans set themselves clear goals and work toward them. People are expected to behave in a disciplined manner, and Germans are bothered by any deviation from the norm. They like clarity and dislike ambiguity.

FRANKNESS

The Germans tend to be straightforward people who say what they think. At times their bluntness may sound rude to the people they are addressing, especially to those other Europeans who, out of a sense of politeness, are more oblique in the way they express themselves.

They are intolerant of bad service and have no hesitation in complaining vociferously if they are dissatisfied, in circumstances where other people might just put up with an imperfect situation in order to avoid a fuss. But Germans see no point in beating about the bush, and no offense should be taken when they express themselves robustly.

GOOD MANNERS

Germans may be direct in their criticisms, but that does not mean they lack good manners: far from it. The more educated men, especially, will stand up when a superior, an older person, or a woman comes into the room or toward them; they will help women on with their coats, and will hold doors open for them. When escorting a woman a man will walk on the outer side of the sidewalk. Germans also have the pleasant habit of giving a general greeting to everyone present when they go into a shop or restaurant.

SENSE OF DUTY

Germans have a great sense of duty. To make a promise and not carry it out is judged as a failure or betrayal of trust, whereas other nationalities in a similar situation might simply shrug it off.

There is a strong sense of community (*Gemeinschaft*) and group identity (*Gruppenzugehörigkeit*), which means that people are willing to subordinate their own interests to the good of all. Everybody is expected to make a contribution to the wellbeing of society, such as in keeping the noise down at night and not dropping litter in public places. There is a strong ecological consciousness all over the country: 50 percent of waste paper and 70 percent of all glass is recycled.

EFFICIENCY AND THOROUGHNESS

The Germans are renowned for being hard workers. Without this ability and persistence West Germany would never have been able to recover so quickly after the war and achieve its *Wirtschaftswunder.*

It is usual to attribute the idea of hard work and thoroughness to the Protestant work ethic, which extols the importance of work in our lives, regarding it as inherently good and character-forming; yet this work ethic is also seen in Catholic areas.

In Germany productivity is high, thanks to the efficiency and thoroughness with which its citizens set themselves targets and

apply themselves in the workplace. They would never dream of taking work home with them or of working excessive hours. It is their view that if you are unable to work in a concentrated, disciplined manner to complete your targets for the day, you are perhaps not up to the job.

STATUS

Status is important to Germans, and particularly to German men, who set great store by status symbols. The clothes you wear, the car you drive, and the house or apartment you live in are all indications of your position in life. Even if you don't own your apartment—and most people do not—you take great pride in its appearance.

The Germans respect people in authority, even though they may criticize them in private. People in important positions are expected to behave in accordance with their status and not compromise it in any way. Hence a boss maintains his dignity in the presence of his subordinates—except, perhaps, at Karneval time—and is unlikely to socialize much with them.

PUBLIC AND PRIVATE LIFE

You might say that Germans lead double lives, inasmuch as they endeavor to keep the world of work and their private lives quite separate. Once the working day is over they like to retreat into their personal space rather than stay on to fraternize with their fellow workers.

They like to make good use of their free time—and they certainly have plenty of it. Vacation entitlements are extremely generous when compared with those in other countries of Europe.

When they relax they do so wholeheartedly, especially in southern Germany where people like to be *gemütlich*—to be comfortable and content in cozy, relaxed surroundings. *Gemütlichkeit* is valued there, as it is in Austria (see page 44).

HEIMAT

Many Germans identify closely with home—the place in which they were born and grew up. Until recently the idea of uprooting themselves and moving to another part of the country or the world would have had little appeal. This sense of regional identity is reinforced by the newspapers they choose to read, which tend to be local rather than national. The federal structure of the country, which gives a considerable amount of autonomy to the state governments, also reinforces regional loyalty.

However, times are changing and ties are starting to loosen. Older people, for instance, are starting to retire to warmer countries, such as Spain, rather than live their final years at home.

RELIGION

Although Germany is a secular state, all residents are obliged to pay the church tax (*Kirchensteuer*), which currently stands at approximately 4 percent. The majority of the population profess Christianity, though there is a growing Muslim minority— principally the Turkish *Gastarbeiter* and their families. The northern parts of Germany tend to be Protestant (or Lutheran) while the south has remained predominantly Catholic, but they no longer go to war for their beliefs as they did in the seventeenth century.

It is quite common, when you enter small communities, to see notices displaying the times of services at the local Protestant and Catholic churches. Most people identify closely with their own faith, even though churchgoing is apparently on the decline.

Festivals and Traditions

Germany has a number of statutory public holidays, plus some that are celebrated only in certain (mainly Catholic) provinces. If a public holiday falls on a Thursday, it is common to take the Friday off and have a long weekend.

HOLIDAYS AND FESTIVALS

January 1	Neujahrstag	New Year's Day
January 6	Heilige Drei Könige	Epiphany
March/April	Karfreitag	Good Friday
March/April	Ostermontag	Easter Monday
May 1	Tag der Arbeit	Labor Day
May/June	Ascension Day	Christi Himmelfahrt
May/June	Pfingstsonntag	Pentecost/Whitsun
May/June	Pfingstmontag	Whit Monday
May/June	Fronleichnam	Corpus Christi
August 15	Mariä Himmelfahrt	Assumption
October 3	Tag der Deutschen Einheit	German Unity Day
October 31	Reformationstag	Reformation Day
November 1	Allerheiligen	All Saints' Day
November (Saxony)	Buss- und Bettag	Prayer and Atonement Day
December 24	Der heilige Abend	Christmas Eve
December 25	Weihnachtstag	Christmas Day
December 26	Zweiter Weihnachtsfeiertag	Boxing Day

THE FESTIVE YEAR

New Year

New Year's Eve is celebrated in style in Germany with dancing, drinking toasts, and fireworks at midnight. Church bells ring out, fortunes are told, and some people exchange good luck charms or special chocolate or marzipan treats.

Epiphany

This festival celebrates the visit to the Christ Child by the three Magi. Children and teenage boys dress up as the kings and go from door to door collecting for charity. Sometimes the letters CMB are chalked on doorways, standing for Caspar, Melchior, and Balthasar, the names of the Magi, and also for the Latin inscription meaning "May Christ Bless This House."

Carnival (Karneval)

Also known as Fasching in Bavaria, this is a time for celebration before the forty days of Lent begin. Preparations often start months before, and parties are held in schools, offices, and homes. Celebrations vary from region to region.

People often process through the streets in fancy dress. On Rosenmontag (Rose Monday), two days before the beginning of Lent, the main parade is held, presided over by a carnival prince and princess. On Shrove Tuesday (known as Fastnacht), there is a grand feast before the fast begins.

Disorder, jollity, and insubordination rule, even in normally staid offices, at this time. Ladies have their fun on Weiberfastnacht, the Thursday before Lent, when they cut the ties of any men they meet.

The Carnival in Cologne

Easter (Ostern)

Good Friday, the commemoration of Christ's crucifixion, is a solemn day for Protestants and Catholics alike, with the churches stripped bare. On Easter Sunday they become a blaze of color as the faithful gather to celebrate the Resurrection.

The *Osterhase* (Easter bunny) is a tradition that dates back to the pre-Christian spring festival. People exchange chocolate Easter bunnies or painted hardboiled eggs, and often decorate their houses with flowers.

Corpus Christi (Fronleichnam)

In Catholic areas this festival is commemorated with street processions and open-air services.

Inside an Oktoberfest drinking tent

Oktoberfest

This is a sixteen-day festival that lasts until the first Sunday in October and is centered on Munich. It is a harvest festival, during which a great deal of beer and wine are drunk. Other wine-growing districts, notably those along the Rhine, also have festivals at this time.

Advent

In this period of preparation for Christmas, children have an Advent calendar, and open one of its small windows each day to display a Christmas-themed picture. Another custom is the *Adventskranz*, a wreath with four red candles, one of which is lit on each Sunday before Christmas.

During this period many towns have picturesque Christmas markets selling gingerbread (*Lebkuchen*), mulled wine (*Glühwein*), spicy Christmas cake (*Stollen*), and colorful decorations.

St. Nicholas' Day

On St. Nicholas' Eve (December 5) children leave out their shoes when they go to bed, in the hope that St. Nicholas (Sankt Niklaus) will reward them for good behavior by filling them with sweets. The following day a figure dressed in red visits children, offering fruit and nuts to the good ones, while his companion, armed with a birch rod and a sack, punishes the naughty ones.

Christmas

On Christmas Eve businesses close early and people hurry home to exchange presents around the Christmas tree. In north

Germany families receive a visit from the *Weihnachstmann* (a Santa Claus-like figure), while in the south the *Christkind* (Christ Child) comes. Many families attend midnight church services.

On Christmas Day there is a family meal, of which the highlight is usually a goose, accompanied by red cabbage and dumplings. Christmas is a time for visiting friends and relations or enjoying oneself in the open air.

TRADE FAIRS

Since medieval times towns and cities have hosted fairs, most with a commercial purpose. These often concentrate on a particular trade and, like the famous Frankfurt Book Fair (Frankfurter Buchmesse), are international in scope.

FAMILY OCCASIONS

On their birthdays children often have parties, to which they invite their friends. Adults might have a modest celebration in their office or at home.

On the eve of a wedding it is customary for the bride and groom to go out with their friends for a *Polterabend* (social gathering), which culminates with the breaking of crockery. Sometimes friends of the groom "kidnap" the bride on the wedding day itself.

Funerals are conducted with great solemnity; many people wear black for the occasion.

Getting to Know the Germans

The Germans, as we have seen, like to keep their professional and social lives separate. They do not generally fraternize with work colleagues, or discuss their personal lives or problems with them. In East Germany especially, under Communism it would have been considered highly dangerous to reveal too much about yourself in case one of your colleagues happened to be a member of the Stasi, the state security service. With the older generation, old habits die hard.

FORMALITY

If you are working with Germans, you can expect a certain formality in your relationships, certainly in the initial stages. You will find that older people in particular will address you as *Sie* (the polite form of "you"), though as a relationship develops this might be dropped for the more familiar *du* form. When addressing children you use the familiar form as a matter of course.

You should also be prepared to address people by their title plus their surname: "*Herr* Braun," "*Frau* Hübner," "*Fräulein* Schmidt." In informal situations people may use first names, but they always use titles in business or professional meetings. If a person has a professional title it is courteous to use it: "*Herr Doktor*," "*Herr Direktor*," "*Frau Professor*."

When meeting people or taking leave of them it is customary to shake hands. Greet them with the words "*Guten Morgen*," "*Guten Tag*," or "*Guten Abend*," according to the time of day. "*Grüss Gott*" ("May God greet you") is used at any time in Bavaria. At the end of the meeting the expression "*Auf Wiedersehen*" is usual.

The younger generation tend to be less formal in their dealings with their peers, but they observe strict protocol when they are addressing their elders.

ACQUAINTANCES AND FRIENDS

Visitors often find it difficult to get to know Germans. Whereas in some European countries it seems easy to strike up an acquaintance with someone, in Germany it is less so. Although they may have an extensive range of contacts—the people they work with or do business with—these are acquaintances rather than friends.

Most people, however, have an inner circle of friends, many of whom they have known since childhood or college days. It may seem difficult to penetrate this tight circle, but it is by no means impossible, and if you manage to establish a relationship you know you have a friend for life.

THE LANGUAGE

Most Germans, especially younger ones, speak excellent English, and many have attended English courses in Britain or the USA; but when relaxing they naturally prefer to speak in their own language. If you are shopping or visiting a *Gasthaus* outside the major towns, you cannot assume that anyone will speak English. It therefore makes sense to know some German before you arrive in the country.

There are plenty of language schools and public educational institutions offering German-language courses, notably the government-financed Goethe Institut, which has branches in many countries; and for private study there is an array of audiovisual courses and distance learning opportunities on the Internet. There's no excuse!

German is an Indo-European language that is closely related to Dutch and English. It is spoken throughout Germany, Austria, and the German-speaking cantons of Switzerland, and is a useful lingua franca in the countries of eastern and southeastern Europe, including Turkey. Proficiency in German will also help your appreciation of a wealth of music and literature, such as the great Wagnerian music dramas, the poetry of Goethe, and the songs of Schubert, Schumann, Mendelssohn, Wolf, and Mahler, to name but a few.

Children are brought up to speak standard German, known as *Hochdeutsch*, but when speaking to one another informally people tend to lapse into their local dialects. In the very north you may hear *Plattdeutsch*, which has similarities with Dutch. The Bavarian dialect is much closer to the German spoken in Austria.

At one time German books were printed in the old Fraktur script, but this is no longer the case. Some years ago German spelling was reformed, but while you will find children are taught the new spelling, older people tend to stick with the spelling they grew up with. It is perhaps worth mentioning that in German all nouns start with a capital letter.

PLACES TO MEET

Younger people may find that discos, nightclubs, and open-air pop concerts are good places to meet like-minded Germans, but these do tend to be noisy places where conversation can be difficult!

A good way to meet people is to join a club. The larger cities have a number of international clubs catering to both Germans and foreigners, and it is worth investigating these. Also, adult education classes are available in a range of subjects, and one can meet many people through these—though if you join a German-language class you are unlikely to meet Germans!

German towns have clubs for sports and other leisure interests, and if you will be staying for any length of time you can make enquiries at the local library or town hall (*Rathaus*) about what is available.

CONVERSATION

Germans enjoy having serious discussions, and can become quite intense when discussing politics, social issues, and philosophy. They do not flit easily from one subject to another, as English-speakers might do. Keep off the topic of work, as Germans do not like to mix business with pleasure.

On the other hand, when eating or drinking they can be very relaxed and jolly, and small talk is perfectly in order. Most topics are suitable for discussion, though older people from the former East Germany are sometimes unwilling to speak about their experiences. Generally speaking, it is fine to talk about your impressions of their country, music, art and culture. It is better not to discuss sex in mixed company.

INVITATIONS HOME

If you are invited to someone's house for afternoon tea (*Kaffee und Kuchen*) or for dinner in the evening, you should consider it an honor. Germans tend not to entertain at home very much, and would generally take people out to a restaurant.

An invitation for afternoon tea usually means arriving at 3:00 p.m. and staying for up to two hours. If you have been invited to dinner, this is likely to begin at around 7:00 p.m., and you are expected to be punctual. Once the meal is over it is customary to sit and chat; to leave early might be considered rude.

It is a nice idea to bring a gift for your host and hostess. Chocolates are very acceptable and so are flowers (but not chrysanthemums or lilies, which are for funerals, or red roses, which are specially for lovers!). A florist will be able to advise you on the kinds of flowers to take and the size of the bouquet. Wine is not a good choice, since many Germans are wine connoisseurs, but good spirits or liqueurs would doubtless be acceptable.

Don't expect to be taken on a tour of inspection of the whole house. You will see only the rooms you are invited into; you may, of course, ask for the bathroom, but everything else is private. Don't look around on your own.

Your hostess will appreciate a note of thanks after the event.

Daily Life

HOUSING

The majority of Germans rent their living accommodation; only about 40 percent own their own homes. Generally the standard of housing is very good, but expensive, with as much as one-third of a household's income going on rent. In the cities apartments predominate, while in the countryside and the suburbs people tend to live in houses, often detached, with gardens and fences around them.

Blocks of apartments often have communal washing machines and driers with specified times for use allocated to each household. Residents may be required to clean the communal areas on a roster basis, and to participate in keeping the surrounding sidewalks clear of snow in the winter.

Apartment buildings in Ostfilden

RULES AND REGULATIONS

Lives are carefully regulated in Germany, with the aim of minimizing inconvenience to other people. For example, the hours of 1:00 to 3:00 p.m. and 10:00 p.m. to 7:00 a.m. are designated "quiet hours," in which you must avoid making excessive noise, which might disturb your neighbors. A rowdy party during the quiet hours could result in a visit from the police. In any case, if you are having a party it is advisable to inform your neighbors beforehand. Sundays are meant to be particularly quiet, which means you cannot use noisy machinery such as a lawn mower, and washing a car in the street may be forbidden at any time by local bylaws.

Other regulations reflect the country's strong ecological credentials. Household waste must not be mixed together: it has to be separated by type into differently colored bags, and refuse collectors may well decline to take garbage if it is in the wrong bag. Supermarkets encourage people to bring their own shopping bags, and don't provide free plastic ones.

FAMILY LIFE

It used to be the tradition that married women remained at home all day to look after the children, do the household chores, and cook. The German poet Goethe once declared that, "the only book a woman needs to read is a cookery book." Things have moved on since his day, and now women make up 50 percent of the workforce.

More married women are now choosing to carry on with their careers, and this was encouraged in Communist East Germany, where extensive childcare facilities were provided. However, there is considerable debate today over whether mothers should have jobs, and many are also deciding to stay at home while their children are young and resume their careers later.

In past decades lifestyles have changed. Although the nuclear family remains the norm, increasing numbers of couples are opting to live together without being married. There has also been a growth in one-parent families.

DAILY MEALS

Germans tend to rise early in the morning—at about 6:30 or 7:00 a.m.—and get to their workplace by 8:00 or 8.30 a.m.

Schools also start around this time. Breakfast consists of bread or rolls, jam, and perhaps ham, cheese, sausage, or boiled eggs. Cereals, such as cornflakes and muesli, are also popular.

Lunch at noon is traditionally the main meal of the day, taken at home where possible, and may extend to three courses. However, for those who travel some distance to work this is not a feasible option. Office workers or others in a hurry might go to a snack bar (*Schnellimbiss*), where customers eat standing up.

Afternoon tea is popular with housewives and children, and consists of tea or coffee with cakes or pastries.

Supper is eaten together in the evening at 6:00 p.m., or soon after. This is normally a lighter meal than lunch and consists of cooked meats, cheese, or fish, with rolls or bread including such German specialties as *Pumpernickel* and *Vollkornbrot* (varieties of wholemeal bread made from rye), often with beer or wine. A more formal dinner would normally start after 7:00 p.m.

SHOPPING

Shopping is as much a recreation as a necessity. People prefer to shop in smaller specialty shops rather than supermarkets, and appreciate good-quality fresh products. Most towns have markets selling flowers, fruit, vegetables, meat, and fish.

Larger stores may be open until 8:00 p.m. on weekdays, but smaller ones are usually closed by 6:00 or 6:30 p.m. Many shops close on Saturday afternoons and all day on Sundays, with the exception of bakeries and gas stations.

Note that many outlets, including gas stations, do not accept credit or debit cards. In Germany cash is still king.

EDUCATION

Education is held in high regard in Germany, and is of a good standard. Most parents want their children to do well at school and become self-reliant and responsible citizens. Schooling is the responsibility of the *Länder* (the provincial governments), and the systems may differ in certain respects according to the province.

School is compulsory between the ages of six and eighteen. Many children attend a local kindergarten before that, from the age of three; this would normally amount to just a few hours a day, but in the former East Germany provision is more extensive. For the first four years of compulsory education children attend a *Grundschule* (elementary school).

The next two years are the *Orientierungsstufe* (orientation stage) to decide on their aptitudes and the future shape of their schooling. Some areas of Germany offer a fully comprehensive system of education whereby children of all abilities are taught in the same school (*Gesamtschule*), but in most of the provinces pupils enter specialist schools at around the age of twelve, after the orientation period.

An estimated 35 percent of pupils attend a *Gymnasium*, which offers a more academic curriculum and leads to a school-leaving exam known as the *Abitur*. Some *Gymnasien* offer a more technical and scientific curriculum than others. Another option is the *Realschule*, which offers a more practical curriculum, and leads to a diploma that will facilitate entry to a commercial or technical college. The third option is the *Hauptschule* (general high school), from which pupils can graduate to the *Berufsschule* (vocational school) or enter into an apprenticeship for training.

Higher education is very varied. The *Technische Hochschulen*, which specialize in science and technology, have an excellent reputation and are a contributory factor to German engineering excellence.

Germany has a wide range of other university-level institutions, and it is not at all uncommon for an undergraduate to switch universities. There have been problems of overcrowding, student studies are less closely supervised than elsewhere, and dropout rates are high. Some students may study for seven years or more before they qualify.

TELEVISION

All the programs shown on German TV are in German, and foreign films and programs are normally dubbed.

The country has three public broadcasters and a number of regional stations. As in other European counties a license fee is payable. Thanks to satellite programming it is possible to view a wide range of programs from outside Germany.

MAIL AND TELECOMMUNICATIONS

Both postal and telephone systems are very efficient. Post offices are open between 8:00 a.m. and 6:00 p.m. on weekdays and until 12:00 noon on Saturdays. You can make international telephone calls from the booth marked "*Auslandsgesprache.*" They also offer banking and mail collection services. Mailboxes are bright yellow.

The fixed telephone system is run by Telekom, and there are a number of cell-phone providers. If you want to use a public telephone you will need a phone card, obtainable from telephone shops and tobacconists. Credit cards can also be used.

As one would expect, Internet usage is developing very rapidly. According to magazin-deutschland.de, 69 percent of German households were online in 2010, and the ever-growing range of Web sites makes it a medium the majority of the population use on a daily basis.

Leisure Time

The Germans have a reputation for working hard, and at the end of the day they like to settle down to talk, read magazines and books, or watch TV. Going out for a drink in the local pub or *Gasthaus* is also popular, and most towns and cities offer a range of entertainment from discos to opera. Most establishments, except those in Berlin, are required by law to close at a certain time.

Workers in Germany enjoy a much more generous vacation entitlement than most other Europeans. They have between four and six weeks' vacation a year, as well as up to fifteen public holidays.

EATING OUT

There is a wide range of cuisines available in all German towns, including Italian, Chinese, French, Turkish, and, of course, German. You'll find international chains, such as McDonald's, everywhere. A *Gasthaus* or *Gasthof* is most likely to serve German food and there are a number of typical dishes from different areas.

Normally in a restaurant you find your way to a table and wait to be served. You may need to call out "*Herr Ober*" (waiter) or "*Fräulein*" (waitress) to attract attention. To ask for your bill (*die Quittung*), you call, "*Zahlen, bitte.*"

TIPPING

A statutory service charge of 15 percent is included in restaurant bills, but it is usual to round up the amount to the nearest euro. If you want to leave more to reward exceptional service in a formal restaurant, 10 percent is normal.

Regional Specialties

Flädlesuppe	a clear soup with pancake strips (Württemberg). The Bavarians call this soup *Pfannkuchensuppe.*
Sauerbraten	braised pickled beef lard with bacon (Rhineland)
Heidschnuckenbraten	roast lamb with potatoes (Lower Saxony)
Thüringer Rostbratwurst	grilled sausage with herbs (Thuringia)
Handkäse mit Musik	pungent cheese served with onion (Hesse)
Salzhering in Sahnesosse	pickled herring in sour cream (Mecklenburg)
Krautwickerl	minced meat rolled into white cabbage (Bavaria)
Westfalische Rebekuchen	cakes made of grated raw potatoes and buckwheat flour (Westphalia)
Pfefferkuchen	gingerbread (Saxony)
Eberswalder Spritzkuchen	deep-fried ring donuts (Brandenburg)

Incidentally, if you want a Frankfurter sausage, especially in Frankfurt, note that it is called *ein Wiener* (a Viennese)!

DRINK

Germany is renowned for its beers and its breweries. There are around 1,500 of the latter, half of them in Bavaria. Some have a *Biergarten* (beergarden), where you can bring your own food and sample the brews, or you can drink in a *Bierkeller* (underground beer cellar), a *Bierhalle* (beer hall), or a *Bierstube* (pub). The waiter keeps a note of the beers you've consumed by recording them on your beer mat.

Beers can be divided by type: *Lager* (which has been slowly fermented by bottom-fermenting yeast); *Pils*, or *Pilsener* (pale lager); *Weissbier* (wheat beer, which may be cloudy); *Kölsch* (top-fermented ale made in Cologne); and *Altbier* (top-fermented, reddish-brown beer).

Germany produces some excellent wines. White wines made from the Riesling grape are particularly highly regarded.

The Rhine and Moselle Valleys are noted for their vineyards, as is the area between the Rhine and the French border, and Franconia, in the north of Bavaria.

CULTURE AND ENTERTAINMENT

Unlike many European countries Germany does not have just one main center of cultural excellence. As we have seen, for many centuries Germany was fragmented into a large number of principalities, each anxious to outshine the others in its cultural activities.

For this reason Germany boasts 120 opera houses and many more theaters, museums, and art galleries. It is home to some of the world's leading orchestras, including the Berlin Philharmonic, the Bamberg Symphony, the Dresdner Staatskapelle, and the three-hundred-year-old Leipziger Gewandhausorchester.

Although Berlin may enjoy a certain preeminence, cities such as Munich, Stuttgart, Leipzig, Frankfurt, and Hamburg run it pretty close, and there are few places where you cannot enjoy great music, drama, and art exhibitions on a regular basis. Cologne (Köln) and Munich are regarded as important centers for the arts.

Most theaters and concert halls take a summer break from June until late September. But that does not signify that cultural life comes to a halt then, for there are a hundred or so music festivals held throughout the country, notably the Bayreuth Festival, which features the operas of Richard Wagner, the Munich Opera Festival, in July, and the Mozart Festival in Würzburg.

Fortunately, the arts are still heavily subsidized in Germany. This means that prices are kept reasonably low, enabling people from all walks of life to attend these cultural events. Unlike many people in other countries today, some Germans still dress very elegantly when they go to the opera or the theater.

STUDENTS, CLUBBING, AND CLOSE ENCOUNTERS

Germany has always been famous for its nightlife. After all, the Beatles first came to prominence through playing in a Hamburg nightclub! There are nightclubs, cabarets, and discos in abundance in Hamburg—and more especially Berlin—that appeal to all tastes and sexual orientations. (Incidentally, with regard to sex, Germans tend to be much less prudish than other Europeans, and there is little, if any, censorship of sexual content in films and plays. They tend to be much stricter with regard to scenes of violence.) Other larger cities, such as Munich, Frankfurt, and Cologne, also boast a varied nightlife, but it is most unlikely that you will be able to dance the night away, since outside Berlin most establishments have a *Sperrstunde*—a closing time enforced by the authorities.

The Mitte district in Berlin's Eastern bloc has always been Berlin's political, commercial, and cultural center. Once a derelict area, it had an artistic renaissance that boasted an array of cheap rents and squatters' communes: young artisans set up galleries and cafés on Oranienburger Strasse, and many forgotten buildings found new purposes as underground party places and ramshackle bars, an alternative hub for Berlin's counter-culture. The Weekend is one of Berlin's quintessential house and techno clubs, with a top location on the thirteenth floor of an old Soviet block on Alexanderplatz.

As Mitte has become more gentrified and thus more "touristy," you will find some of the more trendy and interesting spots in Prenzlauer Berg and Friedrichshain. With its cobbled boulevards and modish cafés, bars, and boutiques, the pretty old Prenzlauer Berg has come a long way from its humble, working-class roots.

Kreuzberg is another area worth exploring. Immigrants initially inhabited the area after the fall of the Wall on the Eastern bloc, and it has since become one of Berlin's hippest quarters, due to the number of artists who moved there and the multicultural influence of the immigrant communities. Together these two communities have inspired a wide range of wonderful places to eat, bars to chill in, public spaces, art

CocoonClub, Frankfurt

shows, concert venues, and live events. The area is also very popular with Berlin's gay community.

Germans often engage in group dates. Different types of bars and clubs are common gathering places for dating couples. Often the man will initiate the date, and if he does so he is expected to pay for the girl. It is acceptable to meet at a specific location or for the man to pick up the girl at her place—but whatever you do, don't be late! German dating customs in general are not so different from those in, say, the USA, but there's a particular point to watch: great store is set on punctuality. So be on time! Keeping your German date waiting ten minutes can mean there'll be no more dates.

SPORTS AND OUTDOOR ACTIVITIES

Germans are great sports enthusiasts, as both spectators and participants. The country has excellent facilities for most activities, including gymnastics, tennis, handball, basketball, shooting, riding, Formula One motor racing, and football. Their national football team always does well internationally.

They are also fond of such outdoor pursuits as mountaineering, walking, jogging, cycling, and riding. With Germany's many rivers, lakes, and extensive coastal area, there is plenty of scope for sailing, canoeing, rowing, and other water sports. Winter sports are also very popular, particularly in the south of the country, with its stunning Alpine scenery.

Getting Around

Germany has an excellent road infrastructure, with well-maintained expressways (*Autobahnen*) extending over 8,700 miles (14,000 km) that are toll-free and have rest stops (*Raststatten*) at regular intervals. *Autobahnen* are designated with the letter "A" on blue signs, while other roads are classified as "R" on yellow signs. Public transport is efficient and well integrated.

There is a comprehensive railway network, run by Deutsche Bahn, with 25,000 miles (40,000 km) of track, some of which passes through beautiful scenery. The trains are punctual and clean, and fares vary according to the type of train. The ICE (Inter City Express) is a high-speed train that runs at up to 175 mph (280 kph). The IC (Inter City) and EC (Euro City) are similar but not quite so fast. Other trains, such as the IR (Inter Regional) and RE (Regional Express), are less expensive and stop at more stations. It is worth enquiring about discounted fares, including ICE Super Saver tickets, the "*Schoenes Wochenende*" ticket, and a range of passes and travel cards.

Bus services, some operated by the railway company, link major and minor centers. The bus station is often situated next to the main railway station (*Hauptbahnhof*).

URBAN TRANSPORTATION

Public transportation in the larger cities is often a mix of trams, trolley buses, buses, suburban railway (S-Bahn), and in certain cases a subway train (known as a U-Bahn). Most of the transportation systems are fully integrated, with buses and trains connecting with one another.

You usually buy bus tickets from a machine, either at a stop or on the bus, but the system varies from place to place. Reduced-rate tickets are normally available for multiple journeys, and it's worth checking up on these.

DRIVING AND WALKING IN TOWN

The Germans love fast cars, and like to show them off on the expressways, where there are long stretches with no speed limit at all. However, there are, of course, rules and regulations; these are rigidly enforced by the police, and drivers should make sure they understand them. The speed limit in towns is 50 kmph (31 mph), and on open roads 100 kmph (62 mph). The "recommended maximum" on expressways is 130 kmph (80 mph). The penalties for drunk driving are severe. The blood alcohol limit is 0.5 mg per ml, but 0.3 mg per ml if you have had an accident. Note also that if you park in the wrong place you may return to find your car has been towed away.

You can drive for up to a year on your existing national driver's license or an international license. EU citizens can obtain a German license after six months in exchange for their national license. The regulations for non-EU citizens may differ. You need to keep your travel documents in the car, also a warning triangle for use in the event of an accident, and a first-aid kit. Seat belts must be worn at all times, and there are special seat belts for children under twelve.

As in other countries in Europe, you normally give way at junctions to traffic coming from the right. You also give priority to cyclists when turning across a cycle path, and to trams. If you are behind a tram when it stops, you must stop too, so that passengers can get off in safety.

Pedestrians should exercise care when using crossings without controls. At crossings with controls, you should wait for the green light. Even if the road is clear, crossing when the light is red is frowned upon.

WHERE TO STAY

If you want comfortable accommodation in Germany there's no need to splash out on an expensive hotel. Anywhere you choose will be of an acceptable standard. Just look out for the signs "*Hotel*," "*Gasthaus*," or "*Gasthof*." A "*Pension*" (guest house) will be cheaper. The local tourist office (*Fremdenverkehrsburo*), which often has a branch at the main station (*Hauptbahnhof*), can advise you or make a booking.

Germany has the largest network of youth hostels (*Jugendherberge*) in Europe, run by the Deutsches Jugendherbergswerk (DJH). If you prefer to rough it a bit, there are more than 2,000 campsites for tents and caravans.

PLACES TO VISIT

Germany has a range of fine cities full of historical sites, of which the major example is undoubtedly Berlin. When it was a divided city, it was fascinating for the visitor to visit both the Western and the Soviet sectors to see the contrast, but now new buildings have sprung up in what was East Berlin, and the contrast is no longer so great.

Schloss Charlottenburg, Berlin

All cities in Germany are worth visiting, notably Hamburg (the main seaport), Cologne, famous for its towering cathedral, Dresden ("the Florence on the Elbe"), Leipzig (with its Bach associations), Munich (the dominant cultural center in the south, famous for its Oktoberfest), and Frankfurt am Main (the leading financial center and the gateway into Germany).

Don't overlook smaller towns such as Heidelberg (famous for its university), Weimar (European City of Culture 1999 and the home of the literary giants Goethe and Schiller), Potsdam (with its beautiful Sans Souci Palace), the Rhineland towns, such as

The Zugspitze mountain in southern Bavaria

Bonn (the former capital of West Germany), Düsseldorf, Koblenz, and Mainz, and the attractive Bavarian cities of Augsburg, Regensburg, and Wurzburg.

The country also has a variety of scenic landscapes ranging from the Baltic coast to the Alps. The Black Forest, famous for cake and cuckoo clocks, the Rhine and Moselle region, known for its fine wines, the Harz mountains where witches are alleged to congregate on Walpurgisnacht, Lake Constance, and the many other lakes in the country are just a few of the delights in store for the visitor.

MEDICAL MATTERS

As one would expect, medical care is first class, and since Germans are demanding patients it needs to be. There is a government health service. EU citizens may use this by registering with the Allgemeine Ortskrankenkasse (AOK), which will issue you with an entitlement document to show a participating doctor. However, it would be sensible, whether you are an EU citizen or not, to take out private insurance for the duration of your stay.

LAW AND ORDER

Security is not a problem in Germany, provided you take suitable precautions—lock your car, keep your valuables in a safe place, and be on the lookout for pickpockets, especially in the larger cities.

Business and Professional Life

Germany is one of the world's leading economies, and its engineering and industrial expertise is second to none. Some companies are industrial giants, but equally outstanding are family firms, which are sometimes described as the *Mittelstand*.

Germans are sticklers for protocol and formality in professional and business life. The worlds of work and play are quite separate, and small talk and jokes have no part in the business process.

BUSINESS STRUCTURE

German businesses tend to be hierarchical with power concentrated at the top. Large companies with more than 500 employees have a supervisory board (*Aufsichtsrat*), which sets the budget and decides strategy, and a management board (*Vorstand*) appointed by the former, which is responsible for day-to-day operations.

In addition, companies of a certain size and public organizations are required by law to have a works council, which has to be consulted, especially on personnel matters. As a consequence it is hard to fire an employee; on the other hand this creates an integrated structure with management and workforce working together for the benefit of the organization.

Jobs are clearly defined within the organization, which has a hierarchical reporting structure. Superiors are expected to give clear and firm instructions to their subordinates, who are expected to comply wholeheartedly with them. There is little scope for initiative.

Many managers will be well qualified in scientific or technological subjects. Some will have worked their way up within a company, starting as apprentices and gaining qualifications along the way. Germans are more likely to stay with the same company for most of their working lives than other nationals.

Because they dislike uncertainty and ambiguity, they place great emphasis on careful planning, consultation, risk analysis, and consensus. Details, facts, and statistics are scrutinized meticulously in order to eliminate risk. This means that coming to a decision is a thorough and lengthy process.

ARRANGING A MEETING

It is advisable to schedule a meeting at least two weeks in advance. This applies also to lengthy telephone conversations, as people like to prepare themselves for whatever might crop up.

Although the working day starts quite early, generally business involving outsiders begins at 10:00 or 11:00 a.m., or in the afternoon. Friday afternoons are definitely out, and so are the months of July, August, and December. Also avoid the times of year when major festivals, such as Karneval or the Oktoberfest, are held.

Make sure that you are well prepared for the encounter, and have plenty of detailed documentation in German to hand out.

MEETINGS

Arrive on time for a meeting. Your German hosts are hard workers who plan their schedules with great care, and unpunctuality on your part would not only make a bad impression but could well disrupt their day.

A good, firm handshake is the normal form of greeting. If there are several people present, greet each one in turn. They will often introduce themselves using their surname, and perhaps offer you their business card. Your own card should clearly state your position and your academic and professional qualifications.

On the whole, Germans like to get down to business as soon as introductions are over. Relationship building does not loom large in business or professional negotiations. They prefer to focus on the matter in hand rather than on personalities.

FAMILY COMPANIES

Many successful companies are family businesses, and members of the founding families are often still in charge and held in great respect. Their decisions override all others, and visitors need to treat the senior members of the firm with deference.

While the atmosphere in these firms may be more *gemütlich* than in larger companies, don't be deceived. They are often in niche sectors, and the reason they have survived is that they are sticklers for quality and make exacting demands on their suppliers.

THE CHANGING FACE OF BUSINESS

Many of the younger managers will have had international experience, perhaps gained by studying at foreign universities and business schools or on foreign internships. This often means they know more about the international business world than the foreigners they deal with know about German business.

As a consequence they may modify their negotiating style in order to accommodate you at a more informal level. However, in meetings where their superiors are present they may revert to the more formal style described above.

PRESENTATIONS

Most senior managers are well qualified in their particular fields and will expect a presentation to be supported by detailed facts and specifications. Don't insult their intelligence—they will be turned off by pure sales talk.

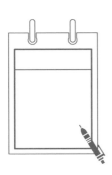

Because they are risk-averse they will want to see proof of the efficacy of the product or service you are offering, supported by testimonials. The more paperwork you can produce, the more positive the result is likely to be.

Expect to be questioned closely both during and following the presentation. The experience may be exhausting, but it is not necessarily a bad thing, since it indicates that your proposals have generated interest. Total silence is the last thing you want.

Be prepared, too, for robust and frank comments. Where business is concerned, Germans do not mince their words.

WOMEN IN BUSINESS

Although women have made great progress in Germany, men are still dominant at the executive level. However, German businessmen are impressed by a woman who has good qualifications and is in a position of responsibility.

Women executives and professionals should dress smartly but conservatively. If you go out for lunch or dinner with a German colleague, it is perfectly acceptable to pay your way.

Chapter 6

IRELAND

Key Facts

THE IRISH REPUBLIC	
Official Name	Eire or Ireland
Capital City	Dublin
Major Cities	Cork, Galway, Limerick
Area	27,000 sq. miles (70,000 sq. km)
Terrain	Plains with rolling hills
Climate	Temperate
Currency	Euro
Population	4.1 million
Language	English, Irish (Gaelic)
Religion	Catholic 88%; Protestant 7%; others 5%
Government	Parliament (*Oireachtas*) has two chambers: the Senate (*Seanad Éireann*) and the House of Representatives (*Dáil Éireann*). The President, elected for seven years, appoints the Prime Minister (*Taioseach*).
Radio and TV	The state-funded broadcaster, RTÉ, has three English-medium TV channels and one Irish-language channel. There are three RTÉ English-language and one Irish-language radio networks and many local stations.
Press	*Irish Times, Irish Independent, The Examiner, The Star*
Electricity	230 volts, 50 Hz.

Internet Domain	.ie
Telephone	Country code: 353
Time Zone	Greenwich Mean Time (GMT/UTC), with summer daylight saving

NORTHERN IRELAND	
Official Name	Province of Northern Ireland
Capital City	Belfast
Major Cities	Belfast, Londonderry, Omagh
Area	5,500 sq. miles (14,000 sq. km)
Climate	Temperate
Currency	Pound sterling
Population	1.6 million
Language	English
Religion	Protestant 60%; Catholic 40%
Government	Elects 17 members to the British parliament. It has its own Assembly at Stormont.
Radio & TV	BBC radio and TV channels plus the commercial Ulster TV
Press	The *Belfast Telegraph* is the leading daily paper.
Internet Domain	.uk
Telephone	Country code: 44
Time Zone	GMT

Map of Ireland

NORTH CHANNEL

NORTHEN IRELAND

Londonderry

LONDON-
DERRY

ANTRIM

DONEGAL

Belfast

Omagh

TYRONE

Armagh

DOWN

FERMANAGH

ARMAGH

Sligo

SLIGO

MONAGHAN

LEITRIM

CAVAN

MAYO

ROSCOMMON

LONGFORD

LOUTH

MEATH

DUBLIN

GALWAY

WESTMEATH

Dublin

Galway

OFFALY

KILDARE

ATLANTIC
OCEAN

LAOIS

WICKLOW

CLARE

CARLOW

Limerick

TIPPERARY

WEXFORD

LIMERICK

KILKENNY

Tralee

Tipperary

Wexford

CORK

Waterford

IRISH
SEA

Killarney

WATERFORD

KERRY

Cork

REPUBLIC OF IRELAND

The Country
and Its People

Ireland, the Emerald Isle, is surrounded by sea—the Atlantic Ocean to the west and the Irish Sea, which separates it from Britain, to the east. It is a compact island, 170 miles (275 km) from west to east at its widest extent and 300 miles (486 km) from north to south. Its greenness is attributed to the ample rainfall and the temperate climate, for the Atlantic, despite its storms, brings with it the warming Gulf Stream. Snow is rare.

Geographically the land is a plateau, surrounded by mountains and hills, with several lakes, such as the three famous Lakes of Killarney, and Lough Neagh in Northern Ireland, the biggest lake in the British Isles. The longest river is the Shannon.

For most of its history Ireland was one country, but that changed nearly a hundred years ago, when the larger part of the island became independent and six of the counties of Ulster chose to

Lakes of Killarney, Co. Kerry

remain part of the United Kingdom. The split has led to generations of strife, especially in Northern Ireland, and anyone visiting this province needs to be particularly aware of the political and historical background.

The Irish have made a huge contribution to the literature of the English-speaking world, with literary giants such as Jonathan Swift (author of *Gulliver's Travels*), Richard Sheridan, Oscar Wilde, James Joyce, William Butler Yeats, Samuel Beckett, C. S. Lewis, and Seamus Heaney. The list of soldiers, politicians, actors, comedians, artists, and composers with Irish roots is seemingly endless.

Most of these made their reputations outside Ireland, as did many millions of others. As a result of large-scale emigration there are as many as seventy million people living outside Ireland who claim Irish ancestry, including several presidents of the United States. This is perhaps why every year there are millions of visitors to this fabled land on the edge of Europe.

A HISTORICAL PERSPECTIVE

Ireland before Cromwell

The Irish people claim Celtic ancestry, and the first Celts appear to have arrived in Ireland in the sixth century BCE. The country was untouched by the Romans, but classical learning and literacy came with the introduction of Christianity and writing in the fifth century CE. Ireland became a beacon of civilization and learning when the rest of Europe was plunged into the Dark Ages following the break-up of the Roman Empire. It became known as "The Land of Saints and Scholars."

Toward the end of the first millennium the Vikings established settlements along the coast, which were eventually dispersed. At the time Ireland consisted of many petty kingdoms that were being consolidated by competing dynasties of overkings. The High King of Ireland had a purely symbolic overlordship, exercising power only within his own realm.

The next invasion came from England, led by Richard de Clare, the Anglo-Norman Earl of Pembroke, known as "Strongbow." He gained control of most of Ireland through alliances, but direct English rule was confined to an area of fifty miles around Dublin.

Henry II consolidated English rule in Ireland and was acknowledged as Ireland's overlord by the High King, Rory O'Connor, King of Connaught, in 1175. King John established civil government independent of Ireland's feudal lords, and English laws were introduced. In Tudor times the whole of Ireland came under direct English control; Henry VIII was the first English monarch to be recognized as King of Ireland.

Elizabeth I fought four wars in Ireland to impose the Protestant Reformation, to which there was considerable resistance, and to protect Britain from a Spanish invasion. Rebellions by Ulster nobles made matters worse. Many Catholics in Ulster were dispossessed and their lands given to English and Scots settlers after the union of the crowns of England and Scotland. The process was known as the Plantation (that is, settlement) of Ulster.

From Cromwell to the Great Famine

The name of Oliver Cromwell brings a shudder to many Irishmen. In 1649–50 the self-styled Lord Protector of England suppressed a rebellion in Ireland with the utmost ruthlessness, killing a third of Irish Catholics in the process. He settled many of his troops in Ireland on lands he had confiscated. Later, hopes that Charles II would restore these lands to their original owners proved forlorn.

After being deposed by the English, Charles' son, the Catholic James II, attempted a comeback and landed in Ireland, where he was given a hearty welcome by the Catholic majority. The city of Londonderry, however, denied him entry when thirteen Protestant apprentice boys locked the gates in his face. James' forces besieged the city for 107 days, but the inhabitants would not surrender. In the following year, 1690, the new king, William of Orange, defeated James at the Battle of the Boyne. The siege and the battle are commemorated every year by the Ulster Protestants.

The Protestant victory led to restrictions on land ownership by Catholics, who were also excluded from Parliament. A rebellion against British rule in 1798 by the (mainly Protestant) Society of United Irishmen was forcibly put down, and Ireland and its parliament became incorporated into the United Kingdom. On a more positive note, Dublin grew into an elegant Georgian city with a vibrant cultural life.

The nineteenth century saw the passing of legislation that guaranteed basic civil rights and freedom to worship, thanks to the campaigning of Daniel O'Connell, a prominent Catholic landowner; but Ireland soon suffered further hardship when the failure of the potato crop led to the Great Famine.

The Path to Home Rule

The Great Famine of 1845–52 is regarded as a defining moment in Irish history. An estimated one million people starved to death, and many survivors chose to migrate to America or elsewhere. The population fell from eight to six million, and continued to decline.

In the 1860s a republican group known as the Fenians waged guerrilla war against the British, while in Parliament Irish MPs, led by Charles Stewart Parnell, campaigned for self-government (Home Rule), but without success. One important concession was legislation that enabled Catholic tenants to own their own land.

In 1905 Arthur Griffith founded the nationalist movement Sinn Féin ("Ourselves Alone.") Many Irishmen volunteered to fight in the First World War, but in 1916 a dissident group seized the General Post Office in Dublin in a doomed attempt to end British rule and proclaim an independent Irish republic. This became known as the Easter Rising. After the War a guerrilla army, the Irish Republican Army, led by Michael Collins, fought against the British Auxiliary forces, known as the Black and Tans.

The struggle culminated in the Anglo-Irish Treaty of 1921, whereby Ireland was given limited self-government, except for six counties in the north that resisted the move. However, the Fianna Fáil party, led by Éamon de Valera, refused to accept the treaty, and when the party came to power in 1932 Ireland became a de facto republic, and consolidated this status in 1948.

Eire Today

In the early years of independence, under Éamon de Valera, Eire was introspective and conservative. It became a backwater, with a low standard of living, where the Catholic Church wielded enormous influence over people's lives. Many Irish people left to find employment in England, which now has a large and thriving Irish population, and elsewhere.

Since the 1960s, and particularly since joining the European Union, Ireland has changed out of all recognition. It has liberalized, its economy has strengthened, and emigration has been reversed. The Catholic Church's grip has loosened and it has become a modern, progressive nation that looks forward to the future rather than dwells on the past.

KEY HISTORICAL DATES

6th century BCE	Celts arrive in Ireland.
3rd century CE	High King Cormac founds an academy.
432	St. Patrick introduces Christianity.
9th century	Vikings seize Dublin and other ports.
1014	High King Brian Baru defeats the Vikings at the Battle of Clondarf.
1170	The Anglo-Norman Earl of Pembroke conquers much of eastern Ireland.
1171	Henry II invades Ireland and consolidates English rule.
1175	High King Rory O'Connor acknowledges Henry as Ireland's overlord by the Tireaty of Windsor.
1210	King John establishes civil government independent of Ireland's feudal lords.
1537	Irish Supremacy Act establishes Church of Ireland with Henry VIII as its head.
1598	Catholic rebellion; Hugh O'Neill defeats the English army at the Battle of the Yellow Ford.
1610	James I establishes Plantation of Ulster with settlers from England and Scotland on confiscated Catholic lands.
1641	Ulster Catholics rebel to recover confiscated lands and kill 12,000 Protestants.
1649	Oliver Cromwell ruthlessly suppresses Catholics.
1689	The deposed James II is welcomed by the Catholics when he lands in Ireland in an attempt at a comeback.
1690	William of Orange defeats James and his Catholic army at the Battle of the Boyne.
1695	Laws restrict land ownership by Catholics. Membership of Parliament restricted to Protestants.
1801	Act of Union incorporates Ireland into the United Kingdom.
1829	The British government emancipates the Catholics.
1845–52	The Great Famine leads to large-scale emigration.
1867	The Fenian uprising against British rule is crushed. Campaign for Home Rule gains widespread support.
1914	First World War begins. Many Irishmen enlist.
1916	Easter Rising in Dublin, leading to executions.
1918	End of First World War. Guerrilla movement fights for Irish independence.
1921	Anglo-Irish Treaty leads to limited self-government for Ireland, but six counties in the north opt out.
1922	Irish Free State proclaimed; IRA split over the Treaty leads to civil war 1922–23.
1939–45	Second World War. Ireland adopts a neutral stance.
1948	Ireland severs ties with the Commonwealth.
1973	Both Ireland and the United Kingdom join the EU.
1998	The Belfast (Good Friday) Agreement.

Northern Ireland Today

Northern Protestants, many of whom are descended from Scottish and English settlers, objected to the principle of Home Rule, which would have meant living in a country controlled by a large Catholic majority. So six of the counties of Ulster that were predominantly Protestant (Londonderry, Tyrone, Antrim, Armagh, Fermanagh, and Down) elected to remain part of the United Kingdom.

This solution did not satisfy Irish nationalists, and in the 1960s guerrilla warfare broke out again. The country became locked in conflict between the Irish Republican Army and the Loyalists (Protestant militia who professed loyalty to the United Kingdom). The British army was sent in to keep the peace, but was regarded by the IRA as having been sent to thwart their ambitions.

The late 1960s saw the start of what are euphemistically described as The Troubles, during which people from the rival communities were routinely murdered, and policemen and British soldiers attacked. Several attempts were made to bring the two parties together and culminated in a ceasefire signed in 1994.

An agreement signed in the following year (the Good Friday Agreement) envisaged a power-sharing Northern Ireland Assembly and cross-border cooperation between Eire and Northern Ireland under the auspices of a North/South Ministerial Council. So far the solution appears to be working. However, tensions have not been completely eliminated, and not everybody in the province is happy to accept the status quo.

GOVERNMENT OF EIRE

The Irish Republic (Eire) consists of the three traditional provinces—Leinster, Munster, and Connaught—plus the counties of Cavan, Donegal, and Monaghan only in the province of Ulster. It is a parliamentary democracy with a president, a prime minister, and two chambers: the Senate (Seanad Éireann) and the House of Representatives (Dail Éireann), whose 166 members are

elected by proportional representation. Elections are held every five years. The main political parties are Fine Gael (meaning Tribe of Ireland) and Fianna Fáil (Warriors of Ireland). The former supported the Anglo-Irish Treaty of 1923; the latter opposed it.

Parliament House, Dublin

GOVERNMENT OF NORTHERN IRELAND

Northern Ireland is part of the United Kingdom and has its own devolved National Assembly in addition to sending representatives to the UK Parliament in London. The main political parties are the Democratic Unionists (the Protestant, Loyalist party) and Sinn Féin (the Catholic, Republican party). Other parties are the Ulster Unionists, the Social Democrats, and the Alliance Party.

LANGUAGE

Irish Gaelic, which is recognized as one of Eire's two official languages, is reputed to be the oldest of the group of Celtic languages, which includes Welsh, Breton, and Scots Gaelic. The alphabet was developed from the Latin script in the sixth century.

For centuries most Irish people spoke Gaelic, but for the last two hundred years or so English has been the dominant language in Ireland and nowadays only 60,000 people speak Irish Gaelic in preference to English. Eighty-five percent of the population speak only English, although Gaelic is taught in schools throughout the Republic. Many Irish people profess an attachment to their national language and incorporate Gaelic expressions into their conversation.

Despite Ireland's compactness you will notice regional differences in the English spoken in Ireland. In Belfast it is said that one can differentiate between a Protestant and a Catholic on the strength of their accents.

Values and Attitudes

The Irish have a reputation for being relaxed, friendly, and amiable. They love talking, have a good command of language, and are excellent raconteurs. They are creative and imaginative, and possess tremendous charm.

They also have a reputation for stubbornness, and for being prepared to fight their cause. They distrust authority, and have a strong sense of their past.

Ireland is even today a predominantly rural island and so, apart from the residents of Dublin and Belfast, the Irish remain country folk steeped in rural traditions. Sixty per cent of the Republic's population, for instance, live away from the main conurbations, some in isolated communities.

RELIGION

Religious affiliation is important in Ireland because it defines your identity. Whereas in many parts of Western Europe churchgoing is declining, churches both in the Irish Republic and in Northern Ireland are packed on Sundays. In Northern Ireland, in particular, the church where you worship often coincides with the political grouping to which you belong.

The roots of the conflict date back to the Protestant Reformation, when Henry VIII broke with the Pope and set up an English Church independent of Rome. At a stroke of the pen all church congregations were expected to transfer their allegiance to the national Church, and in England, at least, the majority of people did so.

Not so in Ireland, of which Henry was nominally king, but where his influence was not so well entrenched. So while the new

Church took over all the properties of the Roman Catholic Church, a relatively small number of people switched. The others continued to worship in the traditional fashion—often in the open air.

The introduction of the new English prayer book made matters worse. The majority of people were Gaelic speakers, and preferred to worship in their traditional way. Those who did not embrace the new faith were deprived of many rights and privileges. During Elizabeth I's reign there were simmerings of discontent, which would fuel Irish nationalism.

The first signs occurred towards the end of Elizabeth's reign, when the Catholic Earl of Tyrone led a rebellion against the English. The English government retaliated by resettling Ulster with English and Scots (after the union between Scotland and England) and dispossessing many Catholics of their lands in the process.

This led to even more dissent, not only among the Catholics but also among the Scots Presbyterian settlers who (like the Catholics) were deprived of various rights and privileges enjoyed by members of the Anglican Church of Ireland. Some of the Presbyterians rebelled against British rule in the nineteenth century, and in the twentieth they fervently opposed the idea of becoming part of an overwhelmingly Catholic Irish state.

So what does this amount to in the twenty-first century? In the Irish Republic the antagonism has died down, and religious sects exist fairly harmoniously together. The Church of Ireland—now disestablished and with a much smaller congregation than the Catholic Church—enjoys considerable respect. Educational provision has not changed much, with most children continuing to attend sectarian schools.

In Northern Ireland antagonism still exists between Catholics and Protestants, with communities still divided, sometimes physically by walls. The militant Catholics, for the most part, now accept that force of arms cannot achieve Irish unity, while the militant Protestants now see that sharing power with Catholics is the only viable option if peace is to be maintained.

However, bitter memories remain, and while relations between the religious communities are now more relaxed, tensions still exist. The Good Friday Agreement represents an uneasy compromise, and education still remains largely sectarian.

MORALITY

In both Irelands moral attitudes are more conservative than in neighboring countries, thanks largely to the influence of the Churches. The Republic used to have draconian censorship laws, and until 1995 divorce was illegal. In both Irelands, abortion is permitted only if the pregnancy threatens the health or life of the mother; terminations are possible only on the British mainland. Contraception is frowned upon in traditional Catholic circles.

Homosexuality was also frowned upon until relatively recently, on both sides of the border. The revelation of child abuse scandals involving Catholic priests have shocked many Irish people.

Sexual attitudes have become more liberal as a result of television, and, particularly, the availability of British television. While the younger generation is more liberal, their elders still have a prudish attitude to sex and prefer not to discuss it openly.

EGALITARIANISM

For much of its history Ireland has been ruled from outside, and mostly not very skillfully. As a consequence most Irish people identify themselves with the oppressed, which means you do not find the social class divisions that exist in England, for instance. Everyone regards everyone else as an equal.

This is combined with a distrust of authority. Many Irish people possess an anarchic streak, and dislike being told what to do. The one exception to this is the Catholic Church, which used to wield enormous authority over how people conducted their lives. While its influence may have waned in recent decades, most Catholics regard their parish priests with great respect, and address them as "Father."

FAMILY VALUES

The family is important to every Irish person, since it provides solace and shelter from the outside world. Given the turbulent history of the island, it is perhaps not surprising that people regarded their families as the only body of people they could trust.

Family members are expected to show loyalty to one another and extend help to them whatever the circumstances. This has been demonstrated in fairly recent times in the way that families offered asylum to wrongdoers in Northern Ireland rather than turning them over to the authorities.

HOSPITALITY

The Irish are a naturally hospitable people who know how to make visitors feel at home. They have a genuine interest in people rather than in material things, and enjoy extending their social circle. They are unfailingly courteous, and have evolved a stress-free lifestyle that allows plenty of time for friendly discourse, whether in the pub or on the racetrack.

CELTIC FOLKLORE

Ireland has a rich store of Celtic folklore, which long predates Christianity. This tradition was initially disseminated orally by wandering bards and later recorded by monks. The translation of Celtic legends into English at the beginning of the twentieth century led to Ireland's rediscovery of its national identity.

Part of this folklore refers to fairies (*sidhe*, pronounced "shee"). Among their number are the *Bean-sidhe* (Banshee), a fairy woman whose wailing portends death; the *Pooka*, a dark horse with flowing mane and smoldering eyes; the *Mornadh* (Merrow), who lives beneath the sea and wears a red cap; and the Leprechaun, a red-coated shoemaker who guards the treasure the Vikings stole from the Irish and keeps it in crocks—hence the term "crock of gold."

HUMOR

The Irish have a reputation for being eloquent, witty, and humorous, and are seldom at a loss for words. They have what is called "the gift of the gab," which, according to an old tradition, can be acquired through kissing the Blarney Stone at Blarney Castle, near Cork, in the south. This facility with words has produced an impressive list of speakers and writers, and it can be no coincidence that both Oscar Wilde and George Bernard Shaw were Irish.

The Irish enjoy telling jokes and listening to them, and often find humor in the most unlikely situations and events. The humor is often self-deprecating or ironic, and they enjoy teasing and trading insults with their friends, but this is essentially gentle humor, and bad language has no part in it. If you are teased in this way, you should take it not as a personal affront but as a compliment. It means you have been accepted into their circle of intimates.

Festivals and Traditions

People on both sides of the border have a certain number of public holidays each year, but they do not always coincide. Surprisingly, the Irish Republic does not have the same range of religious holidays as the Catholic countries of southern Europe. This could be a reflection of the fact that the Roman form of Christianity never really took root in Celtic Ireland.

HOLIDAYS AND FESTIVALS

January 1	New Year's Day
March 17	St. Patrick's Day
March/April	Good Friday
March/April	Easter Monday
First Monday in May	May Day Holiday (Labor Day)
Last Monday in May	Spring Bank Holiday (NI only)
First Monday in June	June Holiday (Eire only)
July 12	Orangemen's Day (NI only)
First Monday in August	August Holiday (Eire only)
Last Monday in August	Late Summer Bank Holiday (NI only)
Last Monday in October	October Holiday (Eire only)
December 25	Christmas Day
December 26	Boxing Day/St. Stephen's Day

THE FESTIVE YEAR

New Year

December 31 is a night for celebration, and for going out on the town with friends. Pubs, clubs, and discos are open late, and on the stroke of midnight toasts are drunk, church bells ring, and fireworks light up the skies.

Shrove Tuesday/Ash Wednesday

On Shrove Tuesday, the day before the beginning of Lent, many Irish people follow the British custom of eating pancakes. The following forty days of Lent are supposed to be a time of abstinence. Many people give up chocolates, sugar, cigarettes, or some other indulgence.

St. Patrick's Day

March 17 is celebrated in Irish communities throughout the world, often with greater ceremony than in Ireland itself. A particular tradition on this day is "the wearing of the green," when people sport a sprig of shamrock, the three-leafed plant that is the symbol of St. Patrick, who used one as a visual aid to explain the Trinity.

St. Patrick's Day, Dublin

Orangemen's Day

July 12 marks the anniversary of the Battle of the Boyne in 1690. Members of the Orange Order, founded in 1795, parade through the streets of Belfast and other towns in Northern Ireland accompanied by brass bands and fife and drum bands.

The remit of the Orange Order is to defend the Protestant religion. This not surprisingly antagonizes the Catholics, who have attempted in the past to disrupt such marches when they pass through Catholic areas.

Christmas

Christmas is celebrated in much the same way as it is in Britain and the USA. Weeks before, stores put up Christmas decorations to encourage customers to part with their money. Santa Claus figures appear in Christmas grottos, or enter a town on a sleigh to turn on the Christmas lights.

Schools and colleges prepare for special concerts and nativity plays, and most establishments—from playgroups to offices—have Christmas parties at which people eat, drink, and are merry. People exchange Christmas cards, often with snow scenes, disregarding the fact that it rarely snows in Ireland.

On Christmas Eve businesses close early and people hurry home to be with their families. Children hang up socks or stockings in the hope that Santa Claus (sometimes known as Father Christmas) will come down the chimney and fill them with presents. Many people go to church to attend the midnight Christmas mass.

The following day is given over to feasting, with an enormous lunch typically consisting of roast turkey, roast potatoes, and vegetables, followed by Christmas pudding (a rich, cake-like fruit pudding) over which is poured brandy, custard, or cream, or perhaps all three! After this many people wish to do no more than have a nap or watch television.

It is increasingly common for the Christmas holidays to last until the New Year, with many organizations closed, or opening with just a skeleton staff during this time.

FAMILY OCCASIONS

The family is dear to every Irish heart, and everyone makes an effort to be present at important family celebrations.

A baptism, when a baby is introduced into the Christian community, provides an excuse for a small family party, even if the baby is unable to appreciate it. Confirmation and first communion, when a person attains full membership of the Church, is a particular cause for celebration in Catholic families.

Weddings are usually very elaborate affairs, and the preference on both sides of the border is for a church wedding. This follows the pattern of weddings in Britain and the United States, with bridesmaids in attendance on the bride, whose the father "gives her away." A reception follows, after which the married couple leaves for their honeymoon.

Funerals are important to Irish people, as anyone familiar with James Joyce's stories in *Dubliners* will attest. People do not hide their feelings. In the past people would sit around the coffin and drink to the deceased, but now it is more usual to wait until after the funeral before the eating and drinking (or "wake") commences. Funerals may be sad occasions, but in Ireland they always end on a high note.

PILGRIMAGES

St. Patrick is much venerated in Ireland, partly because he did not challenge old beliefs but gave them a new Christian dimension. One example is his ascent of Croagh Patrick, the mountain in County Mayo that was originally sacred to the pagan god Crom. When he came down he declared the summit sacred to the Christian God. Every year thousands of pilgrims come here on the last Sunday in July to climb, often barefoot, to the oratory at the top.

Lough Derg (the Red Lake) is also associated with St. Patrick. It is here that he had a vision of Purgatory. Pilgrims visit the lake for three days, following the stations of the Cross.

Another place of pilgrimage, also in County Mayo, is the village of Knock, where in 1879 several local people had a vision of the Virgin Mary silhouetted against the church. The village now boasts a large basilica and an airport.

Getting to Know the Irish

Ireland is sometimes known as "The Land of a Thousand Welcomes," and there is plenty of truth in this. The Irish have a reputation for being friendly, warm, and easy-going, especially with strangers. So it is not difficult to strike up a conversation with someone in a train, shop, or pub. They enjoy having a chat, which is why service in restaurants can seem irritatingly slow if you are in a hurry.

When entering a public space it is a good idea to extend a greeting to all present. A friendly initial approach could be the prelude to an absorbing conversation.

GOOD MANNERS

There is a charming, old-fashioned courtesy about the Irish, both young and old. They may be warm and friendly, but they are also polite and softly spoken, and they expect others to behave similarly. Loud, aggressive, or arrogant behavior makes them uncomfortable.

They dislike confrontation and often resort to humor in order to defuse a potential conflict. To avoid hurting people with a refusal, for instance, they will sometimes express themselves ambiguously rather than tell the truth. Upsetting people is regarded as very bad manners.

In common with the British, they like their personal space. They are not prone to great shows of affection, but appreciate a firm handshake. Kissing, hugs, and pats on the back are out until you get to know a person really well.

JOINING IN

As in the UK, there are countless clubs and associations you can join, and this can be a good way of meeting people. Normally visitors are welcome to join these, though there are some, with political or religious undertones, that it might be advisable to avoid. There is also a wide range of evening classes, from academic subjects to handicrafts. If you are planning to stay a long time in either Ireland, you might like to take up classes in Gaelic.

COMMUNICATION

The Irish dislike pretension and insincerity, so it is best to be frank and open with them. However, that does not mean being brash or curt; an nonconfrontational approach is preferable. Bad language should definitely be avoided.

The Irish appreciate modesty and can be suspicious of people who boast about their achievements, though there is no harm in mentioning them in passing. It is far better to be self-deprecating and make use of understatement, as the British do.

Given the general dislike of authority, you should always treat an Irish person as an equal. Like most people they appreciate a little flattery.

The Irish pride themselves on their eloquence, and often express themselves quite lyrically. They will frequently use stories and anecdotes to make a point, and welcome any stranger who exhibits a similar facility.

INVITATIONS HOME

If you want to drop in on someone, do. The Irish tend to be more relaxed about unannounced visits than other people in Northern Europe, but it would probably be more sensible to call them beforehand to ask if it would be convenient.

If you receive an invitation to a party or dinner in someone's home, enquire discreetly if this is a special occasion. If it's a birthday or a wedding anniversary, it would be a good idea to take along a present, preferably gift-wrapped. In any case, you ought to take a gift, which need not be extravagant or expensive, for the hostess. A bottle of wine or spirits is particularly appreciated, or a box of good-quality chocolates. Flowers are another possibility, but these need to be chosen with care. Don't give lilies, as they are used at religious festivities, and don't give red and white flowers, which are customary at funerals. If you know there will be children there, you might wish to bring small gifts for them, too.

As in Britain, a formal invitation may state two times, such as "7:30 for 8:00 p.m." This means that you don't have to arrive on the dot of 7:30, but you should make every effort to arrive before 8:00, so as not to hold up the proceedings.

Table manners will be relaxed and informal, but avoid resting your elbows on the table. As in most of Europe, people tend to use a knife and fork at the same time, but you don't have to. Don't smoke, unless you see other people doing so.

If it is a very informal occasion you might offer to help with clearing the table or washing up, particularly if you are a woman, although your offer is likely to be refused. Social occasions can be quite drawn out in Ireland, especially when the conversation is flowing freely, and could go on until midnight. Leaving early might suggest you have not enjoyed the evening.

Daily Life

HOUSING

A two-story house is the dwelling of choice for people on both sides of the border, but in the cities apartments are becoming more commonplace, though not as much as in other European countries.

In Northern Ireland you will find that certain areas of cities are the preserve of a particular sectarian community, and because of past strife barriers have been erected to separate the communities from one another.

THE HOUSEHOLD

At one time the extended family was the most important social structure. With the move of people to the cities the pattern is changing, though people still keep in touch with their rural roots.

No longer do you have the dominant father figure; families have become more democratic in structure and less conservative. Religious observance is still at a high level, but in recent years the influence of Catholic teaching on family life has greatly diminished. Examples of this are the now widespread use of contraception and the extent of sexual activity outside marriage.

Couples rarely have more than two children these days, and they try to ensure that they have a good education. Children are always included in social gatherings, and noisy or unruly behavior is tolerated to a greater degree than in other parts of Europe.

SHOPPING

Shopping hours are normally 9:00 a.m. to 5:30 p.m., but in smaller towns many stores may close for lunch as well as on one afternoon during the week, usually a Wednesday or a Thursday. Some supermarkets remain open until late.

Many shops open on Sundays in the Republic, but this is not yet common in Northern Ireland. Also, while the euro is used in the Republic, sterling remains the currency of Northern Ireland, though in border areas both may be accepted.

TELEVISION

Many people enjoy television in the evening, which is provided by both public and commercial broadcasters. In the Republic the state broadcasting authority is Radio Telefís Éireann, which has two television channels.

Northern Ireland receives the same TV and radio programs as the rest of the United Kingdom (including BBC and ITV). Transmissions can be received throughout most of the Irish Republic, and many southern Irish tune in to these because they offer greater variety than is available on national channels.

EDUCATION

The educational system is similar on both sides of the border, with most children going to church schools.

In the Republic 90 percent of primary schools (known as National Schools) are run by the Catholic Church, while most of the rest come under the aegis of the Church of Ireland. After completing primary school pupils go on to secondary, vocational, community, or comprehensive schools; 60 perccent of these schools are the more academic secondary schools which are, for the most part, sectarian.

Education is compulsory from six to sixteen, but most pupils study for longer. The Republic is particularly proud of its record in education: 81 percent of pupils complete the secondary level of education and 60 percent move into higher education.

In Northern Ireland education, which starts at five years old as in the rest of the UK, is also organized along sectarian lines. However, there has been an attempt to introduce nonsectarian schools, known as integrated schools, and at the last count there were around sixty of these in the whole province.

Northern Ireland's educational system is also good, and is reckoned to achieve higher standards than in the rest of the United Kingdom.

Ireland's oldest university is Trinity College, Dublin, founded in 1591 to promote the Anglican cause, and whose alumni have made

a significant impact on the culture of the British Isles. It is now known as Dublin University (not to be confused with Dublin City University). The federal National University of Ireland has colleges in the main cities of Ireland, including Dublin.

Northern Ireland's oldest university is Queen's University, Belfast. The University of Ulster was created in the 1960s.

Both countries have highly regarded technological institutes.

Campanile, Trinity College, Dublin

NEWSPAPERS

On both sides of the border people are avid newspaper readers, with five morning papers and a total of 300 in all. *The Irish Times*, published in Dublin, is a serious paper with a liberal bias, while the other Dublin paper, *The Irish Independent*, has a more populist style. *The Examiner* is published in Cork.

The two Belfast morning papers reflect the political/religious divide in the province. The *Belfast News Letter* is the Unionist/Protestant newspaper, and its rival *The Irish News* supports the Catholic/Nationalist cause. Some London-based newspapers publish Irish editions.

MAIL AND TELECOMMUNICATIONS

Post offices are open from 9:00 a.m. to 5:00 p.m. on weekdays in both countries, but only in the morning on Saturdays. When sending mail to the other side of the border, international postal rates apply. Mailboxes are green in the south, red in the north.

Both Irelands have efficient telephone systems, both fixed line and cellular. Remember that telephoning between Northern Ireland and Eire counts as an international call, and the international dialing code has to be used in both instances.

Cell phone usage is high on both sides of the border, and public telephones often accept credit and debit cards as well as coins.

The Irish are enthusiastic users of the Internet, for which there are several service providers.

Leisure Time

The Irish enjoy their leisure time and find many outlets for their energies. They are fond of the outdoor life and are particularly addicted to horse racing. Socializing with friends is important.

EATING OUT

Both parts of Ireland are enjoying a catering renaissance, and in the larger towns and cities you will find restaurants offering a wide range of national cuisines. For more traditional fare, try the typically quaint and friendly Irish pub, which is still very much the center of Irish nightlife, and a great place for meeting people, catching up on local gossip, and generally having a good time.

At one time Irish pubs were essentially drinking places, with sawdust on the floor, which no decent woman would enter. Nowadays they are social centers for both sexes and the Irish pub formula has taken the world by storm. They are so ubiquitous that no description is really necessary. Many offer live performances of traditional Irish music in the evenings. One matter is worthy of note. Although the Irish have a reputation for heavy drinking, judged by international standards they are quite modest consumers of alcohol, and incidents of drunkenness are much less common than in Britain. Here drinking is more of a social activity.

TIPPING
In a restaurant it is usual to leave a tip of between 10 and 15 percent, unless a service charge has been added to the bill.

FOOD

The food will be similar to that available in other parts of the British Isles, including breakfasts with fried eggs, bacon, sausages, and black pudding, though these are now giving way to much healthier options. Ireland also has an abundance of fresh local produce (including salmon, trout, beef, and vegetables) from which dishes are prepared.

Potatoes have long been a staple of the Irish diet, and visitors may like to sample potato specialties such as boxty (potato pancake), colcannon (mashed potato with cabbage and onion), and Dublin Coddle (a thick stew of interlayered sausages, bacon, onions, and potatoes, cooked in a ham stock). Irish stew, by contrast, is made from lamb, onions, potatoes, and other root vegetables.

The Irish also make some well-known breads. Soda bread is made from wheat flour and buttermilk, with bicarbonate of soda added as a raising agent, and baked on a griddle. Bannocks are soda bread made with oatmeal, barm brack is a spiced bread, and potato bread has mashed potatoes mixed into the flour.

DRINK

The usual range of drinks is available in both Irelands, including

two with particular Irish associations.

Whiskey, spelled with an e, is an Irish invention, according to the Irish, though the Scots (who spell their national drink without an e) may beg to differ. While the evidence of Irish monks distilling *uisce beatha* (water of life) is scanty, Ireland can certainly boast the oldest whiskey distillery in the world at Bushmills, in Antrim.

The other drink is Guinness, a dark beer made from roast barley. Although it is traditionally regarded as an Irish drink, it seems that it did not originate in Ireland at all, but in Covent Garden Market in London, where it was a popular drink among the (mainly Irish Catholic) porters. However, Guinness brewed at Arthur Guinness' brewery in Dublin is particularly prized because of the quality of the water.

CULTURE AND ENTERTAINMENT

Of all the Irish cities Dublin has the most to offer, especially with regard to drama. Here you will find the famous Abbey Theatre,

Waterfront Hall, Belfast

which now specializes in classical drama, the Gate Theatre, and the Gaiety Theatre, which is Dublin's oldest. The National Concert Hall is the main classical music venue, and also hosts jazz and traditional folk music events.

Belfast boasts a brand new concert hall, the Waterfront Hall, and provides a wide range of other entertainment, notably at the Grand Opera House, which dates from 1895.

A number of other towns have become famous for their festivals. Wexford has an annual opera festival, which often features seldom-performed operas, while Galway has an arts festival during the months of July and August. Dublin hosts an international film festival every spring.

With half its population below the age of twenty-five, it is not surprising that Ireland has witnessed an explosion of youth culture. Pop groups, such as U2, Boyzone, and Take That, have achieved tremendous success and there are plenty of others lining up to succeed them.

STUDENTS, CLUBBING, AND CLOSE ENCOUNTERS

Dublin, especially, has a thriving nightlife, with nightclubs, comedy clubs, discos, and cabarets galore. There are also late-night bars that are open until the early morning. Some of these cater to the young and trendy, while others have a slightly older clientele and may turn away people who are not smartly dressed.

Belfast also boasts a number of establishments catering to different tastes, including jazz and blues, traditional folk music, and contemporary pop.

Dublin's nightclubs usually open at around 10:00 p.m., and close at 3:00 a.m. The dress code depends on the type of club, but most have a "no sneakers" policy, and if you have had too much to drink you won't be admitted. Don't forget your ID. Nightclubs in general are becoming a little scarce of late, due to the influx of the "super pubs" since new licensing laws were introduced. These are very large pubs that have multiple bars and dance floors, which can now stay open as late as the nightclubs. As mentioned above, typical old-fashioned Irish pubs are still to be found, and are known for their warm, friendly atmosphere.

Most of Dublin's restaurants and pubs are located in Temple Bar, an area popular with tourists all year-round. Georges Street offers a good alternative from the stag and hen night groups that turn up in their scores to Dublin, with a great selection of some of the city's best bars. Parallel to Georges Street is one of the city's main strips, South William Street. Wexford Street and Baggot Street are two more of the hotspots.

Chatting up, or getting chatted up, is relatively easy these days in Dublin. Dublin is in the throes of a sexual revolution, and its newfound promiscuity sees feisty, redheaded girls and dark-haired, dashing young fellows getting together. Unnerving yet discreet, the Irish are approachable, open, and most of all enjoy having a good time. So the best philosophy to take on here in the hope of meeting somebody would be "When in Rome…". Don't let your inhibitions get the better of you—ask your interest out, perhaps for a casual evening with a group of friends. A fun night out to a pub with live music and a little dancing, or a walk around the city and a nice meal is the norm for an initial romantic meeting in the city.

SPORTS

The Irish love the outdoor life, and enjoy sports—both playing and watching. Here are some of their favorites.

Horse Racing

The Irish adore horses and horse racing, and many leading trainers, breeders, and jockeys in Britain are Irish. Ireland boasts no fewer than twenty-eight racecourses, and race meetings regularly attract thousands of spectators.

Rugby

Rugby, which involves picking up the ball rather than kicking it, has a keen following in Ireland, which has produced some outstanding players. International matches are especially popular. The Ireland team recruits its players from both Northern Ireland and the Republic.

Soccer

Although a number of Irish players play for English teams, soccer is not as popular in the Republic as in other countries of Western Europe. In Northern Ireland, by contrast, it is very popular; team affiliation is often along sectarian lines so you may have the spectacle of Protestants and Catholics battling it out on the football field.

Gaelic Sports

The Celtic Revival movement in the late nineteenth century played a significant role in bringing these sports to prominence and led to the foundation of the Gaelic Athletic Association in Croke Park, near Dublin (named after its first president, who was a Catholic bishop of Cashel). Games normally take place on Sundays.

Gaelic Football uses a round ball that can be kicked or thrown and is played by teams of fifteen players. It bears a strong resemblance to Australian football and American football.

Hurling is a game that is supposed to have predated St. Patrick's arrival in Ireland. Teams of fifteen players battle it out to score goals using hurleys, which are similar to hockey sticks. The goalposts are similar to those used in rugby.

Other Sports

As in the United States and Britain, golf is very popular, and the island has an unusually large number of golf courses. Thanks to the purity of the water in Ireland's rivers and lakes fish thrive there—and so do anglers.

Getting Around

Rail is a fast, cheap, and convenient means of travel in Eire, where the state railway, Irish Rail, connects all the main locations except Donegal. There are also express trains linking Dublin and Belfast.

Northern Ireland has a much less extensive rail service, but it does have a good bus network, Ulsterbus.

URBAN TRANSPORTATION

Dublin has Luas, a brand new and very efficient light rail tram system. DART (Dublin Area Rapid Transport) connects the center with the suburbs. The city also has an extensive bus network. You need the correct change for the autofare system, or a travel pass. Nitelink buses, which charge a flat fare, operate through the night.

The public transport system within Belfast is known as Metro and provides bus services only.

Luas tram in Dublin

DRIVING

The rules of the road in Ireland are the same as in Britain: you drive on the left and give priority to traffic coming from the right.

Speed limits in the Republic are expressed in kilometers per hour. Within cities and towns it is 50 kmph (31 mph), on open roads it is 100 kmph (62 mph), and on expressways 120 kmph (74 mph). Distances are also expressed in kilometers, except on older signposts. In Northern Ireland speed limits and distances are expressed in miles and are the same as elsewhere in the United Kingdom. Throughout Ireland the drink-driving limit is 0.8 mg per ml.

The roads are generally good throughout Ireland. Northern Ireland has two expressways, but since much of the island is rural normal roads suffice, and traffic is remarkably light—so light, in fact, that in Antrim and Cork they play bowls in the road on Sundays! So beware of steel balls in motion there.

WHERE TO STAY

Both Irelands offer a good range of hotels, guesthouses, and bed and breakfast accommodation, which can be booked in advance through tourist information offices. Between June and September pressure on accommodation is heavy, especially in Dublin.

There are plenty of camping and caravan sites, and both countries have a network of youth hostels.

MEDICAL MATTERS

Citizens of European Union countries are eligible for treatment under the state health services of both countries on production of a European Health Insurance Card. For others, it would be sensible to take out private health insurance.

LAW AND ORDER

Both countries are relatively safe, though it is wise to take precautions, especially in urban areas. Don't walk alone late at night, particularly down badly lit streets, don't carry valuables about with you, don't leave bags unattended, and beware of pickpockets.

Visitors to Northern Ireland have no need to fear for their lives. Even when the Troubles were at their height, not one foreign visitor was killed.

Dublin Castle

PLACES TO VISIT

Dublin has a population of one million and is the only substantial city in a predominantly rural country. It is famous for its Georgian architecture and its castle. It boasts a number of excellent museums, including the National Museum, the National Art Gallery, and the Chester Beatty Museum with its extensive collection of Oriental art. There are guided walks throughout the city, including one that retraces the route taken by Leopold Bloom in James Joyce's novel *Ulysses*.

Belfast, which once had a larger population, has more of an industrial heritage than Dublin and is more Victorian in character.

Belfast Castle

The Lisburn Museum has a substantial exhibition devoted to the linen industry, and there is an interesting heritage center inside Belfast Castle, which bears a strong resemblance to Balmoral Castle in Scotland.

Most of Ireland's large towns are on the coast. Cork is the second largest city of the Republic, and is famous for its whiskey, gin, stout, and the temperance movement, the Pioneers, that was founded here. Nearby are Blarney Castle and the famous Blarney Stone. Galway in the west is the gateway to the

Aran Islands, and other towns worth a visit are Wexford, Waterford, and "medieval" Kilkenny.

Londonderry, now renamed Derry by the City Council, is "the prettiest looking town I have seen in Ireland," in the words of Thomas Carlyle, and its city walls are still intact. The Tower Museum gives an insight into the city's turbulent history, including the Siege of Londonderry.

Much of the island is unspoiled countryside, and most visitors appreciate driving along uncongested roads to see such sights as the Giant's Causeway, the Aran Islands, Killarney and its lakes, and the Hill of Tara, as well as elegant country houses such as Bantry House in County Cork.

Giant's Causeway, Co. Antrim

Business and Professional Life

The Irish Republic's economic fortunes seemed to have changed for the better after it joined the European Community (later the European Union) in 1973. What was once one of the poorest countries in the EU, with a predominantly rural workforce, has become become one of its more prosperous members—a "Celtic Tiger," in fact.

Inward investment from the USA, Japan, Britain, and Germany brought modern light industry to the country, which is now particularly strong in electronics and software development and has a well-educated workforce. Tourism also took off in a big way.

Allied Irish Bank offices in Dublin docklands

However, the global recession that started in 2008 exposed fatal flaws in the country's economy, and the government has had to take severe measures to cope with a soaring deficit and a banking crisis. It will clearly take time for the country to recover its previous robust economic health.

North of the border, some of the province's traditional industries have suffered a decline, and the tense political situation deterred investors. Things are starting to look brighter now, but the growth, as in the south, is largely in the service sector. Agriculture and food processing are important earners in both parts of Ireland.

BUSINESS CULTURE

Business culture has changed over recent decades with the arrival of several large international companies. Many brought their own corporate culture with them, but this will inevitably have been modified to blend in with the Celtic way of life.

Traditional Irish businesses still tend to be hierarchical, with one key decision maker who issues instructions to his staff. However, as the younger generation of well-educated managers rises from the ranks, more democratic managerial styles are taking root.

Long-term planning is a foreign notion to many Irish employees, who distrust plans and prefer to improvise. In this respect they resemble their neighbors across the Irish Sea.

MAKING CONTACT

Because personal relationships are so important in Ireland, your first contacts with a company are best made through a third party, who can advise you on the best approach. Both Eire and Northern Ireland being relatively small countries, you will find that everyone has a wide range of contacts.

When scheduling a meeting, it is best to avoid the months of July and August, as this is when most people take their holidays. Important festivals, such as St. Patrick's Day, are also best avoided.

You should allow plenty of time for any negotiations, as the Irish like to conduct business in a fairly leisurely manner, looking at a matter from every possible angle. You may find that younger managers have a brisker approach.

It is wise to confirm appointments by telephone or e-mail the day before your meeting.

BUSINESS ETIQUETTE

Formal dress is normally worn for business meetings, but once the meeting has started, it is not long before the jackets come off and formality is cast aside.

It is helpful to carry business cards to give to the people you meet. Don't worry if you don't receive one in exchange; not all Irish people use them.

Normally you will be addressed by your surname in the early stages of the relationship, especially by older businesspeople. However, younger managers may address you by your first name right from the start.

Personal relationships are important to the Irish, and your hosts will be just as interested in you as in what you are offering them. They will be delighted if you return the compliment and ask them polite questions about themselves.

The Irish are naturally courteous and softly spoken. Confrontation, or a "hard sell" approach, will usually prove counterproductive.

MEETINGS

You should arrive punctually for any meeting you have set up, but don't take it amiss if the proceedings start late. As in the countries of southern Europe, the Irish have a more flexible approach to time.

Greet your hosts with a firm handshake and look them in the eye. You should be prepared to exchange pleasantries before getting down to the serious business. They will expect you to open up, and you should avoid short replies.

If you are giving a presentation you should keep it brief, illustrate your points with anecdotes if you can, and allow plenty of time for

questioning. Discussions can often become protracted as everyone in the room will want to make a contribution.

Inevitably, there are people who will wander from the point. In such cases you should exercise patience rather than attempt to impose a structure on the deliberations. If you try to impose deadlines, you may well put people's backs up.

It is sometimes difficult to gauge the outcome of a meeting.

Politeness is often regarded as more important than telling the absolute truth, so it will not always be clear if the response is negative or not. If the response is noncommittal, this could signify that you are being turned down.

A relaxed atmosphere should not lull you into a false sense of security. The Irish can be remarkably astute and tenacious in business, and you should never underestimate them.

BUSINESS ENTERTAINMENT

As in southern Europe, business matters and social life often overlap, and if you are invited out don't hesitate to go. This could represent a golden opportunity to clinch a deal. The Irish are often more outgoing in a relaxed atmosphere, whether imbibing a glass of Guinness or out on the golf course. Some of the most important decisions are made outside the office rather than in it, so it would be unwise to assume that you are off duty the moment you walk out of the building.

If you are invited out to dinner, be prepared for a long haul. After dinner your host may well take you on to a pub or club, and your evening might continue into the early hours.

WOMEN IN BUSINESS

Although Ireland has had two women presidents, there is still a feeling that a woman's place is in the home—among the older generation, at least. It is therefore unusual to find a woman in a position of authority in Irish companies, although the situation is changing slowly.

However, that should not deter businesswomen and professional woman from abroad. You are likely to be received courteously and listened to attentively. The Irish respect women who dress conservatively—in skirts rather than trousers—and who behave with decorum. While it is perfectly acceptable for you to order a beer, make it a small glass rather than a pint!

Chapter 7

ITALY

Key Facts

Official Name	Repubblica Italiana (Italian Republic)	**Radio and TV**	The state-funded broadcaster RAI has three TV channels and three radio channels. There are several commercial broadcasters. The PAL-BG system is used.
Capital City	Roma (Rome)		
Major Cities	Milano (Milan), Torino (Turin), Napoli (Naples), Bologna, Genova (Genoa), Firenze (Florence), Venezia (Venice), Palermo		
		Press	Regional press with national distribution: *Corriera della Sera* (Milan), *Il Messaggero* (Rome), *La Repubblica* (Rome), *La Stampa* (Turin)
Area	116,319 sq. miles (301,245 sq. km)		
Terrain	Mountainous in north and center; plains and rolling hills		
Climate	Mediterranean, but cooler in mountain areas	**English-language Media**	The *International Herald Tribune* has an *Italy Daily* section covering Italian news. *Wanted in Rome* is an English-language news and listings magazine. *L'Osservatore Romano* (Vatican) has a weekly English-language edition.
Currency	Euro		
Population	60 million		
Language	Italian. Many regional dialects. Also German, French, Slovenian, Friulian, Ladino		
Religion	Roman Catholic 93%; Protestant and others 7%	**Electricity**	230 volts; 50 Hz. Two-prong plugs used
		Internet Domain	.it
Government	Parliamentary democracy, with president as head of state, and prime minister as head of government. Elections held every five years	**Telephone**	Country code 39. For international calls dial 00.
		Time Zone	CET (GMT/UTC + 1) with daylight saving in summer

Map of Italy

SWITZERLAND
AUSTRIA
HUNGARY

TRENTINO-
ALTO ADIGE
FRIULI-
VENEZIA
GIULIA
SLOVENIA

• Trento

VALLE D'AOSTA
LOMBARDA
VENETO
• Trieste
CROATIA

Aosta
• Milano
Venezia

• Torino
PIEMONTE
EMILIA-
ROMAGNA
• Bologna
BOSNIA AND
HERZEGOVINA

• Genova
LIGURIA

FRANCE
LIGURIAN
SEA
Firenze
MARCHE
• Ancona

TOSCANA
• Perugia

UMBRIA

CORSICA
LAZIO
• L'Aquila
ABRUZZI
ADRIATIC
SEA

• Roma
MOLISE
• Campobasso

CAMPANIA
• Bari

Napoli •
• Potenza
PUGLIA

BASILICATA

SARDEGNA
TYRRHENIAN SEA

CALABRIA

• Cagliari
• Catanzaro

IONIAN
SEA

MEDITERRANEAN
SEA
• Palermo
SICILIA

• MALTA

The Country and Its People

Italy consists of twenty regions, from Trentino-Alto Adige in the north to Calabria in the south, including the islands of Sardinia (Sardegna) and Sicily (Sicilia). Its mainland is a long peninsula shaped like a boot, which stretches down into the Mediterranean, flanked by the Ligurian and Tyrrhenian Seas on one side and the Adriatic on the other.

The mainland has frontiers with France, Switzerland, Austria, and Slovenia, and both the northern part and the central spine are mountainous. Only a quarter of the country could be described as low-lying. The climate is Mediterranean but it is cooler in the north and in the mountains. There are two small independent enclaves: San Marino and Vatican City.

Landscape in Tuscany

Italy has a long and proud history. It was the cradle of one of the world's great empires, whose monuments still stand two thousand years later. It was also the scene of one of the most exciting eras of artistic endeavor—the Renaissance, when Italian artists, musicians, scientists, and literary figures revolutionized the arts and the way we look at the world. Today in matters of style and taste Italy still continues to lead the world.

Yet Italy as we know it today is a relatively young country—not even a hundred and fifty years old. After the fall of the Roman Empire the country became a collection of kingdoms, duchies, and city-states that often came under foreign rule. This has given rise to a remarkable diversity. Italians tend to think of themselves as Florentine, Milanese, Roman, Neapolitan, or Venetian first, and Italian second.

A HISTORICAL PERSPECTIVE

By the first century BCE Rome had brought the whole of the Italian peninsula under its control, including the Veneti, the Etruscan, and the Latin peoples, and set about creating an empire that would stretch from Britain to the Caspian Sea.

After the fall of the Roman Empire in the fifth century CE

the Church in Rome gained in authority, and in 800 CE Italy, France, and Germany were briefly united into a single Christian empire under Charlemagne—the precursor of the Holy Roman Empire.

Relations between later emperors and popes deteriorated, and many cities broke away to govern themselves, often becoming fierce rivals. In the fifteenth century most of Italy was divided into the Kingdom of the Two Sicilies, the Papal States, and the city-states of Venice (Venezia), Florence (Firenze), and Milan (Milano).

Statue of the first Roman Emperor, Augustus, c. 20 CE

Thanks to the wealth and influence of the Borgias in Rome, the Medici in Florence, and the Sforzas of Milan, the arts flourished.

In the sixteenth century Italy became involved in the dynastic struggles of the leading powers of Europe and came under the control of the Spanish Habsburgs. After the Treaty of Utrecht in 1713 Austria gained control of most of the country except for the Kingdom of Naples, which came under Spanish Bourbon rule.

From Napoleon to Liberation

The years 1796–1814 saw Napoleon's conquest of Italy. He installed his brother Joseph as King of Naples (Napoli), and created a new Kingdom of Italy for himself out of the remaining territories. Under the Code Napoléon, Italy became a modern, centralized state.

After Napoleon's defeat in 1815, the despotic old regimes were largely restored, and Italy was divided up again. Soon the Italians were clamoring for an independent, united Italy, in a movement called the *Risorgimento* (Resurrection).

Rebellions broke out in a number of places, and the utopian Giuseppe Mazzini founded the Young Italy movement. Mazzini's most celebrated disciple was the flamboyant Giuseppe Garibaldi, who had started his long revolutionary career in South America. On the diplomatic front, Count Camillo Cavour enlisted British and French support, enabling King Victor Emmanuel II of Sardinia to liberate much of the country. By 1870 the mission he had started was complete: Italy was united and free. with the exception of those areas under Austrian rule until 1918.

Giuseppe Garibaldi, c. 1861

Colonialism and Fascism

The first decades of independence were by no means glorious. Italy colonized Eritrea and later Libya, and fought with the Allies in the First World War, for which it was awarded Trentino, South Tyrol, and Trieste.

The postwar years were marked by inflation, unemployment, and considerable popular unrest. One outcome was the rise of the right-wing populist Fascist movement led by Benito Mussolini, who marched his Black Shirt militias on Rome, where King Victor Emmanuel III appointed him prime minister.

In the following years the Fascist regime brutally suppressed all opposition. On the credit side Mussolini stabilized the economy, improved working conditions, and instituted a public works program.

Benito Mussolini, 1938

KEY HISTORICAL DATES

793 BCE	Foundation of Rome.
44 BCE	Assassination of Julius Caesar.
27 BCE	Augustus becomes Roman Emperor.
324 CE	Christianity becomes the state religion under Constantine.
476	Last Emperor of Rome is deposed.
800	Pope Leo III crowns Charlemagne Emperor of the Romans.
873	Saracens gain control of Sicily.
1271	Marco Polo sets off on his journey to China.
1088	First European university is established at Bologna and granted a charter by Frederick Barbarossa.
15th century	The Renaissance.
1528	Habsburg Emperor Charles V takes over most of the country.
1713	Austria becomes the dominant power in Italy.
1801	Napoleon conquers Italy and introduces the Code Napoléon.
1831	Mazzini founds the Young Italy movement.
1848–9	Insurrections occur throughout Italy.
1859	King Victor Emmanuel starts the liberation of Italy.
1870	Unification of Italy.
1922	Mussolini comes to power.
1940	Italy enters the Second World War on Germany's side.
1943	Mussolini resigns; Italy surrenders to the Allies.
1946	Italy votes to abolish the monarchy.
1957	Treaty of Rome establishes the European Economic Community (later the EU), with Italy as a founder member.

He went on to conquer Abyssinia and Albania, offered assistance to General Franco in the Spanish Civil War, and allied Italy with Nazi Germany. The Second World War proved disastrous; Italy suffered defeats in Greece and North Africa, and Mussolini was removed from power and forced to flee.

The new Italian government surrendered to the Allies in 1943, but the Germans occupied north and central Italy, where they were to remain until 1945. King Victor Emmanuel abdicated in favor of his son the following year, but his reign lasted little more than a month, for the Italians voted to become a republic in 1946.

Italy Today

The new republic suffered considerable political instability. During the *anni di piombo* (years of lead) from 1960 to the 1980s, left-wing activists committed acts of terrorism. The Mafia, too, was active, exerting control over businesses and politicians and murdering those who stood in their way.

An anti-corruption campaign in the 1990s led to the emergence of more mainstream political parties. Political extremists from both right and left have been excluded from recent governments, which have alternated between centre-left and centre-right coalitions.

Economically, Italy has done well, and now ranks among the top five economies in Europe. It is a major exporter and boasts an extremely successful tourist industry. However, a considerable gap in living standards still exists between the prosperous north and the more backward south, known as the Mezzogiorno. Northerners are regarded as industrious, whereas southerners are more laid-back and traditional in their ways.

GOVERNMENT

Since 1946 Italy has been a multiparty republic with an elected president as head of state and a prime minister as head of government (who is the leader of the party or coalition with the majority in parliament). There are two legislative chambers—the Senate, with 325 members, and the 633-seat Chamber of Deputies. The twenty regions enjoy considerable autonomy.

THE REGIONS OF ITALY, WITH THEIR CAPITALS
(starting in the northwest)

Valle d'Aosta	Aosta
Piemonte (Piedmont)	Torino (Turin)
Lombardia (Lombardy)	Milano (Milan)
Trentino-Alto Adige	Trento
Veneto	Venezia (Venice)
Friuli-Venezia Giulia	Trieste
Liguria	Genova (Genoa)
Emilia-Romagna	Bologna
Toscana (Tuscany)	Firenze (Florence)
Umbria	Perugia
Marche	Ancona
Lazio	Roma (Rome)
Abruzzo	L'Aquila
Molise	Campobasso
Campania	Napoli (Naples)
Puglia (Apulia)	Bari
Basilicata	Potenza
Calabria	Catanzaro
Sicilia (Sicily)	Palermo
Sardegna (Sardinia)	Cagliari

Values and Attitudes

Italy is not as homogeneous a country as some European states, and attitudes vary according to area. The people of Alto Adige, for instance, have more in common with the Austrians, the region having been part of Austria until the end of the First World War. The Sicilians and Neapolitans lead a more traditionally Mediterranean way of life. The industrial cities of the north are between the two extremes. So the information given in this chapter needs to be treated with care.

THE FAMILY

The role of the family is paramount in Italian life—think of the Montagues and Capulets in *Romeo and Juliet*. Fortunately, family loyalty no longer extends to vendettas, except among the Sicilian Mafia, but it is still a powerful force for stability in a country that has experienced many vicissitudes over the past century.

Family firms make up the majority of Italian businesses, and have often been in the same family for generations. The sense of family normally extends to the workforce, with the proprietor feeling he is responsible for their wellbeing.

Italians like to talk about their families and usually carry around photographs of them. When they eat out it is usually as a family; children are always included in the group. Yet the idea of the large, extended family is a thing of the past. Many couples now choose to have just one child, for reasons of economy.

Most Italians have a close circle of friends, many of whom they have known since childhood, and in a sense friends become part of the extended family—people you can trust and rely on.

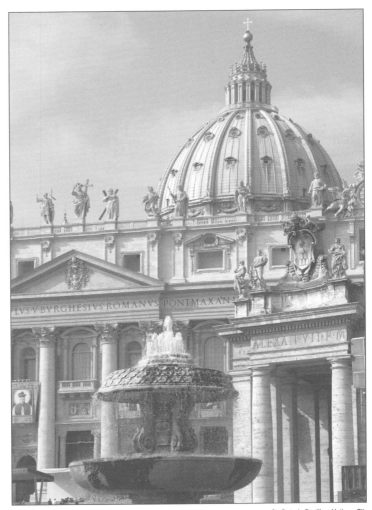

St. Peter's Basilica, Vatican City

RELIGION

Italy may be officially a secular state, but religious beliefs and traditions still play an important part in the lives of Italians, even those who profess atheism. The Roman Catholic Church, with its headquarters in Vatican City, is the dominant player here. The country has a higher proportion of Catholic churches per head of population than any other country in the world.

The Roman Catholic Church is a hierarchical institution that still wields tremendous authority, and although regular attendance at church has waned, the word of the Pope and the local priest still counts for a great deal. Catholics are expected to conform to its strictures, even if they sometimes choose to ignore one or two (such as the Church's views on abortion and contraception).

Yet in some respects the Church is remarkably tolerant. It recognizes that human beings make mistakes, and is prepared to forgive and forget. The Italians follow its lead and tend to overlook even major transgressions.

SOME SUPERSTITIONS

The Italians are devout, and often superstitious.

- Some ward off the evil eye by extending their index and little fingers, keeping the others folded down; others by wearing a horn-shaped charm as a pendant.
- Peacock feathers are unwelcome in the house because the "eye" in the feather looks like the evil eye.
- There are a number of superstitions connected with death, such as putting salt under the head of the corpse in the coffin to safeguard the person against returning as a ghost.
- The number thirteen is not unlucky in Italy, except at dinner parties; but the number seventeen is.
- Italians touch iron (not wood) to ward off bad luck, and eat *gnocchi* (small potato dumplings) on September 29 for good luck.

STYLE

Italians are stylish in the way they dress, the cars they drive, the restaurants they eat in, and the way they present themselves generally. They admire people who flaunt their wealth, even if their reputations are dubious. It is no coincidence that the country boasts so many leading fashion houses. To Italian eyes your appearance reveals the kind of person you are, and if you dress shabbily or unfashionably you will be thought a dismal figure.

NOISE

One overriding impression many visitors have, particularly of southern Italy, is the noise level. Motorists blow their horns with great abandon, people shout and sing in the streets at night, radios and TVs blare out at full volume, and in restaurants people engage in loud and animated discussions. A quiet night out is completely foreign to an Italian.

FORMALITY AND DEFERENCE

The Church is a hierarchical institution, and so is Italian society. People show deference to their bosses and people in authority, such as the captains of Italian industry and their families, to other people who have achieved success, and to older people.

This deference is evident in their formal and courteous manner of communication with each other, and their use of elaborate language to smooth over difficult situations. Sometimes this strikes other nationalities used to a more direct approach as obsequious.

LOCAL PATRIOTISM

Italians have a strong sense of community, and still tend to relate much more closely to their locality and region than to their nation. Moving away from the places and people they grew up with can be a wrench, and even those who have emigrated to distant shores remain loyal to their roots, keeping in touch with the latest events and returning whenever they can.

They are inordinately proud of their local cuisine and traditions—often with good reason—and they enjoy taking strangers around to introduce them to the delights of their area. They turn out in droves to support their local football team.

While they may refer to themselves as Italians outside their country, they will refer to themselves as, for example, Venetians, Florentines, or Calabrians within its boundaries.

BUREAUCRACY

One enduring legacy Napoleon left to Italy was an extensive bureaucracy; but bureaucracy Italian-style is slow and time-consuming. Too often in the past, government jobs were awarded for political services rendered rather than on merit, with the result that government offices seem bloated and staffed by time-servers.

Italians get as frustrated with bureaucracy as visitors to their country, and have a profound mistrust of formal institutions as a whole. In order to expedite matters they often employ a *faccendiere* (fixer) to cut through the red tape for them. Others try to beat the system or just disregard the rules.

Festivals and Traditions

As in most southern European countries, many of the public holidays in Italy have religious origins. In addition to national holidays there are local ones, where everyone has a day off, usually to celebrate the festival of the patron saint of the area.

For example, St. Peter and St. Paul being the patron saints of Rome, the Romans have a holiday on June 29. In addition they take April 21 off to celebrate the legendary founding of their city by Romulus in 753 BCE.

When a public holiday occurs in the middle of the week, it is customary to extend the holiday into the weekend.

HOLIDAYS AND FESTIVALS

January 1	Capodanno	New Year's Day
January 6	Epifania	Epiphany
February/March	Carnevale	Carnival
March/April	Pasqua	Easter Day
March/April	Lunedì dell'Angelo/Pasquetta	Easter Monday
April 25	Festa della Liberazione	Liberation Day
May 1	Festa dei Lavoratori	Labor Day
June 2	Festa della Repubblica	Republic Day
August 15	Ferragosto /Assunzione	Assumption
November 1	Ognissanti/Tutti i santi	All Saints' Day
December 8	Immacolata Concezione	Immaculate Conception
December 25	Natale	Christmas Day
December 26	Santo Stefano	St. Stephen's Day

THE FESTIVE YEAR

New Year
This is a time for partying. Traditionally it is also the time for people to discard unwanted possessions and buy new.

Epiphany
On Twelfth Night, in commemoration of the visit by the Magi to the Christ Child, Italy has a little old lady, Befana, who stuffs children's socks with gifts of sweets.

Carnevale
In the ten days before the beginning of Lent, a time of fasting and abstinence, it is carnival time in many towns and cities. Some put on medieval fairs. Venice in particular is famous for its masked balls and gondola processions. On Martedo Grasso (Mardi Gras, or Shrove Tuesday) Venetians put on cloaks, tricorne hats, and masks before they go out to circulate the streets incognito.

Holy Week
Many people take off the whole of the week leading up to Easter. This is the time when plays about Christ's passion are performed. On Palm Sunday, celebrating the entry of Jesus into Jerusalem,

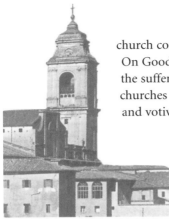

church congregations process with palm crosses or leaves. On Good Friday there are processions with a statue of the suffering Christ. Also on this day services are held in churches focusing on the Stations of the Cross; paintings and votive statues are covered with black cloth.

Easter Day

Easter is the most important Christian festival, celebrating Christ's resurrection. The black cloths are taken off the statues, the churches are decorated with flowers, and the church bells summon the faithful to mass. Families get together and celebrate with a festive meal.

Liberation Day

Italians celebrate the end of the German occupation in 1945 with processions through the streets and the laying of wreaths on war memorials.

Labor Day

In some Italian towns trade unions and political parties organize processions to mark the international day of the worker.

Republic Day

This celebrates the founding of the Italian Republic in 1946, with speeches and the National Anthem.

All Saints' Day

This is another religious festival that venerates Christian saints and martyrs. On the following day, All Souls' Day (Il Giorno dei Morti) it is customary for people to visit cemeteries and lay wreaths and flowers—often chrysanthemums—on their family graves. People often eat cookies called *ossi dei morti* (bones of the dead).

Festival of the Immaculate Conception

The Virgin Mary, the mother of Christ, is especially revered in Catholic countries, and this day is marked by religious processions and church services.

Christmas

The traditional time of Christ's birth is regarded as an important celebration, which Italians like to spend with their families, enjoying festive food and exchanging presents. Many people attend mass on Christmas Eve, and children expect to be visited during the night by the gift-laden "Babbo Natale" (Santa Claus).

Local Festivals

Most Italian towns have an annual *festa* (festival) that may last

several days. Among the most important are the Regata in Venice in September, and the Calcio Storico Fiorentino in Florence (a sixteenth-century costume parade). In Siena on each of two dates, July 2 and August 16, the great traditional event known as the Palio takes place, in which riders race ten horses bareback three times around the Piazza del Campo. The Palio is preceded by a few hours of spectacular pageantry.

In addition to these historical events are the various arts festivals held throughout the year, especially in the summer, when life moves out into the open air. The most famous of these in the Venice Film Festival, the world's oldest. Others are the Festival of the Two Worlds (Festival dei due Mondi) in

Palio procession (above) and banners (right)

Spoleto and the Festival of Italian Song (Festival della canzone Italiana), and the Festival di Sanremo, in San Remo.

FAMILY OCCASIONS

A birth in the family is celebrated by placing a rosette—pink or blue—on the door of the house. The baby is normally baptized in church soon after birth, as is customary in most southern European countries.

Confirmation, followed by First Communion, is another major event in a child's life. Most Italians are named after saints, and celebrate the festival of that saint with a party and perhaps by taking a day off work.

On their wedding day most couples first go to the town hall for the official ceremony, following this with a nuptial mass in church, then return home to prepare for the reception. In some villages it is the tradition for the couple to walk to the village square and saw a log in half to demonstrate their ability to cooperate. Releasing a pair of doves is a more modern tradition. At the reception a toast "*Per cent'anni*" ("May you live a hundred years") is proposed, to wish the couple a long life together, and the feasting begins. The guests may form a circle to dance a *tarantella*, a traditional folk dance, and are presented with sugared almonds to take home.

Funerals are somber affairs, and those attending them wear dark clothes. At one time the Catholic Church forbade cremation, but has now withdrawn its opposition to this.

Until the funeral the body is often kept at home in an open casket so that relations, friends, and neighbors can come to pay their respects. On the day of the funeral it is customary for everybody, not just the close family members, to follow the pallbearers into the church where the funeral mass is held. It is not usual to finish off the proceedings with a wake.

Getting to Know the Italians

The Italians are used to foreigners. The country has been invaded several times by foreign armies, and over the centuries tourists have flocked to Italy to admire the treasures of Florence and Rome, to float along the canals of Venice, and to enjoy the delights of the Italian Riviera.

MAKING CONTACT

The countless foreign invasions could well have led to a bunker mentality, for it is not easy to strike up a relationship with Italians. For one thing the family has priority; for another they already have a close circle of friends with whom they socialize. Their initial

reserve should not be regarded as xenophobia, though. Italians from outside the area will receive similar treatment at first.

One way of penetrating Italian society is to do as the Italians do. Use the local shops and get to know the shopkeepers; visit bars and cafés regularly. People will soon recognize you and start to exchange pleasantries with you.

THE LANGUAGE

Although many Italians speak English and other languages, they naturally prefer to speak their own, which is why learning Italian is a must. If you have to resort to English, you need to speak clearly and avoid idioms.

Italian is not a difficult language to learn, especially if you have some knowledge of French, Spanish, or Latin. There are many language schools both in Italy and abroad that offer courses in Italian, and if you live in a capital city you may have a government-sponsored Italian Institute on your doorstep.

Italian is a Romance language that developed from Latin. The standard written language is based on the dialect of Florence, but the spoken language differs from region to region.

Apart from being the national language of Italy, Italian is one of the official languages of Switzerland, and is spoken in France, close to the Italian border. In addition there are 1.5 million Italian speakers in the USA and a similar number in South America.

In the border areas in northern Italy you will come across other languages, including French, German, Slovenian, Ladino, and Friulian.

FORMS OF ADDRESS

As in many European languages, there are two words for "you": *lei* and *tu*. *Lei* is the polite, or formal version, which you use until you are invited to use the less formal *tu*. When addressing younger people the *tu* form is quite acceptable.

Do not use someone's first name until they invite you to do so. Address a man as *Signor*, followed by his surname, and a woman as *Signora*. *Signorina* may be used for a younger woman.

CONVERSATION

Italians enjoy talking, and are demonstrative communicators. They have no compunction about expressing their feelings or airing their grievances, and arguments can become quite heated. It helps if you are a good listener.

They can talk knowledgeably about most topics, including the arts, food, their region, and especially their local football team. It is best to listen politely and not contradict them, even if you strongly disagree.

Religion, politics, and the Second World War are best avoided, and in mixed company you should steer away from any risqué topics.

JOIN A CLUB

In the major cities you will find a number of expatriate and international clubs that offer opportunities to socialize not only with expatriates, but with Italians as well. These clubs often have their own premises and sports facilities. Otherwise, sports or fitness enthusiasts may wish to enroll in a gym or sports club, where regular attenders gradually get to know each other. If you attend a church each week you will soon meet the regular congregants.

EXPERIENCE THE NIGHTLIFE

Italy enjoys a Mediterranean climate, and Italians love to spend the evenings out of doors, strolling along the streets and piazzas, conversing with one another, and frequenting bars and restaurants. On occasions like this people are at their most relaxed, and therefore very approachable. There is also a lively club scene.

INVITATIONS HOME

There can be a downside to having new Italian friends, in that they will expect you to meet up with them on a regular basis, which might be a strain for anyone accustomed to having plenty of time to themselves. But in Italy that is what friends are for, and it would be considered churlish if you failed to turn up for weddings, funerals, birthdays, and so on. You cannot just drop out of a relationship for a while and then expect to revive it months later.

If you are invited to a person's home, you should regard it as a great honor. It means you are gaining an entry into their inner circle of friends.

It is advisable to dress formally and smartly, unless advised not to, and although punctuality is not vital you should avoid arriving very late. A gift for the hostess is always appreciated, such as good-quality chocolates or pastries, gift-wrapped. Flowers are also very acceptable, but do not bring chrysanthemums, which are associated with funerals. Italians tend to be knowledgeable about wines, so this may not be such a good idea, unless you are sure you are offering them a very superior vintage.

Eating and drinking commence when the host proposes a toast (*brindisi*) and everyone clinks glasses and says "*Salute!*" ("Cheers!"). After the party it is good manners to send a note of thanks, saying how much you enjoyed the occasion.

Daily Life

Clearly there will be differences in the way people live in different parts of Italy. Life in rural areas, and particularly in the south, will be more placid than it is in the cities and industrial centers. And in the prosperous north people generally enjoy a higher standard of living than their compatriots in the south, where the unemployment rate is double.

HOUSING

Although the birth rate is declining, Italy suffers from a housing shortage. Most city dwellers live in quite small rented apartments, which makes it difficult to uphold the tradition of the extended family. However, it is quite usual for several branches of the same family to live in the same neighborhood.

In the suburbs, the smaller towns, and the countryside people are far more likely to live in houses that they own, some of which may be large enough to accommodate three or four generations of the same family.

THE HOUSEHOLD

The large Italian family is now a thing of the past. Italy's birth rate is one of the lowest in Europe (after Spain), with many couples now opting to have just one child rather than several. Yet having a child is regarded as important, since it gives one a stake in society.

Italians adore children, especially their own, and spoil them dreadfully. Boys, in particular, are used to getting their own way and make a fuss when they don't. Parents are often very protective of their daughters, the more so in southern Italy, where girls are brought up strictly and are unlikely to be allowed out on a date without a chaperone. Despite the sometimes-lurid use of scantily clad models on Italian TV programs, many Italians have a guarded attitude to sex.

It is not unusual for children to live with their parents well into their twenties, or until they get married. With a housing shortage to contend with, it is sometimes a case of having to.

DAILY ROUTINE

A typical weekday starts with breakfast (*prima colazione*) at around 8:00 a.m., which is a light meal consisting of biscuits, croissants, and coffee or tea. After that parents go to work and children to school.

The Italians are enthusiastic shoppers, and make regular visits to markets, where they have access to plenty of good-quality fresh produce that is usually cheaper than that found in stores and supermarkets. Bargaining is quite usual. Supermarkets are much less common in Italy than in many other countries, as old shopping habits die hard.

Lunch begins at around 1:00 or 2:00 p.m., and can last as long as three hours in the south, where it is the largest meal of the day. Workers who cannot get home for the meal will spend less time over lunch; in the north shorter lunch breaks tend to be more usual.

Supper may start as early as 8:00 or as late as 10:00 p.m., and is usually a lighter meal than lunch.

Television is an important form of relaxation, and Italians are reputed to watch four hours of it a day—more than anywhere else in Europe. There are three TV channels run by the state broadcaster RAI, plus a number of commercial channels, many owned by Silvio Berlusconi, whom people accuse of using them to further his political ambitions. There are also satellite channels.

SHOPPING

Small shops open at around 8:30 a.m., but many, especially in the south, take an extended lunch break lasting up to three hours. Some stay open until 8:00 p.m. Supermarkets and department stores, however, tend to stay open all day. Banks open between 8:30 a.m. and 4:00 p.m., and some open on Saturday mornings, but opening times vary from place to place.

In Italy most transactions are in cash and many smaller establishments don't accept either credit or debit cards. Most banks have ATMs for withdrawals of money, which are called *bancomats*.

EDUCATION

Education is compulsory from the ages of six to fifteen, but many children attend infant school from the age of four. Children attend primary school until they are eleven, and middle school from eleven to fourteen. After obtaining the middle school diploma they have a choice of schools: a classical high school, a scientific high school, a linguistic high school, a technical high school, an art high school, a music conservatory, an academy of dance or drama, or a commercial institute. Pupils wishing to train as teachers attend the *istituto magistrale* or the *scuola magistrale*.

At the age of eighteen pupils take the *maturitá* examination, which enables them to go on to higher education and study for a *laurea*, which takes three years, plus an additional two years for a *laurea specialistica*. Italian universities are state-funded. Some of them date back many centuries, the oldest being the University of Bologna, founded in the eleventh century. However, a medical school at Salerno existed a century or so earlier.

THE ARMED FORCES

There is no compulsory military service; conscription was phased out in 2005, and Italy now has an all-volunteer military force.

NEWSPAPERS

Italians are not especially avid newspaper readers, and most rely on TV and radio for their news. Daily newspapers are regional and local, rather than national, and include *Il Corriere della Sera* in Milan (Italy's oldest newspaper, founded in 1876), *Il Giornale* (also based in Milan), *La Repubblica* (Rome), *La Stampa* (Turin),

and *Il Mattino* (Naples). The main business newspaper is *Il Sole 24 Ore* (Milan) and there is no popular press as such. *Panorama* and *L'Espresso* are highly regarded weekly news magazines, and the Catholic magazine *Famiglia Cristiana* has a wide readership.

MAIL AND TELECOMMUNICATIONS

The Italian mail service is not always reliable, and Italians opt for using registered mail or private couriers. Post offices are generally open from 8:30 a.m. to 6:30 p.m. on weekdays and may close at 1:00 p.m. on Saturdays. They offer a wide range of transactions, including foreign exchange. Postage stamps are available from tobacco kiosks (*tabacchi*) as well as post offices, which often have long lines of waiting customers.

The state telephone company, Telecom Italia, is responsible for the installation of telephone lines, but it is possible to use another provider. Telephone charges are among the highest in Europe. Italians also use cell phones extensively. To use an orange public telephone you need a phone card, but in some bars you may find a *telefono a scatti*, where you can make a call and pay the barman for the units you have used.

Leisure Time

Italians like to make the most of their leisure, and since the climate is warm for most of the year, they spend much of their time out of doors sitting outside bars and watching the world go by.

Italy is, of course, a renowned center of fashion, and if you want to go shopping you will find plenty of elegant boutiques. However, Italian clothes do not come cheap in these, or even in the department stores.

EATING OUT

Italians like to eat out as a family, and there is a range of establishments available, including the *ristorante* (restaurant) and the *trattoria*, which is a small, family-run restaurant with a more limited menu. The *taverna* or *osteria* is the simplest option. Most offer a choice between an à la carte menu and a cheaper and more restricted *menu turistico* or *menu a prezzo fisso* (fixed price). These establishments are normally open from 12:00 noon to 3:00 p.m. and 7.30 to 11:00 p.m. They are closed on one day a week.

The *pizzeria* is another option, as is the *rosticceria*, which serves meat roasted on a spit. A *tavola calda* is a bar serving hot food, and a *gelateria* is an ice cream parlor. Some wine shops also serve food.

A complete Italian meal normally proceeds along the following lines. First comes the starter (*antipasto*), which often consists of cold meats and marinated vegetables. Next is the first main dish (*primo*), which will be pasta, risotto, or soup. The second main dish (*secondo*) follows, which will be meat or fish. Cooked vegetables may be served with or after this dish. After that come cheese and fruit, followed by dessert and coffee.

Italians usually drink wine with their meal, often starting with an *aperitivo* of a light white wine, still or sparkling, progressing to a white or red wine with the meal, and then a *digestivo* (brandy or a liqueur) to round it off.

TIPPING

In restaurants a service charge of about 12 percent is added to the bill. Sometimes Italians leave a few euros for the waiter. It is customary to round a metered taxi fare up to the nearest euro.

FOOD

Italian food is varied and healthy, which is probably why Italians live to such a great age. Wherever you go you will find an abundance of fresh seafood and vegetables. Pasta dishes are especially popular in the south, whereas in the north risotto and polenta are more popular. Italy is renowned for its cheese (*formaggio*), notably p*armigiano Reggiano* (parmesan) from the Emilia Romagna region, *gorgonzola* and *grana padano* from Lombardy, *mozzarella* from Campania, *pecorino sardo* from Sardinia, and *fontino* from Piedmont.

Every region has its own local dishes, of which it is extremely proud. Here are a few highlights to sample on a gastronomic journey around the country:

pizza napoletana in Campania
minestrone alla genovese in Liguria
risotto alla milanese in Lombardy
fave a cicoria (dried broad bean purée with chicory) in Puglia
bistecca alla fiorentina (T-bone steak) in Tuscany
porchetta (roast piglet stuffed with rosemary) in Umbria
tagliatelle al ragú (pasta with meat) in Emiglia-Romagna
triglia alla livornese (mullet in tomato sauce) in Tuscany
amatriciana (tomato, bacon, and chilli sauce) in Lazio
canederli (noodle soup) in Trentino-Alto Adige

DRINK

The Greeks called Italy "Oenotria," the land of wine, and it ranks with France as the leading wine producer in Europe. As in France, there is a classification system for wines: DOCG, DOC, IGT and *vino da tavola*, in order of eminence.

The quality of even the lesser Italian wines has improved remarkably in recent decades, and most wine lovers are pleasantly surprised when they sample wines produced in the locality they are visiting. The country is especially famous for its red wines, such as Chianti, Barbaresco, Brunello di Montalcino, Gattinara, and Taurasi; but its white wines, such as Soave, Orvieto, and Pinot Grigio are gaining favor.

The Italians also make fortified wines and liqueurs, such as Marsala (a sweet wine from Sicily), Limoncello (a lemon liqueur from the Amalfi coast), and Amaretto (almond liqueur). Beers, such as Peroni and Moretti, are light lagers, and are sometimes obtainable on draft (*alla spina*).

Italians prefer to drink bottled mineral water rather than tapwater, and fresh or bottled fruit juices are obtainable everywhere.

Italy could also be known as the land of coffee, since Italians are avid coffee consumers. It is served in a number of different ways, the most popular being the following.

caffé espresso	a small, strong black coffee
caffé lungo	a longer drink, weaker than an *espresso*
caffé macchiato	black with a dash of milk
caffé latte	large with plenty of milk
cappuccino	coffee with frothy milk
caffé freddo	iced black coffee
caffé corretto	black coffee with a liqueur added

CULTURE AND ENTERTAINMENT

Nearly every town of note has its own opera house, of which La Scala in Milan, the Teatro San Carlo in Naples, La Fenice in Venice, the Teatro Massimo in Palermo, and the Teatro dell'Opera in Rome are the most celebrated. In the summer opera moves into the open air—to the amphitheatre in Verona, for instance, which can seat an audience of 25,000.

Open-air concert in the piazza in front of the Duomo, Spoleto, Umbria

Apart from opera, there are plenty of theaters where one can see plays by renowned dramatists such as Dario Fo and Luigi Pirandello. Classical music concerts are held regularly all over Italy, and there are a number of summer festivals, such as the Festival of Two Worlds in Spoleto, and Umbria Jazz in Perugia.

Cinemagoing continues to be popular. Italy has, over the years, produced many outstanding film directors—notably Federico Fellini, Michelangelo Antonioni, Luchino Visconti, and Vittorio de Sica, as well as Sergio Leone, responsible for a series of "spaghetti Westerns." The famous Venice International Film Festival takes place annually in August.

STUDENTS, CLUBBING, AND CLOSE ENCOUNTERS

Rome doesn't see the real fun start until after dinner. Many bars and cafés are open until 1:00 or 2:00 a.m., and sometimes have live or canned music. Clubs, known as *discoteche*, don't usually open until 10:00 p.m. or later, and carry on into the early hours.

The wine bars and cafés around Piazza Navona and Via della Pace tend to be the most chic, while there's a bustling scene with a more mainstream vibe around Campo de Fiori. Irish pubs are popular with Italians and expats, with a few choices around Monti district, which also has some other bars.

The biggest concentration of nightclubs lies in the Testaccio and Ostiense districts. You will find bars, pubs, live music venues, and clubs. It is not rare to spot the new trend of resto-bars, the so-called *ristodisco*, where you can eat and dance.

There is a gay scene with some saunas and clubs, and many nightclubs have weekly gay nights.

The weekly *Roma C'è* publication (out on Wednesdays, also online) is a good source of information on Rome's nightlife.

For something a little different, visit the Centri Sociali squatter arts venues that are often located away from the center. One of the most cutting-edge locations for live music is Brancaleone, attracting an alternative and dressed-down crowd with concerts, film showings, art exhibitions, and club nights.

With their big reputations as great lovers and snappy dressers, the Italians are firm believers in passion and romance, and pride themselves on their appearance. Generally, Italian men have an ongoing relationship with the woman they plan to marry and provide for while having casual dates with others before actually tying the knot. Italian women also engage in lighthearted relationships and affairs with men.

Gender roles are heavily ingrained in the Italian psyche, so it may come as no surprise that dating is led by the man. These roles are best adhered to at the beginning of a new relationship, so that the male or female Italian will feel comfortable. Males are chivalrous; they will open doors, pay for things, and ask for a kiss. And women should respond to a man's ego in kind—laugh at his jokes or make some witty comebacks!

Italians believe you can meet "the right one" almost anywhere. They find their dates in the piazza, at the beach, on the ski slopes, at school, at work, in a nightclub, through their families, or next door. Shared interests such as a love of soccer or Latin dance, which is becoming popular in Italy, often help to spark romance.

SPORTS

Italians enjoy sports, particularly soccer. The country has produced some of the world's most talented footballers, and boasts some of Europe's leading teams, such as Juventus, AC Milan, and Lazio. The most successful teams come from the north and have armies of followers.

With so many Alpine skiing resorts in the north of the country, Italians love winter sports; and the long coastline and many lakes are perfect for sailing, swimming, windsurfing, and other aquatic sports. Formula 1 motor racing is a popular spectator sport—not surprisingly, perhaps, considering one of the leading sports car manufacturers, Ferrari, is Italian. Italy can also boast success in cycling.

Spring and summer bring everyone on to the beach, where swimming and water sports are popular.

Getting Around

Italy has an extensive state railway network, Trenitalia, which connects most places and is reasonably priced. Fares differ according to the type of train. On the ETR 450 and Eurostar (Italia) seats must be booked in advance, and a supplement is payable. *Espresso* and *diretto* trains do not incur a supplement; they stop at the main stations only, while the *locale* is a slow train that stops everywhere.

There are various discounted fares on offer, but if you buy your ticket on the train you face a 20 percent surcharge. Tickets must be validated on a machine on the station platform before boarding the train.

Santa Giustina railway bridge, Trentino-Alto-Adige

The intercity coach services offer a cheaper alternative to train travel, and there are excellent ferry services between the mainland and the islands and on the lakes. Buy tickets from a booking kiosk.

URBAN TRANSPORTATION

You will find subways (*Metropolitana*) in Genoa, Milan, Naples, Palermo, and Rome. Metro tickets can also be bought at tobacconists and newsstands, and last for sixty to seventy-five minutes from the time of validation. It is cheaper to buy a book of ten tickets or a one-day or weekly travel pass.

In all cities except Rome these tickets can also be used on buses. As you enter the bus you have to validate your ticket in a machine. You will see that people don't wait in an orderly line, but surge forward as the bus arrives.

You can find a taxi at a taxi stand or by calling. Tip by rounding the metered fare up to the nearest euro.

DRIVING

Traffic tends to get very congested, especially in cities such as Naples and Florence. Fortunately, some city centers have been turned into traffic-free zones.

Italian drivers may be fast and skillful, but show little consideration to other road users and break all the rules, including speed limits. The top speed on expressways (*autostrade*) is 130 kmph (80 mph), on open roads 110 kmph (68 mph), and in built-up areas 50 kmph (31 mph). Most of the expressways are toll roads; you take a ticket when you enter and pay when you exit.

Drivers must use dipped headlights at all times, even during the daytime. Children must wear seat belts, and young children must have a special seat. The drink driving limit is 0.5 mg per ml. The police (*carabinieri*) and traffic police (*polizia stradale*) are empowered to issue demands for fines on the spot for speeding, or for not carrying your driver's license, the car's registration document, a fluorescent jacket, or a warning triangle in your car.

Drivers with an EU driver's license who become resident will need to apply for an Italian license if they are planning on staying more than a year.

WHERE TO STAY

Italy offers a wide range of places to stay, particularly in the main cities and tourist resorts, and rates often vary according to the time of year. There is often little to choose between an *albergo* (hotel) and a *pensione* (guest house), which is usually family owned. Both have a star rating system.

Other options are *locande* (inns), *affittacamere* (rooms in private houses), and religious establishments. Several convents and monasteries offer hospitality to tourists at modest rates, and you do not have to take a vow of celibacy before taking up the offer!

Italy has a well-developed network of *ostelli per la gioventú* (youth hostels), though some can be very spartan, and everywhere you will find campsites. Walkers in the Alps and Apennines have recourse to mountain huts known as *rifugi* (refuges), many of which are run by the Alpine Club of Italy.

MEDICAL MATTERS

The Italian state health service is good in parts. All visitors are entitled to free emergency medical treatment in a public hospital. EU citizens have access to the same range of medical services as the Italians on production of their European Health Insurance Card, but not everything will be free. The Unita Sanitaria Locale (local health unit) can provide you with the necessary information. Some form of private medical insurance is advisable.

SAFETY

Italy is a relatively safe place, but cities like Rome and Naples and other places on the tourist beat attract petty thieves and pickpockets, so care needs to be taken, especially in crowds. Young women traveling alone in some tourist spots, and especially in the south of the country, may find themselves pestered by young males, which may be flattering at first but can become a nuisance. The best policy is to ignore them and walk away.

PLACES TO VISIT

Rome, the Eternal City, is a
must for all visitors to Italy
with its architectural legacy
stretching over two
millennia. Here you will
find the ruins of the
Roman Forum and the
Colosseum. The Trevi Fountain,

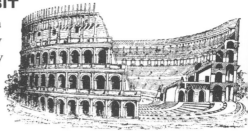

the Piazza di Spagna with the Spanish Steps, and the Villa
Borghese and its museum are among the city's chief delights.

In the heart of Rome lies Vatican City, a small enclave covering
an area of only 110 acres (0.4 sq. km), which is the base for the
central administration of the Roman Catholic Church. Its main
attractions are St. Peter's Basilica and a museum housing the
Sistine Chapel and countless art treasures. This is all that is left of
the Papal States, established by Pope Innocent II, that once
stretched from the Tyrrhenian Sea to the Adriatic.

Florence, the capital of Tuscany, is full of Renaissance treasures
that include the Tuscan Gothic cathedral of Santa Maria del Fiore,
with its giant dome designed by Brunelleschi, San Lorenzo
Church by the same architect, Giotto's Campanile, the Baptistry of
San Giovanni with its famous East Door, and the 700-year-old
Palazzo Vecchio, still in use as the City Hall. The Tuscan city
of Pisa, famous for the *campanile* of its twelfth-century
Gothic cathedral—the Leaning Tower of Pisa—was the
birthplace of Galileo.

Venice, the former city-republic that grew to dominate
the Adriatic in the sixteenth century, has a number of
attractions, not least its extensive canal network. The
Piazza San Marco, with St. Mark's Basilica, is a magnet
for many tourists, as also is the Palazzo Ducale (the
Doge's Palace), with its remarkable art collection.

Naples is often regarded as the capital of the south
of Italy, and has an extensive National Museum
containing Greek and Roman artworks. It is close
to the Roman cities of Pompeii and Herculaneum,
which were buried when Mount Vesuvius erupted
in 79 CE, and the beautiful islands of Capri
and Ischia.

Bay of Naples with Mount Vesuvius

Italy has many other cities, all fascinating in their own right. Milan is the business centre of the country, but also has the world's second-largest cathedral and one of its greatest opera houses. Bologna is home to Europe's oldest university, the Church of San Petronio, and the eleventh-century Torre degli Astinelli. If you want to venture further back in time, take a trip to Ravenna to see the sixth-century Byzantine Church of San Vitale.

Visitors are asked to bear in mind that churches and cathedrals are places of worship, and one should respect convention and dress appropriately when entering one. Women are no longer obliged to cover their heads; but both men and women are expected to be decently covered and not to wear casual clothing such as shorts or baseball caps.

Business and Professional Life

Italy, like Germany, has experienced an economic miracle, thanks in no small part to the dynamism of its family firms. It is considered one of Europe's leading economies, and may be even larger than estimates suggest if the black economy (unreported in statistics or tax returns) is taken into account.

Some of the family firms, such as Fiat, Benetton, Versace, Armani, and Pirelli, are enormous, and the families enjoy considerable prestige. Italy also has a substantial state-owned industrial sector, with political appointees in many of the most influential positions.

BUSINESS ETIQUETTE

Italians appreciate good manners and courtesy, and visiting businesspeople will do well to be on their best behavior and treat everyone with consideration.

The further north you go in Italy, the more formally people will behave. It is customary everywhere, however, to shake hands both on meeting and on taking leave. If you are meeting a group of people you need to ensure you leave nobody out. As a business relationship develops, greetings may become more cordial. If an embrace replaces the handshake, that means the relationship is well and truly established. Visitors who are unaccustomed to such shows of affection in a business relationship may find this off-putting, but do avoid stepping back, or you may be thought cold and unwelcoming.

Remember the formal forms of address, as described on page 297. Note also that the title *Dottore,* or *Dottoressa,* should be used where appropriate for senior graduates.

BUSINESS STRUCTURE

Italian managers have a much more comprehensive remit than their counterparts in northern Europe. They not only have to run the business and keep an eye on the bottom line, but they are expected to look after their employees' welfare as well. An employee with a problem will always look to his boss to sort things out.

This paternalistic approach is obviously much easier in family companies, where the head of the firm may well have known his or her employees since childhood. However, it permeates Italian organizations, which tend to focus as much on people as on business strategy.

SETTING UP A MEETING

Good relationships are of paramount importance to Italians. They prefer to do business with people they know rather than with complete strangers, so it makes sense to use whatever contacts you have to effect introductions for you.

It is best to make arrangements in writing and to follow the letter up with a phone call or e-mail. The best times for a meeting are mid-morning, from 10:00 a.m., or mid-afternoon, after 3:00 p.m., since some companies have a lengthy lunch break.

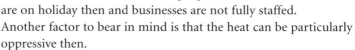

The month of August is not a sensible time for a business visit, as most people are on holiday then and businesses are not fully staffed. Another factor to bear in mind is that the heat can be particularly oppressive then.

If you want to impress your hosts, you should dress stylishly— and this goes for both men and women. Italians tend to judge people by the clothes they are wearing, and first impressions are important. Also take with you plenty of documentation, written in Italian if possible, which will impress them even if they do not take the trouble to read it.

MEETINGS

Although the Italians are more flexible about time than other Europeans, you should endeavor to arrive in good time for a meeting. To do otherwise, unless you have a very good excuse, could suggest sloppiness on your part.

Don't expect to get down to brass tacks right at the beginning. The first five minutes at least will be devoted to an exchange of pleasantries and general discussion. This is the means whereby your hosts get to know you better, which is an important part of doing business in Italy.

Meetings tend to be informal affairs, with no agenda to speak of. Italians are sometimes accused of preferring style to substance. They do, however, like to go carefully into the details of any proposal, and this can take some time, particularly as there may be many people involved who all like to have a hand in the discussions.

PRESENTATIONS

Any presentation you make must be stylish and eloquent, but if it is not supported by some convincing arguments or facts, they may well call your bluff. At the end of the session it is quite likely that they will wish to take your proposals away and analyze them carefully. Offer them as much written information as possible, and make sure it is clearly and neatly presented.

DECISIONS

Italians like to take their time considering proposals, and it would be optimistic to expect instant decisions. If you try to hurry them along or suggest deadlines it will only antagonize the people you are hoping to convince.

BUSINESS ENTERTAINING

Italians often combine business with pleasure, and a meal is regarded as an ideal way with which to conclude a business deal. You should expect invitations to lunch or dinner, and also to issue invitations yourself.

If you are hosting the occasion it is sensible to ask your business colleague's secretary to recommend a restaurant that would meet with her boss's approval. The most important guest usually sits either at the middle of the table or on the right of the host.

WOMEN IN BUSINESS

There are relatively few women in managerial positions, but the situation is changing, particularly in the north of Italy, where women form a larger proportion of the workforce. In small family firms, however, it is quite usual for female members of the family to play a prominent role.

In the professions, women are making their mark, notably in academia. It is worth remembering that women were admitted to universities as students and teachers as long ago as the eighteenth century—considerably earlier than in many other European countries.

If you are a visiting businesswoman you will be treated courteously. You will not encounter any male chauvinism, and if you have sensible, logical proposals you will be listened to with respect.

Chapter 8

THE NETHERLANDS

Key Facts

Official Name	Koninkrijk der Nederlanden (Kingdom of the Netherlands). Short form: Nederland	**Government**	Constitutional monarchy, with a bicameral parliament, the Staten-Generaal. Members of the upper house, or First Chamber, are elected by the country's twelve provincial councils. Members of the Second Chamber are directly elected every four years by proportional representation.
Capital City	Amsterdam		
Major Cities	Den Haag (The Hague), Rotterdam, Utrecht, Maastricht		
Area	16,036 sq. miles (41,534 sq. km)		
Terrain	Mostly coastal lowland and reclaimed land (polders). Nearly 25% is below sea level. Some hills in the southeast	**Radio and TV**	The Netherlands Broadcasting Association coordinates broadcasting. The PAL B system is used for TV transmissions.
Climate	Temperate with relatively mild winters		
Currency	Euro	**Press**	*De Volkskrant, De Telegraaf, NRC Handelsblad*
Population	16.7 million. The most heavily populated country per square mile in Europe	**English-language Media**	Several publications cater to expatriates and businesspeople.
Ethnic Makeup	Dutch 81%; other European 5%; Indonesian, Turkish, Moroccan, Caribbean, and Surinamese 14%	**Electricity**	220 volts, 50 Hz. Two-prong plugs used
		Internet Domain	.nl
Language	Dutch, Frisian	**Telephone**	Country code 31. For international calls dial 00.
Religion	Unaffiliated 42%; Catholic 30%; Dutch Reformed 11%; Calvinist 6%; other Protestant 3%; Muslim 6%; other 2%	**Time Zone**	CET (GMT/UTC +1) with daylight saving in the summer

Map of the Netherlands

The Country and Its People

> "God made the world, but the Dutch made Holland."

The Netherlands, to give the country its official name, is in northeastern Europe and straddles the mouths of three great European rivers: the Rhine (Rijn), Meuse (Maas), and Scheldt. To the east lies Germany, to the south Belgium, and to the north and west the North Sea, with a coastline 280 miles (451 km) long.

"Nederlanden" means lowlands, and the country is in fact so low-lying that nearly 25 percent of it is below sea level. The Dutch have a reputation for being resourceful—and they have needed to be, in order to protect their country from encroachment by the North Sea. Hence the elaborate system of dikes, the first of which

was built in the early thirteenth century. There are, however, hilly areas the further southeast you go. The climate is temperate, and it rains frequently. In January and February it sometimes gets cold enough for the canals to freeze over.

Occupying an area of 16,033 square miles (41,526 sq. km), the Netherlands is the most densely populated country in Europe. Many of its residents are concentrated in the great conurbation of Amsterdam, The Hague (Den Haag), Rotterdam, Utrecht, and their surrounding towns, known as the Randstad, which is the entrepreneurial powerhouse of the country. But there is also a more traditional rural hinterland.

This is the country that produced the humanists Erasmus and Grotius, and painters of the caliber of Rembrandt, Vermeer, Franz Hals, Van Gogh, and Mondriaan. The Dutch also established a global empire, and founded a number of international companies that have become household names today. Intelligent, cosmopolitan, outward-looking, enterprising, tolerant, and modest, with a strong concern for justice and human rights, they are people worth getting to know,

A HISTORICAL PERSPECTIVE

In Roman times the area we now call the Netherlands was populated by Batavians and Frisians, both Germanic tribes. After the fall of Rome, Saxons settled the east while the Franks overran the south. By the eighth century the Franks had imposed Christianity on almost all the country.

The Emperor Charlemagne installed counts and princes to administer different areas of the Netherlands, but after his death several feudal lords asserted their independence, and it was not until 925 that the whole of the Netherlands was incorporated into the Holy Roman Empire.

In the fifteenth century the Low Countries (today's Netherlands, Belgium, and Luxembourg) came under the rule of the Dukes of Burgundy. A number of towns, notably Bruges, Antwerp, and later Amsterdam, had become important centers for trade, were virtually self-governing, and were sufficiently powerful to resist efforts to impose control from the center. Amsterdam became the primary trading port in Europe for grain from the Baltic region, which it distributed to the major cities of Belgium, northern France, and England.

In the sixteenth century, through inheritance and conquest, the Low Countries became possessions of the Habsburg dynasty under Charles V. In 1549, Charles, now Holy Roman Emperor, granted the Seventeen Provinces of the Netherlands status as a unified entity, separate from both the Empire and France. On the division of the Habsburg domains in 1555, however, the Netherlands passed to Spain.

This was a time when the Roman Catholic Church was under attack from the Protestant reformers, and Charles sought to reassert the Church's authority throughout the Empire, including the Low Countries, introducing the Inquisition and the death penalty for all heresy.

The Struggle for Independence

Charles' son, Philip II of Spain, appointed mainly Protestant Dutch nobles as *stadhouders* (stewards, or place holders) to govern the Dutch provinces, but his rule was harsh and remote. A group of nobles presented a request for more lenient treatment, without success.

By now the ideas of Calvin and other reformers had taken root and Protestant mobs began attacking Catholic churches. Philip retaliated by sending in an army to put down dissent, and large-scale executions resulted.

One of the *stadhouders*, William of Nassau, Prince of Orange, refused to renew his allegiance to Philip in 1567, and conspired to free the Netherlands from Spanish rule. The Spanish under the Duke of Alba inflicted heavy defeats on his rebel army, so William took to the high seas where he and his so-called "Sea Robbers" raided Spanish merchant ships.

Slowly but surely, he began to make headway. In 1579 the seven northern rebel provinces signed a treaty, the Union of Utrecht, which is regarded as the foundation charter of the Dutch Republic, and two years later declared their independence. Eventually, in 1648, Spain recognized Dutch independence but kept the Catholic south, which would eventually become Belgium.

Expansion and Occupation

The Dutch Republic was governed by an aristocracy of city-merchants called the regents. Its cities and provinces were self-governing with a large degree of autonomy. Sovereignty lay in the various provincial assemblies and in the Estates-General, in which representatives from the provinces decided on matters important to the Republic as a whole. The function of the office of *stadhouder* changed from feudal representative to that of the highest executive official of each province, albeit with extra prerogatives. In time the office became hereditary and the preserve of the House of Orange.

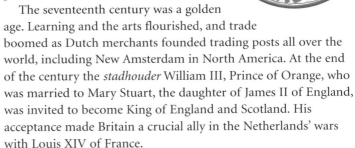

The seventeenth century was a golden age. Learning and the arts flourished, and trade boomed as Dutch merchants founded trading posts all over the world, including New Amsterdam in North America. At the end of the century the *stadhouder* William III, Prince of Orange, who was married to Mary Stuart, the daughter of James II of England, was invited to become King of England and Scotland. His acceptance made Britain a crucial ally in the Netherlands' wars with Louis XIV of France.

The following century saw clamor for greater democracy from the Patriots, a group of reformers inspired by the rebellion against British rule in America; the movement was crushed with Prussian military help. In 1795 the armies of revolutionary France invaded and set up the Batavian Republic, giving the Dutch a brief taste of democracy. In 1806 Napoleon created the Kingdom of Holland, installing his brother Louis Bonaparte as king.

At the Congress of Vienna in 1815 the original seventeen states of the Low Countries were merged into the United Kingdom of the Netherlands under King William I, son of the last *stadhouder*. Differences soon emerged and eventually, in 1830, the Catholic southern states seceded to become Belgium. After that the country prospered and modernized both its industry and its institutions.

The Netherlands remained neutral during the First World War, but Germany refused to acknowledge its neutrality in the Second World War and bombed it into submission. The country emerged from the war in a very sorry state.

KEY HISTORICAL DATES

925	The Netherlands incorporated into the Holy Roman Empire.
1300	Amsterdam gains city status.
1464	Regional assemblies meeting as the States-General resist Philip the Good of Burgundy's centralizing policies.
1519	Emperor Charles V unites the Netherlands.
1530	Charles V becomes Holy Roman Emperor and introduces the Inquisition into the Netherlands to suppress Protestantism.
1568 and	William I, Prince of Orange, begins a struggle for independence religious freedom.
1579	The northern provinces conclude the Union of Utrecht. The Catholic south remains loyal to Spain.
1561	In the Act of Abjuration they declare their independence from Spain.
1759	Union of Utrecht creates the United Provinces of the Netherlands.
1602	The Dutch East India Company is founded and Dutch merchants begin to establish trading colonies worldwide.
1648	Peace of Westphalia. Spain acknowledges independence of the Dutch Republic.
1677	William III, Prince of Orange and *stadhouder*, marries Mary, daughter of the English King James II.
1688	William and Mary are formally offered the English throne.
1689	William becomes King of England.
1795	Revolutionary French invade the Netherlands, which Napoleon later incorporates into the French Empire.
1815	After Napoleon's defeat the seventeen provinces of the Netherlands are reunited under King William I.
1830	Belgium secedes from the grouping.
1848	William II agrees to democratic reforms.
1939–45	Second World War. Netherlands is invaded by Germany, despite its declaration of neutrality.
1948	Benelux customs union is formed.
1952	Netherlands becomes a founder member of the European Coal and Steel Community.
1958	The European Economic Community is formed.
2002	The Dutch guilder is replaced by the euro.

The Netherlands Today

The country was devastated by the Second World War, but with help from America's Marshall Plan the Dutch worked hard to reestablish themselves, and succeeded.

In 1948 they formed a customs union with Belgium and Luxembourg. The following year they joined NATO, and in 1952 the European Steel and Coal Community. In 1958 the country became one of the founder members of the European Economic

Community, which at the Treaty of Maastricht in 1991 became the European Union. The prosperity that resulted from the economic recovery enabled the government to fund social programs and create a paternalistic welfare state.

The 1960s also saw a reaction against the staid Calvinist attitudes of the past and the liberalization of laws regarding homosexuality, divorce, abortion, soft drugs, prostitution, and euthanasia. The role of the individual became more important and traditional social bonds were loosened.

The economic resurgence led to labor shortages. An influx of immigrants helped to overcome this difficulty, but created new social problems, particularly when unemployment started to rise. The initial relaxed policy of multiculturalism, in which the country incorporated foreign cultures into its way of life, has now been superseded by one that encourages immigrants to assimilate into Dutch society.

GOVERNMENT

Since 1848 the Netherlands has been a constitutional monarchy. Queen Beatrix is the current head of state, and it is she who appoints the prime minister.

The Hague is the seat of government and the administrative center of the country. The parliament, known as the States-General (Staten-Generaal), has two chambers. The First Chamber (Eerste Kamer, or Senaat) comprises seventy-five members elected for four years by the provincial assemblies; and the Second Chamber (Tweede Kamer) has 150 members directly elected every four years by proportional representation.

There are twelve provinces: Drenthe, Flevoland, Friesland (Fryslan), Gelderland, Groningen, Limburg, Noord-Brabant, Noord-Holland, Overijssel, Utrecht, Zeeland, and Zuid-Holland.

Values and Attitudes

Dutch people usually make a favorable impression on outsiders. They are neither pushy nor arrogant. They seem quiet, unobtrusive people, who don't insist on getting their own way, can be relied on to carry out their duties in an exemplary fashion, and never make a fuss. How is it that they appear to be such paragons? The answer, strange to relate, lies in religion. Considering that a large number of Dutch people nowadays profess no religious beliefs at all, this may seem an odd claim. But back in the sixteenth century the ideas of the French-born Swiss Protestant theologian Jean Calvin attracted many adherents.

Calvin's doctrine of predestination, his insistence on a strict moral code, his contention that all men are equal and should accept their place in the world, and his belief that individuals should help others and strive to improve themselves, struck a chord. His ideas appealed to the wealthy burghers, who were the opinion-formers of the time. They liked Calvin's proposed separation of Church from state, and objected to paying exorbitant taxes to the Church and a Spanish king.

RELIGION

Despite the fact that church attendance has declined drastically since the heady days of the Reformation in the sixteenth century, nearly 60 percent of the population profess allegiance to a religious faith.

Although the predominantly Roman Catholic part of the country seceded in 1830 eventually to become Belgium, there is still a sizable Catholic community in the Netherlands that tends to

be more liberal and less rigid in outlook than Catholics elsewhere in Europe—perhaps due to Calvinist and Humanist influences.

The main Protestant Church is the Reformed Church (Nederlands Herformde Kerk), which is the direct descendant of the Dutch Reformed Church founded in the sixteenth century. Its followers profess fairly liberal mainstream views, though perhaps not as liberal as those of the Lutherans across the border in Germany.

The other significant Church is the Gereformeerde Kerk, which split off from the Reformed Church in the nineteenth century when a neo-Calvinist scholar, Abraham Kuyper, advocated a return to the strict Calvinist principles of the Reformation. Its adherents refrain from work on Sundays and aim to follow biblical teachings to the letter.

HUMANISM

There is another influence at work on the Dutch character that is also rooted in history: humanist ideas, and in particular the teachings of the great scholar Erasmus, who believed that mankind was intrinsically good, and who advocated non-violence and a humane outlook. Confrontation

should be avoided; instead one should strive to reach consensus.

EGALITARIANISIM AND CONFORMITY

How, then, do these principles play out in people's lives? There is no great divide between rich and poor in the Netherlands, or certainly not one that you would notice. It stems from the Calvinist teaching that all men are equal in the sight of God and that riches are meaningless. People deserve to be treated with respect and to be regarded as equal partners.

Living cheek-by-jowl in a small country means that you need to be careful not to rock the boat. It is regarded as unseemly to try and grab attention, because this would imply you are claiming to be superior. Conforming to the social norms is regarded as essential for the wellbeing of society.

VERZUILING

This is an unusual concept peculiar to the Dutch, often translated as "pillarization" or "columnization." It evolved in the nineteenth century, when Dutch society split along religious lines into separate communities that coexisted alongside one another, like the pillars holding up the roof of an edifice.

Each "pillar" contained a spectrum of social classes and ran its own institutions, including schools, churches, political parties, and even sports clubs. It was felt that separate development would help to reduce friction between people of different persuasions.

Although this concept is no longer a force to be reckoned with, *verzuiling* continues in the education system, with many private schools operated by interest groups but financed by the state.

MODESTY AND RESERVE

The Dutch have much to be proud of—including their business prowess, their democratic institutions, and their resourcefulness—but they prefer not to draw attention to themselves. They are, on the whole, modest folk.

To strangers they may appear reserved and formal. They exercise considerable self-control and avoid discussion of matters of a personal nature. Excessive displays of emotion are regarded with disapproval, and are associated with superficiality and insincerity.

However, that does not mean that the Dutch never let their hair down; in the company of friends they can be extremely relaxed and can get boisterous. "*Gezellig*" is the word they use to describe this feeling of warmth and comradeship.

DISCIPLINE AND THRIFT.

Hard work and resourcefulness are key to the Netherlands' success. Throughout history the Dutch have had a struggle on their hands—against the threat from the sea, and against occupation by a succession of conquerors.

They set about taming the North Sea, and reclaimed large tracts of land from it through a network of dikes. Their hydrological engineers are considered the best in the world.

The Dutch are also shrewd businessmen who used their trading acumen and nautical skills to establish a thriving maritime overseas empire. Today the Netherlands remains a leading trading nation, exerting considerable influence on global commerce.

Yet they are keenly aware that good fortune does not always last. This is why they prefer to put some of their earnings aside, and are unlikely to go out on wild spending sprees. They dislike extravagance and waste, and are strong advocates of recycling.

CLEANLINESS

Visitors to the Netherlands are always impressed by the cleanliness and tidiness of the towns and houses. Housewives endeavor to keep their houses spick-and-span; those who don't are likely to be told off. The origins of this practice lie, of course, in the Calvinist belief that cleanliness is next to godliness.

TOLERANCE

This is an extremely tolerant society. The Dutch are prepared to tolerate views that are at variance with their own and to accommodate them in order to achieve some form of consensus.

This pragmatic approach is exemplified by the "pillarization" concept, according to which it was acceptable for different communities to develop side-by-side, and by the policy of multiculturalism that was initially applied to its immigrant population.

They are open-minded where sex is concerned, and are also tolerant toward drug use and euthanasia—while not necessarily condoning these practices.

SENSE OF COMMUNITY

Community spirit is strong in the Netherlands, where nearly everyone gets involved in some form of communal activity. Participation helps to maintain social harmony, and those who opt out run the risk of being regarded with suspicion or disdain.

Concern for the less fortunate, such as vulnerable members of society, has led to the establishment of support groups, often staffed by volunteers. Everybody is encouraged to make a contribution to the wellbeing of the greater community.

The country has not been unaffected by outside influences and changing fashions. Dutch society is perceived as being more permissive and consumerist than it once was. But the way the majority of people live their lives has not changed dramatically. They may have more cash to spend, but their sense of social responsibility and concern for justice and fairness persist.

Festivals and Traditions

As in other European countries, many of the public holidays have religious origins; but there are other festivals, unique to the Netherlands. Some of these provide an opportunity for people to visit places of interest; others are communal celebrations.

HOLIDAYS AND FESTIVALS

January 1	Nieuwjaarsdag	New Year's Day
February	Carnaval	Carnival
March/April	Goede Vrijdag	Good Friday
March/April	Eerste Paasdag	Easter Sunday
March/April	Tweede Paasdag	Easter Monday
April 30	Koninginnedag	Queen's Day
May 1	Dag van de Arbeid	Labor Day
May 4	Dodenherdenking	Remembrance Day
May 5	Bevrijdingsdag	Liberation Day
May/June	Hemelvaartsdag	Ascension Day
Second Saturday in May	Nationale Molendag	National Windmill Day
Late May	Vlaggetjesdag	"Flag Day" celebrating the first herring catch
May/June	Tweede Pinksterdag	Whit Monday
November 11	Sint Maarten's Dag	St. Martin's Day
December 5	Sinterklaas	St. Nicholas's Day
December 25	Eerste Kerstdag	Christmas Day
December 26	Tweede Kerstdag	Boxing Day

THE FESTIVE YEAR

New Year

New Year's Eve is the occasion for much jollity and fireworks. People drink a toast and shake hands at midnight before going out to a street gathering to set off fireworks. Apple fritters (*appelflappen*) and doughnuts filled with raisins (*olliebollen*) are typical New Year's fare.

Carnival

The weekend before the beginning of Lent is given over to parties and merrymaking, particularly in the Catholic communities. Parades are held, with all the participants in bright costumes. The festivities in Noord-Brabant, Limburg, Amsterdam, and The Hague are particularly notable.

April Fool's Day

As in Britain and in Germany, this is a day for playing tricks on people to make an "April fool" of them.

Queen's Day

This is a public holiday that commemorates the birthday of

Queen Juliana of the Netherlands, who reigned from 1948 to 1980, when she abdicated voluntarily in favor of her daughter Beatrix.

People fly the tricolor and festoon their houses with the orange ensign of the royal House of Orange. Many towns hold fairs at which families put up stalls and sell off their unwanted odds and ends, reflecting the Dutch passion for recycling.

The Queen and her family pay official visits to at least two towns on this day, when you will hear the Dutch National Anthem being played.

Dressing up as royalty

Remembrance Day

May 4 is the day when the Dutch remember those killed in the Second World War. Flags are flown at half-mast; memorial services are held; and at 8:00 p.m. a two-minute silence is observed.

Liberation Day

May 5 commemorates the liberation of the Netherlands by Allied forces in 1945. Flags are flown again, but not at half-mast.

National Windmill Day

Many of the country's working
windmills fly a blue pennant on this
day and are are open to the
public, often with
demonstrations.

Vlaggetjesdag

At the end of May in Scheveningen,
The Hague, the Dutch celebrate the first
herring catch of the season—in a big way. Go along and join in!
See the boats race in, sample a delicious fresh herring, watch the
dancing, and enjoy the many other sights and sounds.

State Opening of Parliament

The third Tuesday in September is always a festive occasion, when
the Queen rides in a golden coach from her palace to open
parliament in The Hague.

St. Nicholas' Eve

One Dutch name that has entered the vocabulary of many
languages is Sinterklaas, better known in the English-speaking
world as Santa Claus. Dutch settlers took this tradition with them
to the United States, and it took root in New Amsterdam (later,
New York).

In the USA the tradition has become part of Christmas, but in
the Netherlands it is observed in early December, when Sinterklaas
visits the major towns, riding a white horse and accompanied by his
servants, the Black Peters (Zwarte Pieten), who throw sweets to the
children and play music.

During the period leading up to St. Nicholas' Eve children put
out a shoe when they go to bed, which Sinterklaas fills with sweets.
The climax occurs on St. Nicholas' Eve (*pakjesavond*, or "presents
evening"), when gifts are exchanged. These are often accompanied
by a poem, supposedly written by Sinterklaas or his assistants,
describing the good and bad points of the recipients' characters.

Christmas

Christmas is traditionally more low-key than St. Nicholas' Eve, with
greater focus on Christ's nativity. People usually have a Christmas

tree in their homes, and many attend Christmas services at church and exchange small presents and cards.

FAMILY OCCASIONS

The family is at the center of life for most Dutch people, who make the most of family occasions. The birth of a child is announced to the neighborhood by decking out the house with blue or pink flags, as appropriate, and a large cardboard stork displaying the name, date of birth, and weight of the new member of the family. Many parents send out cards announcing the birth and inviting people to drop by at certain times. Visitors normally take a small gift for the baby and flowers for the mother.

Weddings take place in the local town hall (*gemeentehuis* or *stadhuis*), and some couples opt for a church wedding after the civil ceremony. A celebratory meal is usually held for the family and a larger party for friends and more distant relatives.

Birthdays are important occasions for celebration, and this will often take the form of an "at home" day. People call, often bringing small gifts, and are served coffee and cake. Alcoholic drinks and savory snacks may follow.

A fiftieth birthday is particularly significant, since it shows that the person has attained maturity and wisdom and can be known as an "Abraham" (for a man) or a "Sarah" (for a woman).

Funerals are important family occasions, when relatives and friends of the deceased gather to pay their respects, often in a church. People dress soberly, but not necessarily in black.

Getting to Know the Dutch

On the whole the Dutch are friendly, sociable people who like to make visitors feel welcome. Living in close proximity to one another, they have learned the importance of establishing harmonious relations with others.

Admittedly, rural folk may not take to strangers immediately, and busy city dwellers often have little spare time to develop relationships, but by and large in the Netherlands you are on friendly territory.

MEETING PEOPLE

Unlike some Europeans, the Dutch do not make a clear distinction between work and their social lives. In this respect they resemble the Americans and British. If you are working with Dutch people it is quite easy to fraternize with them after work or in your free time.

Another idea is to join a club. Clubs are popular in the Netherlands and they cater for every activity imaginable, including sport, bridge, music, and handicrafts. The local town hall will be able to provide you with a list of clubs in your area. If you live in a cosmopolitan city, such as Amsterdam, you will find expatriate clubs where you will meet people who speak your own language and may be able to introduce you to their Dutch friends and associates.

Evening classes are another popular activity, which enable you to learn something and give you the opportunity to meet people. Adult education is provided by *Volksuniversiteiten* (literally, people's universities) and by further education colleges.

GREETINGS

The Dutch observe certain formalities, and a quick wave or a smile will just not do. When you meet people, shake hands, smile, and look them in the eye.

If you are introducing yourself, give your full name (first name and surname). That gives them the option of addressing you by either. So if they use your first name, you can do likewise. However, it is best to address older people by their surname.

Shaking hands is a well ingrained habit here, as in most of Western Europe, and you will find in company that you are expected to shake hands with everyone, on both arrival and departure.

"Goede morgen," "Goede middag," and *"Goede avond"* are the main greetings, though foreigners experiencing difficulty in pronouncing the guttural *g* can get away with "Hallo." *"Tot ziens"* is the way to say goodbye.

It is a well-established custom to greet everyone—shop assistants and customers— when entering a small store.

LANGUAGE

One of the remarkable things about the Dutch is their fluency in English. Indeed, most of them seem to speak it better than many English people or North Americans. And being very cosmopolitan in outlook they appear to enjoy speaking it.

However, that does not mean that it is pointless to learn their language. It you make an attempt it will be much appreciated, though you should not be offended if the person you are talking to switches into English if he or she senses you are struggling.

There are various opportunities to learn Dutch, including courses offered by the *Volksuniversiteiten*. It is not a difficult language to learn for an English- or German-speaker.

When speaking other languages some Dutch people may sound abrupt or insistent. In Dutch they use short words that soften the tone, but these are missing when they switch languages, and no offense should be taken.

The Dutch call their language *Nederlands* (Netherlandic) or *Hollands* (Hollandish), since the standard language is based on the dialect of North and South Holland. In the Middle Ages it was known as *dietsc*, meaning "the language of the people," as distinct from the language of religion and learning, which was Latin.

Like English and German, it belongs to the West Germanic group of languages and it is identical with the Dutch (or Flemish) of Belgium. It is the official language of the country and spoken by 90 percent of the population. A small proportion of the population (2.2 percent) living mainly in the northern province of Friesland speak Frisian, which has official status there.

CONVERSATION

The Dutch enjoy good conversation and sessions can get very lively indeed. Most topics are permissible, but you would be wise to steer clear of the subject of money—such as how much people earn, or what they are worth—and matters of a personal nature.

The Dutch are good at small talk but even better in discussions that enable them to express their opinions. They will discuss any subject under the sun, including religion, sex, politics, and events in their locality. Some of their comments will be extremely direct, but you should not take offense.

They will often be interested to hear your opinions, but of course you should guard against saying anything derogatory about the Netherlands itself.

INVITATIONS HOME

The Dutch are hospitable people, and you may well receive an invitation to someone's home. This is an opportunity not to be missed, and you should accept immediately, since it demonstrates that they value your company and are putting themselves out to be friendly.

The invitation could, especially on a weekend, be for morning coffee, which will no doubt be accompanied by cake or pastries—though don't take anything until the plate is offered to you.

You may be invited to a drinks party (*borrel*), in which case don't expect a meal, although there may be savory snacks (*borrelhapjes*). These parties usually start at 7:30 or 8:00 p.m., and it is advisable to eat before you go.

If you receive a dinner invitation, you might be asked to arrive as early as 6:30 p.m. This is unlikely to be a mistake, and you should make every effort to arrive on time—but don't be early.

It is the convention in some circles for the men to remain standing until the women are seated. Eating and drinking will commence after the host has proposed a toast—*proost*—at which you should raise your glass.

The Dutch use their knife and fork together. To show you have finished eating it is customary to lay them down close together and parallel to each other on the right side of the plate. Leaving them crossed signifies that you have not finished eating. You should try not to leave any food on your plate.

Your host or hostess will appreciate a small gift. Chocolates, a book, a potted plant, or flowers would be most appropriate. Gifts are usually opened when received. With flowers you need to be careful: give an odd number, but not thirteen, which is considered unlucky. Don't give lilies and chrysanthemums, because they are associated with funerals.

A note of thanks is appreciated after the event.

Daily Life

The Dutch enjoy a high standard of living, and their quality of life is good. Theirs is a well-organized society where people lead civilized lives with a good work/life balance.

HOUSING

Many families live in apartments, but houses are becoming increasingly popular. Both may strike visitors as small and cramped—space is at a premium—but the Dutch use it efficiently. For instance, they often use the attics as a living space.

As we have seen, the Dutch are very particular about keeping their homes clean and tidy. The appliances used tend to be small, in order to fit into the cramped space.

Apartment complexes usually have rules regarding the use of public areas, designed to minimize friction between the different householders. Tenants generally have to make a contribution to the upkeep of the communal areas.

THE HOUSEHOLD

The family is seen as the basis of social structure. Women tend to stay at home while their children are small rather than go out to work. They encourage their children to mix with others and there are plenty of youth groups for them to join. Parents may indulge their offspring a little, but they are not overprotective, feeling that they should learn to fight their own battles.

They also refrain from criticizing their children, but try to guide them by the example they set. The children are encouraged to help with the housework.

DAILY ROUTINE

Families rise at around 7:00 a.m. on weekdays and breakfast together before going their separate ways. Breakfast is a substantial continental-style meal typically consisting of ham, cheese, jam, yogurt, a boiled egg, and cereal, together with coffee, tea, or fruit juice. Office workers usually arrive at work at 8:00 a.m. or soon after, and the school day usually starts at 8:30.

Lunch is a light meal, typically a sandwich and soup, or fried eggs, and while some children manage to get home for lunch, others take a packed lunch to school. They arrive home at about 3:30 p.m. and have a snack. They may then have homework to do, or else engage in extracurricular activities.

The main meal of the day is the evening meal, served at 6:00 p.m., if not before, when the whole family arrives home. This is a cooked meal consisting of potatoes, other vegetables, and meat or fish. Rice, pasta, and noodle dishes are also popular.

Evening is a time for relaxation, when many people watch TV or listen to the radio. National broadcasting is coordinated by the Dutch Broadcasting Association, but some households can receive programs from other countries via cable TV. Going out is popular and many Dutch enroll for evening classes.

SHOPPING

There are two words for shopping in Dutch: one is *winkelen*, which means shopping for pleasure in department stores and boutiques; and the other is *boodshchappen*, or shopping for necessities at food shops, markets, and supermarkets.

Most shops are open from approximately 9:00 a.m. to 6:00 p.m., and many open late one night a week. Many are closed on Sundays, but that tradition is slowly changing. In Amsterdam and tourist areas shops often stay open until late in the evening and open on Sundays, too.

When shopping for essentials the Dutch favor small specialty shops, which are abundant and varied. Most towns have a weekly market selling fresh food, and occasionally flea markets spring up where traders and the general public sell cheap or secondhand goods. Note that a *drogisterij* (chemist) sells general products and non-prescription medicines only. If you have a prescription you need to take it to an *apotheek* (pharmacist).

The Dutch do not wait in line in a shop, as one would expect, but tend to push and shove. Some shops have introduced dispensers with numbered tickets, to determine the order in which customers are served.

EDUCATION

Education is compulsory and free from the ages of five to sixteen. Many children start elementary school (*basisschool*) at the age of four, and start secondary school when they are twelve, with the more academic ones enrolling at a *gymnasium*.

All education is state-funded, although it is not always provided by the state. Instead different sections of the community, including the churches, educate their children separately, according to the "pillarization" tradition. However the curriculum is the same, regardless of the school, though the values may be different.

In the secondary school they take the same subjects for the first three years and then begin to specialize, depending on the career they plan to take up. There are three options: MAVO, or prevocational education, which lasts until they are sixteen, after which they attend vocationally oriented further education classes part-time; HAVO, which prepares pupils for higher professional education until the age of seventeen; and VWO, which prepares pupils for university. A fourth option is VBO, lasting for four years and offering a basic secondary education and instruction in practical skills.

The oldest university, Leiden, was founded by William of Orange in 1575 and originally taught Dutch Reformed theology, science, and medicine. The others, in chronological order of their foundation, are Groningen, Utrecht, Limburg, the University of Amsterdam, the Erasmus University of Rotterdam, the Free University at Amsterdam, Nijmegen, and Brabant. There are technological universities at Delft, Eindhoven, and Enschede, and an agricultural university at Wageningen.

Higher education is not free, and most students live at home with their parents in order to keep down costs.

THE ARMED FORCES

There is no compulsory military service; the country now has an all-volunteer force, which includes women.

NEWSPAPERS, RADIO, AND TV

The Dutch are great newspaper readers, with *De Telegraaf* boasting the largest circulation and *Het Financeele Dagblad* the main business newspaper. *Elsevier* and *Vri Nederland* are weekly news magazines.

TV and radio programs are made by a number of different interest groups, and are allocated air time in proportion to their importance on NOS, the public broadcasting company, which runs three TV stations and five radio channels. Commercial broadcasters include RTL and SBS, and foreign programs are accessible by cable and satellite.

MAIL AND TELECOMMUNICATIONS

The mail service is efficient, and post offices are open from 8:30 a.m. to 5:00 p.m. on weekdays and on Saturday mornings. Postage stamps are also obtainable from newsagents, souvenir shops, and tobacconists. Mailboxes are red.

The main telephone provider is KPN-Telecom, but there are others that may provide better deals. Most public telephones use phone cards and sometimes credit cards. To dial an international call, start with the prefix 00.

The Dutch are avid users of the Internet, and Internet cafés abound. The Internet domain is .nl.

Leisure Time

The Dutch work up to 37.5 hours per week, and have five weeks' annual vacation, which means they have plenty of free time at their disposal. They are enthusiastic travelers, visiting neighboring countries and places further afield, and relish the outdoor life.

EATING OUT

There is a wide choice of restaurants, including establishments that function as cafés offering light snacks by day and transform themselves into something grander in the evenings. The country is particularly known for its Indonesian and Chinese food.

In most restaurants you choose your table, but in upmarket establishments you expect to be shown to your place. To call a waiter, say "*Pardon, meneer,*" or a waitress, "*Pardon, juffrouw.*" Since 2009 smoking has been banned in restaurants and bars.

FOOD

Dutch food tends to be plain but wholesome, and is closer to British food than French or Belgian cuisine. Among the typical dishes are:

Bitterballen	fried meatballs coated with breadcrumbs
Erwtensoep	pea soup
Flensjes	pancakes, often filled with ragout
Kroketten	meat or shrimp croquettes
Nasiballen	fried rice balls
Poffertjes	small pancakes served with sugar
Stampot	thick stew
Uitsmijter	fried eggs, ham, and cheese on bread

Since the Netherlands is a maritime nation there is a particularly good range of seafood, including mussels, smoked eel, and shrimp. Raw herring with diced onion is a particular favorite; you take it between your thumb and your forefinger, tilt your head back, and swallow it.

TIPPING

Tipping is not required in snack bars and cafés. In restaurants, 5 or 10 percent is enough for good service, but if a service charge is already included in the bill, the Dutch tend not to tip at all.

DRINK

The Dutch brew and drink several beers, including lager, dark beer, fruit-flavored beer, and wheat beer. They are also known for their gin (*jenever*), *advokaat* (eggnog), and liqueurs, such as cherry brandy.

Coffee tends to be strong, unless you specify *koffie verkeerd* (wrong coffee), which is milky. Mineral water, fruit juices, and iced tea are also widely available, as is imported wine from a wide number of countries.

Be warned! If you want a cup of coffee, go to a café, snack bar, or restaurant. The places called "coffee shops" sell small quantities of soft drugs to adults over eighteen for personal use.

CULTURE AND ENTERTAINMENT

The Dutch have long held the view that everyone should have access to the arts, and their country has a number of first-class venues for concerts, opera, ballet, drama, and film. One of the most famous is Amsterdam's Concertgebouw, where the renowned Royal Concertgebouw Orchestra performs regularly. There are no fewer than three major ballet companies: the Netherlands Dance Theater, Het Nationale Ballet, and the Scapino Ballet of Rotterdam.

You will also find more popular forms of entertainment, such as nightclubs, discos, and bars offering live music. Amsterdam is famous for its nightlife, and especially for its red light district and its gay/lesbian scene. Other Dutch towns are much tamer by comparison. The police maintain a strong presence after dark in Amsterdam, and it is not dangerous.

Don't overlook the various festivals held throughout the year. They include the International Film Festival in Rotterdam in January, the Holland Festival in Amsterdam in June (featuring music, drama, and dance), the annual open-air pop festival in The Hague, also in June, and the North Sea Jazz Festival in The Hague in July—reputed to be the best outside the USA.

STUDENTS, CLUBBING, AND CLOSE ENCOUNTERS

As evening falls, Amsterdam starts to sparkle. The city's cinemas and theaters are busy, and the clubs, cafés, and restaurants fill up with cheerful, friendly people. The Red Light District, not far from Dam Square, is renowned for its peepshows and coffee shops,

drawing in hordes of tourists. At the Leidseplein square you'll find cinemas, theaters, a casino, and clubs, all of which bustle at night. Rembrandtplein is another busy square, with lots of bars, pubs, more clubs, and other entertainment venues nearby. For a more chilled-out vibe there is the old quarter of Jordaan, which has lovely cafés and restaurants packed with locals.

Dance clubs in Amsterdam don't open until midnight, but buzz until 6:00 a.m.— though Amsterdam does love an after-party, and you can find crowds continuing till noon.

Eindhoven is a lively college town, with lots on offer for the culture-hungry, and shopping and fun for travelers. During the spring and summer it comes alive with festivals, there is a flourishing art scene, and the nightlife happens around the Plaza Futura, De Markt, and Stationsplein.

Holland's egalitarian society means that some of the typical European gender rules are blurred, and the rules of the romance game are a little different. Women tend to be a bit more forthcoming than their European neighbors when it comes to starting a conversation with a man, or asking him out. Depending on the visitor, this can either be rather daunting or a refreshing change. Either way, Dutch men take a more passive approach to romance. The financial expectations of the gender roles have also become more modern, and a man is certainly not expected to pick up all the bills for a date. A fifty-fifty approach is usual.

The Dutch take flirting quite seriously, though, and little is left unsaid or to the imagination. Once chemistry is confirmed there is no suspense. Both parties will express their wishes and arrange a date. Going so far as to establish what one is expecting and what the other should expect is not uncommon at this stage.

SPORTS AND OUTDOOR ACTIVITIES

The Dutch are great sports-lovers, and enjoy taking part in a wide range of activities. With the country's network of rivers and canals, its coastline, and its lakes, it is not surprising that boating, canoeing, and sailing are all popular.

This is very much a cycling nation, and people use their bicycles not only to get about but also for cycling trips along the many designated cycle routes (*fietsroutes*).

There is a strong interest in horse riding, and riding schools organize treks for proficient riders. There are also plenty of nature reserves to ride or ramble around.

All manner of team sports are played in the country, and the Dutch are particularly renowned for soccer, speed skating, hockey, tennis, and volleyball, with clubs for these activities in most towns.

Getting Around

The Netherlands is a compact country, and is easy to get around. There is a highly efficient railway system, the Nederlandse Spoorwegen, which runs express trains (*sneltreinen*), and slower trains (*stoptreinen*) that stop at all or most of the stations en route. You can get almost anywhere in the country from Amsterdam within two and half hours by fast train. Needless to say, the trains are well-maintained and the carriages spotless.

It is advisable to buy your ticket before boarding the train, from either a ticket office or a ticket machine. If you leave it until you are on board it will cost you double. There are various concessionary fares offering big savings, and you should enquire about these.

There is also an extensive bus network. If you are planning to explore cities and towns other than Amsterdam, it is worth buying a *strippenkaart*, a multiple-journey ticket, which is valid on local public transportation all over the country, except in Amsterdam.

URBAN TRANSPORTATION

Both Amsterdam and Rotterdam have underground railways, which connect with bus and train services. In Amsterdam the *strippenkaart* has been replaced by a chip-based travelcard. This is called the *OV Chipkaart*, and is being rolled out across the country.

On starting and ending your journey you will need to swipe your card on a designated card reader.

Taxis can be hired at ranks or ordered by phone, and in some cities it is possible to hail them in the street. If traveling by train you can make use of the *treintaxi* service, which can be paid for when you get your train ticket. This is a shared taxi service that covers a certain area:

you and others take a special *treintaxi* from the station where you alight, and will be dropped off in turn at your destinations.

DRIVING

You may drive on your own driver's license for up to six months, after which you must either take a driving test or exchange your license for a Dutch one before the six months are up. Bear in mind that exchanging driver's licenses can be a lengthy process.

Traffic rules are similar to those in other European countries, and infringements are dealt with strictly. Note that cyclists have the right of way—there are a great many of them, and not all obey the rules of the road. If when turning right you have to cross a cycle path, take particular care.

Warning triangles as well as your car documents should be carried in the car in case of an accident. At unmarked junctions you should give way to traffic approaching from the right, except at traffic circles where you see dragon-tooth markings on the road, in which case you give way to traffic already on the circle. You should approach junctions with flashing amber traffic signals with caution. Trams always have priority over motor vehicles.

Seat belts must be worn at all times and children below the age of three must travel in a safety seat in the rear of the car. Children between three and twelve should travel in the rear, or, if there is no room for them there, in a special safety seat in the front.

Note that in some residential areas speed limits can be as low as 30 kmph (18 mph). In built-up areas the speed limit is normally 50 kmph (31 mph); on secondary roads 80 kmph (49 mph); on expressways it is 100 kmph (62 mph) through urban areas and 120 kmph (75 mph) elsewhere.

The drink-driving limit is 0.5 mg per ml.

CYCLING

The country is exceptionally flat, which means that one of the eco-friendliest means of transportation—cycling—is also the most popular. There are millions of bicycles and cyclists in the country, with plenty of well-designed cycle tracks that have their own traffic signals and signs. These should be used wherever they exist; cycling on the footpath is not allowed.

If you are riding a borrowed or rented bike, it is sensible to test the braking system first, as some have back-pedal brakes. Every bike must have a functioning headlight, rear light, and bell, and cyclists are expected to observe the same rules as other road users.

You can take a bike on a train with you. If it folds up, it can be carried free; if not, you have to pay for its transportation.

The Dutch take to cycling at a young age, and it is quite common for teenagers to ride ten miles (16 km) to school and back.

WHERE TO STAY

Accommodation is plentiful and is normally of a very acceptable standard, whether you choose to stay in a hotel or a guest house (*pension*). You will not find many bed and breakfast establishments.

Other accommodation is provided by the national youth hostels association, at campsites, and near the coast in *trekkerhutten* (camping huts). Boat rental is another possibility.

MEDICAL MATTERS

The state health service scheme (ANOZ Verzekeringen) is good, but does not cover every eventuality. EU citizens wishing to use it need to present their European Health Insurance Card at the outset. Normally you are expected to pay for non-urgent treatment and reclaim it later. Private travel insurance is recommended.

LAW AND ORDER

The Netherlands is a relatively safe country to visit, but this does not mean that you should not take reasonable precautions. In the major cities, especially Amsterdam, you need to beware of petty thieves who prey on tourists and try to engage you in conversation. This is not a problem in the countryside and in the smaller places.

PLACES TO VISIT

Rembrandt House
Museum, Amsterdam

If you only have a restricted amount of time in the Netherlands your priority must be to visit the great art museums, such as the Rijksmuseum in Amsterdam with its fine collection of paintings by Rembrandt and Vermeer, the Van Gogh Museum, also in Amsterdam, the Mauritshuis in The Hague, with paintings by Holbein, Rembrandt, Vermeer, and Hals, the Museum Boijmans van Beuningen in Rotterdam, and the Franz Hals Museum in Haarlem.

The Hague has other attractions in addition to its art museum, notably the Binnenhof complex around the thirteenth-century Knight's Hall, and the Peace Palace, now home to the International Court of Justice,

Amsterdam, however, is the most popular tourist magnet, with its extensive canal network, its fine rows of merchant houses, its vibrant entertainment scene, and its museums, not least the Anne Frank House, where the young Jewish girl and her family hid from the Nazis.

Rotterdam is the world's largest and busiest port, and a harbor tour will give some idea of its immensity. The city has plenty of other attractions, including a wealth of interesting architecture, such as Piet Blom's cube-shaped houses.

In the spring a tour of the country's flowering bulb fields is a must, and there are plenty of smaller towns of considerable interest, such as the ancient university town of Leiden, Delft, famous for its pottery, and Maastricht (where the landmark treaty was signed ushering in the European Union), which has the fine Romanesque church of Onze Lieve Vrouwebasiliek.

Business and Professional Life

Given the geographical position of their country, it was inevitable that the Dutch would be a trading nation. They are situated at the mouth of three major European rivers, and for centuries goods have arrived by ship here to be loaded on to barges for onward transportation to central Europe.

Despite its small area, the Netherlands also has an extensive agricultural and horticultural sector, and is one of the world's largest exporters of poultry and dairy products, house plants, and flowers. It is home to companies large and small, including the electronics giant Philips, Royal Dutch Shell, and Unilever, the latter two jointly owned with the UK.

The port of Amsterdam

BUSINESS PRACTICE

Egalitarianism reigns in Dutch business circles and respect between managers and staff is mutual. Normal office hours are 8:00 a.m. to 5:30 p.m., with many employees working flexitime or part-time, which offers better opportunities for married women.

Most Dutch managers are well qualified and extremely competent, having probably been through a lengthy apprenticeship and on-the-job training before moving on to a position of authority. They could well be on a fixed-term contract, which means they have every incentive to perform.

There is no rigid distinction between home and the workplace as in Germany, but like their neighbors they plan their schedules carefully. They do not normally like to work late but will take work home if absolutely necessary.

MAKING CONTACT

Although the Dutch are accustomed to doing business with foreigners, they don't tolerate any sloppiness. To set up a meeting it is best to send a letter couched in formal and polite terms and using correct titles. Even e-mails need to be formal in tone.

The business community is fairly close-knit, so if you are planning to establish relations with a Dutch company you are more likely to succeed if you can get an introduction or endorsement from a third party, rather than adopting a "cold-calling" approach.

Bearing in mind that the Dutch take a long-term view in business and professional matters, in your introductory correspondence you will need to demonstrate how the relationship would be mutually beneficial over a period of time.

SETTING UP A MEETING

Most managers and other professionals operate a tight schedule, and appointments often need to be made well in advance. It is best to avoid the summer months (June to October). Even if the people you need to see directly are at work, some of the members of staff who will need to be consulted are likely to be taking their holidays at this time.

It is normal to write suggesting a meeting and to confirm the arrangements nearer the date by e-mail or telephone; but sometimes speedier action may be called for.

You should prepare for the meeting with great care, or you could be caught out in a question-and-answer session. The people you are dealing with are likely to be well-educated and highly knowledgeable about your product and service—and about the products and services of your competitors.

Your business cards should state your job title and your qualifications—the more the merrier. You also need to have at your disposal a wealth of data, brochures, and recommendations.

MEETINGS

On no account should you arrive late for a meeting. It will disrupt your host's schedule and will count as a black mark against you. If there is any likelihood of a delay you should telephone.

If there are a number of people in the room when you arrive you should shake hands with all of them and introduce yourself, exchanging business cards if they take the initiative.

Then it is straight down to business, skipping the social niceties. At this stage they are not as concerned about who you are as what you have to offer.

Normally there will be a carefully planned agenda for the meeting, which will be adhered to scrupulously.

PRESENTATIONS

The Dutch appreciate detail and plenty of factual information, and are turned off by a "hard sell." They may stop you from time to time to ask for clarification. Elaborate claims and flamboyant body language are not appreciated—the Dutch are more impressed by clear facts and rational argument.

You should not take offense if, at the end of your presentation, you receive a barrage of challenging questions or comments. The Dutch are renowned for their bluntness, and see no reason to mince their words. Any criticisms they make are designed to elicit extra information to enable them to arrive at an informed decision; they are not trying to catch you out.

Your best defense is to reply as robustly as you can to counter their remarks. If you have been overstating your case, you can be sure this will be discovered. For this reason it pays to be clear and honest rather than to dodge the issue, which would merely rouse their suspicions.

NEGOTIATIONS

The Dutch are past masters at negotiation. Their general aims are to get favorable deals, with long-term profits, and to establish long-term relationships. They expect to debate details and terms closely, and may put pressure on you to make quick decisions. If everything is clearly laid out and to their satisfaction, however, they are willing to compromise.

DECISIONS

Don't expect an instant decision. Dutch organizations are run very democratically and anyone likely to be affected by the decision has the right to have their say—and they generally use that right. This inevitably slows the process down.

Once a decision has been reached, it is never changed. Even people who may have disagreed will finally go along with the proposals. Expect the formalities to be completed quickly.

BEING SOCIABLE

Whereas some Europeans like to keep work and home life quite separate, the gregarious Dutch enjoy going out for a convivial evening with their colleagues. If you are invited along, you should grasp the opportunity. If you do not accept, they might regard you as standoffish, and the relationship could cool.

WOMEN IN BUSINESS

The Netherlands is an egalitarian society, and an effort is made to assist women with careers by means of generous maternity rights, job shares, and part-time appointments. While many women with families choose to stay at home when their children are small, the doors to the jobs market remain open.

However, more and more women are making it to the top by sheer ability and intelligence.

Chapter 9

PORTUGAL

Key Facts

Official Name	República Portuguesa (Portuguese Republic). Short name: Portugal	**Radio and TV**	There are public and private radio stations. The state broadcaster's TV channels are RTP1 and RTP2, and there are also privately run cable and satellite channels. TV works on the PAL BG system.
Capital City	Lisboa (Lisbon)		
Major Cities	Porto (Oporto), Coimbra, Faro		
Area	35,520 sq. miles (92,000 sq. km)		
Terrain	Mountainous north of the River Tagus; rolling plains in south	**Press**	*Publico*, *Diário de Notícias* (Lisbon), *Jornal de Notícias* (Oporto), *24 Horas* (Lisbon)
Climate	Maritime temperate climate: cool and rainy in the north; warmer and drier in the south. Madeira and the Azores are similar.	**English-language Media**	The *Portugal News* and the *Algarve Resident*, also both online
		Electricity	230 volts, 50 Hz. Two-prong plugs used
Currency	Euro	**Internet Domain**	.pt
Population	10.7 million	**Telephone**	Country code 351. For international calls dial 00. The local area code must be dialed before all numbers, even local ones.
Language	Portuguese. Also Mirandese and Barranquenho dialects		
Religion	Roman Catholic 85%; Protestant and others 15%		
Government	Democratic republic. The president is head of state and the prime minister head of government. The unicameral parliament, the Assembleia da República, has 230 members elected for four years.	**Time Zone**	Portugal (mainland and Madeira) is in the Western European Time (WET) Zone, which is the same as GMT/UTC. Daylight saving in summer

Map of Portugal

MINHO RIVER

VIANA DO CASTELO

PENEDA-GERÊS

MONTEZINHO

BRAGA

VILA REAL

BRAGANÇA

PORTO

Porto

DOURO RIVER

Ovar

VISEU

GUARDA

AVIERO

SERRA DA ESTRELA

Coimbra

COIMBRA

LEIRIA

CASTELO BRANCO

Fátima

TAGUS RIVER

SANTARÉM

PORTALEGRE

LISBOA

Torres Vedras

SINTRA

Lisboa (Lisbon)

ÉVORA

GUADIANA RIVER

SETÚBAL

BEJA

FARO

Loulé

Faro

SPAIN

ATLANTIC OCEAN

Ponta Delgada

AZORES

Funchal

MADEIRA

The Country and Its People

Portugal consists of the mainland on the western side of the Iberian Peninsula and the archipelagoes of the Azores and Madeira in the Atlantic Ocean. Madeira is famous for its fortified wine, as is the city of Oporto (Porto), which stands at the mouth of the Douro River. The Douro and the Tagus are the main rivers of the country, both rising in Spain and flowing into the Atlantic.

Mainland Portugal has a land border with Spain to the north and east and an Atlantic coastline. The scenery is extremely varied for such a small country, with a mountainous interior that includes the Serre de Estrela mountain range. It has a maritime climate that is temperate in the north and becomes more Mediterranean in character the further south you go. Madeira and the Azores both enjoy Mediterranean climates.

Coastline near Lagos, in the Algarve

Given its long Atlantic coastline, Portugal's orientation has been seaward, rather than toward continental Europe, particularly since the fifteenth-century age of exploration presided over by Henry the Navigator. Portugal was the first European country to acquire extensive overseas possessions, in Africa, South America, and Asia.

The days of empire have gone, but the legacy remains. Around 230 million people around the world speak Portuguese, of whom Portugal accounts for just below eleven million. A few decades ago it was the poorest country in Western Europe, but since joining the European Union it has modernized and prospered, and has become a popular tourist designation.

The Portuguese tend to be quiet, modest people for whom personal relationships matter a good deal. They are fairly conservative in outlook, especially in the more remote areas, and great respecters of tradition. But that does not mean that they shun modernity. They have been enthusiastic members of the European Union since 1986, and in recent decades have made great strides in education and business life.

A HISTORICAL PERSPECTIVE

Portugal was populated by Celts and Lusitanians when the Romans invaded the Iberian Peninsula in 219 BCE. The Romans held sway for seven hundred years, implanting their language, from which Portuguese would evolve. Germanic tribes supplanted the Romans in the fifth century, and were themselves driven out by the Moorish invasions of the early eighth century, which brought Spain and Portugal under the Umayyad Caliphate.

Moorish rule was tolerant of other religions. It produced a brilliant multiethnic civilization and brought technical advances to the region. The Moors' architectural influence is still evident in the Algarve. Their power began to wane when the Christian Kingdom of León liberated parts of the Iberian Peninsula in the twelfth century. An independent Portuguese kingdom emerged in 1139, when Afonso Henriques (known as the Conqueror) defeated the Moors at Ourique, although they were not driven out of the Algarve until 1249.

In the fourteenth century Portugal's independence came under threat from the Kingdom of Castile. But the Spanish were defeated by João I at Aljubarrota with the help of archers from

England, and he formed an alliance with England. His son, Henrique (Henry the Navigator), founded a nautical school at Sagres and started to finance voyages of discovery.

Expansion and Mixed Fortunes

This marked the start of Portuguese expansion, leading to the discovery of Madeira (1419), the Azores (1427), Cap Verde and Guinea (1456), and São Tomé (1471). Bartolomeu Dias rounded the Cape of Good Hope in 1488, and in 1497 Vasco da Gama reached Calicut, in India. Three years later Pedro Álvares Cabral reached what is now Brazil.

But the expulsion in 1497 of the Jews, the country's commercial class, led to a decline in Portugal's fortunes. Under João III Jesuit influence grew, leading to the establishment of the Inquisition in Lisbon (Lisboa) in 1536. King Sebastião's abortive crusade against the Moors in Morocco resulted in his death and Spanish domination for the next sixty years, during which the country's infrastructure was ruined and the overseas empire abandoned.

Portugal regained its independence in 1640 and João IV was proclaimed king. A peace treaty was signed with Spain, trading links were established with England, and gold and diamonds were discovered in Brazil. But João almost bankrupted the country with his extravagant spending.

The newly found prosperity was shattered by the Lisbon Earthquake of 1755, which destroyed the city and killed 20,000. But the reformist prime minister, the Marquis de Pombal, rebuilt the city, reorganized the country's economy, introduced secular education, and expelled the Jesuits and the Inquisition. A Spanish invasion was repulsed, with English assistance.

The Nineteenth and Twentieth Centuries

When the unstable Queen Maria I came to the throne in 1777, she dismissed De Pombal and reversed many of his reforms, but when Napoleon's army invaded Portugal in 1807 the royal family fled to Brazil, where they formed a government-in-exile. The French were forced out of Portugal by an Anglo-Portuguese force led by Sir Arthur Wellesley, later the Duke of Wellington.

In 1820 Liberals forced the King to accept constitutional government, but the move was reversed by an army coup. The country suffered another setback when Brazil declared its independence in 1822, and in 1832 a civil war broke out between Liberals and the Absolutists, known as the War of the Two Brothers (Pedro IV and Dom Miguel), which the Liberal faction won. The nineteenth century was a period of economic decline and political turmoil that saw the rise of socialist, anarchist, and republican parties.

In 1907 King Carlos I suspended the constitution, installing João Franco as dictator. Three years later a revolution led to the declaration of a republic. Portugal entered the First World War on the side of the Allies. The devastation of the war led to a coup in 1917. This was followed by another in 1928 by General Gomez da Costa, which led to the installation of António de Oliveira Salazar as president in 1933. Salazar kept Portugal out of the Second World War, but it subsequently became embroiled in a costly war with its colonies.

"Proclamatioin of the Republic of Portugal," 1910

The Salazar dictatorship lasted until 1968. His successor, Marcello Caetano, instituted social and economic reforms, but his failure to democratize led to a left-wing military coup in 1974, known as the Carnation Revolution, which instituted democratic reforms. Political parties mushroomed, exiles returned, and the ruling junta handed over power to a provisional government. The following year, Portugal granted independence to all of its African colonies and in 1986 entered what is now the European Union.

Portugal Today

After a long period of dictatorship, when the country was absorbed in preserving its empire in Africa and Asia, it finally turned away from its colonies toward Europe.

The current constitution was adopted on April 2, 1976, and subsequently revised to place the military under strict civilian control. It trimmed the powers of the president, and laid the groundwork for a stable, pluralistic, liberal democracy. Provision was made for the privatization of nationalized firms and the government-owned communications media.

KEY HISTORICAL DATES

219 BCE	Romans invade the Iberian Peninsula, which they call Iberia.
416 CE	Vandals and Visigoths start to supplant the Romans.
711	Moors overrun the Iberian Peninsula.
868	Vimara Peres establishes an autonomous county of Portugal in the north.
1139	Afonso Henriques overcomes the Moors at Ourique and becomes king of an independent Portugal.
1249	Moors finally defeated by Afonso III.
1387	João I forms an alliance with England.
1415	Henry the Navigator founds a nautical school in the Algarve.
1519–21	Magellan circumnavigates the world.
1536	The Holy Inquisition is established in Lisbon.
1580	Philip II of Spain occupies Portugal.
1640	Portugal regains independence from Spain and João IV is crowned king.
1688	Peace Treaty with Spain.
1703	Methuen Treaty strengthens ties with England.
1755	The Lisbon earthquake.
1807	Napoleon's troops invade Portugal.
1810	Anglo-Portuguese forces defeat French at Busaco.
1822	Brazil becomes independent.
1832–4	The War of the Two Brothers.
1907	King suspends the constitution.
1910	Portugal becomes a republic.
1926	Military coup establishes a dictatorship.
1949	Portugal becomes a founding member of NATO.
1974	The Carnation Revolution leads to the re-establishment of democracy.
1986	Portugal joins the European Community.

GOVERNMENT

Portugal is a republic, with a president and a prime minister. The prime minister puts together a council of ministers, which needs the president's approval. There is just one parliamentary chamber, the Assembleia da República, which has 230 representatives. Elections are held every four years. A former prime minister became the president of the European Union in 2004.

Mainland Portugal consists of eighteen districts, each named after its capital. Listed from north to south, they are: Viana do Castelo, Braga, Vila Real, Bragança, Porto, Aveiro, Viseu, Guarda, Coimbra, Leiria, Castelo Branco, Santarém, Portalegre, Lisboa, Setúbal, Évora, Neja, and Faro. There are two autonomous regions: Azores and Madeira.

Values and Attitudes

Portuguese society is close-knit and family-oriented, and the people sometimes give the impression that they are suspicious of strangers and feel insecure in the company of people they don't know. This could be the result of the country's relative isolation from Europe in the decades before 1974.

But attitudes are softening, particularly among the young, who did not live through the difficult times, and in areas that welcome large numbers of foreign tourists, such as the Algarve. Essentially, the Portuguese are a warm, gregarious, and fun-loving people.

THE IMPORTANCE OF FAMILY

Although the Portuguese tend to have fewer children these days, the concept of the extended family is deeply rooted. Grandparents, uncles, aunts, and cousins play an important role in everyone's lives, and it is quite usual for an extended family to live in the same area.

It is also normal to have three or more generations of a family living under the same roof, and for young people not to leave the family nest until they marry, perhaps in their mid-twenties. Marriage is still the norm in Portugal, and people are extremely fond of children. Parents are prepared to make tremendous sacrifices for their offspring, and are often very indulgent toward them.

Discretion is the watchword, and people prefer to resolve problems and disputes within the family rather than discuss them with others or seek outside help.

WARINESS

It generally takes time for the Portuguese to strike up friendships. They like to be with people they know and trust—family and close friends—and tend to keep strangers at arm's length until they get properly acquainted. However, once the initial wariness wears off friendships can develop.

NATIONAL IDENTITY

The Portuguese tend to be critical of their governments and politicians, and family life always takes precedence over involvement in public life. Most people are more interested in improving their own circumstances than working for the general good, although the country has a number of public-spirited leaders who have proved the exceptions to the rule.

Visitors would be wise not to join in when Portuguese people start lambasting their country's shortcomings. That would merely serve to put them on the defensive. For deep down the Portuguese are strongly patriotic. They are proud to have been an independent country far longer than their larger neighbor, Spain, with which they have a strong rivalry. They are also proud of their institutions and their literature. The country was ecstatic when the national football team made it to the final of the UEFA Euro 2004 championship.

MACHISMO

Portuguese men come across as being extremely macho, especially behind the wheel of a car and in each other's company, although at home it is often the women who really rule the roost. Men are very protective of their own womenfolk, and behave with great courtesy in female company.

ATTITUDES TOWARD FOREIGNERS

In general, the Portuguese are mild-mannered and tolerant. In their colonies they gained a good reputation for the relatively benign way the native peoples were treated. However, they also have a reputation for bluntness and don't mince their words, about non-Europeans especially. In most cases no offense is meant or should be taken.

Generally speaking, they welcome foreigners who make an attempt to understand their customs and language and try to fit in. They can be somewhat straitlaced, though, and take exception to nudity and women sunbathing topless, although on the Algarve and elsewhere there are secluded beaches set aside for nude bathing.

RELIGION

Religion plays an important role in the lives of the Portuguese,

especially the older generation and those living in rural communities. The overwhelming majority are Roman Catholic and, as we shall see in the next chapter, Christian festivals and rites, such as baptism, are observed with considerable devotion.

People make pilgrimages to sacred shrines, notably the shrine of Fátima near Leiria (see page 368); and everywhere—in people's homes, in public buildings, and by the roadsides—you will find crucifixes and images of saints.

There are churches belonging to other denominations in the Algarve and in the main cities, some of which cater mainly to non-Portuguese.

FORMALITY

Manners are taken seriously in Portugal, and loutish behavior is frowned on. Young people are taught to respect their elders and stand up and greet them when they come into the room.

NOSTALGIA AND FATALISM

The Portuguese have a quality that is often summed up in the word *saudade*. It is a sense of fatalism, and acceptance that what will be will be. At the same time it has a nostalgic element—a yearning for the past, or what is utterly unattainable. This mournful, bittersweet fatalism is the flip side of a people who, on the surface, seem to have hardly a care in the world.

Festivals and Traditions

The Portuguese love celebrations and public holidays. Many of these are religious in nature, reflecting the strong influence of Catholicism. Others commemorate historical events.

There are around a dozen statutory holidays (*feriados obrigatorios*) in Portugal, when banks, post offices, shops, and businesses are closed. If a holiday falls on a Sunday, it is not usual for people to take the following day off in lieu.

In addition to the national holidays many towns have their own holidays, when there are celebrations in honor of the local patron saint.

HOLIDAYS AND FESTIVALS

January 1	Ano Novo	New Year's Day
February	Entrudo	Carnival
March/April	Domingo de Ramos	Palm Sunday
March/April	Sexta-feira Santa	Good Friday
March/April	Páscoa	Easter Sunday
April 25	Dia da Liberdade	Liberation Day
May 1	Dia do Trabalhador	Labor Day
May/June	Corpo de Deus	Corpus Christi
June 10	Dia de Portugal	Portuguese National Day
August 15	Assunção de Nossa Senhora	Assumption
October 5	Dia da República	Proclamation of the Republic
November 1	Todos os Santos	All Saints' Day
December 1	Dia de Restauracão	Restoration of Independence
December 8	Imaculada Conceição	Immaculate Conception
December 25	Natal	Christmas Day

THE FESTIVE YEAR

New Year

The Portuguese see the New Year in with fireworks, dancing, and shouting, and set aside the first day of the year for leisure and relaxation. Twelfth Night (or Epiphany) is also an excuse for celebration, when "kings' cakes" (*bolo rei*) are baked with a lucky charm and bean inside. Tradition has it that the person who finds the bean has to buy the next year's cake!

Carnival

Carnival, held on the day before Lent begins, is an excuse to party, either privately or in public. Celebrations vary from place to place. In Loulé in the Algarve, for instance, there is a three-day street carnival on the lines of Carnival in Brazil.

Palm Sunday and Holy Week

Palm Sunday marks the beginning of Holy Week (Semana Santa), and many parishes hold processions commemorating Christ's entry into Jerusalem. Parish priests visit people at home, and children give their godparents flowers. Other processions are held during Holy Week, in which statues of Jesus and Mary are carried. Good Friday is a day of fasting and reflection, and processions that reenact Christ's Passion.

Easter Day

Easter Sunday, the most important feast in the Christian year, is a time for celebration, when people attend mass at church in the morning and follow it with a family get-together over a special meal. The custom of giving children chocolate Easter eggs and bunnies has taken root here. The day also marks the start of the bullfighting season.

Liberation Day
This is a political occasion commemorating the peaceful 1974
Carnation Revolution that ended the dictatorship. It is marked by
parades and speeches.

Labor Day
This is a more muted affair.

Corpus Christi
This is a popular religious occasion in Portugal, as in other Roman
Catholic countries, with special services and processions.

Portugal's National Day
Also called Camões Day, this day
honors the country's national poet,
Luís de Camões (1524-80), who wrote
a wide range of poems, including
sonnets, odes, eclogues, elegies, and
songs, as well as plays. He is best
known for his ten-canto epic poem
Os Lusiadas ("The Lusiads"), which
describes Vasco da Gama's discovery
of the sea route to India and praises
the Portuguese people; in it Camões,
who spent years as a soldier in Africa
and India, glorifies those who live
dangerously.

Luís de Camões

The Feast of the Assumption
This feast day is observed with religious ceremonies, especially in
the north of Portugal.

Proclamation of the Republic Day
This day commemorates the founding of Portugal's first republican
government in 1910.

All Saints' Day
This is an important religious occasion, when people light candles
in churches and place flowers on the graves of the departed. It is
also the anniversary of the fatal Lisbon Earthquake of 1755.

Restoration of Independence Day
This celebration recalls the day in 1640 when Portugal regained its independence from Spain.

The Feast of the Immaculate Conception
This feast day is another public holiday when the faithful attend mass.

Christmas
Christmas Day is a holiday, and so, unofficially, is Christmas Eve, when people attend midnight mass (*miso do galo*). This is followed by a meal. On Christmas Day families have a festive lunch, which usually features cod and perhaps turkey, followed by rich desserts and sweet pastries. Town centers have Christmas illuminations, and many people at home decorate a Christmas tree and set up a nativity scene (*presépió*). It is also a time for relations and friends to visit.

SUMMER RELIGIOUS FESTIVALS

In pre-Christian times the indigenous inhabitants of Portugal would celebrate the Summer Solstice. Festivities such as this are now held in honor of saints, of whom the most popular are Santo António (St. Anthony), São João (St. John), and São Pedro (St. Peter). People decorate their balconies with lights, streamers, wild leeks, and pots of basil, and come together to eat grilled sardines and green cabbage soup (*caldo verde*), drink wine, and ask the saints to bring them good luck. These festivals take place between June and August.

St. Anthony is closely associated with Lisbon, and in June the city organizes Santo António weddings, in which impoverished engaged couples participate in a public wedding ceremony, after which the brides offer their bouquets to the saint's statue and a reception is held for them at the city's expense. In the evening there is a colorful parade down the Avenida da Liberdade (Liberty Avenue).

St. John is a popular saint in the north, and on St. John's Day (June 23) in Oporto people jump over small fires and make wishes. A regatta is held and there are many outdoor fairs and parties wth dancing and fireworks.

In September Sintra holds the Festa da Senhora da Consolacão, in honor of Portugal's patron saint.

OTHER LOCAL FESTIVALS AND TRADITIONS

Virtually every locality in Portugal puts on a lavish festival of its own.

The Marian shrine at Fátima

In May there is an annual pilgrimage to Fátima, where the Virgin Mary appeared to three children in 1917. Between September 6 and 9 people make pilgrimages to the baroque shrine of Nossa Senhora des Remedios at Lamego.

A number of events are especially popular with tourists, such as the flower festival in Madeira in late April, and Algarve's music festival, which lasts from May to July.

A tradition known as *queima das fitas* (ribbon-burning), dating from the nineteenth century, is followed by students in May. After they have finished their exams, they process to the main square and burn the ribbons they tie up their books with. Much jollification accompanies the ceremony, especially in Oporto and the ancient university town of Coimbra.

FAMILY OCCASIONS

Baptisms

A few days after birth an infant is taken to be received into the Church, and the priest normally performs the rite of baptism during a church service. Afterward the family retires for a large celebratory meal, to which guests often bring gifts for the infant.

Weddings

Marriage in Portugal represents the union not only of a man and a woman but also of their two families. The Portuguese are sticklers for tradition, and a man normally approaches his prospective father-in-law to ask for his daughter's hand in marriage.

A few months before the wedding is due to take place, there is a formal engagement party called a *pedido* (proposal). The bride's family invites the groom and his family for a meal, and the groom proposes to the bride, placing an engagement ring on her finger.

On the day of the wedding proper the bridal party takes breakfast together and accompanies the bride to the church for the ceremony. After the reception the guests often go to visit the newlyweds at home, and celebrations may continue well into the night.

Funerals

Women wear white or black at funerals, and black ties are normal for the men. Refreshments are often served after the service, giving the mourners an opportunity to offer their condolences to the bereaved. Seven days after the funeral a mass is held to pray for the deceased.

Getting to Know the Portuguese

Mention has already made of the apparent reserve shown by the Portuguese toward people they don't know. This should not be regarded as hostility. They can be as warm and friendly as any other nationality once they open up, and you shouldn't feel discouraged if you are not on first-name terms after the first encounter.

People living in some areas, notably those in the Algarve, are accustomed to dealing with visitors from other countries. Those in remoter areas tend to be suspicious at first—even of their fellow Portuguese. They live in close-knit communities that may seem impenetrable.

THE LANGUAGE

Being able to communicate in Portuguese is a definite plus. People will respond to you more readily if they feel you are making an effort to communicate with them on their own terms.

While younger people are likely to have some knowledge of English and are willing to try it out on strangers, they are the exception. Middle-aged people are more likely to have learned French at school.

It is not difficult to find language schools and audio-visual courses that teach Portuguese—which is, after all, a major world language. Some will concentrate on Brazilian Portuguese, which differs in certain respects from the Portuguese of Portugal and is spoken by a very large number of people.

Spanish is widely understood in Portugal. In fact, one can hear Spanish and Portuguese people communicating with one another in their respective languages without too many problems. If you don't speak Spanish, French may be a useful substitute.

Portuguese is spoken by 230 million people around the world; aside from Portugal it is spoken in Brazil, and also in Africa, in countries such as Angola, Mozambique, Guinea-Bissau, and São Tomé. There are also Portuguese-speakers in Goa, East Timor, and Macau.

Portuguese is a Romance language, derived from Latin, but subjected over time to various linguistic influences, including Arabic, Greek, French, and English. Standard Portuguese is based on the Lisbon dialect, but there is considerable regional variation. There are five versions: Northern Portuguese (Galician), Central Portuguese, Southern Portuguese, Insular Portuguese, and Brazilian Portuguese.

Galician, the dialect of northwest Spain, has a special status, being the official language of the *communidad autonoma* of Galicia. In former times Gallego-Portugues, as it was known, was favored by courtly poets throughout the Iberian peninsula and had a much wider audience than it has today.

Brazilian Portuguese differs from European Portuguese both grammatically and in pronunciation, and it is spoken more slowly, with the words enunciated with greater clarity.

European Portuguese makes considerable use of nasal vowels, indicated in writing by the use of the *tilde* (~) or by the m or n following the vowel. The Portuguese speak quickly, often leaving out vowels or whole syllables, and its throatiness sometimes leads it to be confused with Slavonic languages.

MEETING PEOPLE

The Portuguese prefer long-lasting relationships to instant friendships, and the more you get to know them the likelier it is they will open up to you. This means maintaining regular contact.

Café society is well entrenched in Portugal, and if you become a regular at a particular café and appear friendly, sooner or later someone will strike up a conversation with you, and perhaps others will join in. A cheerful "*Bom dia*" ("Good day"), "*Boa tarde*" ("Good afternoon/evening") or "*Adeus*" ("Good-bye") will help break the ice.

Show an interest in the people you meet. Ask about their health—but be prepared for a long, graphic description of all their ailments! If they have children, focus on them, since the Portuguese adore children.

If you are in Portugal for any length of time, you could join a club. There are plenty of sports clubs, for example, where people feel more at ease and more ready to socialize with strangers.

If you are still having problems in making contact with Portuguese people, don't overlook the various expatriate clubs in the larger centers. These will have members who have considerable experience of the country and who could doubtless suggest useful contacts.

GOOD MANNERS

The Portuguese dislike bad manners, so visitors should be careful not to cause offense, even inadvertently. Turning your back on someone is bad manners, as are lounging about in public with your feet on the furniture, using rude language, wearing shorts, and failing to cover your arms in churches and other religious buildings. Although smoking is widespread, it is courteous to ask permission before lighting up.

FORMS OF ADDRESS

As is the case in other Romance languages, care should be taken when addressing other people. The familiar form of you (*tu*) must not be used, except to animals and children, until you become really well acquainted. The more formal *você* (pronounced "vossi") is used. In very formal situations people are addressed by their professional titles. Ordinarily you would first address a man as "*Senhor*" and a woman as "*Senhora,*" after which you may then, if you know their first names, use them in the form "*Senhor* Luis," or "*Dona* Maria," for example.

GREETINGS

Women will greet each other with a kiss on one cheek or both, while men shake hands and may hug each other, or give a pat on the back, if they are particularly close friends. Some men will observe the old-fashioned courtesies and kiss a woman's hand.

When taking leave of a person the phrase "*Com licença*" ("Excuse me") is often used.

MAKING CONVERSATION

The Portuguese express themselves with gestures as well as words, especially when the conversation becomes animated and the noise level rises. However, foreigners should be wary of using hand gestures themselves, as some are considered rude.

People look each other in the eye: not to do so would suggest you have something to hide. There is also plenty of physical contact in the form of hugs, pats on the back, and the grasping of hands.

Most people enjoy a good joke, and may stand up and move around when telling a story. They have a good sense of the ridiculous and like making fun of others as well as themselves. Their preference is for slapstick rather than more subtle brands of humor, so irony is likely to be lost on them.

INVITATIONS HOME

The Portuguese enjoy entertaining at home. It is an opportunity to show off their heritage. Unless they make clear that the occasion will be formal, you should assume that the dress code is "smart casual."

On arrival it is customary to greet everyone. Bring a gift for the hostess. Wine, chocolates, or flowers are very acceptable, provided the flowers are not carnations. (Red carnations symbolize the 1974 Revolution.) If there are children in the family, presents for them are also welcome.

Good table manners are essential. No elbows on tables, for example, and use the knife as well as the fork, European-style. Don't hesitate to praise the food that has been prepared for you.

After the party, it is polite to telephone or write to your hostess thanking her for her hospitality.

Daily Life

HOUSING

In the cities people tend to live in apartments; in the suburbs and away from the urban centers houses are more common. The older

apartments usually have draughty rooms with high ceilings, which means they are expensive to heat during the damp winters. Newer buildings are more compact and better insulated.

Rents are not regulated, which may account for the fact that the Portuguese prefer to own their homes. As a result, owner-occupation is more common here than in some other European countries. Second homes in the country or on the coast are also popular.

The traditional houses of northern Portugal are built of granite and have thick walls. Further south, brick and limestone are the preferred materials, while in the Algarve clay and stone are used, and the houses have a distinctly Moorish look.

THE HOUSEHOLD

While the father is the titular head of the family, it is the woman (or *dona de casa*) who runs the household. Portuguese women tend to be very houseproud and to criticize others who don't reach their exacting standards. Girls are expected to help out at home.

The mother is very much in charge of bringing up the children, on whom she lavishes much affection combined with strict discipline. Children are expected to observe strict codes of behavior.

Grandparents also have a hand in a child's upbringing, particularly if they live under the same roof. Working mothers prefer to leave their children in the care of their grandmother rather than put them in daycare nurseries, certainly until the children are about three.

Housewives usually insist on using fresh (not frozen) ingredients in their cooking, and they prefer to buy them from neighborhood shops (*mercearia*) or a market (*mercado*). Hypermarkets stocking virtually everything and open long hours have made a big impact in recent years.

DAILY ROUTINE

Portuguese families usually have breakfast together at 8:00 a.m. before going their different ways. The lunch break starts at 1:00 p.m., and usually lasts an hour and a half. The work schedule is interrupted by numerous coffee breaks, either at the workplace or in nearby cafés.

After work people return home. In summer families go out for walks together either before or after the evening meal.

BUREAUCRACY

Many Portuguese (as well as foreigners) complain about the problem of dealing with government bureaucracy. Countless forms have to be completed, and long waits are common in government offices. Often several visits are necessary in order to obtain the documents you need.

In order to speed up the bureaucratic process the government has established *loyas do cidadao* (citizens' shops) in some of the urban centers.

THE MEDIA

Of the daily newspapers the most widely read are *Diario de Notícias* in Lisbon, *Jornal de Notícias* in Porto, the liberal learning *Publico*, *24 Horas,* and *Correio da Manha. O Jogo* and *Record* are sports papers. *Semanário Económico* and *Expresso* appear on weekends and concentrate mainly on business and finance. *Resident* and *Portugal News* are the main English-language newspapers.

There are four national TV channels; two are state-owned and the others privately owned. Further channels are available on satellite and cable. There is also a wide range of radio stations.

EDUCATION

For many decades the Portuguese educational system lagged behind those of other Western European countries, but in recent years the country has been making up for lost time.

Education is now compulsory between the ages of six and fifteen, and preschool classes are also available. Fees for state schools are means-tested and the country also has a large number of private schools for those who can afford them. The school day lasts from 9:00 a.m. to 5:00 p.m., with extracurricular activities when classes are over.

Education is not compulsory after the age of fifteen, but many students go on to secondary school. Portugal has a number of state-financed and private universities and polytechnics that set entrance examinations for potential applicants. Fewer than 20 percent of the student population enter higher education.

THE ARMED FORCES

Portugal now has an all-volunteer military establishment. In 2004 compulsory military service was abolished, but young men have to register with the military authorities on their eighteenth birthdays and attend an information session on national defense. Certain military careers are now open to women.

OPENING HOURS

Banks are open on weekdays between 8:30 a.m. and 3:00 p.m., the main ones being the Banci Expirito Santo, Caixa General de Depositos, and Millennium-BCP. However, most have ATM (*Multibanco*) machines.

MAIL AND TELECOMMUNICATIONS

The Portuguese postal service is very reliable. Post offices are open from 8:30 a.m. to 6:30 p.m. on weekdays and until 1:00 p.m. on Saturdays, and are indicated by the letters CTT. You frequently have to wait in line there, so you may prefer to buy stamps from newsstands and bookshops. Letters can be posted in the red mailboxes.

Portugal has an up-to-date telephone system. There are more than four million fixed-line telephones in operation, and an astonishing thirteen million cell phones. The main operator is Portugal Telecom. There is considerable competition between the three cell phone providers, Optimus, TMN, and Vodaphone, which helps to keep rates low.

Internet use is relatively recent, but Portugal is unusual in that there is coverage virtually throughout the country. There are several service providers, of which Portugal Telecom and SonaeCom are the largest. Portugal's internet domain is .pt.

Leisure Time

Leisure is an important part of Portuguese life, and people will find any excuse for a party. Big family occasions and other social events, particularly involving eating and drinking, are dear to their hearts.

CAFÉ LIFE

Cafés are at the heart of Portuguese social life, and you will hardly ever see an empty one. On weekdays they are frequented by office workers eager to get away from the daily grind and indulge in their favorite beverage: coffee. It is not unusual for people to have five or six cups a day, in a coffee house, or alternatively in a cake shop or *salão de cha*.

café	espresso
bica (in Lisbon)	espresso
cimbalino (in the north)	espresso
café curto (short coffee)	a short, strong coffee
café italiano	a short, very strong coffee
café comprido or *cheio*	a longer drink
carioca	weak coffee
pingo or *garoto*	regular coffee with a hint of milk
galao or *café com leite*	white coffee in a glass

EATING OUT

Portuguese people enjoy eating out in restaurants either for lunch (*almoco*), between noon and 3:00 p.m., or for dinner (*jantar*), which takes place at any time between 7.30 and 10:00 p.m. or even later.

Tipico restaurants specialize in local cuisine, whereas *masqueiras* offer principally seafood. *Churasqueiras* are restaurants that serve grilled food. Taverns (*tascas*) also sometimes offer good food. A set meal (*ementa turistica*), which usually includes a drink, works out cheaper than ordering à la carte. Restaurants often place appetizers, such as bread, olives, and cheese, on the table; these are included in the cover charge.

TIPPING

There are no rules regarding tipping. It is unnecessary in cafés, but in restaurants the Portuguese might leave up to 5 percent. Foreigners may be expected to leave more.

FOOD

The Portuguese make some very tasty soups and stews. Examples are *caldo verde* (green soup), which consists of potato purée and shredded cabbage; aromatic fava bean stew; *feijoada*, a stew of beans, beef, and/or pork, sometimes containing various smoked meats or sausage; and *cozido*, a pork and beef stew with vegetables and herbs.

There are a number of delicious meat dishes, including roast lamb; smoked pork; *presunto fumado* (smoked ham); *chouriço* (sausages); *espetada mista* (the Portuguese equivalent of shish kebab); and *bife na frigidera* (fried beefsteak with a sauce). *Frango no churrasco* (barbecued chicken) is another popular dish, and is often served with *piri-piri*, a spicy sauce.

As befits a country with a long coastline, there is a superb range of fish and seafood dishes. Among the most popular are grilled sardines; *espadarte fumado* (smoked swordfish); *ameijoas* (clams); *mexilhões* (mussels); *caldeirada* (seafood stew); and *bacalhau* (salted cod)—Portugal's national dish. Other favorites are *Ameijoas na cataplana* (steamed mussels with sausages, tomato, onion, wine, and herbs); *lulas recheadas* (squid stuffed with rice, olives, tomato, onion, and herbs); and *lampreia* (lamprey), a freshwater fish available only in the spring.

Many Portuguese desserts originated in convents, hence names such as Abbot's Pudding, Nun's Belly, and Heaven's Lard. There are also regional delicacies, such as *pastel de nata* (a cream pastry) from Belém, *ovos moles* ("soft eggs," made from sweet egg paste in Aveiro), and marzipan desserts in various shapes from the Algarve.

Barrels of port awaiting shipment

DRINK

The two most famous drinks associated with Portugal are port and madeira, both fortified wines. Brandy was initially added to wines to prevent them from going sour in transit, and the grapes from which port is made (around forty varieties in all) come from the scenic Upper Douro Valley with its many terraced vineyards. This is the oldest demarcated wine region in the world. Many of the wine cellars in Gaia, across the river from Oporto, offer wine tastings.

Madeira comes in four varieties: white Sercial from the island's highest vineyards is drunk as an aperitif; Verdelho, a medium-dry tawny, is traditionally taken with madeira cake—what else? Bual is dark, rich, and nutty, while Malmsey is a sweet, dark wine. George, Duke of Clarence, is traditionally supposed to have drowned in a barrel of Malmsey, as described by Shakespeare in *Richard III*.

Portugal also produces some very palatable table wines, the most prestigious of which bear the designation DOC. This means that it has been grown in a particular region and subject to stringent production controls. *Vinho regional* can be just as good, but is subject to fewer rules.

Among the best-known wines are Vinho Verde, a slightly sparkling wine from the Minho region north of Oporto, Dão from an inland region south of the Douro, wines from the Estremadura region north of Lisbon, and the sweet Moscatel de Setúbal.

Beer drinkers are well served by local breweries. Mineral water is also available, as either *com gas* (sparkling) or *sem gas* (still).

CULTURE AND ENTERTAINMENT

In Lisbon the Fundação Calouste Gulbenkian is the main center for orchestral concerts and ballet, while the Teatro Nacional puts on plays. The leading theater in Oporto is the Teatro Rivoli, which also boasts an impressive new Casa da Música.

Pop concerts are held in the larger centers, and the cinema is popular among the young. Although Portugal has its own film industry whose directors have won awards at Cannes, most movies that are shown come from Hollywood.

Musical entertainment is to be found in many restaurants, particularly in the *fado* houses of Lisbon, which serve food and drink and offer a novel experience.

FADO

Fado means "fate," and a genre of music called by this name developed in Lisbon in the early nineteenth century. It expresses *saudosismo*, a unique Portuguese trait that is a blend of longing and sorrow. Fado songs are accompanied on the *guitarra* (a flat-backed instrument shaped like a mandolin with eight, ten, or twelve strings arranged in pairs) and *viola* (a Spanish acoustic guitar that provides rhythmic accompaniment). The first great *fadista* (*fado* singer) was Maria Severa (1810–36).

Fado guitarist António Chainho

STUDENTS, CLUBBING, AND CLOSE ENCOUNTERS

Whether you prefer dancing to a live band or the sounds of electronic beats, Lisbon provides a wide variety for all tastes and desires. The major dance spots are concentrated near the Tagus in

Avenida 24 de Julho, between downtown and Belém, in the docklands below 25 de Abril Bridge to the west, and across from Santa Apolonia train station to the east.

Most locals begin their night with a long dinner and then bar-hop for a couple of hours. The dancing clubs get going after 2:00 a.m., and no hard-core reveler leaves before dawn.

Check out the fado music scene's *saudade* in the heart of the Bairro Alto, probably the most "happening" area of Lisbon for nightlife. Lots of clubs and bars are located along Rua da Atalaia and Rua Diario de Notícias. Go underground to Lisbon's legendary Hot Clube in Algeria Square, and you'll find the best of Portugal's jazz musicians demonstrating their art.

The riverfront is home to international dance clubs, live jazz bars, and gay-friendly venues, and the rejuvenated docks of Alxantara and Santo Amaro attract media types and a young, fashion-conscious crowd. Lux, by Apolonia Station, is another favorite. It can be an expensive night out in the larger clubs—or just go for pure music on the riverfront.

Tucked away in northeast Lisbon, Nations Park has plenty of evening options for which you don't have to dress to impress. Catch a concert at the Atlantic Pavilion, then stay and dance after dinner in the restaurant-bars by the Lisbon International Fair, where you'll find lots going on.

Young people in Portugal tend to socialize in mixed groups, and are much more relaxed, both socially and morally, than their parents' generation. Still, they are more conservative than their peers in Spain. Like the Spanish, they can be physically demonstrative and verbal, but in a less intense, more restrained manner. They are open to meeting people from other cultures and very willing to try to speak foreign languages. You may find language a barrier, though. Spanish and English may be the second and third foreign languages taught at school, but not very many Portuguese are fluent in them.

There is greater equality between the sexes today than ever before. Young Portuguese women may take the initiative in inviting a man for a date, but they still like to be treated chivalrously. The man normally pays, and should certainly do so if he has invited her. If she has invited him, though, they can split the bill.

Appearance is important when going out on a date, If going clubbing you should dress elegantly in a casual style, paying attention to detail and good taste. Branded accessories, such as watches and cell phones, are status symbols, and noticed.

SPORTS

The Portuguese are extremely fond of sport, and their best-selling newspaper, *A Bola*, is devoted to the subject, especially football (soccer). Most towns have their own football team, but the leading clubs are Benfica in Lisbon and FC Porto. The Portuguese national team enjoys a high reputation, and Portuguese players can be found playing for major clubs across Europe.

Being blessed with mild weather and a coastline some 497 miles (800 km) long, Portugal offers a wide range of water sports, including windsurfing, surfing, and sailing, and hosts a number of international competitions. Golf and tennis are popular, and the Portuguese are keen cyclists and ramblers.

Bullfighting (*corrida*) in Portugal is less gory than the Spanish spectacle. A team distracts the bull with capes, preparing it for the mounted *cavaleiro* (main bullfighter), who is followed by a further team of eight who have to overcome the bull with their bare hands at the end, but are often tossed aside by it. The bull does not actually meet his death in the bullring but is led out at the end with a herd of cattle.

Getting Around

Mainland Portugal has a well-developed public transport system with around 1,740 miles (2,800 km) of railway track and around 44,117 miles (71,000 km) of paved roads. The main international airports are at Lisbon, Oporto, and Faro (for the Algarve). Madeira and the Azores have airports on most of the islands.

The Portuguese state railway, Caminhos de Ferro Portugueses, or CP, is a very effective way of getting around. The pride of the railway system is the *Alfa Pendular* trains, which link Lisbon, Coimbra, and Oporto, and for which seats can be reserved up to thirty days in advance. The *rapido* trains are almost as fast, whereas the regional and interregional lines tend to be slower.

The high-speed Alfa Pendular train in Lisbon

Rail travel in Portugal is cheaper than in most other countries in Western Europe, and, although express trains attract a supplementary charge, the fares are extremely reasonable. Savings can often be made by traveling midweek or buying a rail pass for one, two, or three weeks that offers unlimited travel over the network.

When traveling from Lisbon, make sure you go to the right station, as the city has four. There are no railways in Madeira or the Azores.

Mainland Portugal has an efficient express bus network operated by Rodoviara Nacional (formerly state-owned, but now privatized) and other companies, which serve places that are not accessible by rail.

URBAN TRANSPORTATION

One of the best ways to travel around Lisbon is by subway (Metro), which operates four lines that link the center to the suburbs and connect with buses and suburban trains. Buses, streetcars, and cable cars also operate throughout the city. You can buy tickets at metro stations and on buses, but it is cheaper to buy a block of tickets or a travel pass such as the Lisboacard.

Oporto also boasts a Metro, though not an underground one, together with buses and street cars. The Andante card can be used on all forms of transportation within the city.

Taxis are a beige color and operate on a meter within cities. For longer journeys the fare must be negotiated with the driver.

DRIVING

The road system has improved beyond recognition over the past two decades, and both highways and expressways are well signed. However, once you move off the beaten track, the roads start to deteriorate.

Tolls are payable on expressways and on the bridges that cross the Tagus River in Lisbon (the Vasco da Gama Bridge and the older 25 de Abril Bridge). For longer distances you collect a ticket from the tollbooth and pay when you exit. Green lanes (a white V in a green square) are for cars equipped with an electronic payment system.

In common with the rest of continental Europe, people drive on the right, pass on the left, and give priority to traffic coming from the right at junctions unless advised otherwise.

A car is a prized possession, and on weekends everyone likes to take to the road. Portuguese driving is erratic at the best of times and is often downright reckless. As a result, Portugal has one of the worst accident rates in Europe.

Perhaps as a consequence of this the police have become much stricter, and among the practices that are illegal are using a cell phone while driving, driving without a shirt or footwear, and driving while drunk. The drink driving limit is 0.5 mg per ml.

You should also carry your international or Portuguese driving license with you. The speed limits are 120 kmph (75 mph) on expressways, 90 kmph (55 mph) on main roads, and 50 kmph (31 mph) in built-up areas.

WHERE TO STAY

Portugal offers a wide variety of accommodation, ranging from five-star hotels to modest guesthouses (*pensão*). Local tourist offices can advise on what is available.

If you would like to stay in a historic building, there is a network of state-owned properties, such as castles and former monasteries, offering high-standard accommodation. These are known as *pousadas*. *Estalegens* are privately owned luxury hotels in buildings of character.

Aparthotels are hotels offering selfcontained apartments, and there are the ubiquitous motels. In the countryside you will find *hoteis rurais*—family-run country hotels. There are numerous campsites, especially in the Algarve, and a network of youth hostels (*pousadas de juventude*).

MEDICAL MATTERS

It is advisable to take out private medical insurance for Portugal since public health centers and hospitals tend to get very crowded.

Basic hospital treatment is free for EU nationals if you produce a European Health Insurance Card and ask to be treated according to EU arrangements. Doctors and dentists charge a nonrefundable fee, but you may get a partial refund on prescriptions. In Madeira you should ask for an official receipt from the doctor who treats you to obtain a partial refund.

The local regional health service office (Administração Regional de Saúde) can offer you further information.

LAW AND ORDER

Portugal is not a dangerous place, and there is little violent crime. However, you are advised, as always, to take the ordinary, sensible precautions such as locking doors, keeping valuables safe, and not leaving baggage unattended.

In urban areas the police force is known as the Policia de Segurança Pública; elsewhere the Guarda Nacional Republicana keeps the peace.

PLACES TO VISIT

In the summer, most Portuguese head for the coast—or for their second homes in the country. The beaches of the Algarve are a strong attraction and now draw a cosmopolitan crowd. However,

*Sesimbra beach,
south of Lisbon*

there are plenty of interesting buildings to see, such as Faro's Convento de Nossa Senhora da Assunção, the first Renaissance building in this region.

The Mosteiro (monastery) de Santa Maria de Alcobaça is a World Heritage Site, and has the distinction of being the largest church in the country. It was built in 1153 by Afonso Henriques to celebrate the capture of the town of Santarém from the Moors. Together with the monastery of Santa Cruz in the university city of Coimbra, it is the first Gothic building in Portugal.

Lisbon is a lively city with plenty of buildings of note and a vibrant cultural life. St. George's Castle, Pena Palace, Belém Tower, and the Jerónimos Monastery are all worth a visit.

Oporto also has a number of attractions, notably the historic city center, the wine lodges, and the Douro Valley.

There are plenty of interesting towns along the coast, and some attractive scenery in the mountainous regions.

Business and Professional Life

From 1920 onward Portugal's economy was in a parlous state. A few wealthy families dominated commerce and industry, and much of the country's resources were wasted on trying to preserve its colonies in Africa and Asia.

The 1974 Carnation Revolution, which restored democracy, has changed the situation for the better. Since joining the European Community (now the European Union) in 1986 Portugal's economy has become diversified and increasingly service-based, with a particularly successful tourist industry. EU grants have financed considerable improvements to the infrastructure, notably roads, bridges, hospitals, and improvements to agriculture.

Many of the seventy or so firms that were formerly state-controlled have been privatized and key areas of the economy liberalized, notably the financial and telecommunications sectors. The country adopted the euro in 2002 along with eleven other EU members, but it remains the poorest country in Western Europe, with a GDP per capita at roughly two-thirds of the EU average.

Productivity and growth have been hampered by a poor educational system, but this is improving. There is strong competition from low-cost producers in Central Europe and Asia for foreign direct investment.

BUSINESS CULTURE

It is difficult to offer hard and fast rules on the way business is transacted in Portugal. However, the majority of companies are small or medium-sized, and often family-owned, which means that they lack a precise management structure.

A number of international companies operate in Portugal, including firms engaged in the production and export of port. The latter may seem relaxed and informal in their conduct of business, but in other areas businesses have to work hard to retain their competitive edge.

Larger Portuguese companies that have been privatized have, for the most part, yet to shed the bureaucratic, compartmentalized structures that were in place when they were state-owned.

BUSINESS CONNECTIONS

Portuguese businessmen prefer to rely on the contacts they have built up over the years, which means that a newcomer is at a disadvantage when presenting himself for business. It will take time to build up trust and be admitted to the inner circle. If you have contacts in Portugal it is a good idea to name-drop, in order to establish your credentials. Who you know can often prove more significant than what you know.

THE WORKFORCE

The Portuguese workforce has a reputation for being loyal and competent, though not especially ambitious. Trade unions are not particularly strong, and rarely show their muscle.

Jobs are imprecisely defined, and people may be asked to undertake certain tasks on the basis of trust rather than because of the position they hold in a company. This can be confusing to the outsider. On the other hand, in the absence of clear job descriptions the Portuguese tend to be resourceful employees, good at thinking on their feet and multitasking. This ability—often referred to as *desenrascado*—is a highly rated quality.

An increasing number of Portuguese study business abroad, and are therefore aware of international business practices. However, the more astute ones combine what they have learned with the traditional Portuguese way of conducting business.

SETTING UP A MEETING

Business hours are generally from 8:00 a.m. to 5:00 p.m. Some firms start later and finish as late as 7:00 p.m. Lunch breaks are often long.

It is not a sensible idea to schedule a meeting for late July or August, since many businesses either close down during this period or operate with only a skeleton staff.

It is also unwise to schedule several meetings for one day, or set yourself deadlines. For one thing, meetings frequently start late (even if you yourself arrive on time) and are likely to be interrupted by coffee and lunch breaks. The Portuguese do not compartmentalize work and private life to the extent that other Europeans do.

Often the best initial approach is through a formal letter, although e-mailing is now starting to become more common.

MEETINGS

Your Portuguese hosts will probably dress quite formally for their working day, and certainly for any kind of meeting, so you are advised to do the same.

Don't expect to get down to business right from the start, as this could be regarded as discourteous. Instead, observe the social niceties and make a little small talk, perhaps offering some details about your travels or your family, and try to find some common ground to help the relationship along. Meetings are opportunities for briefings and discussions, and are unlikely to end with decisions. Even when there is an agenda, it is unlikely to be closely adhered to.

If a senior member of the firm is present at a meeting, the other participants will defer to him (this person is more likely to be a man than a woman) and conduct themselves with decorum. With no senior member to defer to, people often become competitive. Everyone will wish to express an opinion, often to contradict a point made by someone else. To get support for your views it may be a good idea to lobby for support beforehand.

Meetings are expected to be friendly affairs, so confrontation is to be avoided at all cost.

FORMALITY

The Portuguese adopt a formal style—certainly in the early stages of a business relationship—and this is reflected in the way people are addressed.

Anyone with a university degree should be addressed as "*Doutor*" (doctor) or "*Senhor Professor*," or, for example, "*Senhora Arquitecta*," if the profession is known. If neither name nor profession is known, the terms "*Senhor*" (Sir) or "*Senhora*" (Madam) can be used with the formal second person pronoun, *você*.

If a senior member of the firm or organization is present at a meeting, make sure you address your remarks principally to him.

PRESENTATIONS

When giving a presentation it is essential to keep it short and to the point. Visual aids can be very effective, particularly if they are labeled in Portuguese. Make eye contact with everyone, but the most senior person in the room needs to be the main focus of your attention. Don't prolong the presentation by giving unnecessary material.

NEGOTIATIONS

Be prepared to be negotiated down from your opening proposal, but don't then expect an instant decision. The Portuguese err on the side of caution and prefer to explore all the options carefully before concluding a deal, since nobody wants to be held responsible for lack of judgment.

CONTRACTS

Portuguese law is based on the Napoleonic code rather than common law, and because this is all-embracing there is no need for business contracts to cover every eventuality, as would be the case in the USA or Britain.

The Portuguese are not particularly litigious, and a handshake generally carries more weight than a legal document.

BUSINESS ENTERTAINING

This is a country where people are quite happy to mix business with pleasure, so if the opportunity arises to socialize with your business partners, it should be grasped.

Normally this will take the form of a meal in a restaurant, and whoever issues the invitation usually pays. The Portuguese are in a more relaxed frame of mind away from their workplace—although they still dress formally—and many deals are transacted over meals.

WOMEN IN BUSINESS

Portuguese women are becoming increasingly prominent in business and the professions, but men still hold the upper hand. Women with children often have to put their careers on hold because paid maternity leave is very short and there is a scarcity of crèches and nurseries to which they can entrust their children. Nevertheless there are many women in senior management positions who have achieved their status through merit and hard work.

Chapter 10

SPAIN

Key Facts

Official Name	Reino de España (Kingdom of Spain)	**Government**	Constitutional monarchy with a bicameral parliament (Cortes Generales) consisting of an Upper and a Lower House. There are seventeen regions with wide legislative and executive autonomy.
Capital	Madrid		
Major Cities	Barcelona, Valencia, Sevilla (Seville), Zaragoza (Saragossa)		
Area	194,620 sq. miles (504,582 sq. km)		
Terrain	Large central plateau (the *Meseta*) and several mountainous regions. Mediterranean and Atlantic coastlines	**Radio and TV**	There are state and private TV and radio stations. The state broadcaster is TVE, and there are a number of commercial and regional stations. The PAL B TV system is used.
Climate	Mediterranean in south; more temperate and wet in north. The *Meseta* and the southeastern coast tend to be dry, with hot summers.	**Press**	National newspapers with regional offices include *ABC, El País,* and *El Mundo.*
Currency	Euro	**English-language Media**	There are many English-language newspapers published in different cities throughout Spain.
Population	43 million		
Ethnic Makeup	Spanish 87.8%; other (Romanian, Moroccan, Germans, Ecuadorian, British) 12.2%	**Electricity**	230 volts, 50 Hz. Two-prong plugs used
		Internet Domain	.es
Language	Castilian 75%; Catalan 12%; Galician 8%; Basque 1%; other 4%	**Telephone**	Country code: 34. For international calls dial 00.
Religion	Roman Catholic 99%. Others include non-Catholic Christians, Muslims, and Jews.	**Time Zone**	CET (GMT/UTC + 1). Daylight saving in summer

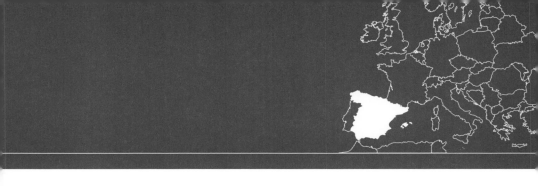

Map of Spain

FRANCE

PYRENEES

Gijón

La Coruña ASTURIAS

GALICIA

CANTABRIA Bilbao

San Sebastián

CANTABRIAN MOUNTAINS BASQUE
COUNTRY

Pamplona

NAVARRA

CATALUNYA
(CATALONIA)

ATLANTIC
OCEAN

LA RIOJA

CASTILLA–LEÓN

Zaragoza
(Saragossa)

Barcelona

COSTA BRAVA

ARAGON

MENORCA
(MINORCA)

Salamanca

Madrid

CASTILLA–LA MANCHA

PORTUGAL

EXTREMADURA

Valencia

IBIZA

MALLORCA
(MAJORCA)

VALENCIA

Badajoz

FORMENTERA

Alicante

Córdoba

MEDITERRANEAN
SEA

Sevilla
(Seville)

ANDALUCIA

MURCIA

Granada

COSTA BLANCA

Málaga

CANARY ISLANDS

Cádiz

COSTA DEL SOL

Ceuta

The Country and Its People

Spain is one of the largest countries of Western Europe, whose beaches attract millions of tourists every year as well as a growing number of permanent residents from northern Europe. Covering four-fifths of the Iberian Peninsula, which it shares with Portugal, it is separated from France by the Pyrenees and has a wide variety of landscapes, including a central plateau on which the capital, Madrid, is situated, making it the highest capital in Western Europe.

In addition to mainland Spain, there are two archipelagoes: the Balearic Islands in the Mediterranean, and the Canary Islands in the Atlantic, off the coast of Africa. There are also two small enclaves in North Africa.

Spain's climate varies according to the nature of the terrain. The northwest and the northeastern coast together with the Balearic

Countryside near Jaén, Andalusia

Courtyard and pool of the Alhambra

Islands are wet; the central plateau and the southeastern coast tend to be dry and subject to hot summers. Winters inland can be cold. The Canary Islands enjoy a subtropical climate with only minor variations in temperature.

The Spanish have a reputation for being confident, extravert, laid back, and noisy—addicted to *fiestas*, *siestas*, and procrastination. Although it may not be so true of the residents of the north, generally speaking, Spanish people are warm and friendly, and know how to relax and enjoy themselves. Work is regarded as a means to an end, rather than an end in itself. The Catalonians and the Basques regard themselves as distinct from other Spaniards.

It was not until 1492 that Spain was finally united, and it quickly became a force to be reckoned with, acquiring an enormous overseas empire and becoming the leading power in Europe. Since then its fortunes have waxed and waned, but after suffering a calamitous civil war in the 1930s, followed by a period of isolation under a dictatorship, the country has transformed itself into a prosperous modern democracy.

A HISTORICAL PERSPECTIVE

Over the millennia Spain has come under a number of influences, starting with the Phoenicians, who established settlements on the coast, and their descendants, the Carthaginians, who penetrated the interior under Hannibal's leadership. The Romans invaded in the second century BCE and incorporated much of the Iberian Peninsula into their empire, constructing roads, bridges, and aqueducts, and bequeathing their language.

With the fall of the Roman Empire the peninsula was invaded by the Visigoths, but they proved no match for the Moors from North Africa who invaded in the eighth century and remained for eight hundred years. They created a multiethnic civilization that enabled art, literature, music, architecture, science, and learning to flourish.

By the fifteenth century Moorish power was declining. When the Christian kingdoms of Aragon and Castile were united through the marriage of Ferdinand and Isabella, the struggle to recover the territory occupied by the Moors—the *reconquista*—came to a head.

Wealth and Influence

The year 1492 was an important one for Spain. The last Moorish stronghold, Granada, fell, and soon after, all Jews who refused to convert to Christianity were expelled. In the same year, Christopher Columbus sailed off to the New World in search of a sea route to the East. In succeeding years Spain acquired an enormous empire in the Americas, and the gold and silver that the *conquistadores* shipped back made the country fabulously rich.

Spain's political power increased when its Habsburg king, Carlos I, whose European possessions already included the Netherlands, Austria, and Naples, was elected Holy Roman Emperor (as Charles V) in 1520. After a turbulent reign, involving wars with France and the Ottoman Turks, and religious conflict in Germany, Charles abdicated in 1556, passing on Spain and the Netherlands to his son, Philip II. By this time most of Spain had become a centralized monarchy, in which the Inquisition, set up to root out heresy, wielded enormous power.

However, the country's prominence was short-lived. Philip was beset with numerous revolts and wars, not least the defeat of the Armada he sent against England in 1588.

In 1701 a dispute between France, the Dutch Republic, and Britain as to Carlos II's successor to the Spanish throne led to the War of the Spanish Succession. The French King Louis XIV's grandson, Philip, became King of Spain, and several former Spanish territories were lost.

From Monarchy to Monarchy

The nineteenth century was a turbulent era, which started with Napoleon's invasion in 1808. He replaced the reigning dynasty with his brother, Joseph Bonaparte, who introduced the Napoleonic regime. This led to the hard-fought Spanish War of Independence, which resulted in the expulsion of Napoleon's armies with British and Portuguese support.

Subsequent civil wars over the succession to the throne reflected opposing liberal and conservative views. A liberal revolution in 1868 deposed Isabella II and elected Prince Amadeo of Savoy, a son of Victor Emmanuel II of Italy, in her stead. Amadeo abdicated in 1873, and a republic was declared to fill the vacuum, but within a year Isabella's son Alfonso XII had succeeded to the throne.

During the course of the century Spain lost most of its overseas possessions, and Spanish society became increasingly divided politically between the landowners and military, supported by the Church, on one hand, and the workers and the middle class on the other.

The military intervened in 1923, and set up a dictatorship under General Miguel Primo de Rivera with King Alfonso XIII's approval. Both Rivera and Alfonso lost the confidence of the people. Rivera resigned and an alliance of political parties decided to end the monarchy and create the Second Spanish Republic.

General Franco, 1959

The 1936 elections were won by the left-wing Popular Front, but the result led to a civil war following a Nationalist uprising under General Francisco Franco that gained control over parts of the country. After an epic struggle during which a million people are reckoned to have lost their lives, the Nationalists emerged victorious. Franco became dictator, and remained in power until his death in 1975.

THE SPANISH CIVIL WAR, 1936–39

The organizers of the insurgency expected a quick triumph, but they had not reckoned with the extent of the support for the government. Civilians, trade unionists, students, and intellectuals from all over Europe flocked to their cause. The Nationalists were forced to seek help from Germany, Italy, and Portugal, and the German bombing of Guernica inspired one of Picasso's best-known paintings.

Franco had nominated Prince Juan Carlos, son of the legitimate heir to the throne, as his successor, and his accession in 1975 ushered in a new era of democracy and prosperity for Spain. The country has benefited greatly through its membership of the European Union and other international bodies, and, despite an abortive coup in 1981 and outbreaks of violence by Basque separatists, it has become one of the most stable countries in Europe.

Spain Today

Spaniards tend to identify more closely with their region than with their country, none more so than the Basques and the Catalonians. Along with the Galicians they have developed separately from the rest of Spain.

culture smart! **spain**

KEY HISTORICAL DATES

9th cent. BCE	Phoenicians establish settlements on the Iberian Peninsula.
218 BCE	Carthaginians under Hannibal establish a presence in Spain.
1st cent. BCE	Romans consolidate their hold on Spain.
5th cent. CE	Fall of Roman Empire. Vandals and Visigoths overrun Iberia.
711	Moors begin their conquest of Spain.
1037	Fernando I unites Leon and Castile for the first time.
1094	El Cid captures Valencia.
1492	Ferdinand and Isabella unite kingdoms of Castile and Aragon.
1512	Navarra united with the rest of Spain.
1519	Carlos I elected Holy Roman Emperor (Charles V).
1556	Philip II succeeds his father.
1561	Madrid becomes the capital.
1713	Spain loses Netherlands and Gibraltar at the Treaty of Utrecht.
1759	Carlos III's accession to the throne ushers in a time of prosperity.
1808	Napoleon's armies occupy Spain.
1868	Isabella II deposed.
1873	Republic declared, but monarchy restored the following year.
1898	Cuba and the Philippines become independent.
1923	Primo de Rivera stages a coup and becomes dictator under Alfonso XIII.
1931	Proclamation of the Second Republic; Alfonso goes into exile.
1936 generals	Republican Popular Front wins the election; nationalist under General Franco rebel and civil war breaks out.
1937	Nazi planes bomb Guernica.
1939	Civil War ends with Nationalists triumphant and Franco as dictator.
1959	Basque separatist movement formed to achieve independence for their region.
1969	Franco nominates Prince Juan Carlos as his successor.
1975	Death of Franco; Juan Carlos accedes to the throne.
1977	First free elections since 1936.
1981	Unsuccessful military coup by Antonio Tejero.
1986	Spain joins the European Community and NATO.

The Basques, in the north, are racially different from the other Spaniards, and their language, Euskera, bears no relationship to any other European language. It was only in the nineteenth century that the Basque country lost its sovereignty and was fully integrated into Spain. The Spanish Civil War and Franco's dictatorship attempted to erase Basque identity; even speaking Basque was declared illegal.

The deprivations led to the formation of a Basque separatist movement, known as ETA, which fought for regional independence. Since the restoration of the monarchy and democracy much of the autonomy the Basques aspired to has been achieved, but there are still extremist elements who wish to achieve total independence, and cause bomb outrages.

Catalonia (Catalunya), on the northwestern coast, also has its own language (Catalan/Castellano), which it shares with Valencia and the Balearic Islands. With its capital, Barcelona, it is the most prosperous area of Spain, and prides itself on its European outlook. The people are hardworking and serious—traits that set them apart. Although subject to Castile and Aragon, Catalonia was more or less self-governing until 1714, when the Bourbon armies moved in and the country came under the direct control of Madrid. Under Franco, Catalan was banned in schools, which the Catalans bitterly resented, but over the past thirty years Catalonia has regained much of its autonomy and Catalan is back in general use.

Galicia, in the northwest, is much poorer than Catalonia and the Basque country. The language, Gallego, was the language of courtly literature in the Middle Ages. However, it does not carry any social cachet these days, and the children there are brought up to speak Spanish. Although General Franco was Galician, he bestowed no special favors on the region.

GOVERNMENT

Spain is a constitutional monarchy with a prime minister (who is normally the leader of the majority party and has the title President of the Government). The prime minister chooses the cabinet (known as the Council of Ministers).

The legislature consists of the Senate and the Congress of Deputies (Congreso de los Diputados). The former has 264 members, of whom 208 are directly elected by popular vote and the other 56 appointed by the regional legislatures. The latter has 350 members consisting of two from the fifty electoral provinces and one each from the North African enclaves; the remaining 248 are elected by proportional representation.

Spain is divided into seventeen regions: from the northwest, Galicia, Asturia, Cantabria, Basque County, Navarra, La Rioja, Catalunya, Aragon, Valencia, Murcia, Madrid, Castilla–La Mancha, Extremadura, Castilla y León, Andalusia, the Balearic Islands, and the Canary Islands; it includes also the autonomous cities of Ceuta and Melilla in North Africa. In addition, every town or district has its own council (*ayuntamiento*).

Values and Attitudes

Values and attitudes are shaped by a number of factors, including climate, geography, and history. The hot climate of southern Spain acts as a disincentive to work in the afternoon and encourages instead a *siesta*; Spain's position on the edge of Europe may account for the sense of isolation that many Spaniards have felt until recently; and the strong arm of the state in the past may have discouraged people from taking the initiative.

Yet Spain is changing fast. Membership of the EU and the influx of other Europeans, as tourists or permanent residents, has exposed the Spanish to other life styles. Travel and education have broadened people's outlook, the power of the Church has waned, and Spaniards are becoming more like other Europeans.

The information in this chapter should be treated with caution. Not every Spanish person indulges in long *siestas* and carouses until after midnight. There are considerable regional differences; a Catalan, for instance, is generally more serious and less laid-back than an Andalusian. Furthermore, people's educational and social backgrounds may well have a bearing on their behavior.

PROCRASTINATION

Outsiders often associate the Spanish with a *mañana* mentality—the tendency to put things off until tomorrow, or the next day. While attitudes are changing, visitors should still come prepared for a flexible concept of time, especially in the southern parts of the country. Government offices in particular can be prone to putting things off, though exaggerating the urgency and making a tremendous fuss can sometimes expedite matters.

RELIGION

Historically, one of the most notorious Spanish institutions was the Inquisition, which clamped down on free thinking and promoted conformity and traditional Catholic values. People were taught under pain of death to accept hardship and suffering in the belief that they would be rewarded in the afterlife.

Spain's rulers were only too glad to use the Church as a means of social control. While other countries embraced new ideas, the Spanish remained in a time warp, and in the twentieth century Franco worked hand-in-hand with Church leaders, making the Catholic Church the state religion to keep change at bay.

Since the death of Franco the floodgates have opened and Catholicism's grip has weakened. Laws have been passed that contravene the Church's teaching, and people no longer feel compelled to attend church regularly, although the elderly and people in rural areas keep the tradition alive. The Catholic Church is now facing a shortage of recruits, and is importing priests from South America.

However, the legacy of centuries cannot be erased entirely. Religion still plays a role in people's lives in the many festivals and traditions that have religious roots, in the magnificent churches and cathedrals that draw crowds of pilgrims every year, and in the fatalistic attitudes of many people.

Spanish soldiers carrying their statue of Christ in Holy Week

THE FAMILY

The family, and more especially the extended family, is extremely important. People respect their elders, and three generations often live under the same roof. Even if they do not live together, it is quite common to find family members living in the same neighborhood.

By and large, families regard it as their duty to care for the elderly and the infirm, but the demands of modern life are forcing changes in attitude, and residential homes for the elderly are now beginning to appear.

The Spanish still like to keep their problems within the family rather than discuss them with outsiders. Mothers who go out to work prefer to entrust their children to family members rather than to strangers.

WOMEN

Since the death of Franco, women's lives have been transformed. Formerly, married women had to seek the approval of their husbands in matters of employment, property ownership, and even travel, and divorce, abortion, and contraception were prohibited by law. But this is not the case today. Spanish women are no longer exclusively confined to the home with a husband making all the decisions. While they are still expected to do the lion's share of the housework, they are enjoying greater independence than any generation before them.

Spanish women are embracing their new freedoms with relish. More women are going on to higher education these days, and many more have jobs. Marriage, it seems, no longer has charms. The marriage rate in Spain is now the lowest in Europe, and the size of the family has also plummeted; it is now the second-lowest in the world.

Spanish women have one singular advantage over their sisters in other countries: they do not have to relinquish their maiden name on marriage. Their children, however, take the name of their father.

CHILDREN

Children are the apple of their parents' eyes, and have considerable affection lavished on them. As a result, they tend to be somewhat spoiled, and often remain at home until they marry, or until work commitments force them to move away. Often they are not expected to contribute to their board and lodging, even if they are in well-paid jobs. On the other hand, they seem to grow up into confident adults.

GOVERNMENT AND BUREAUCRACY

The Spanish have an innate distrust of government and bureaucrats. Despite efforts to decentralize and make the system more responsive to people's needs, politicians and officials are perceived, rightly or wrongly, as seeking to line their own pockets.

Government offices at national, regional, and local levels are lethargic and unhelpful places, characterized by long lines of people waiting to speak with offhand officials. Quite simple matters may involve visiting a number of different offices. For this reason many people employ a fixer (*gestor administrativo*) to handle the paperwork for them, but this of course entails paying a fee.

INDIVIDUALISM

The Spanish are individualists, with very little civic or public spirit. People are more concerned to further their own interests than those of the community as a whole. They do not join organizations readily, and are suspicious of those who claim to be acting from altruistic motives.

Associated with this individual outlook is a sense of pride and honor. People are proud of their achievements, their family, and their region, and it is important not to dent their pride in any way by making, for example, disparaging comments about Spanish politics, which might be taken personally. They themselves, however, are as inclined to criticize aspects of Spain as the next man.

TOLERANCE

Under the Franco regime there was no political debate and strict censorship was imposed. Modern Spain is completely different. People engage in intense debates about political issues, and remain friends even if their views are diametrically opposed. Political pluralism is flourishing in the country today as a result of this tolerant attitude.

The removal of state censorship has had both good and bad consequences. Among the less welcome results are a growth in pornography, the blatant use of sex in advertising, an excess of violence on TV and in the cinema, and sensational news reporting. However, such criticisms could also be directed at other countries.

A large number of foreigners now live in Spain, with few problems. They are appreciated for the prosperity they have brought to once small fishing communities, and while some of the locals may envy their wealth, incidents against foreigners are few.

This tolerance, however, is not extended to gypsies, who are regarded with considerable suspicion. Immigrants from Africa are not particularly welcome either, although they played an important role as laborers during Spain's construction boom.

A CAREFREE ATTITUDE

One of the endearing traits of the Spanish people is their carefree manner and appetite for life. If they are having a good time they seek to prolong it. After all, why go to bed if you are having fun?

For this reason the streets of Spanish towns often resound with laughter until long past midnight. Moreover, it is loud revelry— people seem to like the sound of their own voices and will often shout to make themselves heard in crowded places.

They are also risk takers, which is why lotteries are so popular. Apart from the *lotería nacional*, which has been running for two centuries, there are plenty of others, regional as well as national. Slot machines and bingo also attract many takers.

Festivals and Traditions

Spain is the country of *fiestas*. Many are religious in origin; some are confined to a particular locality. Others commemorate historical events or have a political purpose. Up to fourteen public holidays may be taken a year, of which nine are fixed days, celebrated throughout the country; regional authorities may add another five. If a holiday falls on a Thursday or a Tuesday it is usual to make a long weekend by taking the intervening day off.

HOLIDAYS AND FESTIVALS

January 1	Año Nuevo	New Year's Day
January 6	Día de los Tres Reyes	Epiphany
March 19	San José	St. Joseph's Day
February/March	Carnaval	Carnival
March/April	Jueves Santo	Maundy Thursday
March/April	Viernes Santo	Good Friday
March/April	Día de Pascua	Easter Day
April 23 (Catalonia)	Día de San Jordi	St. George's Day
May 1	Día del Trabajo	Labor Day
June		Corpus Christi
June 23	San Juan	St. John's Eve
July 25	Día de Santiago	St. James' Day
August 15	Asuncion	Assumption
October 12	Día de la Hispanidad	National Day
November 1	Todos los Santos	All Saints' Day
December 6	Día de la Constitución	Constitution Day
December 8	Inmaculada Concepción	Immaculate Conception
December 24	Noche Buena	Christmas Eve
December 25	Día de Navidad	Christmas Day
December 28	Santos Inocentes	Holy Innocents Day

THE FESTIVE YEAR

Epiphany

Parades are held on January 5, in which the three Magi ride on horses or camels and throw sweets to children. Then children put food out for the kings when they go to bed, hoping they will leave gifts for them. Presents used to be exchanged just on this day, January 6, but the newer tradition of Santa Claus is catching on, and children often receive gifts on Christmas Day as well.

St. Joseph's Day

San José, on March 19, used to be a holiday throughout Spain, but most regions have replaced it with festivals to their local patron saints. It is still observed in Valencia, with a display of *las fallas*— giant papier-maché figures—and fireworks.

Carnaval

A number of European countries have a period of festivities before the start of the Lenten fast. Many places in Spain have carnival processions the weekend before Shrove Tuesday, while in others the celebrations last a whole week. One of the most exuberant and creative celebrations takes place in the port city of Cadiz.

Semana Santa

The week leading up to Easter is marked with processions, some very elaborate, with lifelike representations of the crucified Christ and the Virgin Mary. Passion plays are performed in certain areas and in Andalusia people sing flamenco songs to the statues.

Statue of the Descent from the Cross paraded in Holy Week

Sant Jordi

Saint George is the patron saint of Catalonia, and the Catalans celebrate his day on April 23 by giving roses to the women and books to the men in memory of the writer Miguel de Cervantes, who died on this day in 1616.

San Fermín

The well-known festival in Pamplona begins on July 7. During the week, before each bullfight, bulls are let loose and dash through the streets, accompanied by many of the onlookers.

Corpus Christi

This day, the first Thursday after Trinity Sunday, is marked in several towns with flowers, especially in Córdoba, where private houses are thrown open to the public, and in Sitges, where streets are carpeted with floral arrangements.

San Juan

This festival on June 23 dates back to pre-Christian times. Bonfires are lit and in some places, such as Malaga, people jump over the fires for luck or walk barefoot over hot coals.

Día de Hispanidad

Spain's National Day on October 12 marks the day that Christopher Columbus is supposed to have discovered America, and may be celebrated with parades and speeches.

Christmas

This is very much a family festival. On Christmas Eve there is a big family supper and people attend midnight mass (*la misa del gallo*) at their local church. Most households have a Christmas crib (*belén*). Christmas Day is given over to a leisurely lunch, with plenty of seafood and marzipan cakes.

Children sometimes now receive presents from Santa Claus at Christmas, as well as from the three kings at Epiphany, which is the more traditional time for this.

Santos Inocentes

December 28 is the Spanish equivalent of April 1, when children play tricks on one another.

PILGRIMAGES

The tradition of making pilgrimages is alive and well, the most famous shrine being the Cathedral of Santiago de Compostela in Galicia. For centuries pilgrims have trodden the same route across northern Spain to visit the tomb of St. James, the patron saint of Spain.

Another famous pilgrimage is made to the statue of the Virgin of the Dew (la Virgen del Rocío) in the hamlet of Rocío in Andalusia. Pilgrims come on horseback and in decorated carts at Pentecost, waiting for the statue to be brought out of the church on the Monday morning and paraded around the fields.

FIESTAS

The Spanish adore festivals, and are masters in the art of celebrating. Andalusia is particularly famous for them. People often stop work for a week to indulge in almost non-stop merrymaking in the streets.

There are parades of giant figures made of papier-maché, and in Catalonia people dressed as devils run through the streets setting off fireworks and are pursued by a dragon. The expulsion of the Moors from Spain is reenacted in many towns, with mock battles taking place between the two sides.

FAMILY OCCASIONS

The family-minded Spanish let no family event pass without a celebration, starting with a child's christening party.

Confirmation is another excuse for an elaborate celebration. Birthdays are important occasions for most Spanish children, and are usually celebrated with parties. Just as important, however, are name days; most Spaniards are named after saints and celebrate on the feast day of their particular saint.

Although the influence of the Church is on the wane, and civil ceremonies are an option, brides still prefer to have a traditional church wedding. Funerals are also conducted in church with great ceremony.

Getting to Know the Spanish

As we have seen, the Spanish are friendly and sociable, and it is not difficult to strike up an acquaintance. The country is blessed with a warm climate—in summer, certainly—which means that much of their leisure time is spent outside in public spaces. They love to party well into the night, and if you are in the habit of going to bed early, you may find yourself having to adapt to local customs.

THE LANGUAGE

Although an increasing number of Spaniards speak some English, especially those who come into regular contact with foreign tourists, few do so fluently, and people naturally feel much more comfortable speaking their own language. If you are hoping to make some Spanish friends during your stay you will stand a better chance if you, too, speak their language.

It is a good idea to acquire some rudimentary Spanish before you arrive, if you can. It is a relatively easy language to learn and pronounce, especially if you already speak French or Italian, or know some Latin. The Spanish government runs a network of cultural centers abroad (Instituto Cervantes) that offer language courses as well as information about the country. Most language schools offer courses in Spanish wherever you are, and there are plenty of institutions in Spain that can cater for your needs.

It is not necessary to go to the trouble of learning Basque, Catalan, or Galician if you are planning to visit these regions, although if you do manage a few expressions you will be an instant success.

MAKING CONTACT

If you have particular interests, such as sports, bridge, or music, you may well find a specialist club to join that will help you to meet Spanish people. Another idea would be to attend a particular church on a regular basis and get to know the other churchgoers.

In the big cities there will be a large, reasonably well-integrated expatriate population, who could serve as a way into Spanish society. You could try to find people with good Spanish contacts who would introduce you to some of the locals.

MAKING CONVERSATION

In Spain you need to drop any inhibitions you might have arrived with. People love to sit and chat, and will welcome any contribution to the conversation, especially if it is not too serious and spiced with humor.

On the other hand you should guard against dominating the conversation, boasting about your achievements, or trying to impress people. On the whole the Spanish prefer people who behave modestly and with decorum. They also appreciate compliments.

Sarcasm or wry humor is unlikely to be understood, and in any case would not be considered funny. Most topics are permissible, but it is best to err on the side of discretion.

FORMALITY

As in most of Europe people use both a polite form and a familiar form to express the word "you." It is best to start off with the polite form, *usted* (in writing, often abbreviated to *Vd.*), except when addressing young children, and only use the familiar form, *tu*, when your hosts use it with you. The plural forms are *ustedes* and *vosotros*.

GREETINGS

It does no harm at all to greet people in the street, or as you enter a bar or a shop. Handshakes are virtually obligatory between men, while women often bestow kisses on friends and acquaintances.

"*Buenos días*" (Good day), "*Buenas tardes*" (Good afternoon or evening) and "*Buenas noches*" (Good night) are the main greetings, followed by *Señor, Señora,* or *Señorita,* if you do not know the person's name. "*Hola*" (Hello) and "*Adios*" ('Bye) are informal greetings you can use with people you know.

On being introduced the Spanish are formal, and older people in particular prefer to maintain a certain reserve; but relations quickly relax. Women greet both sexes with a kiss on both cheeks; men shake hands, slap each other on the back, and hug each other.

The Spanish are also disconcertingly direct and dispense with common courtesies, such as "please," "thank you," and "excuse me." Men are never slow to compliment a woman on her good looks and some may call out comments in the street.

INVITATIONS HOME

Most invitations will be to public places, such as restaurants or bars, but from time to time you may be invited into someone's home. This is a rare privilege, and you should make an effort to be on your best behavior.

If a meal has been prepared in your honor, be sure to show an interest in the food you are eating and compliment the hostess. It is a nice gesture to bring along a small gift, such as chocolates or flowers.

Daily Life

HOUSING

There has been a pronounced exodus from the countryside over the past fifty years, and now three-quarters of the population live in the towns and cities. Most people live in apartments, which they own rather than rent.

The idea of rural life still appeals, however, and there is a high rate of second-home ownership; on the weekends many city dwellers head for their country retreat. In rural areas most people live in houses that reflect the character of the region. Andalusian houses built around patios are distinctly Moorish in style.

THE HOUSEHOLD

The man may be the head of the household, but it is the woman who presides over the domestic arrangements, assisted by her daughters, if she has any.

Modern husbands sometimes lend a hand with the household

chores, and with more women working outside the home today such help is welcome. In large households grandmothers also help in the preparation of food.

Spanish people like their food fresh, so many women prefer to shop on a daily basis, using local shops, which usually close for most of the afternoon and then reopen from 5:00 to 8:00 p.m. Most towns have a covered market selling fresh produce. Bargaining is the norm.

DAILY ROUTINE

For the Spanish the day starts at 7:00 or 8:00 a.m., no matter what time they have gone to bed. People generally eat a light breakfast of toast with white coffee (*cafe con leche*), and have a sandwich and fruit juice or coffee later in the morning. Work normally stops at 1:00 p.m., when people return home for a substantial lunch followed by a lengthy break—the famous *siesta*. This may be followed by what we might call tea (*la merienda*)—which is in fact probably coffee, with a sandwich or cake. After this many people resume work at 5:00 p.m. for another three hours, possibly calling in at a *tapas* bar on the way home.

Dinner (*la cena*) starts late—at 9:00 p.m. or possibly later—and is usually lighter than lunch. Younger children probably have their meal earlier and are in bed before dinner is served. People tend to stay up until well past midnight.

Old Library, University of Salamanca

EDUCATION

Education is highly prized in Spain, and parents hope their children will go on to college or university.

Education is compulsory from the ages of six to sixteen, but many children begin their education at the age of three. The school day for young children lasts from 9:00 a.m. to 1:00 p.m. and 3:00 to 5:00 p.m. Secondary school starts at 8:00 a.m., but one afternoon a week is completely free.

Around half the schools are privately run, but receive funding from the state. Government schools are more strictly controlled by the state.

Some college or university students receive government grants, but around half of them work to support their studies. Spanish universities tend to be overcrowded, but with the drop in the birth rate the situation is likely to ease soon.

THE ARMED FORCES

Compulsory military service came to an end in 2001, and Spain now has a volunteer army.

NEWSPAPERS, RADIO, AND TV

Spain has around ninety daily newspapers, including regional papers, some of which are published in Basque or Catalan. Of the nationals, *ABC*, based in Madrid, is the oldest, having been founded in 1903; *El País* has a left-wing orientation, and *El Mundo* is a popular tabloid. *Marca* is a widely read sports paper. Barcelona's *La Vanguardia*, published in Spanish, was founded in 1881, while the leading paper of the Basque region is *El Correo*. Sunday newspapers have a particularly large circulation, led by *El País Seminal*. Celebrity magazines, like *¡Hola!*, have a wide following.

The national broadcasting company is TVE, and there are a number of commercial and regional stations, such as Antena 3.

MAIL AND TELECOMMUNICATIONS

The postal service is fairly good, with post offices (*correos*) open on weekdays from 9:00 a.m. to 2:00 p.m.; to 1:00 p.m. on Saturdays. There is a wide range of services. Postage stamps are also obtainable from tobacconists (*estanco*). Mailboxes are painted yellow.

There are a number of telephone service providers using lines rented from Telefonica. Telephone numbers consist of nine digits including the area code. The national code is 34. Public telephone kiosks (*cabinas*) take coins or phone cards (obtainable from tobacconists). Cell phones are popular.

Around two-thirds of Spaniards use the Internet, and broadband is widely available. There are Internet cafés in most urban centers. Spain's Internet domain is .es.

Leisure Time

Spanish people are not solitary souls. They love spending time with family and friends, and they would rather go out to enjoy themselves than stay at home. Perhaps that is why Spain has so many public festivals.

SHOPPING FOR PLEASURE

One of their great pleasures is to stroll around the shops, either with specific purchases in mind or simply to window-shop. Like other businesses, most shops close in the afternoon to reopen at around 5:00 p.m. They normally close on Sundays.

EATING OUT

People delight in eating out—and it is quite normal to pop into a bar on their way home after work or before the main meal for a

light bite. These snacks are called *tapas,* and the popularity of *tapas* bars is now spreading to other countries.

There is a huge variety of *tapas*, from portions of Spanish omelet (*tortilla de patatas*) to small fried fish (*pescadito frito*). In traditional bars the clientele may throw their napkins on to the floor when they have finished.

The serious eating is reserved for lunch and dinner, when at least three courses are the norm. Restaurants range from the cheap and cheerful to expensive and upmarket, but the latter do not always serve the best dishes. Most restaurants offer a fixed price menu (*menú del día*) for lunch. The à la carte menu offers a wider choice of food but is more expensive.

TIPPING

The bill normally includes a service charge. If it doesn't, round the bill up, or leave a tip of around 5 percent. It is customary to offer taxi drivers and hairdressers a similar amount.

FOOD

Spanish food is remarkable for its variety, and there is considerable regional variation. Seafood is especially popular, not only on the coast but also as far inland as Madrid, thanks to a very efficient distribution system. Among the foods worth sampling are:

cocido madrileño	meat stew from Madrid
paella	saffron rice with seafood from Valencia
butifarra	meats and sausages from Catalonia
gazpacho	cold tomato and garlic soup from Andalusia
cochinillo	suckling pig
bacalao al pilpil	cod fried in garlic
chorizo	paprika sausage
pulpo a la gallega	Galician octopus
jamón serrano	cured ham

DRINK

One of Spain's most famous exports is sherry, from Jerez de la Frontera in Andalusia, close to the port of Cadiz. This is wine fortified with brandy. The driest and palest sherries are the *finos* and the *manzanillas*, which have a salty tang. *Amontillado* is a softer, darker sherry often made from old *fino*. *Oloroso* is heavier and darker and is the basis of many of the good sweet sherries.

The area is also well known for its brandies, known as *coñac*, which tend to be sweeter than the French equivalent, but no less palatable. At the end of a meal people may well have coffee laced with brandy or some other spirit—*un carajillo de coñac*.

Spanish table wines should not be overlooked. Their quality improves from year to year and wines from less famous regions are starting to compete with the red wines of Rioja and Navarra, close

to the French border. The Basque country produces some refreshing white wines, and Catalonia has a number of highly regarded whites, including the sparkling *cava*. Spanish beer is also good, but is rarely drunk at meal times.

The traditional toast used to be "¡*Salud y pesetas!*" ("Health and money!") but now that Spain has entered the eurozone the *pesetas* may have become redundant!

Although the Spanish enjoy drinking wine and brandy, drunkenness is rare. People are aware of their limits and frown on those who let their drinking get out of control.

CULTURE AND ENTERTAINMENT

Live theater and music are popular in Spain, and there are opera and ballet in the larger cities. It is perhaps not surprising that Spain, and especially Catalonia, has produced opera singers as great as Plácido Domingo, José Carreras, Victoria de los Angeles, and Montserrat Caballé.

Theaters such as the Teatro de la Commedia in Madrid and the Teatro Nacional de Catalunya in Barcelona put on a wide range of drama by both foreign playwrights and homegrown talent such as Lorca and Lope de Vega. The Teatro Real is Madrid's opera house and its equivalent in Barcelona is the Gran Teatro del Liceu. Spain has also developed its own unique form of musical drama: *zarzuela*.

ZARZUELA

This form of musical play was first performed at the royal residence of La Zarzuela near Madrid in the seventeenth century. *Zarzuela* consisted of spoken dialog, songs, choruses, and dances. Lope de Vega and Pedro Calderón de la Barca were among leading playwrights to work in this genre.

The mid-nineteenth century saw a revival in interest in the form, and it became a witty, satirical drama that included folk music and dance. Nowadays a distinction is drawn between the lighthearted one-act *zarzuela* (*genero chico*) and the longer, more serious version of up to four acts.

The major centers also put on concerts, both pop and classical, and musical festivals are held throughout Spain, especially during the summer. It is worth remembering that Spain has produced a number of fine composers, among them Enrique Granados, Isaac Albéniz, and Manuel de Falla.

Art lovers have plenty to see in Spain. Bilbao is famous for its innovatively designed Guggenheim Museum, and the Prado in

The Guggenheim Museum, Bilbao

Madrid, with its famous collection of paintings by Goya, El Greco, and Velázquez, is regarded as one of the world's great art galleries. Fans of El Greco should include a visit to Toledo, where the famous painter worked. Catalonia has museums devoted to two of her famous sons: Pablo Picasso and Joan Miró.

NIGHTLIFE

The nightlife in Spain is vibrant, especially in the cities and along the coastal strip, where you can walk along the beach or drink till the small hours. There are places to dance the night away; some of these offer live music, others a disco and a DJ. Most of them charge an entrance fee, and their drinks are more expensive than those in the bars. In the early morning you can move on to a bar or café for a breakfast of hot chocolate and doughnuts.

Entertainment of a more authentically Spanish kind can be found in flamenco clubs (*tablaos*), and it is sensible to ask around to find out where the best exponents of this art are appearing.

FLAMENCO

Flamenco originated in the fourteenth century among the Andalusian gypsies (*gitanos*), and has its roots in Andalusian, Arabic, and Jewish folk song. By the late eighteenth century flamenco schools had been established in Andalusia.

Originally the music was vocal, accompanied by rhythmic hand clapping (*toque de palmas*) as dancers improvised on basic movements, but today guitars play an essential role. The male dancer's steps are intricate, with toe and heel clicking, while female dancers rely more on hand and body movements in a manner reminiscent of classical Hindu dances. Among the greatest modern exponents are the guitarist Paco de Lucia and the dancer Joaquín Cortés.

STUDENTS, CLUBBING, AND CLOSE ENCOUNTERS

Madrid and Barcelona set the nightlife style in Spain. Though these cities play host to some legendary nightclubs, it's not all about dancing and drinking. Late evening meals see families out socializing for hours, and groups of friends sip coffee, beer, or wine in restaurants and cafés till the early hours. The bars in Old Town Barcelona provide a mixture of tourist spots and more local and trendy venues. In Spain the terms café and bar are almost synonymous, with a *bodega* specializing in wine and a *cerveceria* serving mostly beer. There's also the Gothic Quarter, which houses more authentic local venues among its labyrinth of alleys.

The hottest nightclubs don't usually open until midnight, with some places waiting until 1:00 or even 2:00 a.m. to open their doors. The trendiest spots, which attract the trendiest DJs, are always opening and closing, changing hands, and moving location, so it's best to talk to locals and check current listings for the latest news to find what you are looking for.

In Madrid you have more choice of entertainment. Around the Gran Via, hotspots and nightclubs are plentiful. La Latina, near to the Plaza Mayor, is a Sunday afternoon favorite, where you will find crowds packed into the bars around Plaza de la Paja, Plaza de San Andrés, and Cava Baja. Chueca is the dynamic hub of gay Madrid. It is the most modern of the *barrios* in décor and style, and the nightlife there is refined. The Salamanca district is the choice location for those with money—keep an eye out for celebrities and models among the flashy cars and designer labels. Alternatively, the Malasaña nightlife represents Madrid's counter-culture, its young, hip, alternative partygoer. The places to go are around Plaza Dos de Mayo, Calle de San Vincente Ferrer, and Calle de la Palma. Calla del Pez, closer to Gran Vía, attracts a slightly more mature and stylish crowd, with some of the best tapas bars, cafés, and jazz bars. Lavapies is Madrid's most recently gentrified area, inhabited by hippies, artists, and a large immigrant population. There are restaurants and nightspots to suit the most eclectic tastes, with a wonderful multicultural vibe.

In order to date someone in Spain you will probably have to work on your Spanish. You will find that young Spaniards are willing to try out their English, but it really is up to you to make the greater effort. Another tip for success in Spain is to pay attention to your appearance and look smart. It may sound superficial, but the Spanish, especially in the bigger cities, pride themselves on their dress sense—this is continental Europe, and one of the world's fashion capitals.

The Spanish are passionate and verbal; their approach to dating is characterized by constant communication and interaction. Most Spanish men will be suave, chivalrous, and courteous to the woman they are genuinely interested in; however, they can be flirtatious to the point of annoyance toward a woman they don't know. Both men and women ask each other out, and it is customary to split the cost of the date at the initial stages. The Internet now plays a part in the dating scene, with social networking becoming widely used.

SPORTS

Football (soccer) is a national obsession; Spaniards love to play it and to watch it. Nearly every town has its local team, which is usually well supported, and the country boasts two of the richest teams in Europe—Real Madrid and FC Barcelona—plus a distinguished line-up of international players.

Basketball has soared in popularity since Spain won a silver medal in the sport at the 1984 Olympics. Tennis has also attracted more followers recently and has produced players of international standing: Rafael Nadal is currently ranked the world champion. Cycling is another favorite pastime, especially in the north of Spain, and all over the country there are golf courses that are second to none.

Swimming, sailing, and other water sports are, of course, very popular along the coast and on the islands, while Formula 1 racing, motor cycle racing, and hockey on roller skates are well-attended spectator sports.

Handball is a popular participatory sport, while the Basque country has a number of sporting activities that are unique to its region.

BULLFIGHTING

One of the most characteristic sports of Spain is the bullfight (*la corrida de toros*—literally, the bull race). This is a national passion, and throughout Spain there are reputed to be four hundred bullrings (*plazas de toros*), where the bullfights are held. People turn up to admire the bravery and the skills of the bullfighter against the bull—a special type known as the *toro bravo*, bred for its aggressive instincts.

The bullfighter (*matador*) is assisted by three *banderilleros* on foot who work with the cape and thrust decorated darts into the bull, and three *picadores* on horseback, who harry the bull with lances.

The *matador* faces the bull alone initially, and is then joined by the *picadores*. The *banderilleros* then appear and stick the lances into the bull's back, and finally the *matador* returns to gain mastery over the bull and effect a kill.

Catalonia banned bullfighting in 2010.

Getting Around

A great deal of money has been invested in Spain's infrastructure over the past two or three decades, and getting around the country has never been easier. Mainland Spain has a comprehensive rail network 15,000 km (9,321 miles) long, run by RENFE, the national rail company. The fares are among the cheapest in Europe—and the trains the slowest. However, the system is being upgraded and new high-speed AVE trains which run on European standard-gauge tracks have been introduced.

Most other trains, including the TALGO express trains, run on the existing wide-gauge track. The fares are higher on fast trains and reservations are advisable, but discounted fares are also available. Apart from RENFE there are a number of small rail companies that operate services—often on narrow-gauge railways.

Privately owned bus companies run services between cities, and these buses are often faster than the normal trains. Advance booking is essential.

URBAN TRANSPORTATION

There is an excellent public transport system. Madrid has a very extensive metro (subway) system, as also do Barcelona, Bilbao, and Valencia. Metros are planned for Seville and Malaga.

Good bus services run in all the major cities and towns, and both Madrid and Barcelona have buses throughout the night. Valencia, Bilbao, and Barcelona also have streetcars.

In most cases you can buy a pass, valid for ten journeys, which works out much more cheaply than buying one ticket at a time, and there are special deals for visitors who are only staying a few days. A season ticket is recommended for longer stays.

DRIVING

Driving in Spain is sometimes hazardous, since local drivers can be aggressive and unpredictable. The rules of the road are similar to those in other countries of continental Europe, including giving priority to traffic approaching from the right. You must not turn left if there is a solid line in the center of the road, and keep an eye out for traffic signals, which are sometimes suspended above the road. Parking spaces are marked in blue, and parking where the sidewalk is yellow is illegal, even though people risk it.

For any traffic infringement, such as speeding, drunk driving, or using a cell phone while driving, you may be issued with an on-the-spot fine. The drink-driving limit is 0.5 mg per ml.

You must carry with you a current driving license, some form of ID, insurance, and the car registration document. You must also carry two red warning triangles, spare bulbs, a first-aid kit, and a fire extinguisher.

The speed limit on *autopistas* (expressways, with the initials AP) is 120 kmph (75 mph); on *autovías* (dual carriageways marked A) and *carretas nacionales* (marked N or CN) with a hard shoulder it reduces to 100 kmph (62 mph). On lesser roads the limit is 90 kmph (56 mph), and in towns it is 50 kmph (31 mph).

Spain has around 1,240 miles (around 2,000 km) of *autopistas*, for which you have to pay a toll to use. At each tollbooth there are three lanes: *Telepago* is for cars fitted with a special chip, *Automático* for paying by credit card or with the exact change; and *Manual* for a booth with an attendant.

WHERE TO STAY

Spain is a top tourist destination, and there is a wide range of accommodation on offer. It is advisable to book in advance, especially in the high season or if it is *fiesta* time. Local tourist offices have accommodation lists.

Paradors (*paradores*) are well worth considering. These are government-run hotels, often in historic buildings, but with a full range of facilities. In country areas you will find *casas rurales*, which are privately run country-house hotels.

Hostales are usually family-run places that are cheaper than hotels, but may not have such facilities as a restaurant or bar. Youth hostels (*albergues juveniles*) offer cheap, basic accommodation.

MEDICAL MATTERS

Health services in Spain are very good. Visitors other than EU citizens are advised to take out private medical insurance. EU citizens are entitled to virtually free treatment, but need to produce a European Health Insurance Card and consult a doctor who works within the Spanish Health Service. The same is true for hospital treatment. Dental treatment is not provided under the state system.

LAW AND ORDER

Generally speaking, Spain is a safe country providing you exercise common sense, like locking your car and keeping your valuables in a safe place. If a problem occurs, contact the local police. There are three main police forces in Spain: the Policia Municipal (Municipal Police), who deal with minor crime and are particularly prominent in tourist resorts, the Policia Nacional (National Police), who deal with serious crime, and the Guardia Civil (Civil Guard), who patrol the highways and rural areas. The Basque country and Catalonia have their own police forces.

PLACES TO VISIT

Aside from its great museums and galleries, the country is full of interesting buildings. In Andalusia there are monuments dating back to Roman times, such as the aqueduct in Segovia and the theater at Mérida, and some outstanding Moorish architecture— the Alhambra Palace and the mosque at Córdoba, to name but two. There is a wealth of religious buildings, notably the cathedrals of Pamplona, León, and Burgos, Santiago de Compostela. and El Escorial, the great monastery palace built by Philip II. When visiting a place of worship it is important to dress appropriately and cover up to avoid causing offense. Shorts, skimpy T-shirts, and short skirts are taboo, and ideally one's arms should be covered, too. Barcelona is full of fascinating architecture, including a number of buildings designed by Gaudí—such as the Sagrada Familia church, consecrated and designated as a minor basilica by the Pope on November 7, 2010, and Palau Guell. The Monestir (monastery) de Montserrat is also well worth a visit. And there are many ancient towns that are a delight to explore, such as the university city of Salamanca, and Toledo. As well as its Roman remains, Segovia has its famous Alcázar, residence of the kings of Castile from the middle ages.

Spain also boasts magnificent scenery, from the Pyrenees to the two island archipelagoes. Walkers are well catered to, with well-marked footpaths all over the country. There are also about two hundred national parks.

The beaches of the islands, as well as those of the mainland, including the Costa Brava, the Costa Blanca, and the Costa del Sol, are a magnet for holidaymakers from all over Europe—it's not difficult to see why.

Business and Professional Life

The Spanish economy flourished after Spain joined the European Union, and the country developed very successful industrial, agricultural, and tourism sectors. However, the property bubble burst in 2008, leading to a sharp downturn in the economy and increasing unemployment.

How you transact business in Spain will depend on where you are. The Catalans are brisk and businesslike—more like the

Banco de España headquarters, Madrid

French; the businesspeople of Madrid are slightly aloof and have a sense of their own importance; the Andalusians are the most laid-back of all and are more likely to transact business over lunch or dinner than in the office.

All have one trait in common: trust. All Spaniards place great emphasis on relationships, and it is difficult to transact any meaningful business until trust has been established. Spaniards like to get to know the people who want to do business with them, which is why socializing is an important item on any visitor's agenda.

BUSINESS PRACTICE

Most companies tend to be small, family-owned businesses where people hold positions by dint of family ties and friendship rather than knowledge and ability. At the other end of the scale are international companies, which put greater stress on competence, and state-owned firms, which are somewhat bureaucratic.

In the past Spain suffered from a lack of managers with professional business skills. The situation is changing as more managers receive business training, either within Spain or abroad—especially France. However, tensions can arise between the new generation of managers who seek greater decentralization of decision making and the more authoritarian older generation.

Most people work a forty-hour week and have a break of two or three hours for lunch. Vacations are generally taken in July and August, which means that most of the decision makers are away during these months and businesses are manned by only a skeleton staff. You also need to be aware of public holidays, which are sometimes an excuse for a long weekend.

THE DECISION MAKER

Traditionally, the man at the top makes the key decisions. Devolved management styles have yet to take root in Spain, except perhaps in the more cosmopolitan Basque country and Catalonia.

The boss (*jefe*) is likely to be a charismatic, paternalistic autocrat who commands the loyalty of his staff. He is the person who issues the orders, which will be clear and detailed. However, not all his subordinates will feel disposed to implement them—and this is a particular feature of government service. The Spaniards tend to follow their own instincts.

The boss's judgments may be intuitive rather than based on cold reason. His role is also broader than the job descripton. He takes an interest in his staff, and often spends time advising them on personal matters in addition to running the company.

NETWORKING

As mentioned above, relationships are important in business, which is why the Spanish go to great pains to get to know people who may become their business partners. For them, the people are more important than the products or services they are offering.

They will want to know about your family, your interests, your aspirations, and your likes and dislikes. They may solicit personal favors. This can be disconcerting to a stranger, but, if you oblige them and help them out, this will be much to your credit and may mark the start of a fruitful relationship that will need to be kept up by regular letters and phone calls.

Once you have established your credentials with one decision maker, doors will open to others. Business deals that can take an age to pull off in other European countries may only take a few days in Spain if the chief players know one another. Having friends in the right places can facilitate many matters.

SETTING UP A MEETING

If you are making an initial appointment, this is best proposed by letter. It should then be confirmed by telephone. As a matter of course, you should do your homework beforehand and make sure your literature and documentation are in Spanish.

You should not assume that the person you are meeting, particularly if he is in a senior position, can speak any other

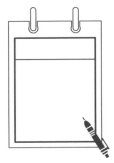

language than his native tongue, although nowadays younger managers usually speak French or English. If you don't speak Spanish yourself, take someone with you who does, who can act as your interpreter. On arrival at the meeting place, give your business card to the receptionist.

FLEXIBILITY

Time is a flexible concept for Spaniards. You should never expect things to start or finish on time, and it is futile to impose deadlines. You may wonder whether it matters if you arrive late for an appointment. It does. While the meeting may start late, you, the visitor, are expected to be punctual.

Business practice may at times seem haphazard, but this is another manifestation of Spanish flexibility. They are masters of multitasking and have no problem in dealing with a number of different matters or people at the same time.

APPEARANCE

As we have seen, the Spanish pride themselves on their appearance, and they expect outsiders also to present themselves in the best possible light. For business meetings dark suits or blazers are the norm, even in the heat of summer. Dressing casually for a meeting could indicate that you are a person of little substance or are not really serious about doing business. Once they get down to business in the office, it is quite usual for jackets to be discarded, but it is for the most senior person present to set the example

They also like to indicate discreetly that they are successful people who enjoy a certain standing, and will notice your own accessories. An expensive watch, gold cufflinks, or a top-of-the-range pen help to create such an image. Status symbols count.

MEETINGS

Most Spaniards prefer a relaxed, informal style of doing business, though they may seem quite formal at first and expect to be addressed as, for example, *Don* Alfonso or *Doña* Antonia.

A meeting may well begin with a long speech in which a person introduces himself and outlines his aims. This could be followed by an equally long response from the other side.

If a number of people are involved it can become a noisy affair, in which people interrupt one another and all speak at once. The participants regard it as an opportunity to air their personal opinions rather than as a decision-making forum. The idea of having an agenda and sticking to it is foreign to many Spaniards.

Finally, the chairman expresses his own view, and the tendency is for everyone to fall in line. Meetings are essentially vehicles for issuing instructions and getting to know people, rather than ways of achieving consensus.

PRESENTATIONS

Presentations should be kept as short as possible, as the Spanish are not particularly good listeners. Besides, they are probably more interested in your mannerisms and attitude than the content of your presentation.

But wherever you are you should avoid overstating your case for the product or service you are offering. A little modesty goes a long way.

Nor should you suggest that you are generally better informed than they are, or make any statements that could be could be interpreted as a criticism of your hosts or their country. Spaniards do not take kindly to people who impugn their personal honor.

BUSINESS ENTERTAINING

Business entertaining is a fact of life in Spain, and it is customary to take clients out to a good restaurant and pay—

unless they insist that you are their guest. This is another way of helping the relationship along, and often the most productive business is done over a meal.

WOMEN IN BUSINESS

Women are starting to make their mark in business and the professions. They now account for a large proportion of university graduates, and while very few of them have made it to chief executive status, it is perhaps only a matter of time before this happens.

Business and professional women expect to be accorded respect. In family businesses they could well be related to the head of the firm and wield a great deal of influence.

Chapter 11

SWITZERLAND

Key Facts

Name	Confederatio Helveticae (The Swiss Confederation). Short national names: Schweiz (German), La Suisse (French), Svizzera (Italian), Svizra (Romansch)	**Religion**	Roman Catholic 41.8%; Protestant 35.3%; Muslim 4.3%; Christian Orthodox 1.8%; other Christian 0.4%; Jewish 0.2%; others 1%; unspecified 4.2%; no affiliation 11%
Capital City	Bern (Berne)	**Government**	Democratic federal republic of 26 cantons. President is head of government and head of state. Bicameral parliament: upper house represents cantons; lower represents the people directly. Swiss system is characterized by referenda.
Major Cities	Basel, Genève (Geneva), Lausanne, Luzern (Lucerne), Lugano, Zürich (Zurich)		
Area	15,940 sq. miles (41,290 sq. km)		
Terrain	Mountainous in west; lowlands and hills in north and east		
Climate	Temperate; varies with altitude. In the mountains, cold, snowy winters, and cool to warm, cloudy, humid summers with occasional showers. In the canton of Ticino, Mediterranean	**Radio and TV**	The national state radio and TV network is the Swiss Broadcasting Corporation. The PAL system is in use.
		Press	National and regional newspapers incl. *Neue Zürcher Zeitung, Tages-Anzeiger, Le Temps*
Currency	Swiss franc	**Electricity**	230 volts, 50 Hz. Three-prong plugs used
Population	7.6 million		
Languages	National and official languages: German 63.6%, French 20.4%, Italian 6.5%. National, not official: Romansch 0.5%. Others 9%	**Internet Domain**	.ch
		Telephone	Country code: 41. For international calls dial 00.
		Time Zone	CET (GMT/UTC + 1). Daylight saving

Map of Switzerland

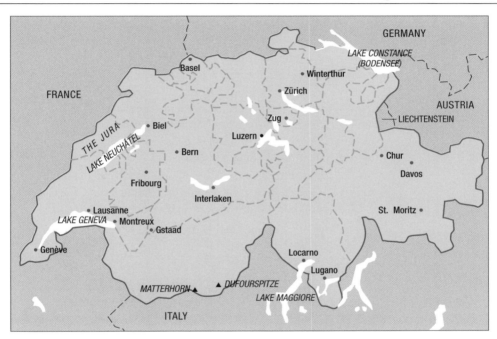

GERMANY

LAKE CONSTANCE
(BODENSEE)

Basel

Winterthur

Zürich

FRANCE

AUSTRIA

LIECHTENSTEIN

THE JURA

Biel

Zug

LAKE NEUCHÂTEL

Luzern

Chur

Bern

Davos

Fribourg

Interlaken

St. Moritz

Lausanne

LAKE GENEVA

Montreux

Gstaad

Genève

Locarno

Lugano

MATTERHORN ▲

▲ DUFOURSPITZE

LAKE MAGGIORE

ITALY

The Country and Its People

Despite its central position, Switzerland stands apart from the other countries of Western Europe. It is not a member of the European Community, it has a policy of strict neutrality, and is regarded as possibly the longest-established, certainly the most stable, democracy in the world. It has four languages (three of them official), and is home to a number of international organizations, including the International Red Cross.

Geographically, Switzerland can be split into three regions: the Jura from Lake Geneva to the Rhine, the Plateau from Lake Geneva to Lake Constance, and the Alps, which account for almost two-thirds of its area but are home to only 11 percent of the population. There are 1,500 lakes, of which Lake Geneva, Lake Constance, and Lake Lucerne are the best-known.

The Sertig Valley, near Davos

All this is in a territory that extends 137 miles (220 km) at most from north to south, and 220 miles (350 km) from east to west.

Switzerland is a land that defies all logic. How could a country in the center of Europe have escaped the conflicts that have beset the continent over the past two centuries? How could people with different languages and traditions live so successfully together? The answers lie in the nature of the Swiss, who, seven hundred years ago, appreciated the need to unite against a common foe while at the same time respecting each other's individual character. Intelligence, shrewdness, independence of mind, and a capacity for hard work have combined to make the country efficient and prosperous.

Among the Swiss who have have made a lasting impact on the world are the composer Honegger, the philosopher Jean-Jacques Rousseau, the educational reformer Johann Pestalozzi, Marie Tussaud of waxworks fame, the writer Johanna Spyri (author of *Heidi*), the psychiatrist Carl Jung, the child psychiatrist Jean Piaget, and the modernist painter Paul Klee. Arguably the people who had the greatest influence of all were the religious reformers Calvin (Swiss by adoption) and Zwingli. Clearly, the Swiss are a remarkable people who are worth getting to know better.

A HISTORICAL PERSPECTIVE

The Long March to Independence

Switzerland's Latin name, Helvetia, is derived from one of the Celtic tribes that lived in the area when it was incorporated into the Roman Empire. After the fall of Rome in the fifth century, Germanic Aleman and Burgundian tribes settled in the territory and later came under control of Charlemagne, who incorporated it into his Frankish Empire, precursor of the Holy Roman Empire.

Under the Treaty of Verdun in 843, Charlemagne's empire was divided among his grandsons and eventually fragmented into a number of self-governing states that paid only lip service to the Emperor.

The election of Rudolf of Habsburg as Holy Roman Emperor in 1273 threatened the independence of these states, including the self-governing Swiss communes of Uri, Schwyz, and Unterwalden. Rudolf sent bailiffs in to administer them on behalf of the Empire, but after his death in 1291 the three communes met to swear an oath of mutual support on the Rütli meadow by Lake

Lucerne. This compact is regarded as the birth of the Swiss Confederation.

The new Habsburg Emperor Ludwig I made another attempt to subjugate the territories, but his Austrian knights were defeated by the Swiss peasants, and in succeeding years more communities flocked to join the Confederation. Eventually the Emperor Maximilian I was obliged to grant them *de facto* independence.

WILLIAM TELL

Wilhelm Tell is Switzerland's national hero, and though doubts exist as to whether he was a real person, the legend is an inspiration to all freedom fighters.

After the Rütli compact, the Habsburg Emperor sought to seize the canton of Uri in order to control the trade routes across the Alps. He sent his bailiff, Hermann Gessler, to the town of Altdorf. Gessler raised a pole in the central square, put his hat on top, and ordered passers-by to bow to it as a mark of respect.

William Tell, a countryman, failed to bow as he walked past the hat, and was arrested by Gessler, who issued him with a challenge. If he could shoot an apple off his son's head, he would be released; if he refused, both Tell and his son would die.

Tell selected two arrows and succeeded in shooting the apple off the boy's head with the first. When Gessler asked what the second arrow was for, Tell said it had been destined for him, Gessler, if the first had killed his son. Gessler was furious and sentenced Tell to life imprisonment in his castle's dungeon. On the way to the castle Tell managed to escape, and killed Gessler with the second arrow.

Neutral and Democratic

Defeat by the French at the battle of Marignano, in northern Italy, in 1515 halted Swiss expansion. By now there were thirteen cantons in the Confederation, and despite being equally divided between Protestantism and Catholicism they remained neutral during the religious wars of the seventeenth century.

At the end of the Thirty Years War the Holy Roman Empire accepted Switzerland's independence and neutrality; but this was threatened when the French revolutionary armies invaded and created the centralized Helvetic Republic, effectively abolishing the cantons, which met with universal opposition.

After Napoleon's defeat at Waterloo the European great powers formally recognized Swiss neutrality and guaranteed it, and the country emerged stronger and more united.

In 1848, following a brief civil war between the Catholic and Protestant cantons, Switzerland adopted a federal constitution. In 1874 the Swiss established the principle of direct democracy through referenda. This was a time when the country was opening up to tourism, thanks to improved transport links. The Swiss were also beginning to apply their skills to precision industries, such as watchmaking, and the Swiss businessman and humanitarian Henri Dunant became instrumental in founding the International Red Cross.

Switzerland's policy of neutrality kept it out of the two major conflicts of the twentieth century. It was chosen as the location of the ill-fated League of Nations and later of the European headquarters of the United Nations. While it is a member of many international organizations, it has shied away from membership of the European Union for fear of compromising its independence and neutrality.

KEY HISTORICAL DATES

1273	Rudolf of Habsburg is elected Holy Roman Emperor and sends bailiffs to administer Uri, Schwyz, and Unterwalden.
1291	Death of Rudolf sparks rebellions. The three communities form a defensive alliance at Rütli meadow in Uri.
1315	Swiss peasants defeat Ludwig of Habsburg's army at Morgarten.
1499	The Swiss gain their independence from the Holy Roman Empire.
1513	Switzerland now comprises thirteen cantons.
1648	The Treaty of Westphalia recognizes Swiss independence.
1798	French armies invades Switzerland and impose a centralized system of government.
1815	European powers recognize and guarantee Switzerland's neutrality.
1864	International Red Cross is established.
1874	A revised constitution establishes the principle of national referendums.
2003	Switzerland joins the United Nations.

GOVERNMENT

Switzerland is regarded as an outstanding example of democracy at work, so it definitely merits a closer look.

Right at the top is the president, who is both head of government and chief of state. Below him is the Federal Assembly, which elects seven members to form a cabinet (the Federal Council), which has executive power.

The Federal Assembly actually consists of two chambers. The Council of States (the forty-six-seat Upper Chamber) has two seats for each canton. There are twenty-three cantons, of which Unterwalden, Basel, and Appenzell are each divided into two semi-cantons, each with its own legislature. The lower chamber is known as the National Council. This is a directly elected body with seats allocated to the cantons according to their population.

Government at the cantonal level is of particular interest. Each canton from the largest (Zurich, with 1,000,000 people) to the smallest (the semi-canton of Appenzell Inner-Rhodes, with a mere 15,000) has its own constitution, legislature, executive, and judiciary. Three of them have ancient democratic assemblies where all the citizens meet annually to choose their council and supreme court. The others are content to have elected representatives.

At the bottom of the pyramid come the smallest and lowest political units, the 3,000 *Gemeinden*, or communes, which have their own elected administrations and in some cases vote on issues in town assemblies.

LANGUAGES

Switzerland has four languages, of which German, French, and Italian have official status, and Romansch has semi-official status. Most Swiss are also fluent in English.

Fourteen of the cantons are German-speaking; Ticino is Italian-speaking; the cantons of Geneva, Jura, Neuchatel, and Vaud are French-speaking; in Bern, Fribourg, and Valais both French and German are used; in Graubünden (Grisons), Switzerland's most easterly canton, half the residents speak German, one-third Romansch, and the remaining one-sixth Italian.

Romansch is descended from the language of the Celtic Rhaetian tribes that peopled the area in Roman times. It is divided into two dialects: Sursilvan, spoken on the west bank of the Rhine, and Sutsilvan, spoken on the east bank.

Linguistic differences are mirrored by cultural differences. People in French-speaking areas would appear to have more in common with their neighbors in France, and the Italian speakers of Ticino with their Italian neighbors, not least Catholicism. The French cantons wanted to join the European Union in 1992, but the German majority vetoed the proposal.

Despite their linguistic and cultural differences, the Swiss have managed to live together harmoniously, respecting each others' regional identities. However, the influx of immigrants is changing the nature of Switzerland and tensions are starting to appear below the placid surface.

THE CANTONS AND THEIR LANGUAGES

Aargau	German
Appenzell	German
Basel	German
Bern	French, German
Fribourg	French, German
Geneva	French
Glarus	German
Graubünden	German, Romansch, Italian
Jura	French
Luzern	German
Neuchatel	French
St. Gallen	German
Schaffhausen	German
Schwyz	German
Soluthurn	German
Thurgau	German
Ticino	Italian
Unterwalden	German
Uri	German
Valais	French, German
Vaud	French
Zug	German
Zürich	German

Appenzell, Basel, and Unterwalden are divided into semi-cantons.

Values and Attitudes

In the case of most of the countries in this volume, national identity is determined to some extent by a common language or religion; but Switzerland does not fit the mould. It has achieved nationhood despite differences in language and religious belief.

These differences makes it difficult to identify traits that could be described as distinctively Swiss, apart from the strong sense of community and local democracy. The tendency is to concentrate on the character of the German-speaking Swiss who represent the majority.

However, one should not ignore the differences. People from the French-speaking parts sometimes appear more anarchic and left-wing than their solid, German-speaking compatriots, with their unswerving confidence in market forces. Ticino has much in common with northern Italy.

RESPONSIBLE CITIZENSHIP

With no strong centralist government, it would be possible for each canton to go its separate way. However, the Swiss recognize that there is strength in unity and are therefore unwilling to jettison a system that has served them well over the centuries. To do so would be irresponsible.

The Protestant reformers Zwingli and Calvin put the onus on individuals to take responsibility for their actions and to conform to the socially accepted norms. Swiss people are still expected to behave responsibly and work for the common good.

This involves fulfilling one's civic duties and adopting a policy of "do as you would be done by."

Switzerland is a small country where everyone lives in close proximity, so it is incumbent on all citizens to respect the rights of others.

CONFORMITY

Allied with the idea of responsibility is the pressure to conform. There are myriad regulations that to an outsider might seem petty or unnecessary, but far from rebelling against them the Swiss recognize they have been put in place for the common good to ensure that society runs smoothly and without disruption.

An example of this lies in garbage collection. All garbage has to be sorted and either taken to a recycling center or separated into bags for collection. There can be financial penalties for those who fail to recycle diligently.

The Swiss are extremely environmentally conscious and set very strict limits on car exhaust emissions. People are also exhorted to switch off their car's ignition when waiting at a crossing or traffic lights.

This does not mean that they are dull and humorless. On the contrary, they very much enjoy humor that is subtle and witty.

HONESTY AND INTEGRITY

Great importance is placed on correct behavior. The Swiss pay their taxes and keep to the rules, and take a dim view of those who don't. You come across unmanned stalls displaying vegetables, fruit, and other produce with an honesty box for payment. If you want to buy a newspaper, you drop a coin in the box and take one. It has been said that the Swiss do not need a police force since they are so good at policing themselves.

If you want an honest opinion, the Swiss will give you one, even if it is not to your liking. It is not that they wish to be offensive, but being truthful and upfront is part of Swiss democracy. People are used to stating their opinions frankly in political forums, so that after discussion some form of consensus can be reached.

CONSERVATIVE VALUES

The Swiss are sometimes accused of not moving with the times. For instance, women did not gain the right to vote at the federal level until 1971, and the country did not join the United Nations until 2003.

This is perhaps less a manifestation of conservatism than a reluctance to change for the sake of change. The Swiss have seen the rise and fall of plenty of nations more dynamic than their own, and have no desire to emulate them. They have done very well for themselves by not following the crowd or the latest fashions.

RESPECT FOR PRIVACY

The Swiss are private people, who like to keep themselves to themselves and respect the personal space of others. This is the reason film stars and others in the public eye are attracted to their country and set up house here. In Switzerland they have the assurance that they will be free from prying eyes or cameras.

One controversial aspect of this respect for privacy is the bank secrecy laws, which protect client confidentiality and which date from 1713. Violation of bank secrecy is a criminal offense, and any banker doing this can face imprisonment and steep fines.

Despite pressure from other countries that fear their citizens are operating bank accounts in Switzerland for tax avoidance purposes, the Swiss have steadfastly maintained their commitment to bank secrecy. However, this confidentiality does not extend to criminals, such as drug smugglers.

LOCAL LOYALTIES

Democracy reaches down to grass roots level in Switzerland. People identify closely with their local area or canton, because they feel they have a stake in their community and ought to support it in every way they can.

This is particularly true of the smaller towns, where everybody knows everyone else and where close friendships develop. Students prefer to study at their local university rather than one some distance away, because they like to maintain ties with their community.

This is not to suggest that the Swiss are entirely inward-looking. On the contrary, they take a great interest in other countries and have a number of international organizations based on their territory. They are also great travelers, who enjoy seeing the world. It is just that at the end of every journey they are content to come home.

WORK ETHIC

The Swiss have always been hard workers, of necessity. Their country is relatively poor in resources, and they have had to live by their wits. In the past this meant, for instance, hiring themselves out as mercenaries to foreign armies, where they gained a reputation for excellence.

Another contributory factor is Protestantism. It is worth noting that the two leading Protestant Reformers, Jean Calvin and Ulrich Zwingli, insisted that work was virtuous.

The Swiss work longer hours than most of their European neighbors, and generally take fewer holidays. In the past they have actually voted against shortening the working week or extending their vacation entitlement. In this respect they differ from their hardworking neighbors, the Germans.

Absenteeism is low; strikes are few and far between; and people turn up for work on time. In the French- and Italian-speaking areas people tend to be a little more casual in their attitude to work, and less prepared to put in extra hours.

RELIGION

Switzerland was a hotbed of religious ideas at the time of the Reformation. However, in the twenty-first century this religious fervor seems to have cooled off.

The country used to be predominantly Protestant, but immigration has boosted the number of Catholics, who now, according to the latest census, outnumber Protestants.

However, both Churches seems to be in decline, in terms of both church attendance and the number of people who believe in God. It would appear that family, job, and sports are more important to the Swiss than their religion.

A Church tax continues to be levied by each canton.

Festivals and Traditions

The Swiss may be hardworking, but they take time off occasionally to enjoy themselves. In addition to the national public holidays listed below there are cantonal holidays.

HOLIDAYS AND FESTIVALS		
January 1	Neujahrstag/Jour de l'An	New Year's Day
January 2	Berchtoldstag/St. Berchtold	
March/April	Karfreitag/Vendredi Saint	Good Friday
March/April	Ostern/Pâques	Easter Day
March/April	Ostermontag/Lundi de Pâques	Easter Monday
May 1	Tag der Arbeit/Fête du Travail	Labor Day
May	Auffahrt/Ascension	Ascension
June	Pfingstsonntag/Pentecôte	Whit Sunday
June	Pfingstmontag/Lundi de Pentecôte	Whit Monday
August 1	Nationalfeiertag/Fête Nationale	Swiss National Day
December 25	Weihnachten/Noël	Christmas Day
December 26	Stephanstag	St. Stephen's Day

THE FESTIVE YEAR

New Year

The New Year is a time for celebration. On New Year's Eve it is customary to light fires on the mountains and for church bells to ring in the New Year.

Epiphany

Le Jour des Troi Rois, or Dreikönigstag, on January 6 is a public holiday in the Catholic areas. People buy special buns, one of which contains a plastic king, which has lucky connotations for the recipient. There is also a tradition of a lucky loaf, which would protect the house from evil spirits.

Fasnacht in Lucerne

Carnival

This is also called Fasnacht, and is a period of merrymaking connected with the beginning of the Christian Lenten fast. The celebrations, involving costumes, music, and satire, differ from canton to canton, but those in Basel are particularly well-known.

On the Monday after Ash Wednesday the street lights are turned out in the early morning and a procession of large decorative lanterns makes its way through the streets, along with masked and costumed figures playing flutes and drums.

In the Lötschen Valley unmarried men dress up as fearsome figures known as the *Tschäggättä*. In ferocious-looking masks, and tunics made from animal skins, they prowl around their villages. The masks are a symbol of anarchy and rebellion against the authority of the Church.

Holy Week and Easter

Chocolate Easter eggs and Easter bunnies are given at Easter, and there is also a tradition of painting hardboiled eggs. In the week leading up to Easter there are a number of local customs: Ticino stages a Passion play, and in Friborg women carry scarlet cushions through the streets bearing the symbols of Christ's Passion. In Nyon the town's fountains are decorated with flowers and eggs, and in Valais canton bread, cheese, and wine are distributed.

Swiss National Day

August 1 is a public holiday that commemorates the Oath of Confederation taken by the three original Swiss cantons in 1291. Meetings are held throughout Switzerland at which the president and local dignitaries make speeches.

Harvest Festival

Toward the end of September, when the cattle are brought down from their Alpine pastures, fairs known as *Chilbis* are held in the major centers, and people attend church to offer thanks to God for the harvest. Stalls are set up in village streets selling traditional fare and serving wine, beer, and coffee. In Stans, the main town of Nidwalden canton, wild figures called the *Butzi*, dressed in skins and moss, chase the children and toss them sweets.

Christmas market in Rapperswil

Traditional St. Nicholas procession in Freiburg

Christmas

Christmas here, as elsewhere in Europe, has a strong commercial element, with stores promoting the event from the end of October onward. Christmas markets spring up in the streets, selling mulled wine, Christmas decorations, and food specialties.

In German-speaking areas children have Advent calendars to open in the run-up to Christmas. Here you also have the tradition on December 6 of St. Nicholas visiting children to lecture them on good behavior while his sooty-faced assistant, Schmutzli, hands out oranges and nuts. On Christmas Eve families tuck into spicy meat *fondue chinoise*, and an angel, the Christkind, brings presents.

In the French-speaking areas Père Noel (Father Christmas) performs this function, and there is likewise much feasting and merrymaking. Some people attend midnight mass, and Christmas Day itself is given over to relaxation.

St. Berchtold's Day

The day after Christmas Day commemorates not a saint, but a duke who founded the city of Bern, the Swiss capital. Duke Berchtold V of Zahringen, to give him his full title, went hunting one day and promised to name the city after the first animal he killed, which was a bear. It is traditional to celebrate his festival by eating nuts and performing folk dances.

LOCAL FESTIVALS

Many cantons have their own special festivals. In April Zurich puts on the Sechselauten parade, which celebrates the arrival of spring and the longer days that allow the diligent Swiss to work until six o'clock. It starts on the third Sunday in April with a parade of children wearing historical costumes. The following day the craft guilds parade through the city and burn a giant snowman stuffed with explosives.

Geneva's Escalade Festival in early December celebrates the city's victory over the Duke of Savoy's Catholic troops in 1602. One intrepid lady is reputed to have thrown a bowl of boiling soup over the enemy as they attempted to scale the city walls; her deed is commemorated with chocolate tureens containing marzipan vegetables.

FAMILY OCCASIONS

On the birth of a child it is customary to present the mother with baby clothes. Sometimes the family put a notice on their door or balcony announcing the baby's name.

The traditional month for weddings is May, which is marked by an official ceremony at the local municipality. If the couple wishes to have a church ceremony this is normally held on the Saturday following, and the day ends with a dinner and dance—which is unlikely to continue into the early hours of the morning because of the stringent noise regulations.

Funerals are held four to seven days after the death, and are arranged with the cantonal authorities.

Getting to Know the Swiss

Before you know them well, Swiss people can often give the impression of being cold and unwelcoming. This could be viewed as a protective shell. They like to keep their public selves separate from their private selves, wanting to be respected rather than liked. The Swiss don't take friendships lightly, and want to size people up before deciding whether to befriend them. Quiet and controlled by nature, they distrust extraverts and may find it difficult to respond to them, preferring more restraint.

This does not mean that relationships must remain frosty for ever. While they may not care to reveal the warm and responsive side of their personality to a stranger, over time they will open up, and when this happens the friendship is real and lasting.

GREETINGS

In Switzerland the greeting you use will depend on where you are. "*Grüezi*" is common between friends in German-speaking Switzerland, "*Salut*" in the French part. "Good-bye" is "*Ade*" or "*Tschüss*," "*Au revoir*," and "*Ciao*" in Ticino.

People shake hands a great deal, when meeting someone and also when taking leave of them. Even children and teenagers do it. Take the first step by introducing yourself, as the Swiss can be reticent about approaching people, though not for negative reasons. They are simply respecting your boundaries.

Kissing—primarily between women or between a man and a woman—is quite acceptable, particularly in the French- and Italian-speaking areas. However, it is not obligatory, and some people prefer to keep their distance even after years of friendship.

FORMS OF ADDRESS

As in most parts of continental Europe there are formal and informal words for "you"—*Sie* and *du* in the German-speaking parts; *vous* and *tu* in the French-speaking areas. In the latter people tend to remain on formal terms for longer than elsewhere.

Sometimes the change from formality to informality is celebrated with a toasting ritual known as *Dudsis* in German and *schmolitz* in French.

OPPORTUNITIES TO MEET PEOPLE

Swiss people have grown up with a group of friends from childhood, and it can be difficult for a stranger to break into this charmed circle.

One way to do this is through fellow-expatriates—the English-speaking community number about 75,000. There are many social

clubs catering for foreigners, especially in cosmopolitan centers such as Geneva and Zurich. The danger with such clubs is that you find yourself interacting with fellow expatriates rather than with the Swiss. However, there will be people with long experience of Switzerland who may be willing to introduce you to their Swiss friends, and smooth the way.

You could join a club or enroll for a course. There are adult education centers in most Swiss towns, teaching all manner of subjects, some of which are operated by Migros Club School, established by the store cooperative Migros.

TAKING THE INITIATIVE

There are times when it pays to be proactive. If you move into an apartment, for instance, it is a good idea to go round introducing yourself to the neighbors. If you don't, they will conclude that you want to keep yourself to yourself, and will naturally respect your privacy.

Another way to meet the Swiss is to patronize your local shops on a regular basis. People are much more likely to chat in a shop than in a supermarket, and it will enable them to get to know you. Always greet people as you enter the shop, and don't be afraid to ask the locals for advice. They will be flattered.

LANGUAGE

English is widely spoken in Switzerland. Many Swiss have studied English abroad to a high standard—and other languages, too—and will appreciate having a chance to practice their foreign-language skills with a native speaker.

Even so, it is appreciated if you make an effort to speak the language of the locality where you are living. To decide which language is appropriate, consult the list on page 439.

Since German is the language of the majority, this may seem the obvious choice. Unfortunately, German-speaking Swiss tend to speak not the standard German (*Hochdeutsch*) taught in schools but an Alemannic dialect known as *Schweizerdeutsch*. This dialect sounds more like Low German or Dutch than standard German, and there are many regional variations. Even the French-speaking Swiss, who have learned *Hochdeutsch* at school, have difficulty following it. So you have every excuse not to speak German in Switzerland.

There is not the same problem in the French-and Italian-speaking regions, and you will get around with much greater ease if you can converse in these languages. Anyone speaking Romansch will be a hit with Romansch-speakers, since foreigners rarely make the effort to learn it.

MAKING CONVERSATION

The Swiss are not over-fond of small talk, and tend to avoid matters of a personal nature. You should therefore steer away from personal questions, at least until you know a person extremely well.

They do, however, enjoy serious discussions and, as mentioned above, can be very direct and forthright in their opinions; on the other hand they will listen respectfully to the ideas of others even if they are diametrically opposed to their own.

Certain topics carry a health warning. On no account should you criticize Switzerland, however much the Swiss may complain about their institutions. Nor should you enquire about the military. On the other hand, many Swiss are cosmopolitan in outlook and interested in what is happening in other countries.

Jokes should be avoided, as they do not travel well. The Swiss have a quiet, witty, often self-deprecating sense of humor and enjoy a good chuckle in the right circumstances.

INVITATIONS HOME

Invitations should always be accepted. It is a sign that you are making some headway in your relationship.

You may receive an invitation to an *apero*, or drinks party. This is an informal get-together that consists of drinks and small canapés, typically starting at 6:00 p.m. and lasting around two hours. People normally turn up soon after the stated time and not to outstay their welcome.

Dinner parties offer a chance to meet the Swiss when they are at their most relaxed. When the food is served it is customary to say "*Bon appetit*" or "*En guete*" before starting. When the host says "*Prost*" or "*Santé,*" everyone raises or clinks glasses and looks their fellow drinkers in the eye before drinking commences.

A small gift for the hostess is always appreciated.

Daily Life

HOUSING

Switzerland is an expensive country to live in, even for the Swiss themselves. As a result the level of house ownership here (30 percent) is lower than anywhere else in Western Europe. People tend to live in rented apartments, with the rent accounting for 25 percent or more of a household's income. All apartment blocks have a basement, used for storage—there is not normally much extra space in the apartments themselves, even for appliances such as refrigerators and washing machines. In any case, refrigerators tend to be smaller than the European average, which means there is limited space for storing food, so instead of making a weekly trip to a supermarket to stock up, many housewives shop daily, or on alternate days.

Many apartment blocks have laundry rooms, where tenants book time in advance or follow a roster. Strict rules govern the use of the washing machines; they must not be used, for instance, during designated quiet hours. Many localities have by-laws designed to prevent excessive noise after 10:00 p.m., and sometimes between noon and 2:00 p.m. In any case, most apartment blocks have their own house rules.

In the suburbs and the countryside people are more likely to live in houses, some of which look very old and picturesque—but don't be deceived by appearances. The interiors tend to be modern since these dwellings undergo frequent renovation and are maintained to a high standard.

THE HOUSEHOLD

It is unusual in Switzerland to find three or four generations of the same family living under the same roof, as happens in southern Europe. Many households, especially in towns and cities, consist of just one or two people, and the elderly often live alone or in retirement homes.

Within a family, the man continues to be the chief breadwinner, while the woman busies herself with household tasks and bringing up the children. It is perhaps for this reason that young Swiss people tend to be more disciplined than their counterparts elsewhere. Most married women take a career break when they start a family as childcare facilities are not very well developed.

As in many other European countries couples are tending to marry later, and it is quite common for them to live together unmarried for some years before tying the knot. A number do not bother to marry at all.

Young people are also remaining at home much longer, rather than fleeing the nest at an early age. This is partly out of financial considerations, given the high cost of living, and because they feel they need to become established in their careers before cutting themselves adrift.

DAILY ROUTINE

The Swiss usually rise at about 7:00 a.m. in order to be at their workplaces by 8:00 or 9:00. Some government offices open as early as 7:15 a.m.

The continental breakfast with croissants (also known as *Gipfeli*) is the norm. Children rarely need to be at school for the whole day, and usually come home for lunch, which is usually the most substantial meal of the day. This is not always possible in large urban centers where both parents are working, so some schools have facilities for children to eat there, but these are few and far between.

In German-speaking Switzerland many establishments close at noon for a lunch break that lasts an hour or more. In the French- and Italian-speaking areas two-hour lunch breaks are common.

Work finishes at 5:00 or 6:00 p.m., and people head for home, often on public transport, which is very efficient. In the evenings many people either go out—evening classes are very popular—or settle down as a family to watch television, though this is not as regular an activity as elsewhere in Europe. The main provider is the Swiss Broadcasting Corporation, which has seven TV channels and eighteen radio stations. The programs cater to all the country's language regions: *Deutschschweiz, Suisse Romande, Svizzera Italiana,* and *Svizra Rumantscha.*

SHOPPING

Swiss women shop every day, partly because they want fresh food but also because, as we have seen, refrigerators are small! Supermarkets are ubiquitous, but many people prefer to frequent open-air markets for fresh fruit, vegetables, flowers, and bakery products. The quality is good and the prices may seem high, but the Swiss are prepared to pay more for quality goods.

Stores are open from 8:00 or 9:00 a.m. until 6.30 p.m. on weekdays, with some closing for lunch. On Saturdays they close earlier, and Sunday opening is virtually unknown. Banking hours are 8:30 a.m. to 4:30 p.m. It is worth noting that credit cards are not used as widely as elsewhere in Europe.

EDUCATION

Education is the responsibility of the cantons, which often delegate the running of the schools to the municipal authorities. As a result teaching will vary from one place to another.

Children enter elementary school at the age of six or seven, but it is quite usual for them to attend kindergarten from four years upward. At the age of twelve they transfer to the higher elementary school for three to five years, depending on which canton they live in, or to a more academic school, called a *Gymnasium* in German-speaking cantons.

At one time, as a matter of course, children learned one of the other national languages at school before being taught a foreign language. So children in French-speaking cantons would learn German, and German children French, and so on, though there was little interest in learning Romansch. The idea behind the policy was to strengthen bonds between the different linguistic regions of the country. But now some German-speaking cantons have opted to teach English before French or Italian.

Around 60 percent of Swiss go on to do an apprenticeship on leaving secondary school, which consists of work experience within an established company or organization, supplemented by attendance at a vocational college for one or two days a week. This system is less popular in the French-speaking cantons. In some cases they move on to more advanced education at a technical school.

Young people who are planning to study at university stay on at secondary school until they are eighteen or nineteen. At this stage they take a leaving exam, the *Matura*, which allows them to attend one of the three universities in French-speaking Switzerland, or one of the five in the German-speaking areas or Fribourg, which is bilingual German and French. Another option is provided by the two Swiss Federal Institutes of Technology in Zurich and Lausanne.

Although it seems to fulfill its purpose reasonably well, the Swiss educational system does not score highly on international comparison sites, and plans are afoot to overhaul the system.

THE ARMED FORCES

Since its inception Switzerland has relied for its defense on a citizens' army, which requires all able-bodied males to be ready to take up arms to defend their country against attack. The tradition lives on in modern Switzerland.

Every Swiss male aged nineteen and above is required to register for military service and follow an eighteen-week course of training. Over the next ten years he has to undergo seven further periods of training, each lasting three weeks.

At one time men were liable for army service until the age of forty-two (or fifty-two in the case of officers), but now most serve only until the age of thirty-four. There is also a small professional army which, apart from defending Switzerland, also helps in international peacekeeping operations. Volunteers, both male and female, can join this at the age of eighteen.

MAIL AND TELECOMMUNICATIONS

The Swiss post office is very reliable, not only delivering mail but also running bus services in the remoter areas. Business hours are normally 7:30 a.m. to 6:00 p.m. on weekdays; the largest post offices are open all day; others may close for a lunch hour. On Saturdays post offices close at 11:00 a.m.

Switzerland has an efficient telephone service run by Swisscom, but other providers may offer more competitive rates. To use a public telephone you will need a phone card, which can be bought at news kiosks or the post office. Cell phones are also used widely.

As one would expect, the Swiss are enthusiastic Internet users, and there are Internet facilities for use everywhere. The Internet domain is .ch.

Leisure Time

The Swiss have less free time than many other Europeans, so they try to make the most of it. In the evenings people go out to meet friends in cafés or to attend evening classes. In the German-speaking areas men often meet up at their guilds, which were formally craft associations but are now social clubs where one can eat, drink, and enjoy convivial conversation. Membership of a guild is by invitation only. On weekends the mountains and lakes are a great attraction.

The Swiss are keen shoppers. Switzerland has a number of luxury department stores, including those along Zurich's premier shopping street, the Bahnhofstrasse. The equivalent in Geneva (Genève) is the Rue de la Rhône.

EATING OUT

There is not much of a pub culture in Switzerland, but there is a café culture, where people meet over coffee for hours at a time to discuss matters of the day and socialize. Cafés also serve alcohol.

The country is celebrated for its restaurants, of which there are plenty, all offering excellent food. You can find them everywhere, even on the tops of mountains! By international standards, meals range from quite expensive to very expensive, but you are always assured of good, fresh ingredients cooked to a high standard.

You should always check opening times. The Swiss lunch early, and many establishments close at 2:00 p.m., though in the French- and Italian-speaking regions lunch can last longer. As noted above, credit cards are not widely used, and restaurants don't always accept payment by this method.

FOOD

Swiss chefs are accustomed to catering to an international clientele, but it would be a pity to confine yourself to familiar fare. Do explore the cuisine of the country.

Switzerland's most celebrated culinary treat is undoubtedly

fondue, a concoction of melted Gruyère or Emmental cheese, wine, and seasoning, into which one dips small pieces of bread or other food on long forks.

There is a huge selection of sausages here, such as *Knackerli*, *Mostmockli*, *Kalbsleberwurst*, *Salsis* (small salami), *Leberwurst* (liver sausage) and *Landjäger*. Another popular dish is *Rösti*,

a fried cake of shredded potato.

The French-speaking cantons are particularly renowned for their fish dishes. *Pieds de porc au madère* (pigs' trotters in Madeira) is a specialty of Geneva, while *viande sechée* (dried beef or pork) is associated with Valais. Graubünden is celebrated for its *Bundnerfleisch* (dried meat with pickled onions and gherkins).

Most of the food dishes in Ticino have a distinctly Italian character, but there are two that could be regarded as specialties of

this canton: *mortadella e lenticchie* (a sausage dish) and *torta di pane* (bread pudding with chocolate and raisins).

Which brings us to pastries and desserts. *Leckerli* is a spiced honey cake associated with Basel; *Gugelhopf* is a cake baked in the form of a tall ring, often with dried or candied fruit and nuts; while *Schaffhauserzungen* are cream-filled cakes, a specialty from Schaffhausen.

DRINK

Switzerland is not generally thought of as a wine-producing country, probably because virtually all its production is consumed within the country itself. Nearly every canton grows grapes for wine making, but around 80 per cent of Swiss wine comes from the French-speaking cantons of Valais, Vaud, Geneva, and Neuchatel, in the west. Ticino produces a Merlot, and the favored grape in the German-speaking part of Switzerland is Müller-Thurgau, named after the Swiss Dr. Müller from Thurgau.

Beer is the drink of preference in the German-speaking cantons; in the French-speaking regions it is mixed with lemonade to make *panaché*.

CULTURE AND ENTERTAINMENT

Most visitors to Switzerland come for the scenery rather than the cultural life. While the entertainment scene may not be as exciting as elsewhere in Europe, the museums and art galleries are as good as you could wish for—and there are over nine hundred of them.

Among the leading ones are the Historical Museum, the National History Museum, and the Paul Klee Museum in Bern,

the Centre le Corbusier and Museum of Fine Arts in Zurich, the Beyeler Foundation and Museum Jean Tinguely in Basel, and the Swiss Transport Museum in Lucerne.

Many of the larger centers offer drama, opera, and ballet, notably Zurich with its Opernhaus and Schauspielhaus, Bern with its cellar theaters (*Kellertheater*), and Geneva with its Grand Theater and Victoria Concert Hall where the famous Orchestre de la Suisse Romande performs.

During the summer the theaters and opera houses take a break and the entertainment moves to the summer festivals, such as the renowned Luzern Festival, held in Lucerne in August and

September. There is an assortment of pop, rock, and open-air jazz festivals, of which the Montreux Jazz Festival is the most famous.

The major cities have a mix of nightclubs, cabarets, bars, and discos, as do some of the livelier ski resorts. Generally speaking, the nightlife is somewhat restrained, and many of these establishments close quite early.

STUDENTS, CLUBBING, AND CLOSE ENCOUNTERS

Zurich is the liveliest city, followed by Basel and Bern. In the French-speaking areas Lausanne and Geneva are the main centers of activity, and in the Italian part, Lugano and Locarno.

New bars and clubs keep opening up in Zurich, especially to the west of Hauptbahnhof in the fourth and fifth districts around Langstrasse and Escher-Wyss-Platz. The majority of bars and clubs close around 2:00 a.m., but some stay open until 6:00 a.m. Information on club nights and other events is listed in "Züritipp," published in Friday's *Tages Anzeiger*.

Along both sides of the Limmat River the bars and venues strewn across the pedestrianized streets of the Old Town are ever popular with visitors of all ages. The trendy side of Zurich is the former industrial northwestern district that is home to many of the city's best nightclubs and restaurants. The alternative and underground party scene is located here. Cutting through Züri-West is Langstrasse, the former Red Light district. It has undergone an exciting transformation, and cool clubs now sit alongside biker bars and strip clubs. Come here for an eclectic melting-pot of fashions, life styles, and attitudes. For Zurich's beautiful and chic, the hippest designer bars and old-style cafés can be found close to Bahnhofstrasse, and if you take a step away from Niederdorfstrasse you will find many delightful small restaurants.

In Switzerland young people tend to socialize in same-sex groups, so getting to meet the opposite sex can be difficult. This generally happens at the workplace, and not in the evenings—people meet for lunch in restaurants or in public places such as parks. On the other hand, Swiss women are independent, strong-minded, and proactive. They expect to be treated as equals and to be consulted. Relationships proceed slowly, starting with a drink, followed by a meal. He offers to pay. If all goes well, he'll continue paying. If she insists on paying, that is not a good sign.

The Swiss are still generally more polite and reserved than people elsewhere in Europe, but the presence of a growing immigrant population is starting to change attitudes all round.

SPORTS AND OUTDOOR ACTIVITIES

Switzerland has plenty of resources for those who like to lead an active life—mountains to climb, lakes to sail or ski on, scenery to walk through, and slopes to ski down in winter.

The Swiss pride themselves on their prowess at winter sports, and they are able to get in plenty of practice. With the nearest ski resort probably less than an hour away from their homes, they can spend every weekend on the ski slopes if they wish. Among the most celebrated ski resorts are Zermatt, Davos, St. Moritz, Verbier, Klosters, Gstaad, and Wengen.

The abundance of large lakes, such as Lake Geneva (Lac

Leman) and Lake Constance (Bodensee), offers plenty of opportunities for those whose hobby is sailing, and Switzerland is now producing world-class yachtspeople.

Hockey, gymnastics, soccer, golf, rock climbing, shooting, and paragliding are just a few more of the popular outdoor activities in Switdzerland.

Getting Around

Switzerland is at the crossroads of Europe, and many international roads and railway routes run across the country, often over Alpine passes or through long tunnels. The Swiss have surmounted numerous obstacles to make traveling around their country a doddle.

Trains run like clockwork, and to the most remarkable places— along the valleys and up to the summits of mountains. The main lines are operated by Swiss Federal Railways (SBB, CFF, and FSS, depending on your language preference). About one-third of the railway track is privately owned, including the Bern–Lotschberg– Simplon line and the Rhaetian railway. Once you get to your destination there are several picturesque mountain railways to choose from, some of them steam-operated.

Cogwheel steam train at the summit of the Brienzer Rothorn in the Bernese Oberland

Postal buses connect some of the remoter areas, and there is also an extensive ferry network on the lakes. In addition to surface transport there are cable cars.

Trolleybus in Zurich

DRIVING

Hairpin bends and steep gradients in the Alpine regions may deter the more timid driver from the plains, and considering the excellence of the public transport system you may feel there is no real need for a car.

Many visitors find driving relatively easy, however. The roads are uniformly good, well-maintained, and well-signposted. Freeways are indicated by green signs, and you must pay a toll and attach a sticker (*vignette*) to your windscreen to travel on these. Other main routes are indicated by blue signs.

Speed limits are 130 kmph (80 mph) on expressways, 100 kmph (62 mph) on other roads, and 60 kmph (37 mph) in built-up areas. Speed cameras are ubiquitous, and speeding drivers are liable to be fined. The same applies to drivers over the drink-driving limit of 0.5 mg per ml, and those who drive through a red traffic light.

Traffic going uphill has priority over traffic coming down, and in winter drivers are required to replace their normal tires with winter ones. In some areas tire chains are needed. You need to carry a red emergency triangle in the car as well as car documentation and a driving license. Switzerland has the most stringent regulation of exhaust emissions in Europe.

WHERE TO STAY

Tourism was more or less invented in Switzerland when northern Europeans, particularly the British, inspired by the accounts they had read about Alpine landscapes, decided to go and see the country for themselves. The canny Swiss recognized that if they could offer their visitors home comforts as well as magnificent scenery the visitors would spread the word and return.

This gave the Swiss a head start over the rest of the world in providing hotel accommodation, and they have never been content to rest on their laurels. The country has some of the best hotel management schools in the world, whose graduates manage many of the world's leading hotels.

In short, visitors have nothing to fear. The accommodation is uniformly excellent, whether you opt for a five-star hotel or settle for a modest bed and breakfast establishment (*pension*). There are also some eighty youth hostels, many of them in the most scenic parts of the country.

Hotel Chateau Gutsch on the hill above Lucerne

MEDICAL MATTERS

Standards of health care are excellent; Switzerland has the best ratio of doctors to patients in the world. The Swiss are long-lived, despite being heavy smokers.

Of course, this comes at a cost, and health insurance premiums here approach the levels of those in the United States. Everyone is expected to have health insurance.

SAFETY

Switzerland is one of the safest countries in Europe, and provided you take reasonable precautions with your belongings you are unlikely to be robbed or mugged.

PLACES TO VISIT

A few people come to Switzerland to climb the Matterhorn or the Jungfrau; others come, with less strenuous intentions, to see the breathtakingly beautiful scenery.

One by-product of the Swiss policy of neutrality is that that its towns and cities have escaped the devastation of war and have been able to preserve their medieval and Renaissance quarters intact. Bern, with its arcades, fountains, and towers, is one of these; another is Lucerne, with its two wooden bridges, the Kapellbrücke and the Spreuerbrücke, which date from the fourteenth and fifteenth centuries.

The resort of Interlaken (meaning "between the lakes"), is surrounded by wonderful scenery, and puts on open-air

performances of Schiller's play *William Tell* every summer. Close by is the Jungfraujoch, with the scenic cogwheel railway leading to the summit. For another scenic journey, take the Glacier Express from Brig to St. Moritz.

The French-speaking areas are also a delight, including the pretty town of Lausanne and the cosmopolitan city of Geneva, where you can have a tour around the Palais des Nations, which once housed the League of Nations and is now the United Nations' base in Europe. And if you would like to sample an Italian–Swiss cocktail, the scenic resorts of Lugano and Locarno (of film festival fame) are well worth a visit.

The "Zytglogge" Tower in Bern

Business and Professional Life

Switzerland is a prosperous and successful country despite having few resources apart from the skills of its people. At one time these skills were military: the Swiss served as mercenaries in a number of European armies. Now they are deployed in tourism, precision engineering, chemicals, food processing, pharmaceuticals, and finance. The country has always ranked high in terms of international competitiveness, and takes pains to ensure that it continues to do so.

BUSINESS STRUCTURE

While Switzerland has a number of large banks, such as UBS, and industrial groups, such as Nestlé, most firms are quite small, with 98 percent employing fewer than five people.

Switzerland enjoys good labor relations. The Swiss dislike confrontation and prefer to settle grievances by negotiation. People take a pride in their work and feel duty-bound to fulfill their responsibilities to the best of their ability.

Swiss organizations are hierarchical, with a clear line of command and well-defined areas of responsibility. Senior managers expect to be presented with well-argued recommendations by their staff on which to make their decisions.

Those in authority are expected to be sound, responsible, and honest in their business dealings. They are also expected to keep their emotions in check and lead a disciplined, blameless personal life. In the close-knit society of Switzerland, if you fall short of these high standards you will be quickly found out.

Helsana Assurances offices in Dübendorf, near Zurich

BUSINESS AND PROFESSIONAL ETIQUETTE

Since the Swiss have trade and professional links with most countries of the world, they have developed a cosmopolitan outlook. This means being multilingual, well-informed, and acquainted with a wide range of business styles, which enables them to meet their contacts on their own terms.

For a foreign professional or businessperson this may seem an ideal situation. However, you are more likely to make a favorable impression if you are willing to respect their business culture and adapt to it. This means keeping things on a formal level.

FORMALITY

The Swiss tend to address each other formally, whether colleague, neighbor, or acquaintance, using surnames, although in some of the multinational companies this is changing, and you may find that people are on first-name terms at meetings.

Until you are well acquainted with people you should address them by their professional titles and surnames—though people would not normally announce their titles when introducing themselves. In German-speaking Switzerland you would use the courtesy titles "*Herr*" to address a man and "*Frau*" to address a woman, or "*Herr Doktor*" or *Frau Doktor*," as appropriate, followed by the surname, for example "*Herr Doktor* Schmidt." In French-speaking areas, use "*Monsieur*" and "*Madame,*" and in Italian-speaking areas, use "*Signor*" and "*Signora.*"

SETTING UP A MEETING

Initial contact is best made by letter, and followed up with a telephone call. Don't be surprised if the manager himself answers the telephone. Swiss executives tend not have perks in the form of secretaries or support staff at their beck and call, and are expected to do much more for themselves than people in equivalent positions in other countries.

The Swiss work long hours, and there are no times of day when you should avoid calling apart from lunchtime, which starts soon after noon. Many Swiss take their holidays in July or August, and in the winter spend a week or two taking part in winter sports. Some businesses close for cantonal festivals, but this is usually only for a day.

MEETINGS

The Swiss are sticklers for punctuality, and you should make every effort to arrive on time. It is also important to arrive well-prepared with plenty of supporting documentation, if appropriate.

On arrival it is customary to shake hands with everyone in the room, and look people in the eye—the Swiss set much store by good manners—but once the introductions are over it is down to the business in hand. There is no room for small talk, or a getting-to-know-you session, certainly in the German-speaking region.

It is not always possible to work out who the senior person is purely from appearance, but you will get some idea of this by observing who speaks first and to whom the others defer. As mentioned earlier, because of the hierarchical nature of Swiss businesses it is the top person in these firms whom you have to convince.

PRESENTATIONS

The German-speaking Swiss prefer low-key presentations that state the facts clearly and intelligibly. They are unimpressed by exaggerated claims or a pushy sales pitch, though their compatriots from the French- and Italian-speaking parts of the country may appreciate a little style.

You should not expect an enthusiastic initial response—or indeed any response— to your proposals. The Swiss will probably listen to you in complete silence, not because they are not interested in what you are saying but because they want to take everything in and think it over.

Expect to be questioned closely on your proposals. Some of the questions may seem quite abrupt and direct. Be assured there is nothing personal in this line of attack; this is simply a determination to leave no stone unturned. The cautious Swiss tend to be risk-averse, and are unlikely to go along with an idea unless they are absolutely convinced that it will work.

NEGOTIATIONS

Don't expect a quick decision; that is not the way things happen in Switzerland. The people you have been talking to will want to take their time to examine all the facts and information before presenting a report to the real decision makers.

Once they reach an agreement in your favor, you can expect some tough negotiating—since the Swiss are known for getting the best possible deals. They are masters of diplomacy, and will drive a hard bargain without ever coming across as aggressive or demanding.

WOMEN IN BUSINESS

For much of the twentieth century Swiss women were second-class citizens—afforded every courtesy, but denied the right to vote until 1971. One canton did not grant full voting rights to women until 1991.

On the whole, the Swiss have a conservative attitude to women in the workplace, and relatively few women make it to boardroom level. Although some married women choose to continue working once they have a family, they are hampered by the lack of childcare facilities.

So a woman holding a high-ranking post is still a fairly rare sight, but it is highly probable that in the future conservative Switzerland will follow its neighbors in opening up more career opportunities to its womenfolk.

Appendix 1: Body Language and Gestures

People communicate not only through words, of course, but also through body language. Many of the ways we communicate nonverbally are common throughout Western Europe—a smile is a sign of welcome; a firm handshake indicates pleasure in meeting somebody, or congratulations; persistent eye contact denotes interest; a nod is a sign of approval; and shaking the head normally signifies disagreement.

In most countries it is considered rude to stare, and pointing a finger at a person is often regarded as impolite—a nod in their direction is much more appropriate. Raising a finger (index or middle) is regarded as a rude gesture almost everywhere. Standing with your hands in your pockets, or putting your feet on the table, is bad manners in virtually every Western European country.

However, there are differences. For example, northern Europeans value their personal space and shy away if a stranger approaches too closely; but in southern Italy, Spain, and Portugal, standing close to someone is the norm. In the Latin countries of Europe, including France, people tend to use their hands much more in order to express themselves. There, good friends will pat each other on the back, shake hands vigorously, grip each other's arms firmly, and even men may kiss each other on both cheeks; elsewhere in Europe people tend to be less demonstrative. Physical contact also tends to be less common among more sophisticated people.

Because of these behavioral differences, Spaniards and southern Italians often perceive northern Europeans as cold and standoffish, while northerners may regard Mediterranean folk as superficial and insincere. Neither perception is correct—one simply has to make allowances for different customs.

Particular care should be taken with hand gestures, as they may well be misinterpreted. Here are a few to be careful with, especially in the Latin countries.

- A thumbs-up sign usually means "OK," or "Well done!" but could be offensive in Italy, Spain, and southern France, as would opening one's palms to a person.
- Joining the index finger and thumb to form an "O" to mean "OK" is regarded as an insult in Italy, Spain, and France, and is not universally understood in others.
- A fist with the thumb poking out between the index and middle fingers is an insult in Italy.

- In Portugal and Spain a clenched fist with first and fourth fingers straightened signifies that a man is a cuckold.
- The "V" sign can denote victory or the number two, provided the palm of the hand faces outward—but is seen as a rude gesture in most countries if the back of the hand faces outward.

Some gestures need to be considered in context. For instance, it is perfectly in order for a football referee to point at a player who has committed a misdemeanor on the pitch, and sign language such as pointing to your mouth to signify that you are hungry is permissible if verbal communication breaks down. The best idea is to observe people's body language carefully to avoid making gestures that might turn out to be inappropriate.

Appendix 2: Emergency Numbers

The European emergency services telephone number is 112.

You can dial this number for police, fire, and ambulance from anywhere in the EU, free of charge, from fixed phones, including pay phones, and cell phones. It is also used in countries outside the EU, including Switzerland.

A trained operator will take and deal with the call. Many operators speak more than one language.

You will be asked for your name, address, and telephone number. This is necessary to identify callers, particularly in order not to report the same incident more than once.

Index

Acknowledgments

A book of this nature is no mean undertaking, and I am greatly indebted to other *Culture Smart!* authors whose books on the individual countries in Western Europe have been a great inspiration and help. They are Charles Abbott (Italy), Sheryl Buckland (Netherlands), Peter Gieler (Austria), Sandy Guedes de Quieroz (Portugal), Mandy Macdonald (Belgium), Kendall Maycock (Switzerland), Marian Meany (Spain), Paul Norbury (Britain), John Scotney (Ireland), and Barry Tomalin (France and Germany). Their works are recommended reading for anyone wishing to explore these particular countries in greater depth.

I am also grateful to Monika Newham, Louise Wilhelm, Alain Krégine, and Daphne Thissen for reading through parts of the book and offering their valuable comments, and to my editor Carolyn Eardley for her tireless efforts in preparing the work for publication.

ROGER JONES